British Naval Aircraft

since 1912

Sea Harrier F.R.S.2 undergoing ship-board trials from HMS *Ark Royal* in November 1990
(Matthew Clement: B Ae Kingston)

British Naval Aircraft

since 1912

Owen Thetford

SIXTH REVISED EDITION

NAVAL
INSTITUTE
PRESS

© Owen Thetford 1958, 1971, 1977, 1982 and 1991

Sixth revised edition 1991

Published in Great Britain 1991 by
Putnam Aeronautical Books, an imprint of
Conway Maritime Press Ltd,
24 Bride Lane, Fleet Street,
London EC4Y 8DR

Published and distributed in the United States
of America and Canada by the Naval Institute Press,
Annapolis, Maryland 21402

Library of Congress Catalog Card No. 90–62896

ISBN 1–55750–076–2

CONTENTS

PREFACE

British Naval Aircraft first appeared in 1958 as a companion volume to my earlier book *Aircraft of the Royal Air Force*, and the same format has been maintained: each main type of aircraft is illustrated with one or more photographs and a three-view general arrangement drawing, accompanied by general narrative on operational history and a technical specification. Once again the aircraft are arranged alphabetically under manufacturers, and thence chronologically in the order of their appearance. An index to the manufacturers appears at the front of the book, a further index at the back of the book listing aircraft under their type names.

Over 100 main types are included, ranging from the Avro 504 to the Wight 'Converted' Seaplane. There are also appendices covering 160 more types of aircraft, airships which came under the control of the Royal Navy between January 1914 and December 1919, and brief particulars of seaplane-carriers and aircraft-carriers which have embarked British naval aircraft.

Whereas the RAF book began with the formation of that Service in April 1918, the present work takes as its starting point the beginning of properly organised naval flying with the creation of the Royal Flying Corps, Naval Wing, constituted by Royal Warrant on 13 May 1912. Whilst not claiming to be utterly exhaustive (a few types presented to the Admiralty by enthusiastic private aviators before this date have not been included), it is nevertheless true that virtually every aircraft used since 1912 by the Naval Wing, the Royal Naval Air Service and the Fleet Air Arm has found a place, including those of foreign origin.

In addition to the technical data presented, every effort has been made to include all relevant information on the units equipped with the various types and the ships in which they were carried. Much new information will also be found in the pages dealing with the more famous aircraft of the 1914–18 and 1939–45 periods, which have been treated at the somewhat greater length warranted by their historical importance.

In preparing this book I have always had reason to be grateful for the generous assistance I have been given by many people. Those who have helped me in the past I have acknowledged in earlier prefaces, but for the present edition I would like to offer my thanks to Mrs Anne Bell, Chief Librarian and Archivist of the Fleet Air Arm Museum; Graham Mottram, Curator of the FAA Museum; Greg Ferguson of British Aerospace, Kingston; Sarah Last of Westland Helicopters; Barry Hawgood of Flight Refuelling Ltd; Alec McRitchie of Shorts' Belfast; Elaine Jones of the Quadrant Picture Library; Alan Williams of the Imperial War Museum; F D Sheppard of the RAF Museum and the public relations and photographic staffs of the Royal Naval Air Stations at Culdrose, Portland and Prestwick. I am especially grateful for the special efforts made by L/A (Phot) Phil Ball of HMS *Gannet*. My thanks are also due to David Brown, Head of Naval Historical Branch at the Ministry of Defence and to Commander T H Boycott, RN, Directorate of Public Relations (Navy) at MoD.

I am also grateful to my wife, Elizabeth, for her assistance in preparing the index and her patience during my prolonged absences at the editorial desk.

London, October 1990   OGT

INTRODUCTORY NOTE

THE DEVELOPMENT OF BRITISH NAVAL AVIATION SINCE 1912

Although the very earliest beginnings of British naval aviation can be traced back to July 1908, when it was proposed that the new post of Naval Air Assistant be established at the Admiralty, it was not until 1912 that heavier-than-air aircraft began to be taken seriously for naval purposes. There are a number of reasons why this should be so. One of the contributory factors was the severe blow suffered by the original plans to foster lighter-than-air aircraft when No.1 Rigid Naval Airship (otherwise known as the *Mayfly*) met with complete disaster in September 1911. As if to emphasise the superior potentialities of the aeroplane, this airship setback was followed soon afterwards by two great milestones in British sea-flying: the first successful ascent from water by a British seaplane on 18 November 1911 and the first take-off from the deck of a British warship on 10 January 1912. The first feat was achieved by Cdr Oliver Schwann flying an Avro biplane (35 hp Green engine) at Barrow-in-Furness; the second by the celebrated Cdr C R Samson (then a lieutenant) in a Short S.38, which, fitted with pontoons, took off from an improvised platform on the foredeck of HMS *Africa* anchored in Sheerness Harbour. The first British flight from a ship under way was also made by a Short S.38 biplane: the date was 9 May 1912. The flight took place from HMS *Hibernia* as she was steaming at about ten knots in Weymouth Bay. Samson had been among the first four officers of the Royal Navy to be selected for flying instruction when, early in 1911, the Admiralty accepted an offer from Mr (later Sir) Francis McClean, a member of the Royal Aero Club, to lend two of his privately-owned aeroplanes and the facilities of the Aero Club's aerodrome at Eastchurch, Isle of Sheppey, for this purpose. Their instructor was Mr George Cockburn, who provided his services free of charge. Lts Samson, Gregory, Longmore, and Gerrard (the last-named being a member of the Royal Marine Light Infantry) were not, however, the

A modified Short S.27 pusher biplane on the launching ramp of HMS *Hibernia* in May 1912.
(Imperial War Museum)

9

first British naval officers to fly: this honour goes to Lt G C Colmore, RN, who qualified at his own expense on 21 June 1910 with Aviator's Certificate No.15.

As mentioned in the preface, properly organised naval aviation in Great Britain did not begin to get into its stride until after the formation of the Royal Flying Corps, with its separate Naval and Military Wings, on 13 May 1912. This arrangement, always unpopular with the Admiralty, lasted officially until the Royal Naval Air Service attained recognition as a separate Service on 1 July 1914: in reality the RNAS had been operating under this title since a few months after the Naval Wing was formed.

By the end of 1912 the Royal Navy had 16 aircraft in service, comprising 13 landplanes (8 biplanes and 5 monoplanes) and 3 hydro-aeroplanes: the term seaplane was not introduced until 17 July 1913. The year 1912 had also witnessed the first experiments in bomb-dropping (Cdr Samson had dropped a dummy 100-pounder from a Short biplane), the transmission of wireless signals from a Short seaplane, the inclusion of aircraft in the annual Naval Review and the establishment at the Isle of Grain of the first of a chain of coastal seaplane stations. By the summer of 1913 further stations had been established at Calshot, Cromarty, Felixstowe and Great Yarmouth, and in July aircraft participated for the first time in the annual naval manoeuvres. A notable event of this period was the operation of two seaplanes from the forward launching platform of the light cruiser HMS *Hermes*. One of these aircraft was a Short Folder: this marked the beginning of the use of aircraft with folding wings aboard ship, a practice which persists to the present day.

At the beginning of 1914 the RNAS had over 100 trained pilots, and from 1 January it became responsible for the operation of all airships which remained under naval control until December 1919. A review of RNAS airships and their activities during this period will be found in the appendices. In the few months that remained before the outbreak of war, the RNAS pressed ahead with characteristic vigour in experiments with armament. Lt Clark Hall did successful firing trials with a 1½-pounder gun mounted in the nose of a Short Gun-Carrier, and on 28 July Lt A M Longmore (later Air Chief Marshal Sir Arthur Longmore) made the first successful torpedo drop from the air in a Short seaplane (160 hp Gnome engine) at Calshot. When war finally began a few days later, the RNAS had on strength a total of 78 aircraft, comprising 40 landplanes, 31 seaplanes and 7 airships. Its strength in personnel amounted to 130 officers and ratings.

By 1 April 1918 (when it was merged with the RFC to form the Royal Air Force) the RNAS had grown to a force of 67,000 officers and men, with 126 air stations at home and abroad and 2,949 aeroplanes and 103 airships on its strength. It had fought not only at sea, from seaplane-carriers and coastal air stations, but in the Dardanelles and on the Western Front. Indeed, the RNAS squadrons based in Belgium and France established a most enviable record: their offensive spirit was demonstrated as early as 22 September 1914, when four aircraft from Cdr Samson's Eastchurch squadron (ordered overseas on 27 August) made the first British air raid on German territory. More details will be found in the following pages of the remarkable pioneering raids by the RNAS on Zeppelin sheds at Düsseldorf and Friedrichshafen and of the commendable foresight shown by the Admiralty in fostering the development of the long-range bomber: the RNAS was the first air service to give practical expression to the

Commander Samson's Eastchurch Squadron of the RNAS at Dunkirk in 1914. The aeroplanes are (left to right): Henry Farman F.20, Samson's B.E.2a (No.50), Sopwith Tractor Biplane and Short No.42. *(G S Leslie)*

coneption of strategic bombing. In air fighting, too, it proved more than a match for the enemy as the narrative on the Sopwith Pup, Triplane and Camel will go to show.

At home stations the task of the RNAS was twofold: it was responsible from 3 September 1914 for the air defence of Great Britain as well as for anti-submarine and anti-Zeppelin patrols over the sea. This somewhat surprising situation came about because the RFC was wholly occupied in France from the outbreak of war and it was not until March 1916 that the RFC established Home Defence squadrons. The exploits of the RNAS flying-boats over the North Sea form an especially exciting chapter of British naval aviation history: their historic achievements are recorded in the main text.

As will be evident from the foregoing remarks, by far the greater proportion of the RNAS effort in the First World War was by seaplanes or flying-boats at coastal air stations or landplanes at shore bases. Aircraft carried in ships played a subordinate rôle: the aircraft-carrier as it is known today did not make its appearance until the closing phases of the war. The aircraft-carrier was evolved by gradual stages from the early seaplane-carrier which originally had no take-off facilities, the aircraft being hoisted over the side to take off from the

No.2 Wing, RNAS at Imbros in 1915: the aeroplanes are Henry Farman F.27s and Nieuport 10 two-seaters. *(G S Haigh)*

11

sea. Later a take-off platform was added, sloping down to the bows to provide a clear run. These platforms were at first used by seaplanes which had wheels (later wheeled trolleys) fitted beneath the floats: only later were landplanes flown from launching platforms. Among the first seaplane-carriers were the converted cross-Channel steamers *Empress, Engadine* and *Riviera*, which were commandeered by the Admiralty on 11 August 1914: these three ships launched the seven seaplanes used in the celebrated Cuxhaven raid of Christmas Day, 1914. Another early seaplane-carrier, the former Isle of Man steamer *Ben-My-Chree*, carried the Short seaplane which on 12 August 1915 made the first successful air-torpedo attack in history while operating in the Dardanelles. These early seaplane-carriers were, nevertheless, of limited value, as they were severely handicapped by their inability to keep station with the Fleet (they had to stop when hoisting their seaplanes overboard), and the seaplanes themselves could operate in only the calmest of seas. The launching platform (first fitted on the pre-war *Hermes*, sunk in October 1914) overcame this difficulty only when the ship was fast enough to provide enough air speed over the deck: some carriers so fitted (eg *Ark Royal*) were too slow and continued to launch their seaplanes the old way. More successful were the carriers *Campania* and *Vindex*, which proved capable of handling the faster single-seaters of the day. On 6 August 1915 a Sopwith Baby on wheeled floats took off from *Campania* for the first time: this was followed by the first normal landplane take-off by a Bristol Scout from *Vindex* on 3 November 1915. Still the problem remained of getting an aircraft back on to the ship, and it was not until 2 August 1917 that this feat was achieved by Sqn Cdr E H Dunning, who flew his Sopwith Pup round the funnel of HMS *Furious* and contrived to alight on the 228-feet-long forward flying-deck. This experiment, and the disaster which overtook Dunning a few

The non-rigid airship S.S.Z.59 landing aboard the carrier HMS *Furious* in 1917. (*Imperial War Museum*)

12

Squadron Commander Dunning lands his Sopwith Pup aboard HMS *Furious* on 2 August 1917.
This was the first carrier landing ever made by an aeroplane. *(Imperial War Museum)*

days later when he repeated it, led to the provision of a flying-on deck 284 feet
long aft of the superstructure. This deck was provided with an early form of
arrester gear comprised of longitudinal wires and transverse ropes weighted with
sandbags and a rope crash-barrier to protect the superstructure. The wires were
engaged by spring-clip hooks on the aeroplane's axle, and a further hook
engaged the transverse ropes. Some aircraft flown from *Furious* at this period
(mainly Pups and 1½ Strutters) had a skid undercarriage instead of wheels. The
system was not a success owing to the eddies and hot-air current set up by the
funnel and superstructure, and *Furious* was modified after the Armistice to have
a flush deck extending from bow to stern. Although *Furious* was not wholly
satisfactory until after this modification had been effected, she could claim to
have been the only carrier of the First World War to have launched a major air
action. This was the famous raid of 19 July 1918, when seven Sopwith Camels
flown off *Furious* made a successful attack on the Zeppelin base at Tondern,
destroying L54 and L60.

The first carrier to enter service with a flush deck already fitted was *Argus*
(converted from the Italian liner *Conte Rosso*), but as she did not begin her trials
until October 1918, she was too late to play any active part in the war. If the war
had been prolonged by a few months, *Argus* would have taken into action a
squadron of 18 Sopwith Cuckoos, the first landplane torpedo-carrying aircraft to
be embarked in an aircraft-carrier.

By 1917 the Admiralty had realised that landplanes, with their superior
performance, offered much better prospects for air operations with the Fleet
than the more cumbersome seaplane. Unfortunately there were not enough
ships with flying-off decks to enable an effective force to be deployed. Other
means were sought, chief among them being the introduction of extemporised
platforms on existing light cruisers and, later, the mounting of short take-off

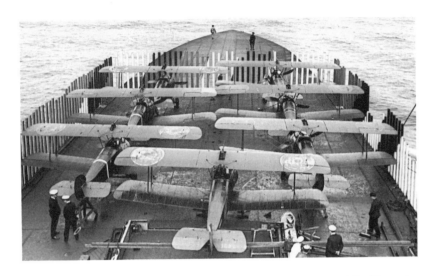

Sopwith 2F.1 Camels on the flying-off deck of HMS *Furious* in 1918. *(Imperial War Museum)*

platforms above the gun-turrets of battleships. The first successful experiment of this kind took place in June 1917, when F/Cdr F J Rutland flew a Sopwith Pup off the light cruiser *Yarmouth*. On 1 October 1917 the same officer repeated his success by flying a Pup off a platform superimposed on the 15-inch gun turret of the battleship *Repulse*: the platform could be turned into wind without the ship altering course and during the take-off was in fact at an angle of 45 degrees from the bow. The final stage in these experiments was achieved on 4 April 1918, when the practice was extended to two-seater aircraft: a Sopwith 1½ Strutter was flown off a turret platform aboard HMAS *Australia*. By the end of the First World War over 100 aircraft were being carried in this way by ships of the Grand

Sopwith F.1. Camels of No.10 (Naval) Squadron seen on the Western Front in 1918.
(G S Leslie)

14

Fleet: 22 light cruisers had been fitted with flying-off platforms and all battleships and battle-cruisers carried a two-seat aircraft on the forward turret platform and a single-seat fighter on the rear turret platform.

One other method of using aircraft at sea remains to be mentioned: the towed lighter. These lighters were designed to be towed behind a destroyer, measured 58 feet long by 16 feet wide, and could reach 32 knots without throwing up sheets of spray. Their original purpose was to convey large flying-boats across the North Sea so as to increase their radius of action over the Heligoland Bight area, but in 1918 it was discovered that they could also be used with 30-feet-long take-off platforms for launching single-seat fighters. The first successful take-off, using a Sopwith Camel, was by Lt S D Culley on 31 July 1918: a few days later he destroyed the Zeppelin L53 by using this technique.

A Camel seen at the moment of take-off from a lighter towed behind a destroyer in the North Sea. *(Imperial War Museum)*

In the years immediately after the Armistice, naval aviation, in common with the rest of the RAF of which it formed a part, shrank to a tiny force; economy was the watchword, and by the end of 1919 it had been reduced to one spotter-reconnaissance squadron, one fighter flight and half a torpedo squadron. There was also a seaplane flight and a flying-boat flight. The next twenty years were to witness a determined campaign by the Admiralty to regain control of naval flying, a campaign which reached a successful conclusion in May 1939, when it could be announced that the take-over from the RAF was complete. This victory was achieved by gradual stages, the first being in 1921, when the Admiralty obtained agreement that naval officers should be trained as air observers. In 1923 a Committee of Inquiry recommended that all observers in naval aircraft should be naval officers and that up to 70 per cent of the pilots should be naval officers with dual RAF and naval rank. In April 1924 the carrier-borne branch of the RAF was named the Fleet Air Arm, a title which is

A Beardmore W.B.III leaves the steep forward launching platform of HMS *Pegasus* in 1918.
(Imperial War Museum)

retained to the present day, though it was abandoned for a period between 1939 and 1953, when the term Air Branch of the Royal Navy, or Naval Aviation, was in vogue officially, though the old title persisted in popular usage. Finally, in 1937, it was announced in the House of Commons that control of the FAA would be handed over entirely to the Royal Navy within two years; all personnel would be naval, and the Admiralty would have its own shore stations for the first time since the days of the old RNAS. The first naval air stations so established were Donibristle, Eastleigh, Evanton, Ford, Hatston, Lee-on-Solent, St Merryn and Worthy Down.

Strength in aircraft grew painfully slowly during the inter-war years. In January 1924 there were 78 naval aircraft in 13 flights: this had increased to 13 flights (128 aircraft) by October 1924, to 24 flights (144 aircraft) by September 1930 and to 26 flights (156 aircraft) in September 1932. On 3 April 1933 the squadron (with 9 or 12 aircraft) was introduced as the basic carrier flying unit and the existing flights (each of 6 aircraft) were merged except for a number which carried on as catapult aircraft in cruisers and capital ships. By May 1935 there were 175 aircraft in 15 squadrons: this had increased to 217 aircraft in March 1936. When war broke out in September 1939 the Royal Navy could muster only 20 squadrons with a total of 340 aircraft, 225 of which were in carriers and the rest in catapult flights.

The inter-war years saw the introduction of five new aircraft-carriers in addition to the two inherited from the war years (*Furious* and *Argus*). These were *Eagle* (1922), *Hermes* (1923), *Glorious* and *Courageous* (1928) and *Ark Royal* (1938). From 1919 until 1922 *Argus* was the only fleet carrier in commission: originally she had no arrester gear, but later a most unusual system was adopted which employed the longitudinal wires (as tried in *Furious*) in

16

conjunction with the deck lift, which was lowered about 9 inches so that aircraft dropped into it and were then finally halted by a sloping ramp. This curious technique led, understandably enough, to a high proportion of accidents, and was shortly superseded by a combination of longitudinal wires and transverse wooden flaps. These flaps were knocked flat by the aircraft as it ran along the deck. This system was little better: it caused a great deal of damage to undercarriages. In 1926 the arrester-gear principle was abandoned and aircraft landed on a plain deck until 1930, when experiments began aboard *Courageous* with transverse arrester wires utilising friction brake-drums with an electrical resetting mechanism. This system was finally perfected in 1933, when hydraulic resetting gear superseded the electrical. This method of deck landing proved completely successful, and became standardised. The arrester wires were engaged by a retractable hook suspended below the rear fuselage, and there was no longer any danger of the aircraft tipping forward on its nose, as was common with the old axle hooks. Initial experiments were conducted with a Fairey IIIF, and the first standard installations of the rear hook were in the Osprey and Nimrod.

Another innovation of the inter-war years was catapult launching of aircraft from ships. Early experiments with catapult launch had been conducted aboard the steam hopper *Slinger* with a Fairey N.9 seaplane in 1917–18, but it was not until October 1925 that a standard FAA aircraft was so launched from a warship. This was by a Fairey IIID seaplane flown by Wg Cdr Burling from *Vindictive*. Thereafter, catapult aircraft were much used for reconnaissance purposes aboard cruisers and battleships, and continued to serve in this rôle until the Second World War. The classic example of the use of catapult aircraft in a naval battle was that of the Fairey Seafox of the cruiser *Ajax*, which spotted for the guns during the Battle of the River Plate in December 1939. During the early thirties an improved type of catapult (then known as accelerator) was introduced in aircraft-carriers. In this type the hydro-pneumatic mechanism was

This photograph of a Parnall Panther aboard HMS *Argus* illustrates well the longitudinal arrester wires, the hinged wooden flaps mounted transversely, the hooks on the axle and the forward hydrovane. The period was 1919–20. *(Imperial War Museum)*

A Fairey IIID seaplane leaves its wheeled launching trolley after taking off from HMS *Argus* in August 1922. *(MoD)*

installed below the deck and the aircraft was pulled off by means of a towing-bridle which ran through a slot in the deck. This system remained in use until superseded by the steam catapult in 1954, by which time, with the increase in all-up weights and wing-loadings, catapult take-off had become the more usual instead of merely an optional technique from a carrier deck. The steam catapult was invented by Cdr C C Mitchell, OBE, RNVR, and enabled the latest jet fighters and strike aircraft to be dispatched even when the carrier was at anchor. Before its introduction, carriers used their accelerators only when free take-off was impracticable due to insufficient wind across the carrier deck

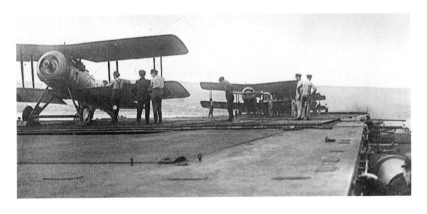

Nieuport Nightjar fleet fighters aboard HMS *Argus* in September 1922. *(MoD)*

or when a large number of aircraft awaiting dispatch restricted the take-off run forward.

Another take-off device, introduced during the Second World War with the advent of heavily-loaded strike aircraft and the faster monoplane fighters, was rocket assisted take-off gear, known as RATOG. Such equipment was, of course, rendered superfluous by the steam catapult.

Until the Spitfire and Hurricane were adopted for carrier duties in 1942, the performance of FAA aircraft had always lagged behind that of their RAF

Blackburn Dart single-seat torpedo bombers of No.461 Flight from HMS *Furious* typify the Fleet Air Arm of the 1920s. *(FAA Museum)*

land-based counterparts. This was due to a number of factors arising out of the peculiar nature of naval work. Firstly, more equipment had to be carried, such as arrester gear, flotation gear (until 1923 this took the form of external air bags with a hydrovane added for good measure), extra wireless, provision for wing folding and so forth: all this meant greater all-up weight, with consequent loss of performance. Secondly, owing to restricted space aboard carriers, there was a tendency to combine two or even three operational functions in one aeroplane: this technique precluded optimum performance in any of the rôles. Single-seat biplane fighters were less handicapped, and were only marginally slower than their land-based equivalents, but the disparity was marked from 1937 onwards, when the monoplane fighter came into general use in land-based squadrons: at the outbreak of war the FAA still had nothing better than the 250 mph four-gun Sea Gladiator. In the reconnaissance rôle, performance had shown an upward trend with the abandonment of the cumbersome three-seat spotter and the introduction of the two-seat fighter-reconnaissance aircraft (typified by the Osprey) around 1932, but this 170 mph biplane was still in service in 1939. For strike purposes, the FAA had from the days of the Cuckoo and Dart pinned its

19

From the mid-twenties until the Second World War most cruisers and battleships of the Royal Navy carried catapult aircraft for reconnaissance purposes. This picture of a Hawker Osprey of No.711 (Catapult) Flight was taken about 1936.

faith in the torpedo: this faith was amply rewarded by such outstanding successes as Taranto in 1940, but it cannot be denied that, technically, deck-landing torpedo aircraft showed little progress in the inter-war years, and it was not until as late as 1943 that all-metal monoplanes (Barracudas) began to replace the antiquated biplanes in the first-line squadrons. In all categories except one (the dive-bomber, represented by the Skua monoplane) the FAA was a force equipped throughout with biplanes when it went to war in 1939, and there was much truth in the charge that it had been unjustly neglected by the

A Blackburn Shark of No.810 Squadron on the deck lift of HMS *Courageous*. Note the mixture of RAF and naval personnel, an arrangement which lasted until 1939. *(Charles E Brown)*

20

powers-that-be. Although the position was largely retrieved by the skill and daring of its aircrews, the FAA's plight received little attention until February 1942, when the public outcry aroused by the escape of the German battleships through the English Channel led to some measure of priority being given to the question of naval aircraft supplies. By the autumn of 1942 the carrier-borne squadrons had begun to receive Seafires (naval versions of the Spitfires), and for the first time possessed a single-seat fighter comparable with any land-based

Famous aircraft: famous ship. Fairey Swordfish of No.814 Squadron flying over HMS *Ark Royal* in 1939. *(Charles E Brown)*

type. These saw action for the first time during the Allied invasion of North-West Africa in November 1942. In 1943–44 the situation was further improved by the large-scale deliveries of Lend-Lease aircraft such as the Corsair, Hellcat and Avenger, and it was these types which formed a large proportion of the British East Indies and Pacific Fleets in the operations leading to the final defeat of Japan.

The events of the Second World War brought full recognition of the value of air power at sea and effected such a revolution in naval thinking that by 1945 the carrier had already begun to assume its post-war rôle as the modern equivalent of the battleship, the backbone of the Fleet. Carriers had proved their ability not only in the classic rôle of providing fighter protection, reconnaissance facilities and strike forces for the Fleet itself, but also showed that there was a place for the smaller carrier as a close escort for convoys and for off-shore operations in support of the Army in beach-head fighting. From 1942 onwards the large Fleet Carrier was progressively supplemented by the Convoy Escort Vessel (about 40 of which were supplied by the USA for the duration of the war), which could be built more rapidly and economically than the full-size carrier. There were also about 20 Merchant Aircraft Carriers (MACships) which were converted merchantmen equipped with only a rudimentary flight deck to accommodate four Swordfish. The smaller carriers proved especially valuable in countering

21

A Fairey Albacore takes off from HMS *Formidable*, a typical fleet carrier of the Second World War. *(Imperial War Museum)*

Swordfish of No.824 Squadron aboard HMS *Striker* prepare for an anti-submarine patrol. This picture gives a good idea of the restricted deck area of a wartime escort carrier. *(Imperial War Museum)*

the U-boat menace, particularly in those stretches of the ocean beyond the range of land-based aircraft of Coastal Command. Of all the U-boats sunk in the Second World War, about half were destroyed from the air.

In August 1945 the FAA had grown to a first-line strength of 1,300 aircraft, with an additional 10,000 in training and second-line duties or in reserve. Strength in personnel amounted to 70,000. Nor was there any shortage of carriers. Apart from the smaller escort carriers obtained under Lend-Lease arrangements there were six Fleet Carriers (*Implacable, Indefatigable, Indomit-*

able, Illustrious, Formidable and *Victorious*) and five of the new class of Light Fleet Carriers completed or on the point of completion (*Glory, Ocean, Theseus, Triumph* and *Warrior*). With the exception of *Victorious*, withdrawn for complete modernisation in 1950 and recommissioned in January 1958, all the wartime Fleet Carriers had been scrapped or reduced to reserve by 1955 and had been superseded by *Eagle* (commissioned October 1951) and the new *Ark Royal* (commissioned February 1955). These 49,000-ton carriers were supplemented by three of 26,000-tons: *Albion, Bulwark* and *Centaur*, laid down in 1944–45 and completed in 1953–54.

The years 1945–56 were to bring far-reaching changes in the technique of deck-flying; changes which marched in step with the spectacular increases in aircraft performance as a result of the changeover from piston engines to jets. The period also provided in the Korean War (1950–53) and the Suez operation (1956) further evidence, if evidence were needed, of the unique ability of the aircraft-carrier to provide effective mobile task forces in localised war situations.

The FAA led the world in experiments with pure jets aboard aircraft-carriers. Within a few months of VJ-Day, on 4 December 1945, a specially modified Vampire had been successfully landed aboard the Light Fleet Carrier *Ocean*. It also led the world in introducing three inventions which enabled the aircraft-carrier to deal efficiently with the faster jets: these were the steam catapult (already mentioned), the angled deck and the mirror landing-sight. The angled deck and the steam catapult were to some extent complementary, in that they enabled flying-off and landing-on to take place simultaneously. With the greater speeds and higher wing-loadings of modern aircraft, it was becoming increasingly difficult to follow the old system, introduced about 1939, of using the first third of the deck for catapult take-off whilst aircraft landing-on used the remaining two-thirds, the two areas being separated by a crash barrier. To increase the deck area was impossible without making the carrier itself much

Fleet Air Arm Corsair fighters prepare to take off from a carrier of the East Indies Fleet for a strike on Sourabaya in May 1944. *(W E Rolfe)*

bigger. The problem was solved by the ingenious method (invented by Capt D R F Cambell, DSC, RN) of splitting the flight deck diagonally: this eliminated the need for a barrier, and meant that aircraft which failed to hook the arrester wires could take off again without encroaching on the space reserved for the forward catapult area. It also had the incidental advantage of leaving an aircraft parking area forward of the superstructure. The first aircraft-carrier of the

With the British Pacific Fleet in 1945. A flak-damaged Firefly of No.1770 Squadron aboard HMS *Indefatigable* is handled by a deck party. *(Imperial War Museum)*

The Vampire, modified for deck flying, which made the first landing by a pure jet aboard an aircraft-carrier in December 1945. The carrier is HMS *Ocean*. *(Charles E Brown)*

24

Supermarine Attackers, the first operational jet fighters ever used by the Fleet Air Arm, seen aboard HMS *Eagle*. Attackers entered service with No.800 Squadron in August 1951. *(MoD)*

Royal Navy with an angled deck was *Centaur*, completed in September 1953.

The mirror landing-sight, developed by Cdr H C N Goodhart, RN, was introduced to overcome the deficiencies of manual control of deck landing by a signals officer, known as the batsman. With the steadily increasing approach speeds of modern aircraft (the Sea Fury piston-engined fighter introduced in 1947 raised approach speeds to 105 mph—they had been less than 60 mph in the days of the Flycatcher) the old type of steepish descending approach at a speed little above the stall, followed by a flare-out and engine-cut, was modified in 1948 to a more nearly level approach at higher speed. The batsman technique, already severely strained by the new approach methods, became finally impracticable when jet fighters lifted approach speeds still higher (not far short of 140 mph), and the introduction of the mirror-sight eliminated the time-lag between the batsman's signal and the pilot's reaction to it, which could be disastrous at such speeds. With the mirror, the pilot received a direct visual guide to his angle of descent relative to the horizontal (indicated by means of lights), and had merely to fly straight on to the deck with no flare-out and no engine-cut until after touch-down. A further refinement of this system was the provision of an audio airspeed indicator (heard in the pilot's earphones), which eliminated the need to watch his instrument panel, and thus deflect his eyes from the mirror-sight during final approach.

The FAA's first operational jet squadron was No.800, which received its Attackers in August 1951. By 1955 the transition to jets in first-line fighter and strike squadrons had been completed: piston-engined aircraft remained only in second-line squadrons and for certain specialised duties such as airborne early warning—radar-equipped aircraft which extended the Fleet's radar range and helped to direct strike forces on to their targets as well as to vector interceptions. An interesting aspect of British naval aircraft equipment policy was the employment from 1953 onwards of turboprop aircraft in the strike rôle (Wyverns) and from 1955 in the anti-submarine rôle (Gannets). Another radical departure in the equipment field was the steadily increasing importance given to helicopters from 1950. Originally, the helicopter's place in naval aviation was that of ship-to-shore communications and 'plane-guard' duties aboard carriers, hovering in the vicinity of the ship during flying operations to rescue any crews unfortunate enough to crash into the sea. As more powerful types of helicopter became available, however, it soon became apparent that this class of aircraft had important potentialities for the anti-submarine rôle, and the FAA's first anti-submarine helicopter squadron (No.845) began operations in March 1954. The helicopter's ability to operate from the deck of any ship, and not merely an aircraft-carrier, extended its usefulness for submarine search and strike even further. An additional helicopter rôle, first demonstrated at Suez in 1956, is that of providing air lifts for assault troops between the decks of carriers and the territory to be invaded.

Traditionally, the main value of a carrier task force has been in providing air support in localised wars: the aircraft-carrier's ability to operate where land bases are not available and the fact that it presents a moving target was urged in its favour by advocates who saw in it an alternative method of launching nuclear-armed strike aircraft against land targets. Whether for use against land targets or enemy fleets, it became Admiralty policy to equip the FAA with aircraft capable of delivering atomic bombs; the Scimitar was the first FAA

A Sea King H.A.S.5 of No.826 Squadron embarks on *Broadsword*-class frigate *HMS Brave* in January 1990. (*RNAS Culdrose*)

26

aircraft capable of carrying a nuclear weapon and also the first swept-wing aircraft in the transonic class to enter FAA service. The first experimental flight of Scimitars was formed at Ford in August 1957, marking the beginning of a new era in naval air warfare.

Entering service shortly after the Scimitar (which replaced the Sea Hawk as the standard single-seat interceptor as well as being equipped for strike duties) was the two-seat Vixen, a transonic all-weather fighter which superseded the subsonic Sea Venom. Both Scimitar and Sea Vixen were armed with air-to-air guided missiles.

Then, in 1962, the Buccaneer strike aircraft entered service, regarded by many experts as the best aircraft of its kind in the world. In terms of aircraft, the Fleet Air Arm had never been better equipped: in the same year it obtained authorisation for its new aircraft-carrier, the CVA-01. A bright future was predicted and a Navy Minister stated, 'The carrier-force will continue to form the backbone of the Navy through the 1970s'.

In February 1966 this vision of the future collapsed with the announcement by the Labour Government that CVA-01 would not proceed on the grounds that it would be too expensive and that the traditional function of carrier-based aircraft could be carried out more cheaply by other means: shore-based aircraft of the RAF would take over the strike-reconnaissance and air defence functions of naval aircraft and would also supply the airborne early-warning facilities hitherto provided by carrier-borne Gannets. It was further suggested that the close anti-submarine protection of naval vessels could be carried out by helicopters operating from cruisers and frigates and that strikes against surface vessels would in future be the province of ship-to-ship guided missiles.

In the White Paper on Defence in 1968 it was announced that 'the carrier force will be phased out as soon as the withdrawals from Malaysia, Singapore and the Persian Gulf have been completed . . .' This was scheduled to take place at the end of 1971.

Then in June 1970 the Conservatives returned to power and many expected that earlier plans to abandon carriers would be completely reversed. In the event, with the publication of the Supplementary Statement on Defence Policy in October 1970, it became apparent that the new Government was only prepared to delay the demise of the aircraft-carrier, extending the life of the new re-fitted *Ark Royal* with its Buccaneers and Phantoms to the late 1970s and phasing out *Eagle* with its Buccaneers and Sea Vixens (it could not take Phantoms without extensive re-fit) in 1972. It was decided not to replace *Ark Royal* with another large fixed-wing carrier.

With the final retirement of *Ark Royal* in December 1978, the FAA was to be without high-performance fixed-wing aircraft in the front line until the summer of 1980, when the Sea Harrier came into service. The deployment at sea of a force of carrier-borne fighter aircraft plus a highly effective force of anti-submarine warfare helicopters (Sea Kings) had been made possible with the successful development of the small 'through-deck' cruiser typified by HMS *Invincible*, launched in May 1977 and HMS *Illustrious*, launched in December 1978. These ships were virtually small aircraft carriers and had their potential considerably enhanced by the installation of a new invention comparable in importance with the angled deck and the mirror landing sight, namely the ski-ramp in the bows, angled at 7 degrees. A similar device, inclined at 12

27

Wessex H.U.5 helicopters of No.848 Squadron with Royal Marines of No.41 Commando on board HMS *Albion* in 1965. *(MoD (Royal Navy))*

degrees, was also installed in HMS *Hermes* when it was re-fitted in 1979. The ski ramps (eventually inclined at 12 degrees) were for the benefit of the Sea Harriers and greatly assisted take-off with heavier war-loads.

A third carrier in the *Invincible* class was launched in June 1981 as HMS *Ark Royal*, but with the financial economies introduced by the Government, *Invincible* was announced as sold to the Royal Australian Navy until the Falklands crisis intervened.

Meanwhile the phased introduction of new and more potent helicopters with improved missiles (Lynx and Sea Skuas) went ahead in over 50 ships, primarily frigates of the Type 21, *Leander*-class, *Tribal*-class and Type 82 and Type 42 destroyers. As a result, the Fleet Air Arm had by 1979/80 become an air force wholly-equipped with vertical or short take-off aircraft, either helicopters or Sea Harriers, including a force of about 100 Sea King anti-submarine helicopters using the most advanced avionics and acoustic sensors available.

In addition to this, and also in support of the NATO commitment of the Royal Navy, the Royal Marine Commando continued to operate in Northern Norway in annual *Clockwork Cell* operations using Sea King Mk.4s carrying Land-Rovers, 105 mm light guns or heavy over-snow vehicles.

The proposed withdrawal of the carrier *Hermes* as part of the Defence cuts in 1981 came as a threat to future Marine operations, and equally unwelcome was the prospect of some 17 fewer frigates being available for Lynx Flights, but plans were confirmed to proceed with such key weapons as the Sea Eagle air-launched anti-ship missile, promising much-augmented strike capacity for the Sea Harrier. In the event, the Falklands crisis of 1982 saw both *Hermes* and *Invincible* spearheading a Task Force in the South Atlantic, adding yet another chapter to the Fleet Air Arm's colourful history.

During the Falklands War, in which the Fleet Air Arm played such a vitally successful rôle, the Sea Harriers destroyed twenty enemy aircraft, including sixteen with the use of Sidewinder missiles. The fighter squadrons involved were Nos.800, 801 and 809. In the anti-submarine and transport rôles, the helicopters performed superbly and Sea Kings alone completed over 2,250 sorties, proving invaluable to the success of the Task Force. Sea Kings were operational with Nos.820, 824, 825, 826 and 846 Squadrons. Also in action were the Wessex helicopters of Nos.737, 845, 847 and 848 Squadrons, mainly in the transport rôle, but HMS *Antrim*'s Wessex succeeded in severely damaging the Argentine

28

submarine *Santa Fe* with depth charges, leaving it to be finally knocked out by torpedoes from HMS *Brilliant's* Lynx and A.S.12 missiles from Wasp helicopters from *Endurance* and *Plymouth*. The new Sea Skua anti-ship missile was used for the first time by Lynx light helicopters from HMS *Coventry* and *Glasgow*. The Lynx were operated by No.815 Squadron and the Wasps by No.829 Squadron.

Despite all these successes, the absence of an airborne early warning facility was a severe hazard and steps were quickly put in hand to remedy this, but too late for Falklands operations. The outcome was the Sea King A.E.W.2 equipped with Searchwater radar which first became operational during the exercise *Ocean Safari* in 1985.

The year 1988 saw the final disappearance of the trusty Wessex and Wasp and plans going ahead to update Sea Harriers (to F.R.S.2 standard for the 1990s), Sea King (to H.A.S.6 standard) and Lynx (to H.A.S.3 and H.A.S.8 standard). This marched in step with the introduction of ever more sophisticated avionics and radars such as Blue Vixen, Sea Searcher, Sea Spray and Sea Owl. New missiles, too, were coming forward and Sea Eagle entered service from 1989.

Following its historic contribution in 1982, the carrier *Invincible* was given a re-fit in 1986/87, followed by *Illustrious* and finally *Ark Royal* and these three ships will continue in the 1990s to ensure that the Royal Navy can operate at least two air groups of Sea Harriers and Sea Kings to keep sea routes open, to mount an anti-submarine force and to provide cover for amphibious landings. Backing this will be the Lynx ASW helicopters in Type 42 frigates and similar ships and Sea Kings in Royal Fleet Auxiliaries (such as *Fort Victoria*). From 1990, Sea Kings were also operated from the decks of Type 22 *Broadsword* class frigates. Ultimately, the helicopter force is to be joined by the new Westland Merlin now under development at Yeovil.

The Fleet Air Arm of today (1990) continues to be one of the most

A Sea Harrier of No.899 Squadron takes off from an inclined launching ramp.
(British Aerospace)

highly-trained and efficient fighting forces in the world and although not large (340 aircraft in thirteen first-line and seven second-line squadrons) it would doubtless give an excellent account of itself if ever called upon to do so.

A Sea King H.A.S.6 of No.824 Squadron formates with a Sea King H.A.S.5, both based at RNAS Prestwick. (HMS *Gannet*)

Fleet Air Arm fighter for the 1990s; Sea Harrier F.R.S.2 on board HMS *Ark Royal*.

Avro 504B (N5273) built by Sunbeam. *(Imperial War Museum)*

Avro 504

For over 15 years the Avro 504 was the standard trainer of the British flying services, and on this fact alone its reputation stands secure in aviation history. It is less often appreciated that in the opening phases of the 1914–18 War it was used in first-line squadrons of the RFC and the RNAS for reconnaissance and bombing and that, with the RNAS, Avro 504s were responsible for one of the most audacious operations of the First World War.

The prototype of the immortal 504 series was tested at Brooklands in July 1913. In general appearance it resembled very closely the thousands of production aircraft that were to follow; the main differences were in the square-section cowling for the 80 hp Gnome engine, the straight top longeron of the fuselage and the fact that lateral control was dependent on wing-warping instead of conventional hinged ailerons. Very early in the 504's career the wing-warping was discarded in favour of normal ailerons and a better streamlined cowling fitted.

For 1913, the Avro 504 presented a thoroughly modern appearance, an appearance matched by a correspondingly good performance. Its sole rival in this respect was the Sopwith Tabloid, which turned out to have an even better performance, but in the event (chiefly due to its adoption as a trainer) the Avro outlived the Tabloid by many years.

The original military orders for the Avro 504 were complicated by the fact that the Admiralty specified a different wing spar from that agreed by the War Office, and until the emergence of the RAF in 1918 this difference between the RFC and RNAS versions remained.

At the outbreak of war in August 1914 the RNAS had only one Avro 504 on its strength, but by the middle of December 1914 No.1 Squadron RNAS (Sqn Cdr A M Longmore) had five more among its equipment. This squadron was sent to France in February 1915 to relieve Wg Cdr C R Samson's famous Eastchurch Squadron, which had been overseas since 27 August 1914 and which had taken delivery of its first Avro 504 on 27 November. The Eastchurch Squadron's Avro lost little time in getting into action, and on 14 December 1914, flown by F/Sub-Lt R H Collett, dropped four 16 lb bombs on the Ostend–Bruges railway.

Routine sorties of this kind, however, would have contributed little to the fame of the Avro 504 as a weapon of war; what focused attention on the type was the magnificent and now historic raid of 21 November 1914, when three Avro 504s of the RNAS bombed the Zeppelin sheds at Friedrichshafen, on Lake Constance. This raid provided a good example of the Admiralty's remarkable foresight in the promoting the use of the bombing aeroplane, a policy which was later pursued with even more vigour in 1916 with the establishment of Nos.3 and 5 Wings for bombing duties.

The RNAS unit which bombed Friedrichshafen formed at Manchester, under the command of Sqn Cdr P Shepherd, in October 1914, and it was decided to launch the attack from Belfort, a few miles from the Franco–Swiss border and about 120 miles from the target. The four Avro 504s concerned were Nos.179, 873, 874 and 875; No. 179 was the first of the type to be made for the Admiralty and hence, by the RNAS system of those days, sometimes used as a designation. The raid was at first delayed by bad weather, but when the aircraft eventually set off, each loaded with four 20 lb bombs, No.873 was flown by Sqn Cdr E F Briggs, No.874 by F/Lt S V Sippe and No.875 by F/Cdr J T Babington. No.179, flown by F/Sub-Lt R P Cannon, was forced to retire owing to a broken tailskid. The raiders flew north of Basle, followed the Rhine at a height of about 5,000 ft, came down to within 10 ft of the water over Lake Constance to escape detection and then climbed to 1,200 ft again about five miles from the target. The three Avros dived to about 700 ft to release their bombs, and the effect was catastrophic. A gas-works exploded and sent gigantic flames into the sky and one of the Zeppelins was gravely damaged. Sqn Cdr Briggs was shot down and taken prisoner, but the other aircraft returned safely. Perhaps the best summary of this truly remarkable achievement is that by Walter Raleigh, the official historian, who wrote in *The War in the Air*:

Avro 504A of the type used in the RNAS raid on the Zeppelin sheds, 1914. *(Imperial War Museum)*

Avro 504C (No.1488) of the RNAS at St Pol. *(Photo from H H Russell.)*

'The pilots deserve all praise for their admirable navigation, and the machines must not be forgotten. There have since been many longer and greater raids, but this flight of 250 miles, into gunfire, across enemy country, in the frail little Avro with its humble horse-power, can compare as an achievement with the best of them.'

Although the Zeppelin sheds were not attacked again, Avro 504s took part in other notable bombing raids. One of these occurred on 24 March 1915, when five aircraft of No.1 Squadron, RNAS, flown by Sqn Cdr I T Courtney, F/Lts B C Meates and H L Rosher and F/Sub-Lts B L Huskisson and F G Andreae, raided the submarine depot at Hoboken near Antwerp and destroyed two U-boats, as well as setting the shipyard on fire.

Avro 504s were also employed as anti-Zeppelin fighters, and on the night of 16–17 May 1915 both the LZ38 and LZ39 were intercepted by Avros flown by F/Sub-Lt R H Mulock (who later commanded No.3 Squadron, RNAS) and F/Cdr A W Bigsworth respectively. Both Zeppelins escaped destruction, but LZ39 was badly damaged by the four 20 lb bombs which were dropped on its envelope as Bigsworth climbed above it over Ostend. One variant of the Avro 504, the 504C, was specially developed for anti-Zeppelin patrols and about 80 were supplied to the RNAS. It had an auxiliary fuel tank in place of the front cockpit, which increased its endurance to eight hours, and frequently carried a Lewis machine-gun firing upwards at an angle of 45 degrees through the centre section.

The Avro 504C (of which 80 were built) shared with the other RNAS variants

Avro 504E (No.9277) of the RNAS. *(Imperial War Museum)*

the 504B, 504E and 504G a distinctive type of tail in which the familiar comma rudder of the 504 was replaced by vertical tail surfaces of elongated pattern. This tail assembly was used only on RNAS 504s; another distinctive feature of naval Avros were the long-span ailerons. The Avro 504B was employed chiefly for training and about 230 were built. The Avro 504G, of which 44 were built, was a gunnery-training development of the 504B and it was fitted with a single, fixed, synchronised Vickers machine-gun forward and a Lewis machine-gun on a Scarff ring aft.

The Avro 504E differed more markedly from the classic 504 configuration than the other RNAS variants. Whereas the 504B, C and G had all retained the 80hp Gnome engine, the 504E had a 100hp Gnome Monosoupape; it also reverted to the straight-top longerons of the original Avro 504. Another noticeable feature of the 504E was the heavy reduction of wing stagger; this resulted from the changed centre of gravity position due to the installation of the

Avro 504K with 100 hp Gnome Monosoupape. *(Imperial War Museum)*

main fuel-tank between the two cockpits and the re-positioning of the rear cockpit further aft. The Avro 504Es served at RNAS flying schools at Chingford, Cranwell and Fairlop.

Mention must be made of two important experiments in naval flying which were undertaken by the Avro 504B and C. The 504B was used in pioneering work on deck-arrester gear and the 504C (under the new designation 504H) became in 1917 one of the first aircraft to be launched by catapult gear: the pilot was F/Cdr R E Penny.

With the amalgamation of the RFC and RNAS to form the RAF in 1918, the Avro 504K was also used at former RNAS training schools, and this type remained in service for the training of FAA pilots during the nineteen-twenties. In 1923, at Leuchars, pilots scheduled for Panther spotter-reconnaissance flights first completed a course on Avro 504Ks, or dual Snipes, so as to accustom themselves to the vagaries of rotary engines; there were no dual-control Panthers. At about the same period all naval officers trained as pilots did their *ab initio* instruction on Avro 504Ks at Netheravon.

UNITS ALLOCATED

No.1 Squadron RNAS (Dover and Dunkirk); No.2 Wing, RNAS (Imbros); No.3

Squadron (formerly Eastchurch Squadron) RNAS (Dunkirk); No.4 Squadron, RNAS (Dover and Eastchurch). RNAS training schools at Chingford, Cranwell, Fairlop, Frieston, Manston, Port Victoria and Redcar.

TECHNICAL DATA (AVRO 504A, 504B and 504C)

Description: Avro 504A: Single-seat bombing aircraft; Avro 504B: two-seat trainer; Avro 504C: single-seat anti-Zeppelin fighter.

Manufacturers (504A): A V Roe & Co Ltd, Miles Platting, Manchester. (504B): A V Roe & Co Ltd, and sub-contracted by Parnall & Sons, Bristol; Regent Carriage Co Ltd, Fulham; Sunbeam Motor Car Co Ltd, Wolverhampton. (504C): A V Roe & Co Ltd, and sub-contracted by Brush Electrical Engineering Co Ltd, Loughborough. Serial numbers allocated were:- (504A):Nos.179, 873–878. (504B):Nos.1001–1050, 9821–9830, 9861–9890, N5250–5279, N5310–5329, N6010–6029, N6130–6159, N6650–6679. (504C):Nos.1467–1496, 3301–3320 and 8574–8603. (504E):Nos.9276–9285. (504G):N5800–5829.

Power Plant (504): One 80 hp Gnome; (504B): one 80 hp Gnome or 80 hp Le Rhône; (504C): one 80 hp Gnome.

Dimensions: Span, 36 ft. Length, 29 ft 5 in. Height, 10 ft 5 in. Wing area, 330 sq ft.

Weights (504): Empty, 924 lb. Loaded, 1,574 lb.

Performance: (504): Maximum speed, 82 mph at sea level. Climb 7 min to 3,500 ft. Endurance, 4½ hr.

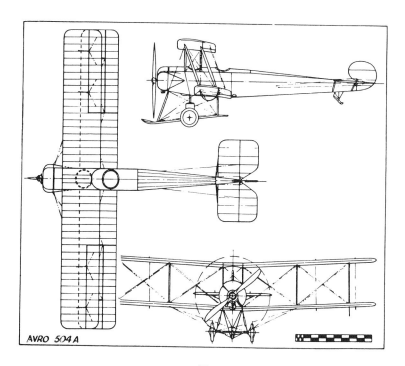

AVRO 504A

35

Armament: The Avro 504 equipped as a bomber carried four 20 lb bombs in improvised racks below the bottom wings and four small incendiaries. For anti-Zeppelin patrols, the Avro 504C had a single Lewis gun firing incendiary ammunition.

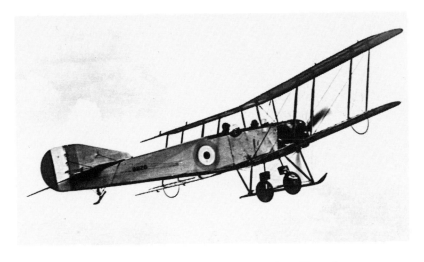

Avro 504B (No.9826) of the RNAS (*Imperial War Museum*)

Bison II (N9848) of No.423 Flight from *Hermes* in 1926. *(FAA Museum)*

Avro Bison

Speaking of the Avro Bison and the Blackburn Blackburn in his book *Flying and Soldiering*, R R Money recalled that, in both types, 'A 450 hp Napier Lion engine towed an unwieldy contraption about the sky.' There is no denying that the Bison, like other British naval aircraft of the early nineteen-twenties, was uncommonly ugly. The cumbersome lines of these early Fleet spotters resulted from the attention given to the needs of the naval observers and wireless operators, who were provided with an enormous cabin, with generous windows, in which to go about their duties with maps, plotting tables, wireless sets and other impedimenta. Welcome as this no doubt was to the naval observer, it resulted in a fuselage of ungainly proportions with an unusually large cross-section, paying little regard to the requirements of aerodynamics. The body of the Bison was set so high that the line from the pilot's cockpit to the airscrew boss ran at a downward angle of about 45 degrees. To assist the pilot when landing and taking off, it was found necessary to fit an aiming-rod parallel with the line of flight.

The prototype Bison I (N153) first appeared in 1921, and a second prototype (N154) was exhibited in the New Types Park at the RAF Display at Hendon in 1923. There was also a third prototype, N155. Production Bisons for the FAA totalled 53, comprised of 12 Mk.Is and 41 Mk.IIs. The Mk.I had the top wing attached to the top of the fuselage: the Mk.II raised the wing on centre-section struts and also introduced a long dorsal-fin extension. The Bison Is were serialled N9591 to 9602 and the Mk.IIs N9836 to 9853, N9966 to 9977, S1109 to 1114 and S1163 to 1167. Avro was building Bisons from 1923 until 1927.

The first Bisons in service went to No.423 (Fleet Spotter) Flight at Gosport, Hampshire, in November 1923 and subsequently embarked in HMS *Argus* in May 1924. The Bison was retired from the FAA in March 1929, when it was finally superseded by the Fairey IIIF in No.421 Flight.

Fleet Spotter Flights: No.421 *(Furious)*, No.421A *(Furious)*, No.421B *(Eagle, Argus* and *Furious)* and No.423 (Gosport, *Argus,* Donibristle, *Eagle* and *Hermes).*

TECHNICAL DATA (BISON II)

Description: Carrier-borne fleet spotter-reconnaissance aircraft with a crew of three or four. Available both as landplane and amphibian. Wooden wings, fabric covered. Steel-framed fuselage with ply and fabric covering. Maker's designation, Type 555.

Manufacturers: A V Roe & Co Ltd, Manchester and Hamble.

Power Plant: One 480 hp Napier Lion II.

Dimensions: Span, 45 ft 10 in. Length, 35 ft 6 in. Height, 12 ft 9 in. Wing area, 620 sq ft.

Weights: Empty, 4,116 lb. Loaded, 6,132 lb.

Performance: Maximum speed, 105 mph at 6,500 ft. Cruising, 90 mph. Climb, 19 min to 10,000 ft. Initial climb, 600 ft/min. Range, 360 miles. Service ceiling, 14,900 ft.

Armament: One free-mounted Lewis machine gun on Scarff ring amidships, and a single fixed Vickers machine-gun forward. Light bomb racks below wings for two 230 lb or four 112 lb bombs.

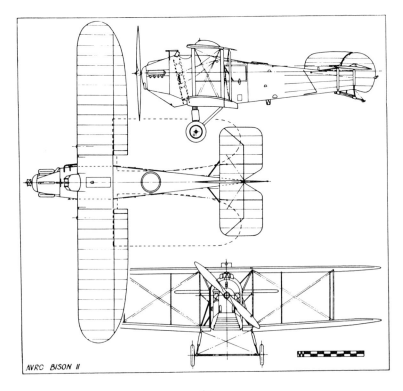

AVRO BISON II

B.E.2c (No.8300) of the RNAS. *(Imperial War Museum)*

B.E.2c

The B.E.2c is more often associated with the RFC, yet over 300 aircraft were delivered to the RNAS, where they were employed for bombing duties, for anti-submarine patrols and for training purposes.

Much has been written about the B.E.2c's dismal failure as a fighting machine with the RFC on the Western Front, its heavy losses in 1915–16 and the 'Fokker fodder' scandal. With the RNAS, however, it earned a somewhat happier reputation, perhaps because it was employed chiefly in theatres of war where the opposition was less vigorous. The RNAS was, in fact, the first service to use the B.E.2c in overseas zones other than France when, in April 1915, two B.E.2cs accompanied the Farmans, Voisins and a Breguet of No.3 Wing to Tenedos to take part in the Dardanelles campaign. In August 1915 they were joined by six more belonging to No.2 Wing, RNAS. All these naval B.E.2cs had 70 hp Renault engines, as fitted in the prototype which first flew in June 1914.

On 13 November 1915 a B.E.2c of No.2 Wing flown by F/Cdr J R W Smyth-Pigott made a daring night-bombing attack on a bridge at Kuleli Burgas spanning the Maritza river, a vulnerable point on the Berlin–Constantinople railway. Smyth-Pigott bombed from 300 ft and was awarded the DSO for his gallantry, though the target was not destroyed.

Many of the B.E.2cs used as bombers by the RNAS had a small bomb-rack beneath the cowling, as illustrated, and some were flown as single-seaters with the front cockpit faired over.

In the United Kingdom the RNAS used B.E.2cs for anti-submarine and Zeppelin patrols from coastal air stations until as late as 1918. On 28 November 1916, off Lowestoft, three B.E.2cs flown by F/Lt Cadbury and F/Sub-Lts Pulling and Fane brought down the Zeppelin L21.

The RNAS received 337 B.E.2cs altogether; 161 with Renault engines, 153 with the RAF 1a and 23 with the Curtiss OX-5. The last B.E.2c (No.10,000) left the Blackburn factory on 3 July 1917.

No.1 Wing, RNAS (Dunkirk), No.2 Wing, RNAS (Imbros and Mudros), No.3 Wing, RNAS (Imbros and Tenedos), No.7 (Naval) Squadron (East Africa). Also coastal air stations at Eastbourne, Hornsea, Great Yarmouth, Port Victoria, Redcar, Scarborough and training schools at Chingford and Cranwell.

TECHNICAL DATA (B.E.2c)

Description: Two-seat bomber and anti-submarine patrol aircraft. Wooden structure, fabric covered.

Manufacturers: Admiralty contracts to Beardmore; Blackburn; Eastbourne; Grahame-White; Hewlett and Blondeau; Martinsyde; Ruston, Proctor; Vickers; Vulcan; and G & J Weir.

Power Plant: 70 hp Renault, 90 hp RAF 1a or 90 hp Curtiss OX-5.

Dimensions: Span, 37 ft. Length, 27 ft 3 in. Height, 11 ft 1½ in. Wing area, 371 sq ft.

Weights: Empty, 1,370 lb. Loaded, 2,142 lb.

Performance: Maximum speed, 72 mph at 6,500 ft. Climb, 6½ min to 3,500 ft; 45 min to 10,000 ft. Endurance, 3¼ hr. Service ceiling, 10,000 ft.

Armament: Renault-engined bombers carried up to four 25 lb bombs under engine nacelle. RAF-engined single-seaters carried two 112 lb bombs or ten 20 lb bombs below the wings.

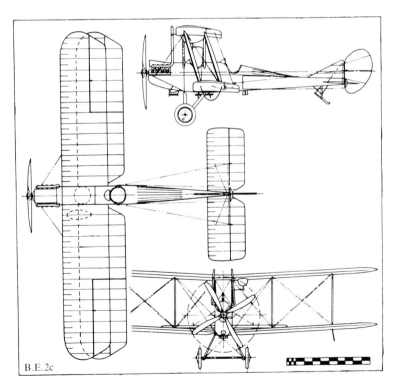

B.E.2c

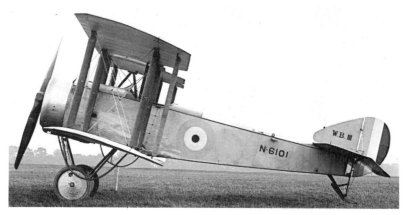

Beardmore W.B. III (N6101). *(Imperial War Museum)*

Beardmore W.B. III

The Beardmore W.B. III was introduced during 1917 and, although it can lay claim to no memorable engagements with the enemy, it is nevertheless interesting historically as an early attempt to produce an aircraft exclusively for carrier-borne flying. It was not an original design, being a derivative of the Sopwith Pup, but the ingenuity that went into its modification for aircraft-carrier work was quite remarkable. The adaptation was the work of Mr G Tilghman Richards, and the manufacturers were no strangers to the Pup, as they had been the first company to build Pups under licence for the RNAS.

The prototype W.B. III (No.9950) was in fact converted from the last batch of Sopwith Pups built at Dalmuir. It differed from the Pup in having folding wings to conserve hangar space aboard ship. Unlike the Pup, the wings had no stagger and the dihedral angle was reduced. The normal centre-section struts were replaced by full-length interplane struts adjacent to the fuselage and the ailerons were operated by control rods, the upper and lower ailerons being rigidly connected by a light strut. This last feature was abandoned in later production aircraft, which reverted to cable controls. Other modifications included wingtip skids and a lengthened fuselage, which was adapted to carry emergency flotation gear, and a remarkable system whereby the undercarriage was retracted to further economise in space when stored.

Two official designations were applied to the W.B. IIIs in service, S.B.3D and S.B.3F. The former indicated an aircraft with an undercarriage which could be jettisoned in the event of 'ditching', the latter a folding undercarriage. Production orders for 100 W.B. IIIs reached Beardmores (N6100 to N6129 and N6680 to N6749), but it is possible that not all were built. On 31 October 1918, 55 W.B. IIIs were officially 'on charge' but only 18 with the Grand Fleet.

UNITS ALLOCATED

Aircraft-carriers *Nairana* and *Pegasus*. RNAS shore stations at Donibristle, Rosyth and Turnhouse.

Description: Single-seat carrier-borne scout. Wooden structure, fabric covered.

Manufacturers: William Beardmore & Co Ltd, Dalmuir, Dumbartonshire.

Power Plant: One 80 hp Le Rhône or 80 hp Clerget.

Dimensions: Span, 25 ft. (10 ft 4 in folded). Length, 20 ft 2½ in. Height, 8 ft 1¼ in. Wing area, 243 sq ft.

Weights: Empty, 890 lb. Loaded, 1,289 lb.

Performance: Maximum speed, 103 mph at sea level; 91 mph at 10,000 ft. Climb, 9 min to 5,000 ft; 24 min to 10,000 ft. Endurance, 2¾ hr. Service ceiling, 12,400 ft.

Armament: One Lewis gun mounted above centre-section firing over airscrew.

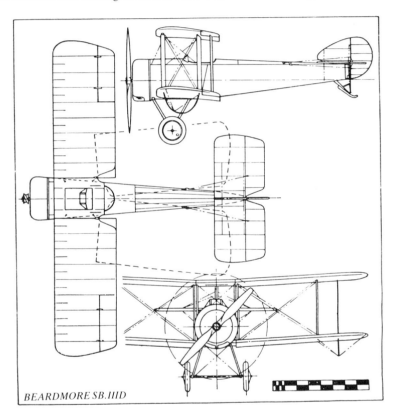

BEARDMORE SB.IIID

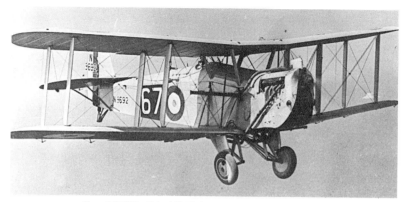

Dart (N9692) of No.460 Flight from *Eagle*. *(FAA Museum)*

Blackburn Dart

The Blackburn Company's association with torpedo aircraft began with the twin-engined G.P. seaplane of 1916 and was continued with the building of 80 Sopwith Cuckoos and the three Blackburn Blackburd prototypes (N113–115), the first Blackburn aircraft specially designed for torpedo-dropping. Next, in 1919, came the Swift. The Swift was the immediate predecessor of the Dart, which it closely resembled, and was exhibited at Olympia in 1920. The prototype (N139) was followed by overseas orders, but none were built for the FAA.

The Dart (prototypes N140, N141 and N142) appeared in 1921 and, like the Swift but unlike the Blackburd, which had to drop its wheels to release its torpedo, featured a split-axle undercarriage, one of the first of its kind. Darts entered service with Nos.460 and 461 Flights in 1923 (initially No.210 Squadron until April), and the type remained with the FAA until 1933, though in diminishing numbers from 1929.

The Dart lent itself well to carrier operation, being easy to land on a deck, and on 6 May 1926 F/Lt Boyce made the first night landing aboard an aircraft-carrier (HMS *Furious*) whilst flying a Dart, N9804. Although it did not have a high performance, the Dart did its job well and enabled the FAA, during its formative period, to develop its theories of torpedo attack. Darts were occasionally used in air-defence exercises, notably in 1931, when aircraft of No.463 Flight operated in night camouflage.

Total Dart production for the FAA was 117, the serial ranges being N9536 to 9561, N9620 to 9629, N9687 to 9696, N9714 to 9723, N9792 to 9823, N9990 to 9999, S1115 to 1120 and S1129 to 1138. Production ceased in 1927. A twin-float seaplane version of the Dart was also built, fitted with a second cockpit and dual control, and a number of these were operated for several years by one of the four RAF Reserve Training Schools of the late nineteen-twenties. The Dart was finally withdrawn in November 1934 and declared obsolete in April 1935.

UNITS ALLOCATED

No.460 Flight (*Eagle*, Mediterranean Fleet, 1923–30); No.461 Flight (Gosport and

43

Furious, Home Fleet, 1923–30); No.462 Flight (Gosport and *Furious*, Home Fleet, 1924–29);No.463 Flight (*Courageous*, Mediterranean Fleet, 1928–33); No.464 Flight (*Courageous*, Mediterranean Fleet, 1927–33). Also served briefly with No.810 Squadron before converting to Ripons after its formation out of Nos.463 and 464 Flights in April 1933.

TECHNICAL DATA (DART II)

Description: Single-seat carrier-borne torpedo-carrier. Composite wood and metal structure, fabric covered.

Manufacturers: Blackburn Aeroplane & Motor Co Ltd, Leeds, Yorks.

Power Plant: One 450 hp Napier Lion IIB or 465 hp Lion V.

Dimensions: Span, 45 ft 6 in. Length, 35 ft 4½ in. Height, 12 ft 11 in. Wing area, 654 sq ft.

Weights: Empty, 3,599 lb. Loaded, 6,383 lb.

Performance: Maximum speed, 107 mph at 3,000 ft. Climb, 600 ft/min. Range, 285 miles. Service ceiling, 12,700 ft.

Armament: Provision for one 18in torpedo beneath the fuselage or equivalent bomb-load comprising two 520lb bombs.

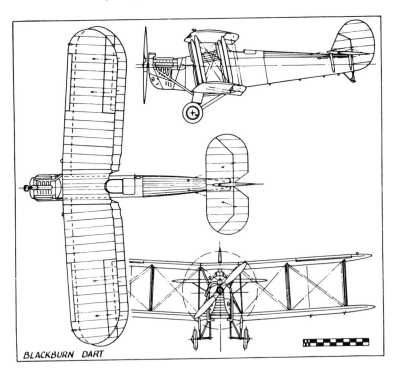

BLACKBURN DART

Blackburn II (N9982) of No.422 Flight from *Eagle*. *(FAA Museum)*

Blackburn Blackburn

The Blackburn Blackburn was a contemporary of the Avro Bison, and when it came to ugliness there was little to choose between the two. Both types were designed for spotting and reconnaissance duties, working in close co-operation with Fleet gunnery, and the bulky, ungainly fuselage resulted in the need to provide a cabin for the navigator/observer and wireless operator. Possibly because the performance suffered so badly, subsequent spotter-reconnaissance aircraft showed less thought for the comfort of the observer.

The Blackburn bore a close relationship to the Dart, and the first of three prototypes (N150, N151 and N152) appeared in 1922. In the Mk.I version the fuselage connected directly with both upper and lower wings; subsequently the gap between the wings was increased by raising the top wing on struts above the fuselage, and the wing petrol-tanks were eliminated. The first unit to be equipped in June 1923 was No.422 Fleet Spotter Flight, which served first in HMS *Eagle* with the Mediterranean Fleet and afterwards in HMS *Argus* on the China Station.

In 1925, the Blackburn Blackburn also entered service with No.420 Fleet Spotter Flight, where it superseded the ageing Westland Walrus, and operated for a time at Gosport before embarking in HMS *Furious* for duties with the Home Fleet.

In May 1929 the Blackburn flights were redesignated Nos.450 and 449 Fleet Spotter Reconnaissance Flights respectively: this was part of a general re-organisation of spotter flights involving the disbandment of the original Nos.420, 421, 422 and 423 Flights and the creation of Nos.440 to 450 Flights inclusive.

Blackburns finally disappeared from the Fleet Air Arm in June 1931, when No.449 Flight re-equipped with Fairey IIIFs in *Furious*. Between 1922 and 1924, a total of 33 Blackburn Mk.Is were built, serialled N150 to 152, N9579 to 9590,

N9681 to 9686 and N9824 to 9835. In 1925–26, the Mk.II was in production, a total of 29 being delivered to the FAA with the serials N9978 to 9989, S1046 to 1057 and S1154 to 1158. The Blackburn was finally declared obsolete in March 1933.

UNITS ALLOCATED

No.420 Flight (Gosport and *Furious*, Home Fleet, 1925–29); No.422 Flight (*Eagle*, Mediterranean Fleet and *Argus*, China Station, 1923–29); No.449 Flight (*Furious*, Home Fleet and *Courageous*, Mediterranean Fleet, 1929–31); No.450 Flight (*Argus*, China Station and *Courageous*, Mediterranean Fleet, 1929–30).

TECHNICAL DATA (BLACKBURN I)

Description: Fleet spotter-reconnaissance aircraft with a crew of three or four. Composite wood and metal structure, fabric covered.
Manufacturers: Blackburn Aeroplane & Motor Co Ltd, Leeds, Yorks.
Power Plant: One 450 hp Napier Lion IIB (465 hp Lion V in Mk II)
Dimensions: Span, 45 ft 6½ in. Length, 36 ft 2 in. Height 12 ft 6 in. Wing area, 650 sq ft.
Weights: Empty, 3,929 lb. Loaded, 5,962 lb.
Performance: Maximum speed, 122 mph at 3,000 ft. Climb, 690 ft/min. Range, 440 miles. Service ceiling, 12,950 ft.
Armament: One Lewis machine-gun on Scarff ring in rear cockpit and one Vickers machine-gun forward.

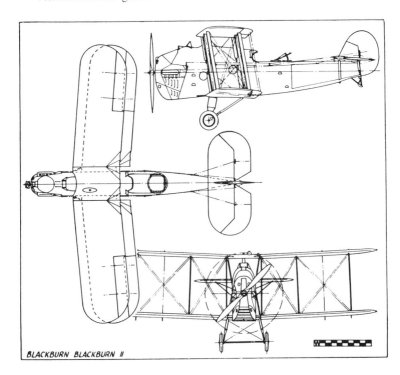

BLACKBURN BLACKBURN II

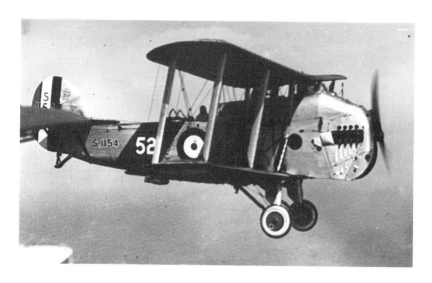

Blackburn II (S1154) of No.450 Flight from *Argus*.

(MoD)

Blackburn Blackburn Trainer

This side-by-side dual-control trainer variant of the Blackburn fleet spotter was known to the FAA as the Bull. Contemporary accounts allege that the drag was such with the side-by-side cockpit that the take-off run was increased to 600 yards, requiring the whole length of Leuchars aerodrome to get airborne. Once in the air, it took 10 minutes to reach 1,000 ft. Two Bulls (N9589 and N9989) were used by No.1 FTS Leuchars. The Blackburn Trainer illustrated (N9589) was a converted Mk.I and retained the split-axle undercarriage and upper wing tank but N9989 was a modified Mk.II. It entered service in January 1927.

47

Ripon IIA (S1564) of No.466 Flight from *Furious (MoD)*

Blackburn Ripon

The Ripon succeeded the Dart as the FAA's standard torpedo aircraft, first entering service with No.462 Flight in February 1929. Its increased radius of action, roughly twice that of the Dart, meant that an observer had to be carried to do the navigation. For this reason its rate of climb was not so good as that of the Dart, though it was faster.

The prototype Ripon Mk.I (N203) first flew on 17 April 1926 and was followed by a second (N204), tested on floats, and a Mk.II prototype (N231). The production version was designated Ripon II and IIA and was of composite wood and metal construction; later an all-metal version appeared under the designation Ripon IIC. A total of 96 Ripons was built for the FAA, and the last aircraft (K2887) was flown in December 1933.

Ripon II and IIA production aircraft were serialled S1265 to 1271, S1357 to 1369, S1424 to 1432, S1465 to 1473 and S1553 to 1574. Mk.IIC aircraft (all-metal) were serialled S1649 to 1674 and K2884 to 2887.

The Ripon was a multi-purpose aircraft; it was fitted with spools for catapulting and could be used for long-range reconnaissance with armament removed and extra fuel tanks installed to give a total endurance of 14 hr.

In addition to succeeding Darts in Nos.460, 461 and 462 Flights, Ripons provided the initial equipment of No.465 Flight formed on 20 March 1931, and of No.466 Flight formed on 31 March 1931. From January 1934 Ripons began to be superseded by Baffins, and the last in service were those of No.811 Squadron aboard HMS *Furious* in January 1935.

UNITS ALLOCATED

No.460 Flight (*Eagle, Glorious*, Mediterranean Fleet 1930–32); No.461 Flight (*Furious*,

Glorious, Mediterranean Fleet 1929–33); No.462 Flight (*Furious*, Home Fleet and *Glorious*, Mediterranean Fleet 1929–33); No.465 Flight (Gosport and *Furious*, Home Fleet 1931–33); No.466 Flight (Gosport and *Furious*, Home Fleet 1931–33); No.810 Squadron (*Courageous*); No.811 Squadron (*Furious*) and No.812 Squadron (*Glorious*).

TECHNICAL DATA (RIPON IIA)

Description: Two-seat carrier-borne torpedo-bomber. Composite wood and metal structure, fabric covered.
Manufacturers: Blackburn Aeroplane & Motor Co Ltd, Brough, E Yorks.
Power Plant: One 570 hp Napier Lion XIA.
Dimensions: Span, 45 ft 6½ in (17 ft 10 in folded). Length, 36 ft 9 in. Height, 13 ft 4 in. Wing area, 683 sq ft.
Weights: Empty, 4,255 lb. Loaded, 7,405 lb.
Performance: Maximum speed, 126 mph at sea level; 118 mph at 15,000 ft. Cruising, 109 mph. climb, 610 ft/min. Endurance (normal), 4 hr. Service ceiling, 10,000 ft. Range, 815 miles with torpedo or 1,060 miles for reconnaissance.
Armament: One fixed Vickers machine-gun forward and one free-mounted Lewis machine-gun aft. Provision for one Mk.VIII or Mk.X torpedo; alternatively one 1,100 lb smoke-container or a bomb-load comprised of three 230/250 lb or three 520/550 lb bombs on universal carriers under wings and fuselage and light series carrier for 20 lb practice bombs below starboard wing.

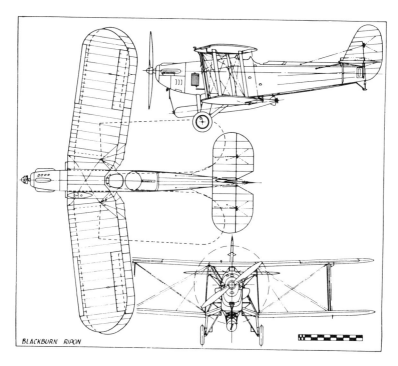

BLACKBURN RIPON

Baffin (S1358) of No.810 Squadron from *Courageous (FAA Museum)*

Blackburn Baffin

The Baffin succeeded the Ripon as the FAA's standard torpedo-bomber, and it was the first of the many Blackburn aircraft supplied for service in carriers to introduce an air-cooled radial engine, all its predecessors having had the Napier Lion. Indeed, the Lion had been used in every FAA aircraft from 1925 to 1932, with the exception of the Flycatcher. The Baffin's use of a radial had a precedent among Blackburn torpedo-bombers in the Beagle (N236) of 1928, which mounted a Bristol Jupiter, but this type never went beyond the prototype stage.

Two prototypes, then known as Ripon Vs, flew in 1932–33, one with a Tiger engine and one with a Pegasus. The type was named Baffin in September 1933 after a production order had been placed. Twenty-nine Baffins were built as such, with the numbers K3589, K3590, K3546 to 3559, K4071 to 4080 and K4776 to 4778 inclusive. There were in addition some 68 Ripons converted into Baffins; these retained their original serial numbers. The last of the true-built Baffins (K4778) was delivered in June 1935.

The first FAA squadron to receive the Baffin was No.812, which relinquished its Ripons in January 1934. Next came No.810 Squadron in July 1934, and No.811 Squadron in January 1935. In 1935 Baffins of No.810 Squadron had the honour of leading the formation of FAA aircraft taking part in the Jubilee Naval Review.

The Baffin offered only a marginally better performance than the Ripon and was in service for only a few years. No.812 Squadron was the last to retain the type, until December 1936. In Nos.812 and 811 Squadrons the Baffin was supplanted by the Fairey Swordfish, and in No.810 Squadron by the Blackburn Shark. It was finally declared obsolete in September 1937.

50

No.810 Squadron (*Courageous*); No.811 Squadron (*Furious*); No.812 Squadron (*Glorious*) and No.820 Squadron's 'A' Flight (*Courageous*).

TECHNICAL DATA (BAFFIN)

Description: Two-seat carrier-borne torpedo-bomber. Composite wood and metal structure, fabric covered.

Manufacturers: Blackburn Aeroplane & Motor Co Ltd, Brough, E Yorks.

Power Plant: One 565 hp Bristol Pegasus I.M.3.

Dimensions: Span, 45 ft 6 ½ in (17 ft 10 in folded). Length, 38 ft 3¾ in. Height, 13 ft 5½ in. Wing area, 683 sq ft.

Weights: Empty, 3,184 lb. Loaded, 7,610 lb.

Performance: Maximum speed, 136 mph at 6,500 ft; 125 mph at sea level. Climb, 480 ft/min at sea level; 600 ft/min at 5,000 ft. Range, 450 miles at 100 mph. Service ceiling, 12,500 ft.

Armament: One fixed Vickers machine-gun forward and one free-mounted Lewis machine-gun on Fairey high-speed mounting aft. Provision for one 1,576 lb Mk.VIII or Mk.X torpedo. Alternatively, six 230/250 lb or three 530 lb bombs could be carried, plus four 20 lb practice bombs.

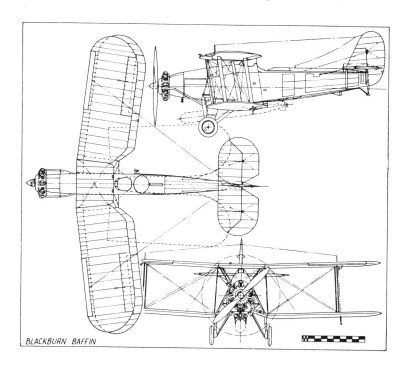

BLACKBURN BAFFIN

Shark II (K8454) of No.820 Squadron from *Courageous*. *(Charles E Brown)*

Blackburn Shark

The Shark was the last of the series of Blackburn torpedo biplanes for the FAA, and it embodied the experience gained with such stalwarts as the Dart, Ripon and Baffin. It had its genesis in the private venture Blackburn B-6 which flew on 24 August 1933. This became prototype (K4295) that made its first public appearance at the RAF Display at Hendon in 1934. It was designed to operate either as a landplane or as a seaplane, and the FAA used both, though the landplane predominated.

Blackburns received their first production contract for 16 Shark Is (K4349 to 4364) in 1934, and in December the type entered service with No.820 Squadron, formerly equipped with Fairey Seals.

The Shark II was the next version, for which K4295 again served as the prototype. A small order for three (K4880 to 4882) in June 1935 was followed by further contracts for 53 Mk.IIs (K5607 to 5659) in September 1935 and for 70 (K8450 to 8519) in January 1936. The year 1936 saw three more first-line squadrons equipped with the Shark, Nos.810, 821 and 822, formerly Baffins and Seals. First-line service of the Shark was to be relatively brief, for by September 1937 it had been wholly replaced by the Fairey Swordfish, and was used thereafter chiefly in the training rôle. The Shark I became obsolete in May 1938.

The final production version of the Shark was the Mk.III (see three-view), which introduced the added refinement of a glazed canopy for the crew. Ninety-five Shark IIIs (K8891 to 8935 and L2337 to 2386) were built to a contract received in January 1937. This variant, which was still widely used for the training of observers and telegraphists at the outbreak of war in 1939, was built to Specification S.19/36. Final production of the Shark for the FAA totalled 238. From July 1938 a number of Sharks were reconditioned at Blackburn's new Dumbarton factory. Sharks on training duties continued in service until October 1943 with No.755 Squadron at Worthy Down.

Nos.810, 820 and 821 Squadrons (all *Courageous*) and No.822 Squadron (*Furious*). *Catapult Flights:* Nos.444, 701 and 705. *Second-line Squadrons:* Nos.753, 755, 757, 758, 767, 774, 780 and 785.

TECHNICAL DATA (SHARK II)

Description: Two/three-seat torpedo-spotter-reconnaissance landplane or seaplane. Metal structure, with Alclad monocoque fuselage and fabric-covered wings.

Manufacturers: Blackburn Aircraft Ltd, Brough, E Yorks.

Power Plant: One 760 hp Armstrong Siddeley Tiger VI.

Dimensions: Span, 46 ft (15 ft folded). Length, 35 ft 2¼ in (38 ft 5 in as seaplane). Height, 12 ft 1 in. Wing area, 489 sq ft.

Weights: Empty, 4,039 lb. Loaded, 8,050 lb.

Performance: Maximum speed: 152 mph at 6,500 ft. Cruising, 118 mph. Initial climb, 895 ft/min. Range, 625 miles with bombs or 792 miles without bombs. Maximum range, 1,130 miles. Endurance, 4.9 hr. Service ceiling (with bombs), 16,400 ft.

Armament: One fixed 0.303 Vickers machine-gun forward and one flexible 0.303 Vickers or Lewis gun aft. One 1,500 lb torpedo or equivalent load of bombs.

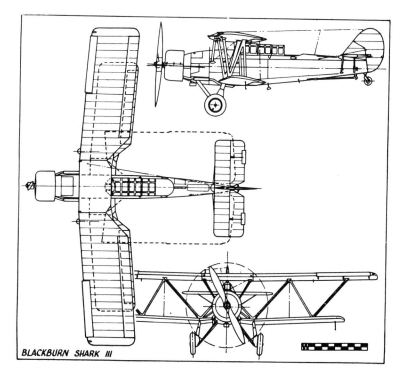

BLACKBURN SHARK III

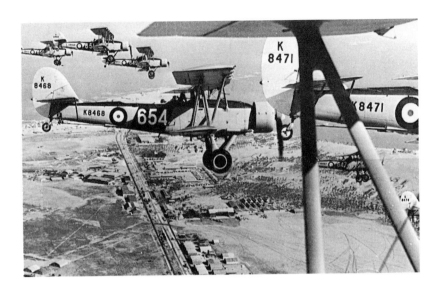

Sharks of No.820 Squadron from *Courageous (FAA Museum)*

(Imperial War Museum)

Blackburn Shark Seaplane

Twin-float verson of the Shark, as used by catapult flights in such warships as *Renown*, *Repulse* and *Warspite*. Length increased to 38 ft 5 in with floats fitted, otherwise technical details similar to landplane.

Skuas of No.803 Squadron from *Ark Royal. (Charles E Brown)*

Blackburn Skua

The Skua will go down in FAA history as its first operational monoplane and also the first British aircraft specifically designed for dive-bombing to enter squadrons. There had been earlier examples of monoplanes for the FAA such as the Blackburn Airedale, a parasol monoplane designed for Fleet spotting in 1926, but none of them had entered service.

Designed to Spec O.27/34, the first prototype Skua (K5178) flew first on 9 February 1937 and was followed by a second prototype (K5179), both aircraft having been ordered by the Air Ministry in April 1935. The designer was Mr G E Petty. The first prototype was exhibited in the New Types Park at the RAF's final Hendon Display in 1937, where it was seen in public for the first time.

In July 1936 the Air Ministry placed a production contract for 190 aircraft, and these Skuas (L2867 to 3056 inclusive) were fitted with the Bristol Perseus sleeve-valve engine and designated Mk.II. The first production Skua II flew on 28 August 1938. Production ceased in March 1940.

The first FAA unit to be equipped with Skuas was No.800 Squadron at Worthy Down in October 1938. They began deck flying in April 1939 aboard HMS *Ark Royal*, the Royal Navy's latest carrier at that time. With the outbreak of war, Skuas were also equipping Nos.801 and 803 Squadrons in *Ark Royal*. The first notable action by a Skua was by one of No.803's aircraft which on 25 September 1939 shot down a Dornier Do 18 flying-boat off Norway, the first enemy aircraft claimed by the FAA in the Second World War. On 10 April 1940 Skuas of Nos.800 and 803 Squadrons based at Hatston in Orkney dive-bombed and sank the German cruiser *Königsberg* in Bergen Fjord. In the Dunkirk evacuation, Skuas of No.801 Squadron operated with Coastal Command from RAF Detling, as dive-bombers and fighters. Skuas were also active off Dakar in September 1940 when aircraft of No.800 Squadron from *Ark Royal* bombed the battleship *Richelieu*.

Skuas remained operational with No.800 Squadron as dive-bombers until November 1940 and as fighters until February 1941, the last victory being over an Italian Cant Z.506 seaplane. After replacement by Fulmars and Sea Hurricanes, Skuas continued for several years as target-tugs based at shore stations at home and overseas. The sole surviving Skua (L2940) is at FAA Museum Yeovilton.

UNITS ALLOCATED

Nos.800 (*Ark Royal*), 801 (*Ark Royal* and *Furious*), 803 (*Ark Royal* and *Glorious*) and 806 (Worthy Down, Hatston, Detling and *Illustrious*). *Second-line squadrons:* Nos. 757, 758, 759, 760, 767, 769, 770, 771, 772, 774, 776, 778, 779, 780, 782, 787, 788, 789 and 791.

TECHNICAL DATA (SKUA II)

Description: Two-seat deck-landing fighter and dive-bomber. All-metal stressed-skin construction. Maker's designation: D.B.1A.

Manufacturers: Blackburn Aircraft Ltd, Brough, E Yorks.

Power Plant: One 905 hp Bristol Perseus XII.

Dimensions: Span, 46 ft 2 in (15 ft 6 in folded). Length, 35 ft 4 in. Height, 12 ft 6 in. Wing area, 319 sq ft.

Weights: Empty, 5,490 lb. Loaded, 8,240 lb.

Performance: Maximum speed, 225 mph at 6,500 ft or 204 mph at sea level. Cruising, 144 to 165 mph at 15,000 ft. Climb, 22 min to 15,000 ft. Range, 480 nautical miles (fighter) or 720 nautical miles (bomber). Endurance, 4 hours (bomber) or 6 hours (fighter). Service ceiling, 19,100 ft.

Armament: Four Browning machine-guns in the wings and one manually-operated Lewis gun in rear cockpit. One 500 lb bomb on ejector arm in recess below fuselage and eight 20 lb practice bombs on light series carriers below wings.

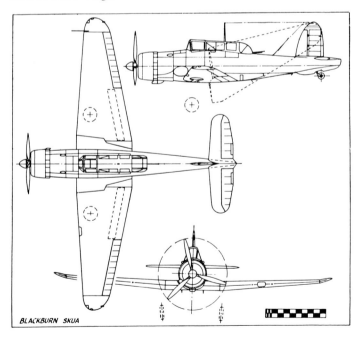

BLACKBURN SKUA

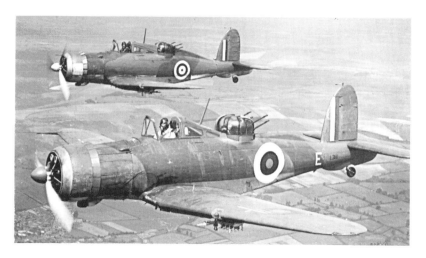

Roc Is from No.759 Squadron. *(The Aeroplane)*

Blackburn Roc

The Roc was the first aircraft ever used in the FAA to be equipped with a power-driven gun-turret. It was designed to meet the requirements of Spec O.30/35 and was intended as a FAA equivalent of the RAF's Boulton Paul Defiant. The tactical concept of a turret fighter, which brought its four guns to bear in broadside attacks on enemy bombers, were subsequently proved to be unsound, and the Roc saw only very restricted first-line service.

The design of the Roc was based closely on that of the Skua dive-bomber; the main points of difference were the slightly widened fuselage to accommodate the Boulton Paul turret and the use of increased dihedral on the wings from the centre-section, with no turned-up wing-tips. A twin-float seaplane variant was produced and appears on page 59.

Manufacture of the Rocs was entrusted to the Boulton Paul factory, after the production order was received on 28 April 1937. The contract was for 136 aircraft (L3057 to 3192 inclusive) and the first flew on 23 December 1938. Production ended in August 1940.

Rocs first entered service with the FAA in May 1939, being issued to Nos.800 and 803 Squadrons at Worthy Down to supplement Skuas. Lacking adequate performance, their brief operational career as shore-based fighters finally ended in June 1940 when No.806 Squadron's Rocs were superseded by Fulmars.

The Roc ended its days on training and target-towing duties with RNAS stations at Yeovilton, Eastleigh, Donibristle, St Merryn, Machrihanish, and Bermuda. The last Rocs in service remained with Nos.771, 772 and 773 Squadrons until April or May 1944.

UNITS ALLOCATED

Nos.800, 801, 803 and 806 Squadrons. *Second-line Squadrons:* Nos.725, 758, 759, 760, 765, 769, 770, 771, 772, 773, 774, 775, 776, 777, 778, 782, 787, 789, 791, 792, 793 and 794.

Description: Two-seat Fleet fighter. All-metal stressed-skin construction.

Manufacturers: Boulton Paul Aircraft Ltd, Wolverhampton.

Power Plant: One 905 hp Bristol Perseus XII.

Dimensions: Span, 46 ft. Length, 35 ft 4½ in. Height, 12 ft 1 in. Wing area, 310 sq ft.

Weights: Empty, 6,121 lb. Loaded, 8,800 lb.

Performance: Maximum speed, 219 mph at 6,500 ft. Climb, 6 min 30 sec to 5,000 ft; 13 min 36 sec to 10,000 ft; 25 min 36 sec to 15,000 ft. Endurance, 4 hours. Range, 480 nautical miles. Service ceiling, 18,000 ft.

Armament: Four Browning machine-guns in electrically-operated Boulton Paul turret amidships. Light series bomb carriers below the wings.

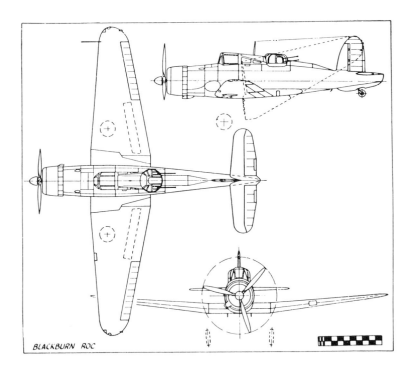

BLACKBURN ROC

Roc seaplane (L3059), converted at Dumbarton in 1939. (*FAA Museum*)

Blackburn Roc Seaplane

This variant was designed to Specification 20/37 as a twin-float seaplane fighter and three Rocs (L3057, 3059 and 3060) were converted at Blackburn's Dumbarton factory in October 1939.

Plans to equip No.805 Squadron with 18 Roc seaplanes were abandoned after the Norway campaign ended and in any event serious problems had been encountered during trials, notably directional instability.

Although seeing no operational service, some examples served in a training rôle with No.765 Squadron at Lee-on-Solent in 1940–41 and with No.773 Squadron in Bermuda in 1941–43.

The Roc seaplane had a length of 39 ft 4 in. Its top speed was 193 mph at 10,000 ft, its climb 1,130 ft/min and its service ceiling 14,600 ft.

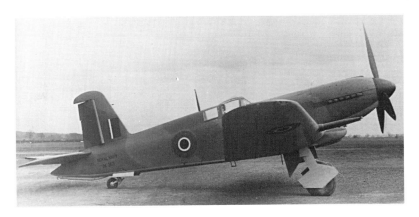

Blackburn Firebrand I

The Firebrand was designed to Spec N.11/40 and the prototype (DD804) flew on 27 February 1942. The second prototye (DD810) did deck landing trials aboard HMS *Illustrious* in February 1943. A third prototype (DD815) and nine production Firebrand F. Mk.I fighters (DK363 to 371) were built, all powered by the Napier Sabre engine. A production aircraft (DK363) is illustrated. Tested by No.778 Squadron at Arbroath and Crail in 1943.

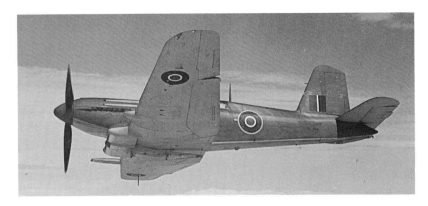

Blackburn Firebrand II

The Firebrand II had the centre section widened by 18 in to accommodate a torpedo between the wheel bays. The prototype (DD810 rebuilt and numbered NV636) flew on 31 March 1943 and 12 production aircraft followed serialled DK374 to 385. A production Firebrand T.F.Mk.II (DK378) is illustrated. One Napier Sabre III engine. Equipped No.708 Squadron at RNAS Lee-on-Solent and Gosport from October 1944 to August 1945.

Blackburn Firebrand III

This Firebrand variant was the immediate forerunner of the Mk.IV and most of the 24 production Firebrand IIIs serialled DK386 to 412 were subsequently converted to Firebrand 4s. The first prototype (DK372) is illustrated. First flight was on 21 December 1943 and a second prototype (DK373) was also built. The Firebrand III, the first variant with a radial engine, mounted the Bristol Centaurus IX and had a smaller fin and rudder than the Mk.4.

The Firebrand III was appraised by No.700 Squadron at Worthy Down and Middle Wallop, by No.703 Squadron at Thorney Island, by No.708 Squadron at Ford, Fearn and Rattray, and by No.778 Squadron at Arbroath and Gosport.

Maximum speed, 348 mph at 12,500 ft. Cruising speed, 299 mph at 10,000 ft. Service ceiling, 31,100 ft.

Firebrand T.F.5 (EK747). *(Crown Copyright Photograph)*

Blackburn Firebrand (Mks.4 and 5)

Although first conceived as early as 1939, the Firebrand did not reach a first-line squadron until 1945, and it saw no action in the Second World War. During these six years its rôle altered from that of a short-range interceptor to a torpedo-carrying strike fighter.

The prototype (DD804) was designed to Spec N.11/40 and, fitted with a Napier Sabre III, first flew on 27 February 1942. It carried no armament, but the second prototype (DD810), which flew 15 July 1942, had four 20 mm guns. By this time, however, it was clear that the Seafire enjoyed a lead in performance and it was decided to utilise the Firebrand's undoubted load-carrying capacity for torpedo work. Accordingly, the Firebrand II prototype (NV636, actually DD810 rebuilt) first flew on 31 March 1943, equipped to carry an 18-in torpedo between the wheel bays in a widened centre-section. Production of the Firebrands I and II was limited to 21, and with the Mk.III a change was made to the Centaurus radial due to the shortage of Sabre engines which were going into Typhoons for the RAF. The prototype Firebrand III (DK372) met the requirements of Spec S.8/43, and first flew on 21 December 1943. It was followed by a second prototype (DK373) and 24 production aircraft (DK386 to 412), but suffered from inadequate directional control at take-off. This was rectified in the Mk.4 by an enlarged fin and rudder, and this variant also introduced a two-position torpedo mounting and wing dive-brakes. Firebrand 4 production totalled 102 (EK601 to 638, EK653 to 694 and EK719 to 740), the first flying on 17 May 1945.

In September 1945 No.813 Squadron at Ford re-formed with 15 Firebrand T.F.4s and became the first FAA squadron to fly single-seater torpedo aircraft since the Dart had been retired in 1933. No.813's Firebrands participated in the Victory Flypast over London in June 1946.

The final Firebrand variants were the Mks.5 and 5A which entered service with No.813 Squadron in May 1947. Detail improvements included horn balanced elevators and longer-span aileron tabs, and the Mk.5A also had powered ailerons. Production totalled 68 (EK741 to 748, EK764 to 799 and EK827 to 850) and there were also about 40 Mk.4 conversions. A final contract for 80 Firebrands was cancelled in 1945. The Firebrand (of which a total of 220 was built) was superseded in the FAA during 1953 by the Westland Wyvern.

UNITS ALLOCATED

No.813 (RNAS Ford, *Implacable* and *Indomitable*) and No.827 (*Illustrious* and *Eagle*). *Second-line Squadrons:* Nos.703, 736, 738, 759, 767, 778, 787 and 799.

TECHNICAL DATA (FIREBRAND T.F.5)

Description: Single-seat deck-landing torpedo-strike fighter. Maker's designation: B-46.
Manufacturers: Blackburn Aircraft Ltd, Brough, E Yorks.
Power Plant: One 2,520 hp Bristol Centaurus IX.
Dimensions: Span, 51 ft 3½ in. Length, 38 ft 9 in. Height, 13 ft 3 in. Wing area, 383 sq ft.
Weights: Empty, 11,835 lb. Loaded, 17,500 lb (maximum).
Performance: Maximum speed, 340 mph at 13,000 ft. Cruising speed, 256 mph. Initial climb, 2,600 ft/min, or 2,200 ft/min with torpedo. Range, 740 miles at 256 mph, or 627 miles at 289 mph. Service ceiling, 28,800 ft.
Armament: Four 20 mm Hispano guns in wings and provisions for one 1,997 lb torpedo, or 2,000 lb of bombs or eight rocket projectiles.

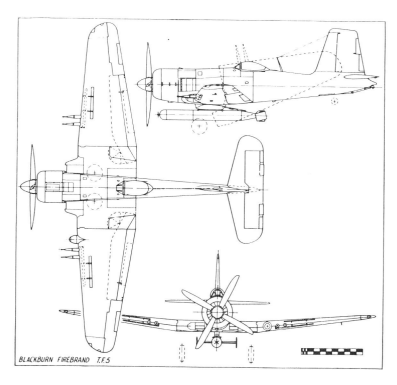

BLACKBURN FIREBRAND T.F.5

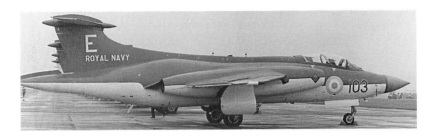

Buccaneer S.1 (XN960) of No.809 Squadron. *(Flight)*

Blackburn Buccaneer S.1

The Buccaneer, originally known as the Blackburn N.A.39, was the world's first specially designed, low-level, high-speed strike aircraft. It was designed by Mr B. P. Laight to an Admiralty requirement for an entirely new carrier-borne weapons system: an aircraft which would be capable of delivering a nuclear weapon by exploiting the vulnerable gap beneath enemy radar defences at a speed in excess of Mach 0.9.

The prototype (XK486) made its maiden flight at Boscombe Down on 30 April 1958, piloted by Lt-Cdr Derek Whitehead, only thirty-three months after the initial contract had been placed. In July 1955 a pre-production batch of fourteen Buccaneers (XK523 to 536) was ordered for development flying, and the first deck landing trials took place on board *Victorious* in January 1960.

In October 1959 an order for forty Buccaneer S.1 was placed, to follow directly after the completion of the pre-production contract. Serial numbers allocated were XN922 to 935 and XN948 to 973.

In March 1961 six Buccaneers were delivered to No.700Z Flight at RNAS Lossiemouth, the Intensive Flying Trials Unit commanded by Lt-Cdr A J Leahy, RN. The first operational squadron, No.801, formed at Lossiemouth in July 1962. Buccaneers of No.801 embarked in *Ark Royal* on 20 February 1963.

In 1965, Buccaneer S.1s of No.800 Squadron from *Eagle* were active with the Royal Navy force in the Indian Ocean enforcing oil sanctions on Rhodesia. They were air-refuelled by Scimitar tankers.

The unique electronic and weapons system of the Buccaneer enabled the two-man crew to carry out a planned operation of extreme accuracy using conventional or nuclear weapons. Extensive incorporation of the area rule configuration delayed the drag rise, and boundary layer control by ejected supersonic air nearly doubled the lift and decreased the approach speed. Steel fittings and components machined from the solid ensured the necessary fatigue strength for prolonged high-speed flight in the turbulent air near the ground. Weapons could be delivered by a conventional direct run over the target or by the newer 'toss bombing' technique, in which the weapon followed a ballistic trajectory to the target, by which time the aircraft was well away from the impact area.

The last Buccaneer S.1 was completed in December 1963.

From 1965, the Buccaneer S.1 was superseded in first-line squadrons by the Buccaneer S.2, details of which appear on pages 256–7.

Nos.800 (*Eagle*), 801 (*Ark Royal* and *Victorious*), 803 (*Hermes*) and 809 (*Victorious* and *Eagle.*) *Second-line Squadrons:* Nos.700 and 736 (RNAS Lossiemouth).

TECHNICAL DATA (BUCCANEER S.1)

Description: Two-seat carrier-borne low-level strike aircraft. Maker's designation, B.103.

Manufacturers: Blackburn Aircraft Ltd, Brough and Holme-on-Spalding Moor, E Yorks.

Power Plant: Two de Havilland Gyron Junior 101 turbojets, each of 7,100 lb static thrust.

Dimensions: Span 44 ft (20 ft folded). Length, 63 ft 5 in (51 ft 10 in folded). Height, 16 ft 3 in. Wing area, 515 sq ft.

Weights: Empty 24,500 lb. Loaded, 45,000 lb.

*Performance:*Maximum speed, 720 mph at sea level. Tactical radius 500–600 miles. Service ceiling: 50,000 ft.

Armament: Conventional or nuclear weapons carried internally in fuselage on large rotating bomb door. Bomb load, 5,000 lb.

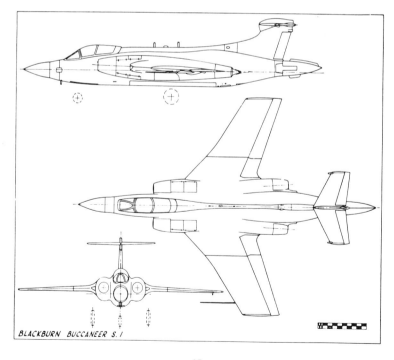

BLACKBURN BUCCANEER S. 1

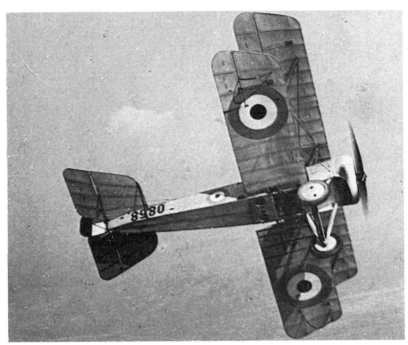
Bristol Scout D (No.8980) of the RNAS.

Bristol Scout C and D

The Bristol Scout occupies a unique position in British naval flying by being the first landplane with a wheeled undercarriage to take off from the deck of an aircraft-carrier. This feat was achieved on 3 November 1915 when F/Sub-Lt H F Towler flew his Scout C (No.1255) from the short flying-deck of the seaplane carrier *Vindex*. Two Bristol Scouts were accommodated, and for stowage they were dismantled. As there were no facilities for landing-on, flotation bags were fitted so that the aircraft could 'ditch' alongside.

The RNAS used both the Bristol Scout C and D, both of which were developments of the original Bristol Scout flown in February 1914. The RFC was the first Service to adopt the type (on 5 November 1914), but the RNAS followed soon afterwards with an order for 24 (Nos.1243 to 1266) on 7 December 1914. Some of these early Scout Cs served with the RNAS on the Western Front in 1915. They were followed by a second batch of 50 Scout Cs (Nos.3013 to 3062).

Later Admiralty orders were for the Scout D, which differed from the C in having shorter ailerons, increased dihedral and wingtip skids further outboard. Of the 80 Scout Ds delivered to the RNAS, the first 60 had 100 hp Gnome Monosoupape engines (Nos.8951 to 9000 and N5390 to 5399), N5400 an 80 hp Le Rhône and the final 19 (N5401 to 5419) the 80 hp Gnome, as on the Scout Cs.

Despite its fine design, the Bristol Scout was handicapped by lack of effective armament. It was used extensively for anti-Zeppelin patrols, both from carriers in the North Sea and from land bases such as Redcar and Great Yarmouth, but with no real success. One method of attack was to climb above the Zeppelin and drop Ranken darts.

The RNAS also employed Bristol Scouts in the Dardanelles campaign, sometimes to escort bombing raids.

UNITS ALLOCATED

No.2 Wing, RNAS (Belgium, Imbros and Mudros); 'A' Flight, RNAS (Thasos). Coastal air stations at Eastchurch, East Fortune, Great Yarmouth, Port Victoria and Redcar. Training schools at Chingford and Cranwell. Seaplane carrier *Vindex*.

TECHNICAL DATA (SCOUT C)

Description: Single-seat scout, land-based or carrier-borne. Wooden structure, fabric covered.

Manufacturers: British & Colonial Aeroplane Co Ltd, Filton and Brislington, Bristol.

Power Plant: One 80 hp Gnome.

Dimensions: Span, 24 ft 7 in. Length, 20 ft 8 in. Height, 8 ft 6 in. Wing area, 198 sq ft.

Weights: Empty, 750 lb. Loaded, 1,190 lb.

Performance: Maximum speed, 93 mph at sea level. Climb, 9½ min to 6,000 ft. Endurance, 2½ hr. Service ceiling, 15,000 ft.

Armament: Anti-Zeppelin aircraft carried 48 Ranken darts. Some Scout Ds had one Lewis gun above the centre-section.

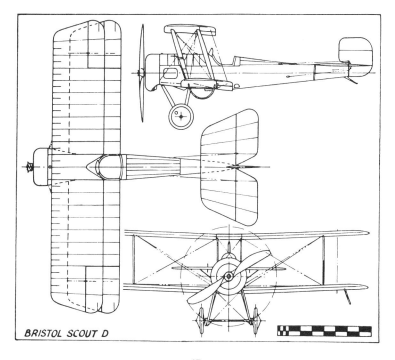

BRISTOL SCOUT D

Jetstream T.2s of No.750 Squadron. *(RNAS Culdrose)*

British Aerospace Jetstream (Mks 2 & 3)

Initially produced as a civil transport by the former Handley Page company, the Jetstream was later taken over by Scottish Aviation which eventually became the Scottish Division of British Aerospace. The Jetstream itself was adopted initially by the Royal Air Force and then from 1978 entered service with the Royal Navy in slightly modified form as a replacement aircraft for the veteran Sea Prince which had served as a 'flying classroom' and in various communications duties for 25 years.

The first Jetstream T.2 for the Fleet Air Arm (XX480) was delivered to the Royal Navy on 21 October 1978. By March 1979 there were six Jetstreams operating alongside six Sea Princes with No.750 Squadron at RNAS Culdrose and the transition to the type was completed by April 1979. With greatly improved avionics and flight performance compared with the Sea Prince, the Jetstream offered naval observers (subsequently to carry on their training in Sea King or Lynx helicopters) the opportunity to operate up to 280 mph at heights up to 26,000 ft.

Sixteen Jetstream T.2s were supplied to the Fleet Air Arm, serialled XX475, 476, 478–81, 483–490 and ZA110–111. All were converted from former Jetstream T.1s for the RAF, the main changes being the incorporation of a new, longer nose for the 45.7 cm Ekco scanner, a Decca Doppler 71 and two navigational consoles inside the cabin for trainee observers.

In 1984 the Royal Navy ordered four additional Jetstreams. Designated T.3, they were powered by Garrett TPE 331 engines and incorporated a ventrally-mounted radar scanner instead of the nose-mounted type of the earlier Jetstream T.2, which permitted an aerodynamically cleaner nose entry. The radar installed in the Jetstream T.3 was of the Racal ASR 360 type.

Jetstream T.3s were serialled ZE438 to 441 and first entered service with No.750 Squadron at Culdrose early in 1986.

UNITS ALLOCATED

No.750 Squadron at RNAS Culdrose, Cornwall.

Description: Multi-purpose crew training and communication aircraft. Crew of 2 plus 2 instructors and 3 trainees. All-metal stressed-skin construction. Maker's designation: Jetstream 201.

Manufacturers: British Aerospace (Scottish Division), Prestwick, Scotland.

Power Plant: Two 940 shp Turboméca Astazou XVI propeller-turbines.

Dimensions: Span, 52 ft. Length, 47 ft 1½ in. Height, 17 ft 5½ in. Wing area, 270 sq ft.

Weights: Empty, 8,741 lb. Loaded, 12,550 lb.

Performance: Maximum speed, 285 mph at 12,000 ft. Maximum cruising speed, 278 mph at 12,000 ft. Initial climb, 2,500 ft/min. Range, 1,382 miles. Service ceiling, 26,000 ft.

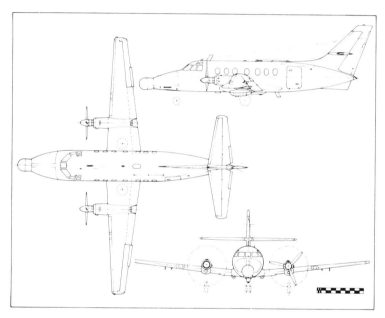

Jetstream T.3 (ZE438) of No.750 Squadron from RNAS Culdrose. (*HMS Seahawk*)

Sea Harrier F.R.S.1 (XZ452) of No.899 Squadron, RNAS Yeovilton. *(British Aerospace)*

British Aerospace Sea Harrier F.R.S.1

The decision of the British Government to order the Sea Harrier for the Royal Navy rescued the Fleet Air Arm from the virtual certainty, until that time, that it would become merely an all-helicopter force, and hence was of paramount historical importance. It was of course bound up with more complex matters concerning the future of the aircraft-carrier or alternative forms of surface warship design and undoubtedly the acceptance of the 'through-deck' cruiser concept, typified by HMS *Invincible*, laid down at the Barrow-in-Furness plant of Vickers Ltd in July 1973, was the deciding factor in determining that the 'fixed-wing' aircraft (albeit a highly unorthodox design) still had a significant rôle to play in naval air power.

Britain's pioneering of the V/STOL aircraft in squadron service in the world's air forces (by the Royal Air Force's land-based Harriers) led inevitably to the idea of operating the aircraft from the decks of warships, and numerous experiments were conducted leading to the first Harrier carrying official 'Royal Navy' markings (XV136) doing trials on board HMS *Hermes* in the English Channel in February 1977. Other aircraft involved in the same trials were XV281 from Boscombe Down, the two-seat XW175 from the Royal Aircraft Establishment at Bedford and the manufacturer's own demonstrator G-VTOL.

In May 1975 approval was finally given for development of the fully-navalised Harrier to proceed and a contract for 24 Sea Harriers (subsequently increased to 34) was placed. First Sea Harrier flight at Dunsfold was by XZ450 on 20 August 1978 and the main differences compared with the RAF's Harrier were the modified front fuselage with raised cockpit and improved avionics (such as the Blue Fox radar eventually installed), deletion of magnesium in exposed areas of the airframe, installation of improved Pegasus 104 engine, addition of autopilot, new nav-attack system and new weapon installations. Intended primarily for the air-defence rôle, the Sea Harrier also offered reconnaissance and strike capacity, hence the designation F.R.S.1.

The first Sea Harrier delivered to the Royal Navy (XZ451) reached Yeovilton on 18 June 1979. This was the second aircraft off the production line. The first (XZ450) had made its first landing on a carrier on HMS *Hermes* on 14 November 1978. Serial numbers allocated to Sea Harrier F.R.S.1s were XZ438–440, XZ450–460, XZ491–500, ZA174–177, ZA190–195, ZD578–582, XD607–615 and ZE690–698. Total production amounted to 57 aircraft.

Sea Harriers entered service with No.700A Squadron of the Fleet Air Arm at Yeovilton in June 1979 and on 31 March 1980 became No.899 Squadron. The first front-line unit, No.800 Squadron, commissioned in March 1980. Second operational squadron with Sea Harriers was No.801 which commissioned in January 1981, subsequently serving in HMS *Invincible*.

No.800 Squadron, the premier fighter squadron of the Fleet Air Arm, took its Sea Harriers on board HMS *Hermes* in June 1981. A third operational squadron, No.802, was originally scheduled to receive Sea Harriers for service in HMS *Illustrious* but this scheme fell victim to the 1981 financial cuts.

The arrival of Sea Harriers in operational squadrons from 1980 ended the unwelcome two-year gap in the availability of high-performance fighters in the FAA since Phantoms departed in November 1978.

With the outbreak of the Falklands crisis in April 1982 and the despatch of the Royal Navy Task Force to the South Atlantic, Sea Harriers of Nos.800 and 801 Squadrons went into action on board HMS *Hermes* and *Invincible* and operated both as interceptors in defence of the Fleet and on low-level offensive strikes on Argentine ships and airfield installations.

Sea Harriers destroyed a total of 24 Argentine aircraft in air combat (Daggers, Mirages and Skyhawks) and put out of action three enemy ships (*Narwal, Bahia Buen Suceso* and *Carcarana*). They flew over 2,300 sorties and lost only two aircraft to enemy action, adding a brilliant chapter to Fleet Air Arm history.

UNITS ALLOCATED

Nos.800 (Yeovilton, *Invincible, Hermes* and *Illustrious*), 801 (Yeovilton, *Invincible*), 809 (Yeovilton and *Atlantic Conveyor*) and 899 (Yeovilton, *Hermes, Invincible* and *Illustrious*). *Second-line Squadrons:* No.700A (Yeovilton).

TECHNICAL DATA (SEA HARRIER F.R.S.1)

Description: Single-seat carrier-borne fighter, reconnaissance and strike aircraft. All-metal stressed-skin construction.

Manufacturers: British Aerospace, Kingston-on-Thames and Dunsfold, Surrey.

Power Plant: One 21,500 lb static thrust Rolls-Royce Pegasus 104 vectored-thrust turbofan.

Dimensions: Span, 25 ft 3¼ in. Length, 47 ft 7 in. Height, 12 ft 2 in.

Weights: Empty, 12,950 lb. Loaded, 26,000 lb.

Performance: Maximum speed, 740 mph. Range, 250 nautical miles radius of action in strike rôle and 400 miles in interception rôle. Service ceiling, 51,200 ft.

Armament: Two fixed 30 mm cannon in underbelly fairings and two underwing pylon-mounted Sidewinder or Sky Flash missiles. Capacity to carry free-fall bombs or (from 1989) Sea Eagle anti-ship missiles with 60 mile stand-off range. Maximum weapon load: 8,000 lb.

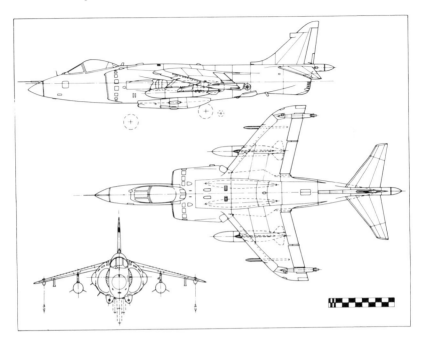

Sea Harrier F.R.S.1 of No.801 Squadron from HMS *Invincible* in 1981. *(British Aerospace)*

Sea Harrier F.R.S.1s of No.800 Squadron from RNAS Yeovilton. (*British Aerospace*)

Sea Harrier T.4N (XZ445) of No.899 Squadron. (*British Aerospace*)

British Aerospace Sea Harrier T.4N

In 1979, with the Sea Harrier F.R.S.1 starting to come off the production line, the Royal Navy placed an order for three Sea Harrier T.4N two-seat trainer variants of the single-seat fighter. These aircraft were to initiate the pilot conversion programme and the first T.4N (ZB604) was handed over to the Fleet Air Arm at Yeovilton on 21 September 1983. It entered service with No.899 Squadron (the Sea Harrier Headquarters Squadron) where it operated alongside the Hunter T.8M. Later, two additional Sea Harrier T.4Ns serialled ZB605 and ZB606 joined the training programme.

The Sea Harrier T.4N first flew in 1982 and was in fact a navalized version of the RAF's Harrier T.4, three of which served with the FAA before their own T.4Ns were delivered.

UNITS ALLOCATED

No.899 Squadron (Yeovilton)

TECHNICAL DATA (SEA HARRIER T.4N)

Description: Two-seat conversion trainer also capable of operational Fleet fighter rôle. All-metal stressed-skin construction.
Manufacturers: British Aerospace, Kingston-on-Thames and Dunsfold, Surrey.
Power Plant: One 21,500 lb vectored thrust Rolls-Royce Pegasus 104 turbofan.
Dimensions: Span, 25 ft 3¼ in. Length, 55 ft 9½ in. Height, 12 ft 2 in. Wing area, 201 sq ft.
Weight: Loaded, 13,600 lb.
Performance: Maximum speed, 740 mph. Range, 2,000 nautical miles. Endurance, 2 hours.

Sea Harrier F.R.S.2 (ZA195) on test from Dunsfold. (*British Aerospace*)

British Aerospace Sea Harrier F.R.S.2

Developed to take advantage of progress in military avionics and weapons technology and capitalising on the outstanding success of the earlier version of the Sea Harrier in the Falklands War, the F.R.S.2 began as a feasibility study in 1983. The prototype (ZA195), a converted F.R.S.1, made its first flight, from Dunsfold, on 19 September 1988. The most obvious change externally was the modified nose radome enclosing a Ferranti Blue Vixen multi-mode fire control radar and a fourteen-inch extension to the rear fuselage just aft of the wings. There was also a small extension to the wingtips. The Blue Vixen radar remedied a shortcoming of the earlier Blue Fox in the F.R.S.1 by offering a 'look-down shoot-down' capability against aircraft or missiles flying below the attacking fighter. It also provided greater surface target acquisition and the ability to engage several targets simultaneously well beyond visual range. Other new features of the F.R.S.2 were a completely new cockpit and head-up display and more formidable armament in the shape of four Hughes AIM-120 (AMRAAM) air-to-air missiles in addition to two 190-gallon combat tanks on the inner wing pylons.

In November 1990, two Sea Harrier F.R.S.2 prototypes (with full war-load and twin drop tanks) completed first sea trials on board HMS *Ark Royal*.

In March 1990 a new contract was signed for 10 new-build Sea Harrier F.R.S.2 aircraft to supplement the 33 converted F.R.S.1s ordered in December 1988. Deliveries of both new and mid-life up-dated Sea Harriers were due to begin late in 1992.

The superlative qualities of the Sea Harrier F.R.S.2, and its ability to dominate the maritime air combat environment, will doubtless ensure its long service with the Royal Navy well into the next century.

TECHNICAL DATA (SEA HARRIER F.R.S.2)

Description: Single-seat carrier-borne interceptor fighter, strike and reconnaissance aircraft. All-metal stressed-skin construction.

Manufacturers: British Aerospace (Military Aircraft) Ltd, Kingston-upon-Thames, Dunsfold and Brough.

75

Power Plant: One 21,500 lb static thrust Rolls-Royce Pegasus 104 (later 106) vectored-thrust turbofan.

Dimensions: Span, 26 ft 7½ in. Length, 48 ft 9 in. Height, 12 ft 2 in.

Weights: Not released.

Performance: Not released.

Armament: For fighter rôle can carry (a) Four Hughes AIM-120 AMRAAM air-to-air missiles (without cannon) or (b) Two AIM-120 inboard and four AIM-9 outboard or (c) Two AIM-120 outboard plus two 30 mm Aden cannon. For strike rôle can carry (a) two Sea Eagle anti-ship missiles or (b) four ALARM anti-radar missiles plus bombs, mines or depth charges. Capacity for WE 177 nuclear bombs.

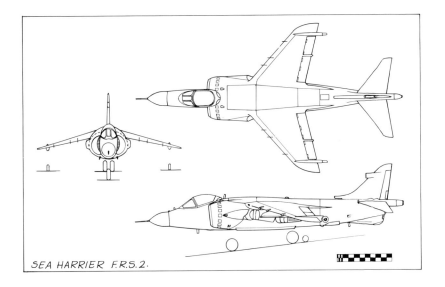

SEA HARRIER F.R.S.2.

Caudron G.4 of the RNAS. *(Imperial War Museum)*

Caudron G.4

This curious-looking aircraft was a twin-engined derivative of the earlier Caudron G.3 (see Appendix), which had served with the RNAS from its very early days. One Caudron G.3 (90 hp Gnome engine) was on the strength of the RNAS on 4 August 1914, when the total muster was 40 landplanes and 31 seaplanes. Subsequently, the type was widely used by the RNAS for pilot training both in Great Britain and in France.

Although used chiefly by the French Air Force over the Western Front and, to a more limited extent, by the RFC, the Caudron G.4 has a definite place in the history of the RNAS. As has been recorded elsewhere, the RNAS was quick to appreciate the value of the bomber in air operations, and as early as March 1916 the Fifth Wing, specially trained for long-range bombing duties, had taken up its station at Coudekerque under the command of Sqn Cdr Spenser Grey. In the absence of more suitable British types, the initial equipment of this Wing comprised French Breguets and Caudron G.4s. Later the Sopwith 1½ Strutter was added. Caudron G.4s also formed part of the equipment of No.4 Wing, which arrived at Petite Snythe from Eastchurch under the command of Sqn Cdr C.L. Courtney on 11 April 1916.

The Caudrons of Nos.4 and 5 Wings, RNAS, were busily engaged during 1916 in day and night raids on German seaplane, submarine and Zeppelin bases in Belgium. On 2 August 1916 they took part in a daylight raid on the enemy aerodrome at St Denis Westrem, near Ghent, at the request of General Trenchard. The 10 Caudrons (plus one Farman) attacked in line astern, directed by Very signals from one of the five escorting Sopwith 1½ Strutters, an early example of 'master-bomber' tactics.

The cumbersome Caudrons remained with the RNAS until the spring of 1917, when the Handley Page O/100 made its appearance. One of their last major operations was against Bruges docks in February 1917 with No.7 Naval Squadron.

Altogether, the RNAS took delivery of 46 Caudron G.4s, the parent firm supplying 39 (Nos.3289–3300 and 9101–9131), and the British Caudron Company seven (Nos.3333–3334, 3894–3895 and 3897–3899).

Nos.4 and 5 Wings, RNAS (Belgium); No.7 (Naval) Squadron.

TECHNICAL DATA (CAUDRON G.4)

Description: Two-seat long-range day or night bomber. Wooden structure, fabric covered.

Manufacturers: Caudron Freres, Rue (Somme), Le Crotoy. Sub-contracted by the British Caudron Co.

Power Plant: Two 80 hp Le Rhône or two 100 hp Anzani.

Dimensions: Span, 55 ft 5 in. Length, 23 ft 6 in. Height, 8ft 5 in. Wing area, 427½ sq ft.

Weights: Empty, 1,870 lb. Loaded, 2,970 lb.

Performance: Maximum speed, 82 mph at 6,500 ft; 80 mph at 10,000 ft. Climb, 33 min to 10,000 ft. Endurance, 4 hr. Service ceiling, 14,000 ft.

Armament: One machine-gun mounted in front cockpit and bombs on racks beneath wings.

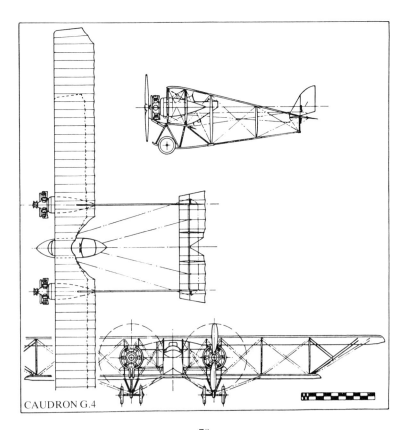

CAUDRON G.4

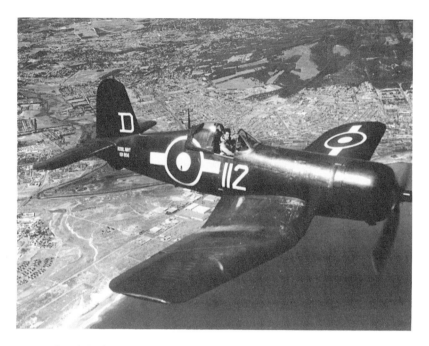

Corsair IV (KD856) from No.1846 Squadron, HMS *Colossus*. *(FAA Museum)*

Chance Vought Corsair

The shortest possible list of truly outstanding Allied single-seat fighter aircraft in the Second World War would have to include the name of the Corsair. It ranks with such classic aircraft as the Spitfire, the Hurricane, the Mustang and the Thunderbolt. Nor is that all: the Corsair can claim one of the longest unbroken records of first-line service of any piston-engined fighter ever built. First in action early in 1943, the Corsair was progressively improved and was still giving a good account of itself during the Korean War and, even as late as 1954, in the fighting in Indo-China. With the FAA, the Corsair had a much briefer history, but no account of this remarkable fighter could ignore its outstanding record in wider service.

The Corsair was first conceived as early as June 1938, when design work began on the XF4U-1 for the US Navy. At the time of its first flight, on 29 May 1940, it was the most powerful naval fighter ever built, with a Pratt & Whitney XR-2800-4 engine of 1,850 hp. The choice of this engine, combined with the need to economise in stowage space for carrier operations, led to the adoption of the characteristic 'inverted-gull' wing. This feature enabled a large-diameter airscrew to be used to absorb the immense thrust, reduced the length of the undercarriage leg and allowed the outer wing panels to be folded upwards whilst still clearing the roof of the hangar below deck. Another technical innovation was the use of spot-welding in the skin covering, reducing surface friction to a minimum. Reduction in drag was further effected by the way in which the inner sections of the wing joined the cylindrical fuselage at right angles, eliminating the need for fillets.

By the time that the first production Corsair flew on 24 June 1942, extensive changes had been effected. The fuselage was lengthened to accommodate additional fuel, and the cockpit was moved aft to a point level with the trailing edge. The twin guns in the fuselage were abandoned, and instead six guns were mounted in the wings, which had previously carried only two. Finally, the new 2,100 hp R-2800-8 engine was installed.

Following deck-landing trials with the US Navy, it was decided to allocate the Corsair for shore duties with the US Marine Corps. Though subsequently used aboard carriers by both the US Navy and the FAA, the Corsair called for skilful handling due to the restricted forward visibility and, for this reason, later models had the pilot's seat raised about 7 in and a large, single-piece canopy fitted.

In US service the F4U-1 Corsair made its first operation on 15 February 1943 at Guadalcanal where it equipped the Marine Corps Squadron VMF 124. Its superiority over Japanese fighters was quickly apparent, and by the end of 1943 the USMC Corsairs had destroyed the impressive total of 584 enemy aircraft.

Meanwhile, delivery of the first batch of Corsairs supplied to the FAA under Lend-Lease agreements had begun. These were the Corsair Mk.Is (JT100 to 194), the equivalent of the F4U-1, and the Corsair Mk.IIs (JT195 to 704), the British version of the F4U-1A and 1D. The first Corsair squadron of the FAA was No.1830, which formed at Quonset, the US Navy base, on 1 June 1943. By the end of 1943 seven more squadrons had been equipped. Based either at Quonset or Brunswick, they worked up in the USA before being shipped to the United Kingdom in escort carriers. Corsair squadrons went on forming in this way right through 1944 and early 1945. No fewer than 19 FAA squadrons received Corsairs, the last unit being No.1853 Squadron, which formed at Brunswick as late as 1 April 1945.

In home waters FAA Corsairs first went into action when aircraft of No.1834 Squadron embarked in *Victorious* joined Hellcats of No.800 Squadron (*Emperor*), Wildcats of No.898 Squadron (*Searcher*) and Seafires of No.801 Squadron (*Furious*) in providing fighter cover for the memorable attack by Fairey Barracudas on the German battleship *Tirpitz* on 3 April 1944. As related in the narrative on the Barracuda, this attack was a resounding success, and further strikes from carriers off the Norwegian coast took place on 17 July and on 22, 24 and 25 August 1944. In the July attack Corsairs of No.1841 Squadron (*Formidable*) provided the fighter cover, and in the final strikes of August 1944 No.1841's Corsairs were joined by those of its sister squadron in *Formidable*, No.1842.

These operations were the work of Corsair IIs, which differed from the Corsair I in having certain modifications to make them suitable for operations aboard British carriers. The improved-visibility cockpit canopy has already been mentioned; additionally the Corsair II introduced clipped wings (of 16 in less span) to accommodate British below-deck hangars and undercarriages with a long-stroke oleo leg. Another point of difference was that the Corsair I had no provision for carrying bombs, whereas the Corsair II could mount 2,000 lb of bombs, or additional fuel in long-range tanks up to a total of 471 gallons.

The Corsair I and II were followed in the FAA by the Corsair III (JS469 to

888 and JT963 to 972) and the Corsair IV (KD161 to 999, KE100 to 117 and KE310 to 429), making a grand total of 1,977 Corsairs manufactured for the Royal Navy and the RNZAF. The Corsair III was the equivalent of the F3A-1 (Brewster-built Corsair). The Corsair IV was built by Goodyear and equated to the FG-1D.

The most important contributions of the FAA Corsairs to British naval operations were against the Japanese with the East Indies and Pacific Fleets during 1944–45. On 19 April 1944, in an attack on Sabang by two Barracuda squadrons from *Illustrious*, Corsairs of Nos.1830 and 1833 Squadrons from the same carrier provided fleet-defence patrols, and repeated these operations on 6 May 1944, when two Avenger squadrons hit Sourabaya, and, on 21 June 1944, when 15 Barracudas struck the Andaman Islands.

In the historic attack on the oil refineries at Palembang on 24 January 1945, 16 Corsairs of Nos.1830 and 1833 Squadrons joined in the destruction of 13 Tojo fighters, and in the period 26 March to 14 April 1945 these units made nearly 400 of the 2,000 sorties flown from the four large carriers of the British Pacific Fleet. During this period of intensive flying the Corsairs carried out daily sweeps in the all-out effort to neutralise the Japanese airfields in the Sakishima Islands.

Between 17 July and 10 August 1945, Corsairs of Nos.1834 and 1836 Squadrons (*Victorious*) and Nos.1841 and 1842 Squadrons (*Formidable*) made a series of strikes in the Tokyo area, and it was during one of these operations that a Corsair pilot earned for the FAA its second VC of the Second World War. The pilot in question was Lt R H Gray, of the Royal Canadian Volunteer Reserve, who on 9 August 1945 was leading a formation of No.1841 Squadron's Corsairs in a strike on Shiogama. Lt Gray, in spite of intense opposition from shore batteries and ships, pressed home his attack on an enemy destroyer lying in the harbour of Onagawa Wan and succeeded in sinking it with a direct hit even

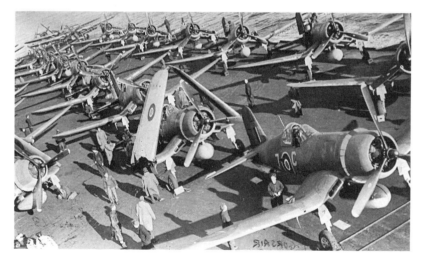

Corsairs of Nos.1834 and 1836 Squadrons aboard *Victorious* with the British East Indies Fleet in 1944. *(Imperial War Museum)*

Corsair II fighters of No.738 Squadron in echelon formation. *(Imperial War Museum)*

although his own aircraft was in flames. Immediately after this gallant attack Lt Gray lost his life as his Corsair plunged into the sea.

With the end of the war against Japan, the Corsair squadrons disbanded fairly rapidly, and by the end of 1945 only four remained. These squadrons (Nos.1831, 1846, 1850 and 1851) stayed with the post-war FAA until the following summer, the last to go being Nos.1831 and 1851, which disbanded on 13 August 1946.

So disappeared the Corsair from the FAA, but, as related above, it continued in production for the US Navy and Marines until 24 December 1952, by which time a grand total of 12,571 had been built. The later versions were the F4U-4B (with R-2800-18W engine and four 20 mm guns), the F4U-5NL all-weather fighter with a radome below the starboard wing, the F4U-5N night-fighter and other specialised variants such as the AU-1 (originally F4U-6), all of which saw extensive service in Korea. The final version, the F4U-7, was exported to France and fought in Indo-China.

A Royal Navy Corsair IV (KD431) is on view at the FAA Museum at Yeovilton, Somerset.

UNITS ALLOCATED

Mk.I Nos.1830, 1831, 1833, 1834, 1835, 1836, 1837, 1838, 1841 and 1848 Squadrons. *Mk.II* Nos.1830 (*Illustrious*), 1833 (Illustrious), 1834 (*Victorious*), 1835 (Brunswick), 1836 (*Victorious*), 1837 (*Illustrious* and *Victorious*), 1838 (*Victorious*), 1841 (*Formidable*), 1842 (*Formidable*), 1843 (Eglinton) and 1848 (Machrihanish). *Mk.III* Nos.1835 (Eglinton), 1837 (Eglinton and Nutts Corner), 1841 (*Formidable*), 1842 (Brunswick), 1843 (Eglinton), 1845 (Eglinton), 1846 (Eglinton) and 1849 (Brunswick). *Mk.IV* Nos.885 (*Indefatigable*), 1831 (*Glory* and *Vengeance*), 1834 (*Victorious*), 1835 (Brunswick), 1836 (*Victorious*), 1841 (*Formidable* and *Victorious*), 1842 (*Formidable* and *Victorious*), 1843 (Colombo and Nowra), 1845 (Archfield, Maryfield and Nowra), 1846 (*Colossus*), 1849 (*Vengeance*), 1850 (*Vengeance*), 1851 (*Venerable* and *Vengeance*) and 1852 (Nutts Corner). *Second-line Squadrons* (*Mk.I*) Nos.700, 732, 738 and 787. *Mk.II* Nos.703, 706, 723, 731, 732, 738, 748, 757, 759, 768, 771, 778 and 787. *Mk.III* Nos.700, 715, 718, 719, 721, 731, 736, 748, 757, 759, 760, 767, 768, 771, 787, 794 and 797. *Mk.IV* Nos.706, 715, 716, 718, 721, 731, 736, 748, 757, 759, 778, 791 and 794.

TECHNICAL DATA (CORSAIR I AND IV)

Description: Single-seat carrier-borne or shore-based fighter and fighter-bomber. All-metal stressed-skin construction.

Manufacturers: Chance Vought Aircraft Division, United Aircraft Corporation, Stratford, Connecticut. Other variants sub-contracted by Brewster Aeronautical Corporation and Goodyear Aircraft Corporation.

Power Plant: One Pratt & Whitney Double Wasp R-2800-8 developing 2,000 hp at 1,500 ft in Mk.I and 2,250 hp at sea level in Mk.IV.

Dimensions: Span, 41 ft. (Mk.I): 39 ft 8 in. (Mk.IV). Length, 33 ft 4 in. Height, 15 ft 1 in. Wing area, 314 sq ft (Mk.I): 305 sq ft. (Mk.IV).

Weights (Mk.I): Empty, 8,800 lb. Loaded, 11,800 lb. (maximum). (Mk.IV): Empty, 9,100 lb. Loaded, 12,300 lb.

Performance (Mk.I): Maximum speed, 374 mph at 23,000 ft. Cruising speed, 251 mph at 20,000 ft. Climb, 10.8 min to 20,000 ft. Range, 673 miles (normal) or 1,125 miles (with extra tanks). Service ceiling, 34,500 ft

(Mk.IV): Maximum speed, 415 mph at 19,500 ft. Cruising speed, 261 mph at 20,000 ft. Initial climb, 2,070 ft/min. Climb, 10.1 min to 20,000 ft. Range, 500 miles (with 2,000 lb of bombs) or 1,562 miles (with no bombs and maximum fuel). Service ceiling, 35,000 ft. Endurance, 4 hours.

Armament: (Mk.I): Four fixed 0.50-calibre guns in the wings. (Mk.IV): Six fixed 0.50-calibre guns in the wings and provision for two 1,000 lb bombs beneath the centre-section.

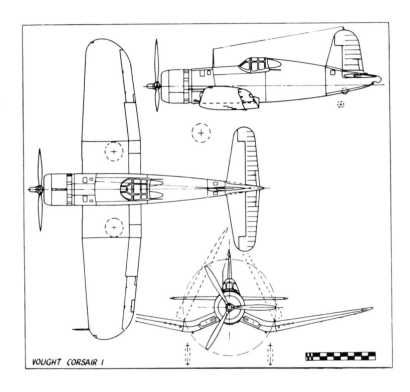

VOUGHT CORSAIR I

Curtiss H.4 Small America (No.3592). *(Imperial War Museum)*

Curtiss H.4 Small America

The H.4 was the first of the Curtiss flying-boats acquired from the USA to enter service with the RNAS. The firm of Curtiss had been the first to produce a successful flying-boat, which flew on 12 January 1912, and in the following year a British agency for Curtiss boats was acquired by the White and Thompson Company of Bognor, Sussex. It was in this way that John Porte, whose name is synonymous with the development of flying-boats for the RNAS during the First World War, first came into contact with Curtiss types and soon afterwards joined the parent company in the USA, for in 1913 he was the White and Thompson Company's test pilot.

If the World War had not intervened, John Porte was to have flown the Atlantic in a flying-boat named *America*. In the event, he re-joined the RNAS as a squadron commander in August 1914 and persuaded the Admiralty to purchase two Curtiss flying-boats (Nos.950 and 951), which were delivered in November 1914. These boats were tried out at Felixstowe air station and were followed by 62 production aircraft, four of which (Nos.1228 to 1231) were built in Britain. Curtiss supplied an initial batch of eight (Nos.1232 to 1239) and a second of 50 (Nos.3545 to 3594). The entire series was given the official designation H.4 and acquired the name Small America, retrospectively, after the introduction later of the larger H.12, or Large America.

Despite numerous deficiencies such as poor seaworthiness, the H.4 boats saw operational service. More important, however, was the contribution they made to the evolution of flying-boats generally as a result of the experiments they underwent at the hands of John Porte, a designer and innovator of genius. The H.4s so employed were Nos.950, 1230, 1231, 3545, 3546 (the 'Incidence Boat'), 3569 and 3580. Various hulls and planing bottoms were tried to improve take-off and alighting characteristics. This knowledge was put to good use in the later Curtiss and Felixstowe flying-boats.

A few H.4 flying-boats were still in service as late as June 1918 when, it is recorded, Nos.1232, 1233 and 1235 were at Killingholme coastal air station.

Description: Reconnaissance flying-boat with a crew of four. Wooden structure with wood and fabric covering.

Manufacturers: Curtiss Aeroplanes and Motors Corporation, Buffalo, Hammondsport, NY. Sub-contracted by Aircraft Manufacturing Co in Great Britain.

Power Plant: Variously, two 90 hp Curtiss, two 100 hp Curtiss, two 150 hp Sunbeam or two 100 hp Anzani.

Dimensions: Span, 72 ft 0 in. Length, 36 ft 0 in. Height, 16 ft 0 in.

Weights: Empty, 2,992 lb. Loaded, 4,983 lb.

Performance: Not available.

Armament: Flexibly-mounted machine-gun in bows and light bombs below the wings.

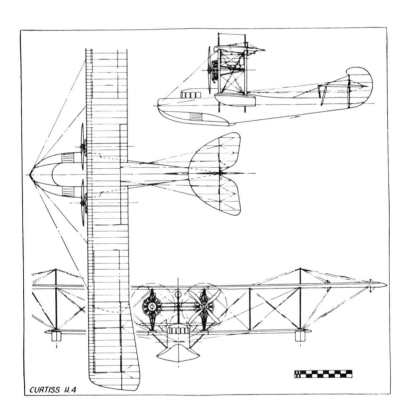

CURTISS H.4

Curtiss H.12 Large America (No.8681). *(MoD)*

Curtiss H.12 Large America

The H.12, known as the Large America, was by far the most famous of the series of Curtiss flying-boats used by the RNAS. It was developed from the H.4 Small America and was both larger and more powerful. Despite a distinguished operational record, related in detail in C F Snowden-Gamble's classic *The Story of a North Sea Air Station*, the H.12 was handicapped by weakness of the hull planing bottom which made take-off hazardous in all but the calmest of seas.

The original power plant of two 160 hp Curtiss engines proved inadequate and was superseded by two Rolls-Royce engines. A total of 71 H.12s reached the RNAS, the first batch being Nos.8650 to 8699 and the second N4330 to 4350. Great Yarmouth air station made its first H.12 patrol with No.8660 on 1 May 1917 and Felixstowe air station with No.8661 on 13 April 1917, initiating the famous 'Spider-web' patrols.

In both its rôles, as an anti-submarine reconnaissance aircraft and as an anti-Zeppelin fighter, the H.12 enjoyed outstanding success. The first of these was on 14 May 1917, when No.8666 from Great Yarmouth, flown by F/Lt Galpin, shot down the airship *L22* about 18 miles NNW of Texel Island. This was the first Zeppelin claimed by a flying-boat. The second Zeppelin to be shot down by an H.12 was *L43*, which fell to Felixstowe's No.8677, flown by F/Sub-Lt Hobbs, on 14 June 1917.

Against U-boats the first success went to F/Sub-Lts Morrish and Boswell, who attacked *UC-36* on 20 May 1917, and the second to H.12s 8662 and 8676, *UB-20* on 29 July 1917. Another victory was scored on 22 September 1917, when No.8695 was instrumental in sinking *UB-32*. Another submarine, the *UC-6*, was claimed by F/Sub-Lts Hobbs and Dickey on 28 September 1917.

Some of the H.12s were modified later in their careers, and were almost indistinguishable from the F.2A. These H.12s were styled 'Converted Large Americas'. On 31 October 1918, when there were 18 H.12 boats still in service, six were of the converted type.

UNITS ALLOCATED

'War Flight' of RNAS, Felixstowe and 'Boat Flight' of RNAS, Great Yarmouth (later No.228 Squadron, RAF). Also at RNAS, Killingholme and with No.234 Squadron (Tresco) and No.240 Squadron (Calshot).

TECHNICAL DATA (CURTISS H.12)

Description: Anti-submarine and anti-Zeppelin patrol flying-boat with crew of four. Wooden structure with wood and fabric covering.

Manufacturers: Curtiss Aeroplanes and Motor Corporation, Buffalo, Hammondsport, NY.

Power Plant: Originally two 275 hp Rolls-Royce Eagle I. Later two 345 hp Eagle VII or 375 hp Eagle VIII.

Dimensions: Span, 92 ft 8½ in. Length, 46 ft 6 in. Height, 16 ft 6 in. Wing area, 1,216 sq ft.

Weights: Empty, 7,293 lb. Loaded, 10,650 lb.

Performance: Maximum speed, 85 mph at 2,000 ft. Climb, 3.3 min to 2,000 ft; 29.8 min to 10,000 ft. Endurance, 6 hr. Service ceiling, 10,800 ft.

Armament: Up to four Lewis guns on flexible mountings and four 100 lb or two 230 lb bombs below the wings.

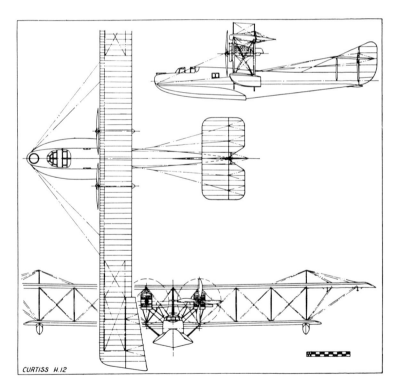

CURTISS H.12

Curtiss H.16 Large America (No.4060). *(Imperial War Museum)*

Curtiss H.16 Large America

The H.16 was an improved and enlarged version of the more famous H.12 and was delivered to Britain in 1918. It represented a notable advance on the H.12, in that it incorporated the stronger and more seaworthy Porte-type hull, thus bringing the American boats into line with their British counterparts, the Felixstowe series, whose design they had originally helped to inspire. The wheel had turned full circle.

The initial Admiralty contract for H.16 flying-boats covered 15 aircraft, N4060 to 4074, fitted with twin 250 hp Rolls-Royce Eagle engines. This was followed by an additional contract for 110 aircraft, N4890 to 4999, but the end of the war saw the last 50 cancelled. The second batch of H.16s mounted twin 375 hp Rolls-Royce Eagle engines.

H.16 Large Americas rivalled the Felixstowe boats in performance, but they figured less in records of the period and no particularly outstanding operations are associated with the type. On 31 October 1918 there were some 69 on charge with the RAF, but 39 of these were in store or with contractors. At about the same time another 50 or so H.16s were operated round British shores by the US Navy. The US Navy versions had twin 330 hp Liberty engines and were based at Killingholme. It is alleged that one of the American H.16s at Killingholme was actually looped by an over-exuberant pilot!

UNITS ALLOCATED

H.16s served with No.228 Squadron at Great Yarmouth and Killingholme, No.230 Squadron (Felixstowe), No.238 Squadron (Cattewater) and No.257 Squadron (Dundee).

TECHNICAL DATA (CURTISS H.16)

Description: Anti-submarine patrol flying-boat with a crew of four. Wooden structure with wood and fabric covering.

Manufacturers: Curtiss Aeroplanes and Motors Corporation, Buffalo, Hammondsport, NY.

Power Plant: Two 375 hp Rolls-Royce Eagle VIII.

Dimensions: Span, 95 ft. Length, 46 ft 1½ in. Height, 17 ft 8 in. Wing area, 1,000 sq ft.

Weights: Empty, 7,363 lb. Loaded, 10,670 lb.

Performance: Maximum speed, 98 mph at 2,000 ft; 95 mph at 6,500 ft; 92 mph at 10,000 ft. Climb, 512 ft/min; 3.7 min to 2,000 ft; 14.6 min to 6,500 ft; 28 min to 10,000 ft. Endurance, 6 hr. Service ceiling, 12,500 ft.

Armament: Twin Lewis machine-guns on ring mounting in bows and amidships. Provision for two further Lewis guns to fire through the side of the hull and for bombs mounted on racks beneath the wings.

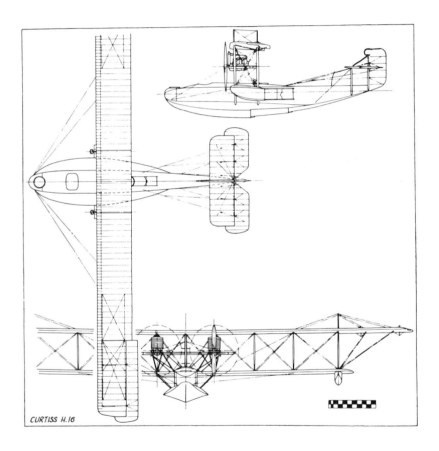

CURTISS H.16

Seamew I (FN475) with landplane undercarriage. *(Crown Copyright Photo)*

Curtiss Seamew

The Curtiss Seamew, as used by the FAA, was the British version of the SO3C-2 Seamew (originally known as the Seagull) of the US Navy. The prototype (XSO3C-1) made its first flight in 1940. It was designed by Don R Berlin in the tradition of the US Navy's medium-powered scout-observation class, convertible for land or seaplane duties, and followed the Curtiss SOC-1 Seagull biplane of 1935. In the event, the earlier biplane, like Britain's Swordfish, outlived its intended replacement and at the end of 1944 about 70 Seagull biplanes remained with the US Navy. The Seamews, on the other hand, had been withdrawn from the US Navy in early 1944, apart from a few converted as target drones.

About 800 Seamews were built in 1941–2 and 250 were scheduled for delivery to Great Britain under Lend-Lease arrangements. Of these aircraft, the first 100 (FN450 to 499 and FN600 to 649) were not all delivered, and it is doubtful if the remaining 150 (JW550 to 699) ever reached the Royal Navy. To these Seamew Is were added a further 11 aircraft known as Queen Seamews. These were numbered JX663 to 669 and JZ771 to 774, and were converted for use as radio-controlled target drone aircraft to supplement the Queen Bees already in service.

Although intended chiefly for catapult launching from warships, the Seamews with the FAA in fact saw no operational service and, although it was once planned to equip No.850 Squadron with the type, from 1943 they were relegated to the training rôle. Most of them served with FAA establishments in Canada and at Worthy Down in Hampshire, where they trained wireless-telegraphist/air gunners. The last Seamews in FAA service were those of No.745 Squadron in Canada which eventually disbanded in March 1945.

The narrow-track spatted undercarriage of the landplane Seamew was fitted to the float attachment, and was so far aft that a steep ground angle resulted. This, by all reports, made for difficult ground handling and landing characteristics, and did not improve the Seamew's popularity.

91

Second-line Squadrons: Nos.744 and 745 in Nova Scotia, Canada, and No.755 at Worthy Down, Hampshire.

TECHNICAL DATA (SEAMEW I)

Description: Two-seat reconnaissance aircraft suitable for catapult launch and equipped with either land or seaplane undercarriage. All-metal stressed-skin construction.

Manufacturers: Curtiss Airplane Division of the Curtiss-Wright Corporation, Buffalo, NY.

Power Plant: One 520 hp Ranger SGV-770-6.

Dimensions: Span, 38 ft. Length (seaplane), 36 ft 10 in; (landplane), 34 ft 2 in. Height, 11 ft 5 in. Wing area, 290 sq ft.

Weights: (seaplane) Empty, 4,284 lb. Loaded, 5,729 lb; (landplane) Empty, 4,113 lb. Loaded, 5,588 lb.

Performance: (seaplane): Maximum speed, 190 mph at 7,500 ft. Cruising speed, 126 mph. Endurance, 8 hr.

Armament: One fixed machine-gun forward and one free-mounted machine-gun aft.

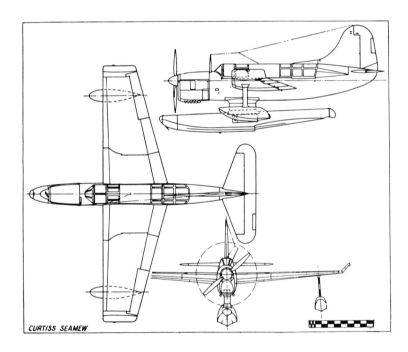

CURTISS SEAMEW

D.H.4 (N5997) of No.2 (Naval) Squadron. *(MoD)*

de Havilland 4

The D.H.4 was the first British aeroplane ever designed specifically for day-bombing duties. In this rôle it excelled, and it remained to the end of the First World War one of the truly outstanding aircraft of its day.

The prototype (No.3696) of 1916 had a BHP engine, but the first production aircraft, which went to the RFC, were powered by the Rolls-Royce Eagle. In the RNAS, D.H.4s first saw service with squadrons in 1917, going to No.2 (Naval) Squadron at St Pol in March and to No.5 (Naval) Squadron at Coudekerque at the end of April. No.2 Squadron specialised in reconnaissance, and spotted for the guns of naval monitors. On 1 April 1918, No.2 became No.202 Squadron, and its D.H.4s photographed the entire defensive system of Zeebrugge and Ostend before the Royal Navy's blocking operations of 22/23 April. Meanwhile, No.5 Squadron's D.H.4s had from July 1917 operated exclusively on day bombing raids, attacking naval targets as well as German Air Force bases at Ghistelles, Houtave and elsewhere.

D.H.4s also served with distinction at RNAS coastal air stations. Great Yarmouth received its first D.H.4 in August 1917 and a year later, on 5 August 1918, a D.H.4 from this station, A8032 flown by Major E Cadbury and Capt R Leckie, shot down the Zeppelin L70 in flames. A few days later, on 19 August 1918, four D.H.4s of No.217 (formerly No.17 (Naval) Squadron) sank the submarine *UB-12*. In the Aegean, Naval D.H.4s bombed the Sofia-Constantinople railway and the cruiser *Goeben*.

UNITS ALLOCATED

Nos.2, 5, 6, 11 and 17 (Naval) Squadrons (later Nos.202, 205, 206, 211 and 217, RAF) in Belgium and Nos.212, 233 and 273 at coastal air stations. 'C' Squadron at Imbros and 'D' Squadron at Stavros, No.220 (Mudros), No.221 (Stavros), No.222 (Thasos), No.223 (Mitylene, Stavros and Mudros) and Nos.224, 226 and 227 (Italy).

Description: Two-seat day bomber, reconnaissance or anti-Zeppelin patrol aircraft. Wooden structure, fabric covered.

Manufacturers: Aircraft Manufacturing Co Ltd, Hendon, London. Subcontracted by F W Berwick & Co Ltd, Westland Aircraft (N5960 to 6009 and N6380 to 6429), and Vulcan Motor & Engineering Co Ltd.

Power Plant: Variously one 200 hp RAF 3a; 230 hp BHP; 250 hp Rolls-Royce Eagle III, 322 hp Eagle VI, 325 hp Eagle VII or 375 hp Eagle VIII.

Dimensions: Span, 42 ft 4¾ in. Length, 30 ft 8 in. Height, 10 ft 5 in. Wing area, 434 sq ft.

Weights (with 250 hp Eagle): Empty, 2,303 lb. Loaded, 3,313 lb.

Performance (with 250 hp Eagle): Maximum speed, 119 mph at 3,000 ft. Climb, 1 min 5 sec to 1,000 ft; 46 min to 16,500 ft. Endurance, 3½ hr. Service ceiling, 16,000 ft.

Armament: Twin, synchronised Vickers forward and one Lewis aft. Bomb load: two 230 lb or four 112 lb, or depth charges.

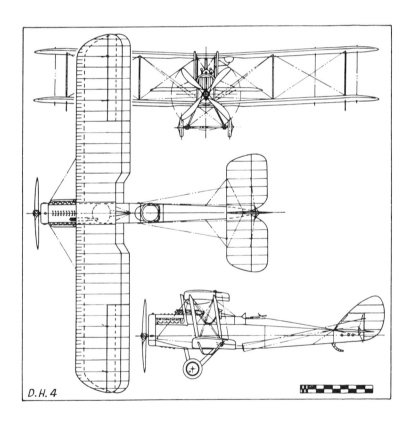

D.H. 4

D.H.6A of No.242 Squadron, Newhaven. *(Imperial War Museum)*

de Havilland 6

The stark, utilitarian lines of the D.H.6 can be ascribed to the fact that it was designed for rapid and simple production in 1916 at a time when the RFC was expanding and needed many more training aircraft in a hurry. Captain (later Sir Geoffrey) de Havilland achieved this purpose admirably, and over 2,200 D.H.6s were built by the parent company and seven sub-contracting firms.

Few aeroplanes can have had so many nicknames, for the D.H.6 was variously known as 'The Sky Hook', 'The Crab', 'The Clutching Hand', 'The Flying Coffin', 'The Dung-hunter' and 'The Sixty'. As a trainer, the D.H.6 saw widespread service at home and overseas during 1917, but was gradually withdrawn with the subsequent standardisation of the Avro 504K.

By a curious turn of events, the D.H.6's decline as a trainer witnessed its introduction in a first-line operational rôle as an anti-submarine hunter with the RNAS. Early in 1918 the Admiralty asked for additional aircraft to patrol off the coast between the Tyne and the Tees, an area where U-boats were doing great damage, and the first two Flights of D.H.6s formed at Cramlington in March. In June 1918 a further 192 D.H.6s were made available for anti-submarine work, and 32 more Flights were established at coastal air stations, five of them operated by the US Navy.

Little success was achieved by the D.H.6s, nor could it be expected with a performance so inferior that, in order to lift a mere 100 lb of bombs, the observer had to be discarded. Modifications such as the introduction of back-stagger and a new aerofoil section on the D.H.6A did little to improve the lack of speed, and D.H.6s fitted with the far from reliable Curtiss OX-5 engine suffered frequent descents in the sea. Fortunately, the type floated for long periods and thus improved the chance of rescue.

On only one occasion did a D.H.6 come near to destroying a U-boat. This was on 30 May 1918, when *UC-49* was attacked, but it crash-dived and made its escape.

UNITS ALLOCATED

Thirty-four Flights allocated as follows: two Flights (Cramlington); five Flights (Humber to Tees); four Flights (Tees to St Abbs Head); four Flights (Portsmouth Group); eight

Flights (South Western Group); six Flights (Irish Sea). After April 1918, organised as Nos.236, 241, 242, 244, 250, 251, 252, 253, 254, 255, 256, 258, 260 and 272 Squadrons.

TECHNICAL DATA (D.H.6)

Description: Two-seat elementary trainer, later used for anti-submarine patrol. Wooden structure, fabric covered.

Manufacturers: Aircraft Manufacturing Co Ltd, Hendon. Sub-contracted by Grahame-White Aviation Co, Gloucestershire Aircraft Co; Harland & Wolff; Kingsbury Aviation Co; Morgan & Co; Ransome, Sims & Jeffries; and Savages Ltd.

Power Plant: One 90 hp RAF 1a, 90 hp Curtiss OX-5 or 80 hp Renault.

Dimensions: Span, 35 ft 11 in. Length, 27 ft 3½ in. Height, 10 ft 9½ in. Wing area, 436 sq ft.

Weights: Empty, 1,460 lb. Loaded, 2,027 lb.

Performance: Maximum speed, 75 mph at 2,000 ft. Climb, 35 min to 6,500 ft. Service ceiling, 6,100 ft.

Armament: Up to 100 lb of bombs below wings.

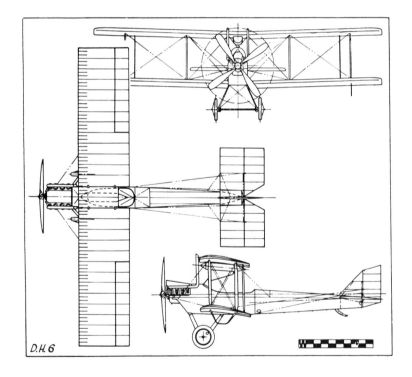

D.H.6

D.H.9. *(Imperial War Museum)*

de Havilland 9

With the exception of the B.E.2c, the D.H.9 was the most severely criticised British aeroplane of the First World War. It was designed as a replacement for the D.H.4 in day bomber squadrons, where it was intended to offer a much wider radius of action. In the event its performance fell far short of expectations, and it was actually inferior to the type it superseded. Although this fact was known before it entered service, it was decided (fantastic as it sounds) to proceed with large-scale production despite protests from commanders in the field. The inevitable results followed. Losses were high, one of the worst incidents being on 31 July 1918, when only two out of 12 D.H.9s returned from a raid over Germany.

The fault lay not in the aeroplane but in the engine, the BHP, which failed to deliver its designed power of 300 hp and remained unreliable to the end. As a result, forced landings were common, and with full bomb-load the D.H.9 could rarely exceed 13,000 ft, leaving it at the mercy of enemy fighters.

The prototype (A7559) flew in July 1917 and production aircraft entered squadrons early in 1918. Although chiefly identified with the Independent Force, RAF, and the raids on Germany, the D.H.9 in fact saw a good deal of service on naval work of various kinds; with RNAS bombing squadrons in Belgium before they became RAF squadrons, on naval co-operation work in the Mediterranean and for anti-Zeppelin and anti-submarine patrols from coastal air stations in the United Kingdom. Some of these latter squadrons (technically RAF, but employed exclusively on maritime duties) retained D.H.9s as late as July 1919, when they disbanded.

During raids on Bruges Docks with the 5th Wing, RNAS, in March 1918, D.H.9s of No.6 Naval Squadron destroyed three cement barges, a submarine, two torpedo boats and a cargo vessel. This unit operated from Petite Synthe until transferred to the RAF on 1 April 1918.

UNITS ALLOCATED

Nos.2,6 and 11 Naval Squadrons (later Nos.202, 206 and 211 Squadrons, RAF) in

Belgium. Sea patrol: No.212 (Great Yarmouth), No.219 (Manston), No.233 (Dover), No.236 (Mullion); No.250 (Padstow), No.254 (Prawle Point), No.260 (Westward Ho!), No.273 (Burgh Castle). *Aegean*: Nos.220, 221, 222 and 223. *Mediterranean*: Nos,224, 225, 226 and 227. *Egypt*: No.269 (Port Said) and No.270 (Alexandria).

TECHNICAL DATA (D.H.9)

Description: Two-seat day bomber, also used for anti-submarine patrol. Wooden structure, fabric covered.

Manufacturers: Aircraft Manufacturing Co Ltd, Hendon, London, and fifteen sub-contractors.

Power Plant: One 230 hp BHP or Siddeley Puma.

Dimensions: Span, 42 ft 4⅝ in. Length, 30 ft 6 in. Height, 11 ft 2 in. Wing area, 434 sq ft.

Weights: Empty, 2,203 lb. Loaded, 3,669 lb.

Performance: Maximum speed, 111½ mph at 10,000 ft; 104½ mph at 13,000 ft. Climb, 1 min 25 sec to 1,000 ft; 31 min 55 sec to 13,000 ft. Endurance, 4½ hr. Service ceiling, 15,500 ft.

Armament: One fixed, synchronised Vickers machine-gun forward and either single or double free-mounted Lewis aft. Bomb-load: 460 lb.

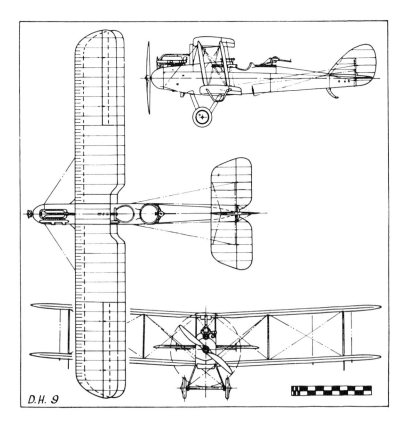

D.H. 9

de Havilland Mosquito VI

The Mosquito VI fighter-bomber entered service with the FAA when it equipped the re-formed No.811 Squadron at Ford in September 1945. It remained shore-based, not being equipped for carrier operations, and gave No.811 Squadron the Mosquito experience it needed before rearming with the Sea Mosquito T.R.33 in August 1946. A Mosquito VI of No.811 Squadron (TE720) is illustrated. Also used by Nos.703, 704, 751, 762, 773, 778, 780, 787 and 790 Squadrons. Two 1,230 hp Rolls-Royce Merlin XXI engines. Loaded weight, 21,600 lb. Maximum speed, 380 mph at 13,000 ft. Range, 1,205 miles. Service ceiling, 36,000 ft. Span, 54 ft 2 in. Length, 40 ft 6 in. Nineteen to FAA.

de Havilland Mosquito T.3

Over 40 of these two-seat dual-control trainers were handed over to the FAA by the RAF and the example illustrated (VT626) has the markings of the Royal Naval Air Station, Brawdy. Served with Nos.704, 728, 762, 780 and 811 Squadrons. Two Rolls-Royce Merlin 25 engines.

Sea Mosquito T.R.33 (TW256) of No.771 Squadron from Lee-on-Solent.

de Havilland Sea Mosquito T.R.33

The Sea Mosquito was evolved to meet the requirements of the Admiralty's Specification N.15/44, the first to be issued for a twin-engined aircraft capable of carrier-borne operations. The pre-prototype of the Sea Mosquito was a converted Mosquito VI (LR359), which, fitted with an improvised arrester gear, became the first British twin-engined aircraft ever to land on the deck of an aircraft-carrier. This notable event took place aboard HMS *Indefatigable* on 25 March 1944, the pilot being Lt-Cdr E M Brown, MBE, DSC. This 'navalised' Mosquito had special large-diameter (12 ft 6 in) four-blade airscrews which gave the Merlin 25 engines a thrust improvement of 5 to 10 per cent: folding wings were not introduced until the second conversion was made on Mosquito VI LR387. This aircraft also had the nose radome.

Production of the Sea Mosquito, designated T.R.Mk.33, started at de Havilland's Leavesden factory late in 1945 and the first aircraft (TW227) flew on 10 November. The first 13 production aircraft had the original type of rubber-block suspension on the undercarriage and fixed wings. The first Sea Mosquito brought up to full Naval requirements (TW241) incorporated folding wings and a Lockheed oleo landing leg which offered a better rebound ratio for deck flying. Two special prototypes (TS444 and TS449) were also built at Leavesden for handling trials at Boscombe Down. Contracts for 97 Sea Mosquitos were later reduced to 50 (TW227–257 and TW277–295).

All production Sea Mosquitos had provision for an 18 in torpedo and for maximum range carried two 50-gallon fuel tanks beneath the wings; alternatively two 30-gallon tanks combined with two rocket projectiles.

Sea Mosquito T.R.33s first entered service with No.811 Squadron at Ford, where they superseded Mosquito VIs in August 1946. They remained with the Royal Navy for just under a year, being disbanded at Eglinton in July 1947.

The Sea Mosquito T.R.33 was followed by the T.R.37, small numbers of which were delivered. This type is dealt with on page 102.

UNITS ALLOCATED

No.811 ((RNAS) Ford and Brawdy). *Second-line Squadrons:* Nos.703, 739, 751, 762, 771, 778 and 790.

Description: Two-sea carrier-borne, or shore-based, long-range strike aircraft. All-wooden construction.

Manufacturers: Watford Division of de Havilland Aircraft Co Ltd, Leavesden, Herts.

Power Plant: Two 1,640 hp Rolls-Royce Merlin 25.

Dimensions: Span, 54 ft 2 in (27 ft 3 in folded). Length, 42 ft 3 in. Height, 13 ft 6 in. Wing area, 454 sq ft.

Weights: Empty, 17,165 lb. Loaded, 23,850 lb.

Performance: Maximum speed, 376 mph at 12,250 ft. Climb, 1,820 ft/min. Range, 1,260 miles. Service ceiling, 30,000 ft.

Armament: Four British Hispano 20 mm guns forward and provision for eight 60 lb rocket projectiles, four beneath each wing. One 18 in torpedo below fuselage or 2,000 lb of bombs comprising two 500 lb bombs internally in the rear bomb-bay and two 500 lb bombs externally beneath the wings.

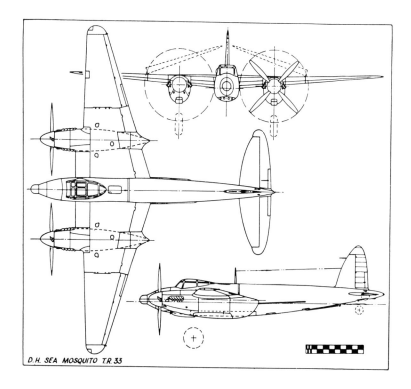

D.H. SEA MOSQUITO T.R.33

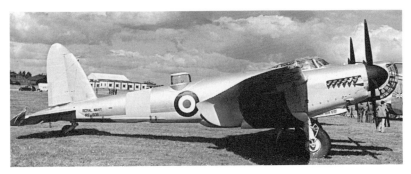

de Havilland Mosquito T.T.39 *(Flight)*

de Havilland Mosquito T.T.39

High-speed shore-based naval target-tug produced to Spec Q.19/45 and converted from the Mosquito B.XVI by General Aircraft Ltd of Feltham, Middlesex. Modifications included lengthened nose, addition of dorsal cupola, and installation of winch gear. Twenty-seven entered service, supplied to No.703 Squadron, No.728 (Malta) and No.771 (Ford). Superseded by Short Sturgeons in 1952. Two 1,650 hp Rolls-Royce Merlin 72/73 or 76/77 engines. Loaded weight, 23,000 lb. Maximum speed, 280 mph (with 32 ft span target) or 292 mph (with 16 ft span target) or 299 mph (with small sleeve target). Endurance of 1 hr with 32 ft target. Span, 54 ft 2 in. Length, 43 ft 4 in.

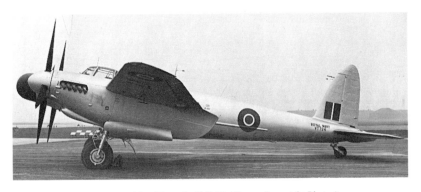

de Havilland Sea Mosquito T.R.37 *(Crown Copyright Photo.)*

de Havilland Sea Mosquito T.R.37

This was a developed version of the T.R.33, 14 of which were delivered to the FAA, serialled VT724–737. Fitted with British ASV radar and an enlarged nose to accommodate larger scanner. Used by Nos.703 and 771 Squadrons. Two Rolls-Royce Merlin 25 engines. Maximum speed, 345 mph at sea level and 383 mph at 20,000 ft. Range, 1,100 miles.

Sea Hornet F.20s from No.728 Squadron, Hal Far, Malta. *(MoD)*

de Havilland Sea Hornet F.20

The Sea Hornet was the FAA's version of the RAF's Hornet long-range fighter, and it became the first twin-engined single-seat fighter to be operated from aircraft-carriers of the Royal Navy. It was evolved to meet Spec N.5/44, and the first prototype (PX212) made its maiden flight on 19 April 1945. This was a converted Hornet I and, like the second prototype (PX214), did not have folding wings. The first fully navalised conversion (PX219) was produced by Heston Aircraft Ltd and was equipped with folding wings, arrester gear, tail-down accelerator gear and special naval radio equipments.

The first production Sea Hornet F.20 (TT186) flew on 13 August 1946 and early production aircraft carried out their Service trials with No.703 Squadron at Lee-on-Solent. The first front-line unit of the FAA to be equipped with Sea Hornet F.20s was No.801 Squadron, which had flown Seafires when disbanded after the war and which re-formed on 1 July 1947 at Ford. After a spell at Arbroath, No.801's Sea Hornets embarked in hms *Implacable* in 1949, and the unit retained these aircraft until re-equipped with Sea Furies in March 1951.

Although No.801 Squadron was the only first-line unit equipped throughout with Sea Hornet F.20s, the type formed the partial equipment of other units. In 1948, two Sea Hornet F.20s joined two Sea Furies and a Vampire of No.806 Squadron to form the composite aerobatic team which toured Canada and the USA with great success.

Total production of the Sea Hornet F.20 amounted to 79 aircraft, the last (WE242) being delivered on 12 June 1951. Serials allocated were TT186–213, TT217, TT218, VR836–864, VR891–893, VZ707–715 and WE235–242.

Sea Hornet F.20s continued in service with second-line units for many years after they had left the first-line of the FAA, and No.728 Fleet Requirements Unit was still using them at Hal Far, Malta, until February 1957.

UNITS ALLOCATED

No.801 Squadron (Ford, Arbroath, Lee-on-Solent, *Implacable* and *Indomitable*); No.806

103

Squadron (two aircraft only); No.809 Squadron (four aircraft only); *Second-line Squadrons:* Nos.703, 728, 736, 738, 739, 759, 771 and 778.

TECHNICAL DATA (SEA HORNET F.20)

Description: Single-seat medium-range carrier-borne strike fighter. Wooden fuselage and composite plywood and light alloy wing.

Manufacturers: de Havilland Aircraft Co Ltd, Hatfield, Herts.

Power Plant: Two 1,960 hp Rolls-Royce Merlin 130/131.

Dimensions: Span, 45 ft. Length, 36 ft 8 in. Height, 14 ft 2 in. Wing area, 361 sq ft.

Weights: Empty, 11,700 lb. Loaded, 15,682 lb.

Performance: Maximum speed, 431 mph at 10,000 ft; 460 mph at 18,750 ft. Climb, 4,000 ft/min. Range, 1,930 miles with auxiliary tanks. Service ceiling, 36,700 ft.

Armament: Four fixed 20 mm guns forward and provision below wings for six 60 lb rocket projectiles or 2,000 lb of bombs or two mines.

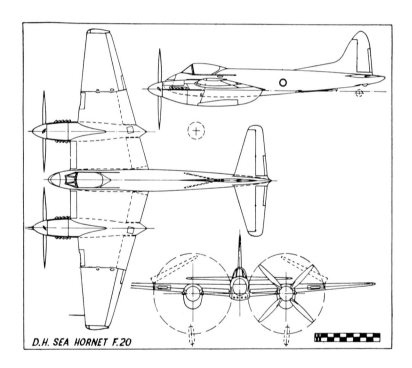

D.H. SEA HORNET F.20

Sea Hornet N.F.21 (VW949) of No.809 Squadron from Culdrose. *(Flight)*

de Havilland Sea Hornet N.F.21

The Sea Hornet N.F.21, the only two-seat version of the Hornet, was produced to Spec N.21/45 and from 1949 to 1954 was the FAA's standard carrier-borne night-fighter. Its comprehensive radar equipment and the presence of a navigator also made it useful as lead aircraft in a strike formation.

As with the single-seat Sea Hornet, the night-fighter was first produced as a conversion of a Hornet I (PX230), the modifications being made by Heston Aircraft Ltd. This aircraft first flew on 9 July 1946; it had the ASH scanner in the nose and flame-damping exhausts, but the folding wings and long dorsal fin fillet did not appear until the second prototype conversion (PX239) was introduced.

Production of the Sea Hornet N.F.21 began with VV430 which flew on 24 March 1948 and total output reached 78, the last aircraft (VZ699) being completed on 3 November 1950. After prolonged tests with the Naval Air Fighting Development Unit and the Service Trials Unit at Ford, the Sea Hornet N.F.21 entered first-line service with No.809 Squadron at Culdrose on 20 January 1949. No.809 Squadron was re-formed specially for the Sea Hornet night-fighter and, until re-equipped with Sea Venoms in 1954, was the only first-line squadron to use the type.

Sea Hornet N.F.21s first embarked with No.809 Squadron in HMS *Vengeance* in May 1950 and formed part of the FAA's first All-Weather Air Group. The range of the N.F.21 was well demonstrated in November 1951, when an aircraft of No.809 Squadron flew from Gibraltar to Lee-on-Solent non-stop at an average speed of 378 mph.

Sea Hornet N.F.21s also served on training duties with second-line squadrons between 1950 and October 1955. Serial numbers allocated to N.F.21s were VZ430–441, VW945–980, VX245–252, VZ671–682 and VZ690–699.

No.809 Squadron (*Vengeance, Indomitable* and *Eagle*). *Second-line Squadrons:* Nos.703, 759, 771 and 792.

TECHNICAL DATA (SEA HORNET N.F.21)

Description: Two-seat carrier-borne night-fighter and all-weather strike-fighter. Wooden fuselage and composite plywood and light alloy wing.

Manufacturers: de Havilland Aircraft Co Ltd, Hatfield and Chester.

Power Plant: Two 2,030 hp Rolls-Royce Merlin 134/135.

Dimensions: Span, 45 ft. Length, 37 ft. Height, 14 ft. Wing area, 361 sq ft.

Weights: Empty, 14,230 lb. Loaded, 19,530 lb.

Performance: Maximum speed, 430 mph at 22,000 ft; 365 mph at sea level. Climb, 4,400 ft/min. Range, 1,500 miles. Service ceiling, 36,500 ft.

Armament: Four fixed 20 mm guns forward and provision for eight 60 lb rocket projectiles or two 500 lb or two 1,000 lb bombs.

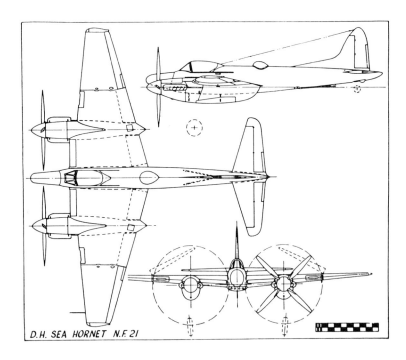

D.H. SEA HORNET N.F. 21

Sea Hornet P.R.22 (VW 930) *(Crown Copyright Photo)*

de Havilland Sea Hornet P.R.22

Photographic reconnaissance version of the Sea Hornet, 22 of which were delivered to the FAA and used by Nos.801, 809, 703, 738, 739, 759, 787 and 1833 Squadrons. Serials were VW930 to 939, VZ655 to 664 and WE245 to 247. Generally similar to the Sea Hornet F.20 described on pages 103–104, but fitted with two F.52 cameras for day reconnaissance or one Fairchild K.19B camera for night reconnaissance. Loaded weight, 16,804 lb (night duties) or 18,230 lb (day duties). Maximum speed, 467 mph at 22,000 ft. Range, 2,050 miles. Service ceiling, 37,500 ft.

Sea Hornet P.R.22 (VZ 658) *(A J Jackson)*

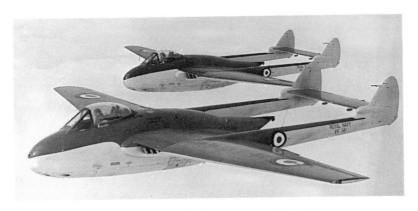

Sea Vampire F.20s (VV141 nearest camera). *(Flight)*

de Havilland Sea Vampire F.20

The Sea Vampire has the distinction of being the first pure jet aircraft ever to operate from the deck of an aircraft-carrier. This event took place on 3 December 1945 aboard HMS *Ocean*, one of the 14,000-ton light fleet carriers of the *Colossus* class. The aircraft was the converted Vampire I third prototype (LZ551) and the pilot Lt-Cdr E M Brown, RNVR. The first deck landing was followed by trials in which fifteen take-offs and landings were completed in only two days.

The production version of the Sea Vampire, the F.20, was a navalised version of the Vampire F.B.5, with the same clipped wings, but strengthened to take increased acceleration and landing loads, and with dive-brakes and landing-flaps enlarged. An 'A' type arrester hook was also fitted in a fairing in the tail of the nacelle, just above the jet outlet. The first production Sea Vampire F.20 (VV136) made its first flight in October 1948 and 20 aircraft were built, serialled VV136–153, VF315 and VG701. They were employed by the Royal Navy for jet familiarisation duties in second-line squadrons and first operated during 'Exercise Sunrise', when Lts G Baldwin, DSC and K Shepherd, of the Carrier Trials Unit, made over 200 deck landings with their Sea Vampires. A solitary Sea Vampire F.20 participated in the Coronation Naval Review in 1953, piloted by Rear Admiral W T Couchman, Flag Officer, Flying Training. An experimental development of the Sea Vampire, designated F.21, was used in the early part of 1949 aboard HMS *Warrior* for deck-landing trials with undercarriage-less aircraft. For this experiment, *Warrior* had rubberised deck surfaces and the aircraft had strengthened undersides to the fuselage to permit landing with the undercarriage retracted.

The Sea Vampire single-seaters made an important contribution to the training of the FAA's first generation of jet pilots, and were followed in service by the two-seat Sea Vampire T.22. A single Sea Vampire F.20 (VT315) flown by Lt-Cdr D B Law DSC was featured in the historic visit to the USA in 1948 by No.806 Squadron's aerobatic display team. It was the first FAA jet aircraft ever seen by the American public.

(*F.20*): No.806 (*Magnificent*). *Second-line Squadrons:* Nos.700, 702, 703, 728, 759, 764, 771 and 787. (*F.21*) Nos.703, 764 and 771.

TECHNICAL DATA (SEA VAMPIRE F.20)

Description: Single-seat carrier-borne fighter-trainer. All-metal stressed-skin construction.

Manufacturers: de Havilland Aircraft Co Ltd, Hatfield, Herts.

Power Plant: One 3,100 lb thrust de Havilland Goblin 2 turbojet.

Dimensions: Span, 38 ft. Length, 30 ft 9 in. Height, 8 ft 10 in. Wing area, 266 sq ft.

Weights: Empty, 7,623 lb. Loaded, 12,660 lb.

Performance: Maximum speed, 526 mph. Climb, 10 min to 25,000 ft. Range, 590 miles at 350 mph at sea level; 1,145 miles at 350 mph at 30,000 ft. Endurance 2 hr at 220 mph at sea level; 2.35 hr at 350 mph at 30,000 ft. Service ceiling, 43,500 ft.

Armament: Four 20 mm guns.

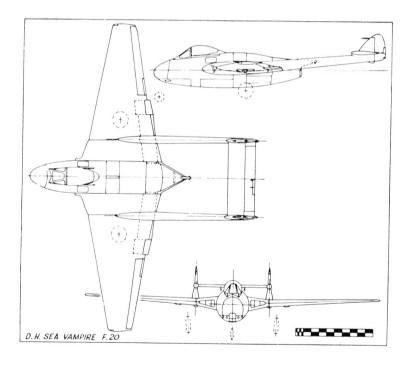

D.H. SEA VAMPIRE F.20

Sea Vampire T.22s (XA 169 nearest camera) from Lossiemouth.

de Havilland Sea Vampire T.22

FAA version of the RAF's Vampire T.11. Production was at the former Airspeed factory at Christchurch and began with XA100 in 1953 and ended with XG777 in May 1955. Total of 74 delivered to the Royal Navy serialled WW458, WW461, XA100–131, XA152–172, XG742–748 and XG765–777. The Sea Vampire T.22 entered service with Nos.802, 806, 808, 809, 831, 890, 891, 892, 893 Squadrons, Nos. 1831 and 1832 Squadrons of the RNVR and the Second-line Squadrons Nos.700, 702, 718, 724, 727, 736, 750, 759, 764, 766 and 781. The aircraft illustrated have the markings of Royal Naval Air Station, Lossiemouth, and belong to No.736 Squadron. One 3,500 lb thrust D H Goblin 35 turbojet. Loaded weight, 11,150 lb. Maximum speed, 538 mph at sea level. Climb, 4,500 ft/min. Range, 840 miles. Span, 38 ft. Length, 34 ft 5 in.

Sea Venom F.A.W.21s of No.890 Squadron. *(Flight)*

de Havilland Sea Venom

The Sea Venom was the Royal Navy's first jet all-weather fighter, and it succeeded the Sea Hornet N.F.21 in carriers during 1954. It was developed initially from the RAF's Venom N.F.2 night-fighter, the prototype of which (G-5-3) was taken over for trials by the Royal Navy as WP227. The first true prototype (WK376) was designated Sea Venom N.F.20, first flew on 19 April 1951, and did its first carrier take-off during trials in *Illustrious* on 9 July 1951. Folding wings were not fitted until the third prototype (WK385) was introduced.

With production, the designation changed to F.A.W.20 the first of which (WM500) flew on 27 March 1953. Forty were built, the last aircraft (WM567) being delivered on 6 June 1955. The F.A.W.20 was followed in production by the F.A.W.21, which introduced the up-rated Ghost 104, power-operated ailerons, American radar, clear-view frameless canopy and, eventually, Martin-Baker Mk.4 ejection seats. The Mk.21 also differed in having no tailplane extensions outboard of the tail booms. The first F.A.W.21 (WM568) flew on 22 April 1954. The final variant was the F.A.W.22, which had the Ghost 104 replaced by the Ghost 105. With the delivery of the last F.A.W.22 (XG737) in January 1958 a total of 256 Sea Venoms had been built for Fleet Air Arm Squadrons. The full serial ranges were WM500 to 523 and WM542 to 567 (F.A.W.20); WM568 to 577, WW137 to 154, WW186 to 225, WW261 to 298, XG606 to 638 and XG653 to 680 (F.A.W.21); and XG681 to 702, XG721 to 737 (F.A.W.22).

Sea Venom F.A.W.20s first entered service with No.890 Squadron, re-formed at Yeovilton on 20 March 1954; the unit converted to F.A.W. 21s before embarking in a carrier. The second Sea Venom squadron was No.809, which from 1949 had been the FAA's only all-weather squadron with Sea Hornets. From 1955 the all-weather force of Sea Venoms expanded, and by the time of the Anglo-French intervention in Egypt in October and November 1956, five squadrons were available for operations in the Eastern Mediterranean. Flying from *Albion* and *Eagle*, Sea Venoms of Nos.809, 891 and 893 Squadrons co-operated with RAF Venoms from Cyprus in large-scale ground-attack sorties and made a notable contribution to the accurate army support operations.

At the end of 1958, three Sea Venoms of No.893 Squadron, embarked in *Victorious*, made the first firings of Firestreak guided missiles by an operational fighter squadron of the Royal Navy. They scored 80 per cent of hits against drone targets off Malta. From the middle of 1959, the Sea Venom was gradually superseded as the Fleet Air Arm's standard all-weather fighter by the Sea Vixen. Sea Venoms were finally retired from carrier duties in December 1960. Ashore, they were finally withdrawn at RNAS Yeovilton in October 1970.

UNITS ALLOCATED

F.A.W.20 Nos.808, 809 (*Bulwark*), 890 (*Albion*), and 891 Squadrons. *Second-line Squadrons:* Nos.700 and 766. *F.A.W.21* Nos.809 (*Albion*), 890, 891 (*Ark Royal*), 892 (*Albion* and *Eagle*), 893 (*Bulwark, Ark Royal* and *Eagle*), and 894 Squadrons. *Second-line Squadrons:* Nos.700, 736, 738, 750, 766 and 787. *Electronic Counter-measures:* No.751. *F.A.W.22* Nos.891 (*Bulwark* and *Centaur*), 893 (*Victorious*) and 894 (*Eagle, Victorious* and *Albion*). *Electronic Counter-measures:* No.831 (*Ark Royal* and *Hermes*).

TECHNICAL DATA (SEA VENOM F.A.W.22)

Description: Two-seat carrier-borne all-weather fighter and strike fighter. All-metal stressed-skin construction.
Manufacturers: de Havilland Aircraft Co Ltd, Christchurch and Chester.
Power Plant: One 5,300 lb thrust de Havilland Ghost 105 turbojet.
Dimensions: Span, 42 ft 10 in. Length, 36 ft 8 in. Height, 8 ft 6¼ in. Wing area, 279.8 sq ft.
Weights: Empty, 10,853 lb. Loaded, 15,800 lb.
Performance: Maximum speed, 575 mph at sea level. Initial climb, 5,900 ft/min. Range, 950 miles. Service ceiling, 40,000 ft.
Armament: Four fixed 20 mm guns and provision for bombs or eight 60 lb rocket projectiles below the wings.

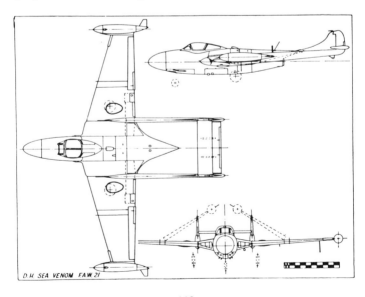

D.H. SEA VENOM F.A.W.21

Sea Vixen F.A.W.1 (XJ520) of No.766B Squadron. *(Flight)*

de Havilland Sea Vixen F.A.W.1

With the Sea Vixen the FAA acquired its first swept-wing two-seat all-weather fighter. It was developed from the D.H.110, which grew out of the requirements of the Naval Specifications N.40/46 and N.14/49, and the RAF's Specifications F.44/46 and F.4/48.

The first prototype D.H.110 (WG236) flew on 26 September 1951 and first exceeded the speed of sound in a dive on 9 April 1952. The second prototype (WG240) flew on 25 July 1952, and did 'touch-and-go' carrier trials from HMS *Albion* in the autumn of 1954. The first fully-arrested landing-on was aboard HMS *Ark Royal* on 5 April 1956, with the semi-navalised intermediate prototype (XF828), built at Christchurch and first flown on 20 June 1955. The first fully-navalised production Sea Vixen F.A.W.1 (XJ474) flew on 20 March 1957. This introduced a hydraulically steerable nosewheel, power-folding wings and a pointed nose radome.

The first production contract for 45 Sea Vixens (XJ474 to 494 and XJ513 to 528) was followed by a second order for 39 in June 1959 (XJ556 to 611) and a final batch of 29 ordered in August 1960 and serialled XN647 to 658 and XN683 to 710, plus a replacement aircraft XP918, brought the final total to 114.

Service trials of the Sea Vixen, with No.700 Squadron 'Y' Flight in *Victorious* and *Centaur*, took place in November 1958. The first operational unit to be equipped was No.892 Squadron (Cdr M H J Petrie, RN), which commissioned at Yeovilton on 2 July 1959, and embarked in *Ark Royal* in March 1960. Then Sea Vixens superseded Sea Venoms in all FAA all-weather fighter squadrons. The introduction of the Sea Vixen was a highly significant event in the Royal Navy. It was not only far in advance of the Sea Venom in performance (with twice the rate of climb, far greater patrol endurance and ceiling) but was also the first British naval aircraft designed as an integrated weapons system and the first to become fully operational armed with guided weapons instead of guns.

The second Sea Vixen Squadron (No.890) formed at Yeovilton on 1 February 1960 and embarked in the new carrier *Hermes* in July 1960. From 1964, the Sea Vixen F.A.W.1 was gradually superseded by the F.A.W.2 (described on pages 254–5). Nearly 70 F.A.W.1s were converted to F.A.W.2 standard at Hawarden and Sydenham.

The last Sea Vixen F.A.W.1s were phased out in May 1968.

UNITS ALLOCATED

No.890 (*Hermes* and *Ark Royal*), No.892 (*Ark Royal* and *Victorious*), No.893 (*Ark Royal*, *Centaur* and *Victorious*), and No.899 (*Hermes*, *Centaur*, *Eagle* and *Victorious*). *Second-line Squadrons:* Nos.700 and 766 (Yeovilton).

TECHNICAL DATA (SEA VIXEN F.A.W.1)

Description: Two-seat carrier-borne all-weather interceptor or strike fighter. Naval Spec. N.139. All-metal stressed-skin construction.

Manufacturers: de Havilland Aircraft Co Ltd, Christchurch, Hants, and Hawarden, Chester.

Power Plant: Two Rolls-Royce Avon 208 turbojets, each of 10,000 lb static thrust.

Dimensions: Span, 51 ft 0 in. Length 55 ft 7 in. Height 10 ft 9 in. Wing area, 648 sq ft.

Weights: Empty, 24,500 lb. Loaded, 41,575 lb.

Performance: Maximum speed, 645 mph at sea level. Mach 0.95 at high level. Initial climb, 16,900 ft/min. To 40,000 ft in 7 min. Service ceiling, 48,000 ft. Maximum range, nearly 2,000 miles.

Armament: Four Firestreak infra-red homing missiles or four Microcell rocket packs plus 28 2 in missiles stowed internally. In the strike rôle, two 1,000 lb bombs were carried.

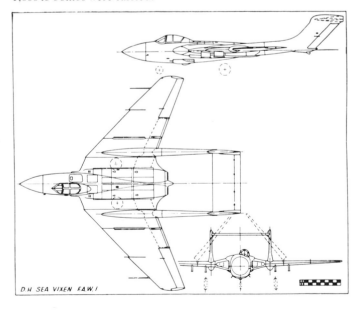

D H SEA VIXEN F.A.W. I

Skyraider A.E.W.1 (WT944) from No.778 Squadron, Culdrose.

Douglas Skyraider

The Skyraider, 50 of which were supplied to the Royal Navy under the Mutual Defence Assistance Programme, first reached Great Britain in November 1951, and it at once filled an important gap in British naval aviation. Its great virtue was its ability to carry nearly a ton of powerful radar equipment, complete with pilot and two radar operators, and to act as an early warning airborne radar picket. No British aircraft capable of doing this job was then available to the Royal Navy and the Skyraider thus occupied a unique position.

The technique of using early warning radar aircraft from carriers was pioneered by the US Navy in the Second World War, initially in the Grumman Avenger. It extended the range of radar well beyond that of the aircraft-carrier's own installations and could protect a fleet at sea from low-flying surprise attacks, as well as providing direction for air strikes and aiding the anti-submarine force.

Characterised by its huge ventral radome, the 'Guppy' version of the Skyraider was designated AD-4W in the US Navy and A.E.W.1 in the FAA. It was one of many variants of the original AD-1 (initially XBT2D-1) single-seat attack aircraft which first flew in April 1945. It was originally conceived in July 1944 as a replacement for the celebrated Dauntless dive-bomber.

The Skyraiders supplied under MDAP were serialled WT943–969, WT982–987, WV102–109 and WV177–185.

The Skyraiders were pioneered in British service by No.778 Squadron at Culdrose, Cornwall, and after intensive operational training, including carrier trials in *Eagle*, were grouped into a first-line unit, No.849 Squadron, in 1952. No.849's Skyraiders operated with a Headquarters Flight, permanently based at Culdrose, and four operational Flights (A, B, C and D), each of four aircraft for detachment as separate units with carriers.

Skyraiders first embarked in a carrier when they joined *Eagle* in January 1953.

During the Suez campaign in 1956 they were in action aboard *Eagle* and *Albion*.

An interesting sidelight on the Skyraider is that, pending its replacement by the Gannet A.E.W.3, it was the last example of a piston-engined aircraft (excluding helicopters) in first-line service with the FAA. It was finally retired from first-line duties in December 1960.

UNITS ALLOCATED

No.778 Training Squadron and No.849 Squadron (RNAS Culdrose).

TECHNICAL DATA (SKYRAIDER A.E.W.1)

Description: Three-seat radar-equipped carrier-borne radar picket. All-metal stressed-skin construction.
Manufacturers: Douglas Aircraft Co Inc, El Segundo, California.
Power Plant: One 3,300 hp Wright Cyclone R-3350-26WA.
Dimensions: Span, 50 ft 0¼ in. Length, 39 ft 3¾ in. Height, 15 ft 8 in. Wing area, 400 sq ft.
Weights: Empty, 13,614 lb. Loaded, 17,311 lb.
Performance: Maximum speed, 345 mph. Cruising speed, 250 mph. Service ceiling, 36,000 ft. Maximum range, 868 miles.
Armament: None carried.

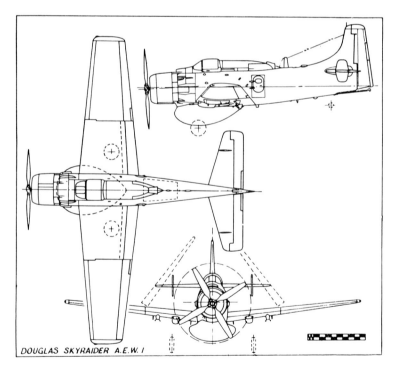

DOUGLAS SKYRAIDER A.E.W. I

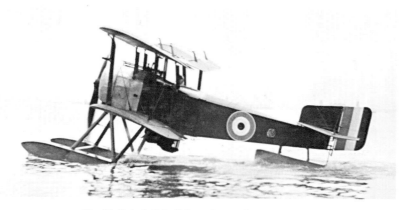

Hamble Baby built by Fairey. *(Imperial War Museum)*

Fairey Hamble Baby

Although in the first place a derivative of the Sopwith Baby, the Hamble Baby was so extensively re-designed by the Fairey Company in 1916 that it must be considered as a separate type, more particularly in view of the incorporation of the Fairey Patent Camber Gear. The introduction of this latter device was a landmark in aircraft development, for it was the first time that trailing edge flaps, to increase wing lift, made their appearance. These flaps extended along the entire trailing edge of each wing and were also used for normal aileron control. They remained a standard feature of Fairey naval aircraft right down to the Seal of 1932.

The original Hamble Baby was converted from a Sopwith Baby (No.8134) and emerged with new wings, incorporating the camber gear, a new set of floats and a re-designed tail reminiscent of the Campania. This square-cut tail became something of a Fairey trademark and was to be seen for many years after the war on such types as the IIID and Flycatcher.

Fifty Hamble Baby seaplanes were built by the Fairey factory, airframes N1320 to 1339 having a 110hp, and N1450 to 1479 a 130hp Clerget engine. By far the majority of Hamble Babies, however, were made under sub-contract by the Bristol firm of Parnall and Sons, which built 130. The Parnall aircraft could be readily distinguished by their retention of the original Sopwith-type floats and tail assembly. The first 56 Parnall-built Hamble Babies were seaplanes, N1190 to 1219 with 110 hp Clerget engines, and N1960 to 1985 with the 130 hp version, but the remainder (ending N2044) were landplanes as illustrated in the Appendix on page 447. These were known as Hamble Baby Converts, and were extensively used for training by the RNAS school at Cranwell.

Hamble Babies gave good service with the RNAS during 1917–18 on anti-submarine patrols from coastal stations at home and overseas, as well as with seaplane carriers, and their ability to carry two 65 lb bombs was a direct outcome of their camber-gear innovation. By the end of the war, however, they were giving way to later types and only 18 remained in service on 31 October 1918.

RNAS Stations at Calshot, Cattewater, Fishguard and Great Yarmouth. Overseas with seaplane carrier *Empress* and at seaplane stations in the Aegean and in Egypt. After April 1918, served with Nos.219 (Westgate), 229 (Great Yarmouth), 249 (Dundee), and 263 (Otranto).

TECHNICAL DATA (HAMBLE BABY SEAPLANE)

Description: Single-seat anti-submarine patrol seaplane. Wooden structure, fabric covered.

Manufacturers: Fairey Aviation Co Ltd, Hayes, Middlesex. Sub-contracted by Parnall & Sons, Bristol.

Power Plant: One 110 hp or 130 hp Clerget.

Dimensions: Span, 27 ft 9¼ in. Length, 23 ft 4 in. Height, 9 ft 6 in. Wing area, 246 sq ft.

Weights: Empty, 1,386 lb. Loaded, 1,946 lb.

Performance: Maximum speed, 90 mph at 2,000 ft. Climb, 5½ min to 2,000 ft; 25 min to 6,500 ft. Endurance, 2 hr. Service ceiling, 7,600 ft.

Armament: One fixed, synchronised Lewis gun forward and two 65 lb bombs on racks below fuselage.

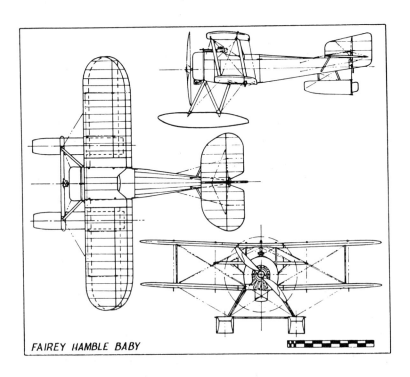

FAIREY HAMBLE BABY

F.22 Campania (N1006) at Calshot. *(J M Bruce.)*

Fairey Campania

The Campania is important in the history of British naval aviation as the first aircraft specifically designed for operation from a carrier vessel. It was designed in 1916, when the Fairey Company was only a year old, and was that famous concern's second type of aircraft. It took its name from the fact that the carrier for which it was designed was *Campania*, a former Cunard passenger liner purchased by the Admiralty in October 1914. *Campania* was commissioned in April 1915, after being converted to carry 10 seaplanes and fitted with a 120 ft flying-off deck above the forecastle. By the time that Fairey Campanias first operated from *Campania* in 1917, the flying-off deck had been lengthened to 200 ft. The Campanias took off with the aid of a wheeled trolley, which was left behind as the aircraft became airborne.

The prototype Campania (N1000) had the Fairey works designation F.16 and mounted a 250 hp Rolls-Royce Mk.IV engine, later named Eagle IV. With the second prototype (N1001) a number of changes were introduced, including an improved wing section, larger fin and rudder and the more powerful 275 hp Rolls-Royce Mk.I (later Eagle V) engine. This version had the Fairey works number F.17 and was the first to be ordered in quantity. With Campania N1006 a change of power plant was necessitated by the temporary shortage of Eagles, and the Sunbeam Maori II was substituted. The Fairey works number changed to F.22 with this modification, but in later production aircraft the Eagle was re-introduced.

Production contracts for 100 Campanias included airframes N1000 to 1009 and N2360 to 2399 from the parent company and N1840 to 1889 from sub-contractors, but only 62 were completed. On 31 October 1918 some 42 Campanias were serving at coastal air stations and with seaplane carriers. Campanias continued to serve for a period after the Armistice, and in 1919 five were aboard the seaplane carrier *Nairana* (together with two Camels) during operations against the Bolsheviks from Archangel.

RNAS Stations at Bembridge, Calshot, Cherbourg, Dundee, Newhaven, Portland, Rosyth and Scapa Flow. HM Seaplane Carriers *Campania, Nairana* and *Pegasus*. After April 1918, Nos.240, 241 and 253 Squadrons.

TECHNICAL DATA (F.22 CAMPANIA)

Description: Two-seat coastal patrol or carrier-borne reconnaissance seaplane. Wooden structure, fabric covered.

Manufacturers: Fairey Aviation Co Ltd, Hayes, Middlesex. Sub-contracted by Barclay, Curle & Co Ltd, of Glasgow.

Power Plant: One 275 hp Sunbeam Maori II or 345 hp Rolls-Royce Eagle VIII.

Dimensions: Span, 61 ft 7½ in. Length, 43 ft 0⅝ in. Height, 15 ft 1 in. Wing area, 627 sq ft.

Weights: Empty, 3,672 lb (Maori) or 3,874 lb (Eagle). Loaded, 5,329 lb (Maori) or 5,657 lb (Eagle).

Performance (Maori II): Maximum speed, 85 mph at sea level. Climb, 7 min to 2,000 ft; 38 min to 6,500 ft. Endurance, 4½ hr. Service ceiling, 6,000 ft (Eagle VIII): Maximum speed, 80 mph at 2,000 ft. Climb, 41½ min to 6,500 ft. Endurance, 3 hr. Service ceiling, 5,500 ft.

Armament: Lewis gun on Scarff ring and bombs on racks below fuselage.

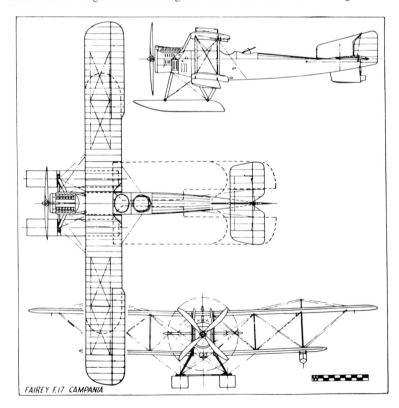

FAIREY F.17 CAMPANIA

Fairey IIIC (N9236). *(Imperial War Museum)*

Fairey IIIC

The Fairey IIIC was a development of the IIIA and IIIB (described and illustrated in the Appendix), and was the last of the Series III to be delivered from the Fairey works before the Armistice of November 1918. In that month the first IIIC was received by Great Yarmouth air station, but it was too late to see any action in the First World War.

Generally considered to be the first general-purpose seaplane for British naval aviation, the IIIC combined the scouting rôle of the IIIA landplane with the bombing duties of the IIIB seaplane. In configuration, too, it merged the features of the two earlier types, having the equal span wings of the IIIA and the float undercarriage of the IIIB. Its advantage over both its predecessors was in the installation of the powerful Rolls-Royce Eagle VIII engine which improved the power:weight ratio by as much as 26 per cent.

The first Fairey IIIC (N2246) left the factory in September 1918 and a total of 35 was delivered. Serial numbers were N2255 to 2259 and N9230 to 9259. Fairey IIICs served both at home and overseas until the autumn of 1921, when they were finally supplanted by the more famous IIID.

Despite a relatively brief Service career, the IIICs did see active service, for they equipped part of the North Russian Expeditionary Force in 1919, based at Archangel. They were taken to the scene of action in HMS *Pegasus* and on 8 June 1919 made a bombing attack on four Bolshevik naval vessels, though without much effect. Later, they attacked enemy rail communications. At least seven IIICs served in action with British Forces in North Russia in 1919. These included N9230, N9231, N9233, N9234, N9238 and N9241. Operations on the Murmansk front are described by Group Capt F E Livock in his book *To the Ends of the Air*, published in 1973.

UNITS ALLOCATED

No.229 (Great Yarmouth) and No.230 (Felixstowe). Also with North Russian Expeditionary Force in HMS *Pegasus* at Archangel and HMS *Nairana* at Murmansk.

Description: Two-seat general-purpose seaplane. Wooden structure, fabric covered.

Manufacturers: Fairey Aviation Co Ltd, Hayes, Middlesex.

Power Plant: One 375 hp Rolls-Royce Eagle VIII.

Dimensions: Span, 46 ft 1¼ in. Length, 36 ft. Height, 12 ft 1¾ in. Wing area, 542 sq ft.

Weights: Empty, 3,392 lb. Loaded, 4,800 lb.

Performance: Maximum speed, 110½ mph at 2,000 ft, or 102½ mph at 10,000 ft. Climb: 2 min 20 sec to 2,000 ft and 18 min to 10,000 ft. Endurance, 5½ hr. Service ceiling, 15,000 ft.

Armament: One fixed Vickers gun forward and one manually-operated Lewis gun on Scarff ring aft. Provision for light bomb-load on external racks beneath the wings.

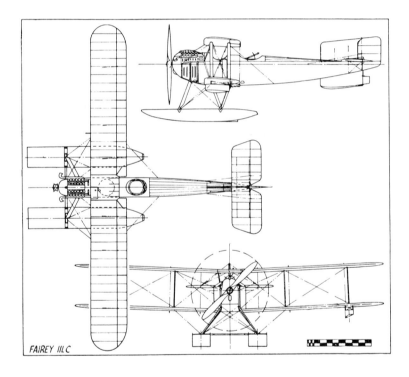

FAIREY IIIC

Fairey IIID (N9749) of No.443B Flight from *HMS Argus*. (*FAA Museum*)

Fairey IIID

From 1924 until 1930 the Fairey IIID was one of the leading types used by the FAA. It was developed from a proven design, the IIIC of 1918, and in due course was succeeded by the classic IIIF. It was the first of the III Series to enter service in large numbers, was strongly built and immensely reliable, and it could be flown either as a landplane from carriers or shore stations, or as a seaplane catapulted from warships.

The first IIID (N9450) appeared as a seaplane and was powered by an Eagle VIII engine. It was flown for the first time by Col Vincent Nicholl, at Hamble in August 1920. Production was ordered to Spec 38/22, and all the first aircraft (N9451 to 9499) had Eagle engines. The second batch (N9567 to 9578) had Lion engines, but the Eagle was installed again in IIIDs N9630 to 9635. Thereafter the Lion engine was standardised, the Lion II being used in the IIIDs N9636 to 9641 and N9730 to 9791; the Lion V in S1000 to 1035 and S1074 to 1108. The last of 176 IIIDs reached the FAA in 1926.

The first units equipped with the IIID were Nos.441 and 442 Flights in 1924. No.441 Flight used landplanes (equipped with arrester hooks on their axles) aboard HMS *Hermes*. which had fore-and-aft arrester wires; this technique led to accidents, and, from 1926, IIIDs were flown without arrester hooks from carrier decks. The IIIDs of No.444 Flight aboard HMS *Vindictive* were seaplanes: a IIID flown by Wg Cdr Burling became, on 30 October 1925, the first standard seaplane of the FAA to be catapulted from a ship at sea.

Both Nos.441 and 442 Flight had relinquished Parnall Panthers to receive IIIDs. In No.440 Flight, the Fairey IIID supplanted Seagull II amphibians in January 1925.

Fairey IIIDs were particularly active in the Far East: those of HMS *Pegasus* carried out an aerial survey of Malaya from Singapore, and in 1927 a special force shipped to Hong Kong in HMS *Argus* went to the aid of the Shanghai Defence Force to protect British interests against rebel Chinese forces. The

IIIDs flew both as landplanes from the Shanghai racecourse and as seaplanes from the Whangpoo River.

UNITS ALLOCATED

No.440 Flight (*Eagle* and *Hermes*), No.441 Flight (*Hermes* and *Eagle*), No.442 Flight (*Argus* and *Hermes*), No.443A Flight (*Furious* and *Argus*), No.443B Flight (*Argus*), No.444 (Catapult) Flight (*Vindictive*) and No.481 Flight (Malta), later No.202 Squadron, RAF.

TECHNICAL DATA (FAIREY IIID)

Description: Three-seat spotter-reconnaissance landplane or seaplane. Wooden structure, fabric covered.
Manufacturers: Fairey Aviation Co Ltd, Hayes, Middlesex.
Power Plant: One 375 hp Rolls-Royce Eagle VIII or 450 hp Napier Lion IIB, or 465 hp Lion V.
Dimensions: Span, 46 ft 1¼ in. Length (seaplane), 37 ft. Height (seaplane), 11 ft 4 in. Wing area, 500 sq ft.
Weights (Lion engine): Empty, 3,430 lb. Loaded, 5,050 lb.
Performance (Eagle engine): Maximum speed 106 mph. Climb 6 min 40 sec to 5,000 ft. Range, 550 miles at 100 mph. Service ceiling, 16,500 ft.
Armament: One Vickers gun forward and one Lewis gun aft.

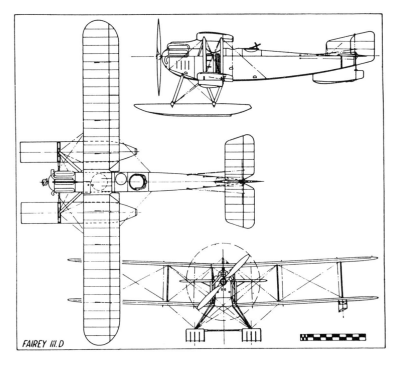

FAIREY III.D

Flycatcher I (N9928) of No.403 Flight from *Hermes*. *(Charles E Brown)*

Fairey Flycatcher

No pilot who flew with the FAA during the early days will ever forget the Flycatcher. This rugged little biplane made an enduring impression on all who flew it: for aerobatics it was superb, it was comfortable to fly, easy to land aboard a carrier and possessed a delightful full-throttle roar that never failed to impress spectators. Its appearance, too, was of a strongly individual character, with marked dihedral on the top wings but none on the bottom wings, a somewhat ungainly undercarriage and a fuselage which, combined with the characteristic fin and rudder, gave the impression of being 'cocked-up' at the rear end. Another feature of the Flycatcher, first seen on the Fairey Hamble Baby and shared with the Flycatcher's contemporaries, the IIID and the IIIF, was the Fairey patent camber-changing mechanism on the wings. Flaps which ran along the entire trailing edges of both wings (the outer sections serving also as ailerons) could be lowered for landing and taking off. These flaps steepened the glide path and shortened both take-off and landing runs, both invaluable aids to deck-flying operations.

For over a decade, from 1923 to 1934, the Flycatcher was a standard first-line fighter of the FAA and, indeed, from 1924 until 1932 (when the first Hawker Nimrods came into service) was the only type of Fleet fighter. Like its stable-mate, the IIIF, the Flycatcher served in all the aircraft-carriers of its day and was also used (like its forebears in the First World War) as a landplane fighter from short take-off platforms mounted on the gun-turrets of capital ships. It was the last Fleet fighter to employ this technique. The land undercarriage was readily interchangeable with twin floats, and in some Flycatchers the floats incorporated wheels which permitted amphibious operations.

125

The prototype Flycatcher (N163) appeared in 1922 and first flew at Hamble on 28 November. Following Service trials at Martlesham Heath, this aircraft went aboard HMS *Argus* in February 1923 for deck trials. For this purpose two steel jaws were fitted on the undercarriage spreader bar to engage the fore and aft arrester wires then in use. This type of arrester gear remained standard on Flycatchers until the fore-and-aft wire system was abandoned about 1926. In this connection it is interesting to note that the Flycatcher was the first FAA aircraft to be fitted with hydraulic wheel-brakes, which reduced the landing run to a mere 50 yards. However, they were not fitted to standard aircraft and it was not until the arrival of the Fairey Seal in 1933 that they were introduced on squadron service.

The Flycatcher was built to Spec 6/22, and the first prototype, fitted with a Jaguar engine, was followed by a second (N164) fitted as a seaplane, and a third (N165), also with Jaguars. The first prototype was later re-engined with a Jupiter, but the Jaguar was adopted as standard in production aircraft. The third prototype (N165) was used for trials with the amphibian type undercarriage. Although no Flycatchers had folding wings, they were built in such a way that the airframe could be dismantled so that no section exceeded 13 ft 6 in in length, thus aiding stowage aboard ship.

Production Flycatchers began to leave the Fairey factory in 1923, and repeated contracts kept the works busy until 1930. A total of 189 Flycatchers was delivered to the FAA, the last aircraft (S1418) being flown to Gosport on 20 June 1930. The serial numbers allocated to Flycatchers were N9611 to 9619, N9655 to 9680, N9854 to 9895, N9902 to 9965, S1060 to 1073, S1273 to 1297 and S1409 to 1418. A number of these aircraft call for special mention. Flycatcher N9678 was the first production amphibian, flown at Northolt on 19 February 1924 by Capt Norman Macmillan. The second amphibian (N9953) was flown at Hamble in October 1925. The Flycatcher seaplane N9913 was used for catapult trials aboard HMS *Vindictive* in 1925.

Flycatchers first entered service with No.402 Flight in April 1923: other standard Fleet fighters at this time were Nieuport Nightjars of No.401 Flight and Parnall Plovers of Nos.403 and 404 Flights. The rotary-engined Nightjars belonged to an essentially 1914–18 conception of the fighter, but the Plovers were radial-engined aircraft not unlike the Flycatcher in general appearance. The Plover, however, could not stand up to the competition of the Flycatcher

Flycatcher pilots practise formation flying. *(Air Ministry)*

126

and was soon eclipsed. In 1924 both Nightjars and Plovers gave way to the Flycatcher in Nos.401, 403 and 404 Flights and two new units, Nos.405 and 406 Flights, received Flycatchers as initial equipment. Other new Flycatcher Flights were No.407 in 1928, and No.408 in 1929. In 1933, with the formation for the first time of squadrons in the FAA, No.801 Squadron (formerly No.401 Flight) retained Flycatchers for a time until superseded by Nimrods and Ospreys.

By 1934 Flycatchers were entirely superseded by Nimrods and Ospreys in first-line Fleet fighter squadrons, and in that year they also disappeared from catapult flights aboard warships, which received Osprey seaplanes. The last units equipped with Flycatchers were No.403 Flight (with five aircraft), which served on the China Station with the 5th Cruiser Squadron, and No.406 Flight (with two aircraft), operating with the East Indies Squadron. No.406 exchanged their Flycatchers for Ospreys in June 1934 and No.403 from May 1934.

The exploits of Flycatchers during their many years of service with the FAA are well described in a most engaging book entitled *Aviation Memoirs*, by Owen Cathcart-Jones. In this book the author recalls incidents in No.403 Flight, serving in HMS *Hermes* around 1926–27, and with No.404 Flight in HMS *Courageous* during 1928. No.403 Flight's Flycatchers were flown as seaplanes from Hong Kong harbour during operations against Chinese pirates raiding coastal shipping. Also to be found in the pages of *Aviation Memoirs* is an account of how the celebrated 'blue note' of the Flycatcher originated. Such was the strength of the Flycatcher's airframe that it could be dived vertically with engine full on until it reached its terminal velocity; in fact it was the first aircraft to be required to undertake such a test by the Air Ministry. If during the course of such a dive the engine was suddenly throttled back, the most curious sound was heard on the ground. It is alleged that a FAA pilot named Aldridge became so proficient at this trick that he could control the sound effects and almost play a tune with his engine. Another explanation of the tremendous noise generated by the Flycatcher in dive-bombing attacks is that the airscrew blades fluttered when pulling out of the dive. Be that as it may, the Flycatcher was always a star turn at air displays where it gave such demonstrations, and it delighted the crowds. The Flycatcher enabled the FAA to develop a tactic known as converging bombing, whereby three fighters attacked the same target from different directions simultaneously, diving steeply from an altitude of about 2,000 ft straight at the objective. Memorable exhibitions of converging bombing were given by Flycatchers at a number of RAF Hendon Displays. Nos.405 and 403 Flights participated in 1928 and No.405 Flight in 1929. For this type of work Flycatchers were armed with four 20 lb bombs with which, it was somewhat optimistically predicted by the Admiralty, they would be able to attack enemy surface units that came within range, in addition to their normal duties of repelling air attack by close patrol above the carrier or fleet.

Aboard aircraft-carriers Flycatchers proved extremely amenable, and it is recorded that on 26 November 1929 a Flycatcher from Hal Far, Malta, landed aboard HMS *Courageous* at night, this being the first night-landing on a carrier deck by a Fleet fighter. Flycatcher flights prided themselves on their skilful handling aboard ship, and the record strike-down and stowage was when six aircraft were landed aboard and stowed in their hangars within 4 min 20 sec. Flying-off operations were no less spectacular. Aboard the carriers *Furious*, *Courageous* and *Glorious*, the fighter flights, known as 'slip-flights', were

Flycatcher N9859.

housed in a forward hangar, and the Flycatchers took off from a 60 ft tapered runway (below the main flying-deck) straight out of their hangar and over the bows. They returned, of course, to the main deck above. Some records claim that a favourite party-piece of the Flycatchers (no doubt unauthorised) was to do a slow roll immediately after leaving the carrier, presumably in this case from the main flying-deck, as 'slip-flight' invariably dropped out of sight below the bows and almost touched the water before gaining height.

Perhaps the oddest sight the Flycatcher presented was when it operated from a land aerodrome as an amphibian. The wheels of this aircraft projected only a little way below the floats and were scarcely visible at some distance as Flycatcher amphibians taxied across the grass. This form of undercarriage was immensely strong, and the amphibians could land and take off from a ploughed field. They were less successful, however, in operating from the water, where they were allegedly reluctant to 'unstick', and the book *Aviation Memoirs* refers to training aircraft 'charging up and down the River Tay near Tayport in a vain attempt to get off the water'.

The Flycatcher was finally declared obsolete in April 1935, and with its passing an era in British deck-flying came to an end.

UNITS ALLOCATED

No.401 Flight (*Argus, Hermes, Furious* and *Courageous*), No.402 Flight (*Eagle* and Courageous), No.403 Flight (*Hermes* and Catapult Flight, 5th Cruiser Squadron, China Station), No.404 Flight (*Furious, Argus* and *Courageous*), No.405 Flight (*Furious, Glorious* and *Courageous*), No.406 Flight (*Furious, Hermes, Glorious* and as Catapult Flight, 4th Cruiser Squadron, East Indies) No.407 Flight (*Courageous* and *Furious*), No.408 Flight (*Glorious)* and No.801 Squadron (*Furious*). Launched from gun-turret platforms of HMS *Barham, Emerald, Enterprise, Hood, Ramillies, Renown, Repulse,*

128

Revenge, Royal Oak, and *Royal Sovereign.* Catapult-launched from HMS *Berwick, Cornwall, Cumberland, Dorsetshire, Kent, Queen Elizabeth, Royal Oak, Royal Sovereign, Suffolk, Vindictive* and *York.*

TECHNICAL DATA (FLYCATCHER I)

Description: Single-seat carrier-borne seaplane or amphibian fighter. Wooden wings with fabric covering and composite wood and metal fuselage, metal and fabric covered.

Manufacturers: Fairey Aviation Co Ltd, Hayes, Middlesex.

Power Plant: One 410 hp Armstrong Siddeley Jaguar IV.

Dimensions: Span, 29 ft. Length, 23 ft (29 ft as an amphibian). Height, 12 ft (13 ft 4 in as an amphibian). Wing area, 288 sq ft.

Weights: Empty, 2,039 lb. Loaded, 3,028 lb (3,531 lb with floats).

Performance: Maximum speed, 133 mph at 5,000 ft (126 mph as a seaplane); 129½ mph at 10,000 ft; 117½ mph at 15,000 ft; 110 mph at 17,000 ft. Initial climb, 1,090 ft/min. 5 min 55 sec to 5,000 ft; 9 min 29 sec to 10,000 ft; 18 min 50 sec to 15,000 ft; 25 min 23 sec to 17,000 ft. Range, 263 miles at maximum speed at 10,000 ft (1.82 hr); 311 miles at 110 mph at 10,000 ft. Service ceiling, 19,000 ft (14,000 ft as seaplane).

Armament: Twin synchronised Vickers guns. Provision for four 20 lb bombs below wings.

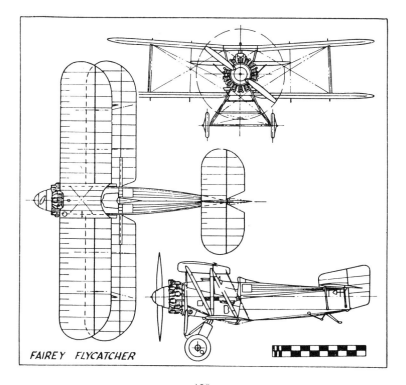

FAIREY FLYCATCHER

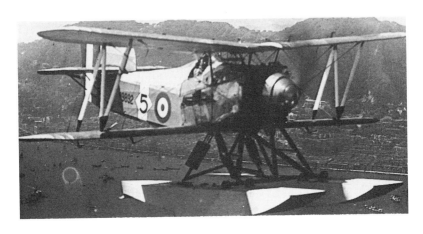

Flycatcher seaplane (N9892) of No.403 Flight from *Hermes*. *(FAA Museum)*

Flycatchers of No.402 Flight from *Eagle* at Hal Far, Malta. *(FAA Museum)*

IIIF (S1189) of No.445 Flight, HMS *Courageous. (MoD)*

Fairey IIIF

The Fairey IIIF is one of the best-remembered types of the FAA's biplane era and, indeed, a classic design in the history of British aviation. It was the last of the renowned Fairey III Series, which began in 1917, and was introduced as a successor to the Fairey IIID. Fairey IIIFs were supplied to the FAA and the RAF proper, and a grand total of 622 was built. Over 350 of these went to the FAA, making the IIIF the most widely-used aeroplane in the FAA between the wars. Between 1927 and 1936 IIIFs served in every aircraft-carrier of the Royal Navy and were a familiar sight at naval air stations from Leuchars to Hong Kong. They were also widely employed as twin-float seaplanes in catapult reconnaissance flights aboard capital ships and cruisers.

The prototype IIIF (N198) was first flown by Capt Norman Macmillan at Northolt on 19 March 1926. It bore a strong family resemblance to the earlier IIID, but was of improved aerodynamic form with a smooth, pointed nose and a streamlined instead of slab-sided fuselage. A Fairey-Reed metal airscrew was fitted and a neat undercarriage replaced the somewhat cumbersome assembly on the IIID. It was fitted out as a three-seater, carrying a wireless-telegraphist/airgunner as well as the pilot and naval observer. All subsequent IIIFs for the FAA were three-seaters, the two-seater going to the RAF. Composite construction was used, with metal tubular fuselage and wooden wings. One feature in which the IIIF differed from its predecessors in the III Series was its tail assembly. The traditional rectangular fin and rudder with a straight sloping line along the top was replaced by a 'stepped' outline resulting from a taller, balanced rudder. This was retained in the early production IIIFs, but was later superseded by an elongated curved fin and rudder with inset balance. The first prototype IIIF was followed by a second (N225) and was built to Spec 19/24.

Production of the IIIF Mk.I for the FAA was preceded by an interim non-standard batch of aircraft from the end of the IIID contract, numbered S1139 to 1148. Of these aircraft, S1147 became the first two-seat general-purpose type and S1148 was allocated for deck-landing trials aboard HMS *Furious* in 1927. Standard production IIIF Mk.Is (S1168 to 1207) were of composite construction and had the Lion VA engine. The first production Mk.I

(S1168) was first flown at Northolt by Capt Norman Macmillan on 18 February 1927.

On 18 August 1927, again at Northolt, Capt Macmillan flew the first IIIF Mk.II (S1208), fitted with the Lion XI engine. Thirty-three of these aircraft were built (S1208 to 1227 and S1250 to 1262), and they were all of composite construction.

Meanwhile, on 2 March 1927, the second IIIF (N225) was flown as the prototype for the Mk.III. The IIIF Mk.III saw the change from composite to all-metal construction, the mainplanes having corrugated drawn-tube spars with pressed ribs clipped on. Production of the IIIF Mk.III began with S1303, which flew on 26 March 1929. The Lion XIA was fitted, and this engine remained standard in the rest of the IIIFs built for the FAA. Serial numbers allocated to IIIF Mk.IIIs were S1303 to 1356, S1370 to 1408 and S1454 to 1463. The final batch of ten aircraft listed were built as dual-control trainers.

The IIIF Mk.IIIM was followed by the IIIF Mk.IIIB, another all-metal variant, which had a strengthened fuselage for catapulting and a number of detail changes. The first IIIF Mk.IIIB (S1474) was flown at Northolt by C S Staniland on 6 June 1930. This was the last IIIF variant for the FAA which took delivery of 166. The Mk.IIIBs were allocated the serial numbers S1474 to 1552, S1779 to 1844 and S1845 to 1865. The final IIIF for the FAA was delivered on 10 September 1932. Total production of IIIFs for the Royal Navy was 352 aircraft.

The Fairey IIIF first entered service with the FAA in 1927, when it superseded the Fairey IIID in No.440 Flight and formed the initial equipment of Nos.445 and 446 Flights. In 1929 IIIFs followed Avro Bisons in Nos.447 and 448 Flights and IIIDs in No.441 Flight. Re-equipment continued in 1931 with IIIFs in place of Blackburn Blackburns in Nos.449 and 450 Flights, and the last remaining IIIDs were also replaced in Nos.442 and 444 Flights. Finally, in

IIIF (S1346) of No.825 Squadron from *Glorious*. *(FAA Museum)*

November 1932, the IIIF was issued to No.460 Flight in place of Blackburn Ripons.

From April 1933, when FAA Flights were merged, IIIFs equipped five spotter-reconnaissance squadrons. No.820 Squadron was formed from No.450 Flight; No.822 Squadron from Nos.442 and 449 Flights; No.823 Squadron from Nos.441 and 448 Flights; No.824 Squadron from Nos.440 and 460 Flights and No.825 Squadron from Nos.440 and 460 Flights. In 1934 the IIIF was largely supplanted by the Seal, but IIIFs remained with No.822 Squadron in *Furious* and No.825 in *Glorious* until 1936. No.822 received Seals in June and No.825 the first Swordfish in July.

As the IIIF was used in aircraft-carriers at a period when the arrester wire technique was out of favour it did not carry any form of arrester hook as standard, but one aircraft was used for early experiments with the rear fuselage type of deck hook later standardised on Seals, Ospreys and other biplanes of the 'thirties. This was a swinging triangular steel frame with a spring-loaded hook at the apex. This hook could be lowered by the pilot when required, and raised flush with the fuselage for normal flight. First ship trials with S1781 took place aboard *Courageous* in 1931, the arrester wires being of the transverse type, instead of the longitudinal system used in the 'twenties when hooks on the axle were in vogue.

Earlier mention has been made of the IIIF's use as a seaplane. In this form it departed from the traditional three-float undercarriage familiar on the earlier III Series seaplanes: instead it used long twin floats providing stability both laterally and fore and aft, thus dispensing with the tail float. The IIIF Mk.IIIB, being stressed for catapult work, was issued in seaplane form for use aboard warships, and it served for several years in this rôle until superseded by the Hawker Osprey. Eight IIIF seaplanes were allocated to HMS *York*, five to HMS *Exeter*, two to HMS *Hood* and one each to HMS *Norfolk*, *Valiant* and *Dorsetshire*. IIIF seaplanes were also used from catapults on aircraft-carriers, including *Hermes* and *Glorious*. Another IIIF Mk.III (S1317) was used for catapult launch experiments at the Royal Aircraft Establishment at Farnborough, whilst three

IIIF Mk.IIIM (S1307) of No.446 Flight, HMS *Courageous*.

133

IIIF Mk.IIIB (S1821) of No.824 Squadron from HMS *Eagle*.

IIIF seaplane (S1509) from No.444 Flight. *(FAA Museum)*

more (including S1536) were modified for radio-controlled pilotless aircraft experiments. These special IIIFs, known as Fairie Queens, had increased dihedral on the wings to aid stability, and had a fully automatic pilot. One of them was shipped out to Gibraltar, where it acted as a target for ships of the Home Fleet. Later it was sent to Malta and was eventually shot down by the guns of the Mediterranean Fleet. Other IIIFs at Hal Far, Malta, were equipped with a windmill-driven winch and towed aerial drogues to provide the Royal Navy with gunnery practice. A similar duty for the Home Fleet was performed by target-towing IIIFs of the Base Training Squadron at Gosport. Other IIIFs at Gosport were used for the training of wireless-telegraphist/airgunners, and at Lee-on-Solent (the School of Naval Co-operation) naval observers were trained.

Although it could also be used for precision high-bombing attacks on enemy fleets (a tactic never taken very seriously by the Admiralty), the IIIF was first

Fairey IIIF (S1189) of No.821 Squadron from *HMS Courageous*. (*FAA Museum*)

and foremost a spotter-reconnaissance aircraft and, with the closely-related Seal, was the last representative of this class in the FAA. Thereafter reconnaissance duties were combined with other work, producing the fighter-reconnaissance aircraft (such as the Osprey) and the torpedo-spotter-reconnaissance aircraft (such as the Shark and Swordfish). All Fairey IIIFs were finally declared obsolete early in 1940.

UNITS ALLOCATED

No.421 Flight (*Furious*), No.423 Flight (*Eagle*), No.440 Flight (*Hermes*, China Station); No.441 Flight (*Argus*, China Station; *Glorious*, Mediterranean Fleet); No.442 Flight (*Furious*, Home Fleet); No.443 Flight; *Furious*, Home Fleet; Catapult Flight, West Indies and South Africa); No.444 Flight (Lee-on-Solent and Catapult Flight, Home Fleet Capital Ships); No.445 Flight (*Courageous*, Mediterranean and Home Fleets); No.446 Flight (*Courageous*, Mediterranean and Home Fleets); No.447 Flight (*Furious*, Home Fleet; *Glorious*, Mediterranean Fleet; 1st Cruiser Squadron and Capital Ships, Mediterranean Fleet); No.448 Flight (*Eagle* and *Glorious*, Mediterranean Fleet); No.449 Flight (*Courageous*, Home Fleet); No.450 Flight (*Courageous*, Home Fleet); No.460 Flight (*Glorious*, Mediterranean Fleet); No.820 Squadron (*Courageous* and *Furious*, Home Fleet); No.821 Squadron (*Courageous*, Home Fleet); No.822 Squadron (*Furious*, Home Fleet); No.823 Squadron (*Glorious* and *Courageous*, Mediterranean Fleet); No.824 Squadron (*Eagle*, Mediterranean Fleet); No.825 Squadron (*Eagle* and *Glorious*, Mediterranean Fleet). *Catapult Flights:* Nos.701, 714 and 718.

TECHNICAL DATA (IIIF MK.IIIB)

Description: Three-seat carrier-borne or catapulted seaplane for spotter-reconnaissance duties. All-metal structure, fabric covered.
Manufacturers: Fairey Aviation Co Ltd, Hayes, Middlesex.
Power Plant: One 570 hp Napier Lion XIA
Dimensions: Span, 45 ft 9½ in. Length, 34 ft 4 in (36 ft 4 in as seaplane). Height, 14 ft 2¾ in. Wing area, 443½ sq ft.
Weights: Empty, 3,923 lb. Loaded, 6,301 lb.

Performance: Maximum speed, 120 mph at 10,000 ft. Climb, 6.4 min to 5,000 ft. Endurance, 3 to 4 hr. Service ceiling, 20,000 ft.

Armament: One fixed Vickers gun forward and one manually-operated Lewis gun on Scarff ring or Fairey high-speed mounting in rear cockpit. Provision for up to 500 lb of bombs below the wings.

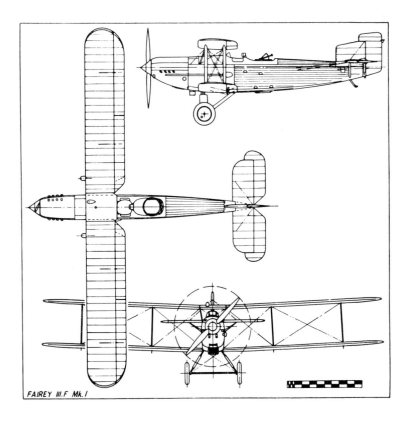

FAIREY III.F Mk.I

Seal (K3481) of No.821 Squadron from *Courageous*. *(Charles E Brown)*

Fairey Seal

The Seal was the FAA equivalent of the RAF's Gordon; both types superseded the IIIF in their respective Services. As with the prototype Gordon, the first Seal was a converted IIIF and was in fact originally known as the IIIF Mk.VI. The conversion was made to Spec 12/29 from a IIIF Mk.IIIB (S1325), and the first flight took place on 11 September 1930. The seaplane version (still S1325) flew for the first time at Hamble on 29 September 1932,

Delivery of the production Seal began in 1933 and continued until March 1935. One aircraft (K3485), from the initial batch of eleven (K3477 to 3487), was taken off the line for modification as the dual-control trainer prototype. Air Ministry contracts totalled 91, the remaining aircraft being K3514 to 3545, K3575 to 3579, K4201 to 4225 and K4779 to 4796.

The first FAA unit to be equipped with the Seal was No.821 Squadron which embarked in HMS *Courageous* in 1933. No.821 Squadron was formed from Nos.445 and 446 Flights in April 1933, and it is possible that a few Seals may have been used before the merger took place. The next Seal squadron was No.820, which converted from IIIFs in June 1934, followed by No.824 Squadron in October 1934. The last to receive Seals, No.822 Squadron, took over No.821 Squadron's aircraft when it re-equipped with Sharks in 1936. No.820 Squadron retained its Seals only to December 1934 when it became the first Shark squadron. Seals left first-line service in April 1937 but some continued in second-line duties until August 1940.

As well as serving in aircraft-carriers, the Seal was also employed in catapult flights in warships as a twin-float seaplane. A notable fact about the Seal is that it was the first Fairey type to be fitted as standard with the swinging, triangular steel frame arrester hook beneath the rear fuselage, engaging transverse arrester wires. It was also the first standard Fleet Air Arm aircraft to employ wheel brakes. This was an improved version of the experimental type tried out on the IIIF.

The last Seals in service were with the RAF and not with the FAA. They flew patrols over the Indian Ocean with No.273 Squadron, based in Ceylon, from August 1939 to April 1942.

UNITS ALLOCATED

No.820 Squadron (*Courageous*); No.821 Squadron (*Courageous*); No.822 Squadron (*Furious*); No.823 Squadron (*Courageous* and *Glorious*); No.824 Squadron (*Hermes* and *Eagle*). *Catapult Flights:* Nos.444, 701 and 702. *Second-line Squadron:* No.753 (Lee-on-Solent).

TECHNICAL DATA (SEAL)

Description: Three-seat spotter-reconnaissance carrier-borne landplane or twin-float seaplane. All-metal structure, fabric covered.

Manufacturers: Fairey Aviation Co Ltd, Hayes, Middlesex.

Power Plant: One 525 hp Armstrong Siddeley Panther IIA.

Dimensions: Span, 45 ft 9 in. Length, 33 ft 8 in as landplane or 35 ft 4 in as seaplane. Height, 12 ft 9 in as landplane or 14 ft 4 in as seaplane. Wing area, 443½ sq ft.

Weight: Loaded, 6,000 lb as landplane or 6,400 lb as seaplane.

Performance: Maximum speed, 138 mph as landplane or 129 mph as seaplane. Climb, 5.34 min to 5,000 ft. Endurance, 4½ hr. Service ceiling, 17,000 ft (or 13,900 ft as seaplane).

Armament: One fixed Vickers gun forward and one Lewis gun aft and provision for up to 500 lb of bombs below the wings.

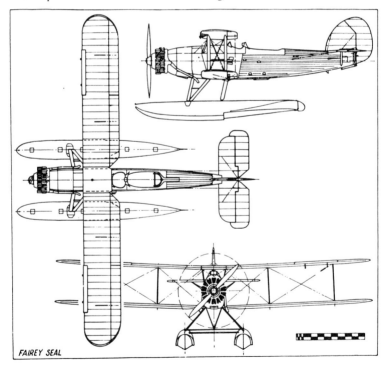

FAIREY SEAL

Swordfish I (L9781) of No.820 Squadron flies over *Ark Royal*, 1939. *(Charles E Brown)*

Fairey Swordfish

The name of the Swordfish will remain imperishable in the annals of the FAA. Few aeroplanes, with the exception of the Spitfire, ever received and deserved such universal acclaim. It was known to everybody as the 'Stringbag'; its achievements became a legend, and it earned the affection and respect of thousands of FAA pilots during its decade of active service with the Royal Navy.

Perhaps the most remarkable thing about this very remarkable aeroplane was its longevity. Although by all normal standards it was already obsolescent at the outbreak of war in 1939, it confounded the prophets by remaining operationally effective until after VE-Day. Indeed, it outlasted its intended replacement, the Albacore, which disappeared from first-line naval squadrons long before the Swordfish, in November 1943. The reason for this unprecedented feat was not immediately apparent, for the Swordfish was slow and altogether antiquated in appearance. The secret lay in its magnificent handling qualities—qualities that made it uniquely suitable for deck-flying and the problems of torpedo or dive-bombing attacks. Perhaps the finest tribute to the Swordfish's flying characteristics has been paid by Terence Horsley in his book *Find, Fix and Strike*.

'You could pull a Swordfish off the deck and put her in a climbing turn at 55 knots. It would manoeuvre in a vertical plane as easily as it would straight and level and even when diving from 10,000 feet the ASI never rose much beyond 200 knots. The controls were not frozen rigid by the force of the slipstream and

139

it was possible to hold the dive within 200 feet of the water. The Swordfish could be ditched safely and even its lack of speed could be turned to advantage against fighters. A steep turn at sea level towards the attacker just before he came within range and the difference in speed and small turning circle made it impossible for the fighter to bring its guns to bear for more than a few seconds. The approach to the carrier deck could be made at a staggeringly slow speed, yet response to the controls remained firm and insistent. Consider what such qualities meant on a dark night when the carrier's deck was pitching the height of a house.'

Time and again the Swordfish proved its worth and fully justified the FAA's belief in the torpedo-bomber as a weapon against enemy navies. The tradition of torpedo aircraft had been kept alive since the early successes of the First World War, but it was not until the Norwegian campaign of 1940 that Swordfish, of Nos.816 and 818 Squadrons in HMS *Furious*, carried out the first, co-ordinated, torpedo attack launched from a carrier in the history of naval warfare. A few months later, at Taranto, other Swordfish brought to fruition a plan first worked out at the Admiralty in 1938, resulting in one of the most brilliant naval victories of the war.

The origins of the Swordfish dated back to 1933, when its forerunner, the Fairey T.S.R.I, took the air for the first time at Fairey's Great West Aerodrome on 21 March. This biplane, produced as a private venture by Fairey, differed from its famous descendant in a number of details, but it already possessed what were to be the essentials of the Swordfish. It had a shorter fuselage, a fin and rudder of higher aspect ratio and, originally, a spatted undercarriage. It was flown both with a Siddeley Tiger and a Bristol Pegasus engine, driving a two-blade airscrew. After promising initial tests, the T.S.R.I was lost in an accident on 11 September 1933, the pilot escaping by parachute. It was followed by the T.S.R.II, which became the Swordfish prototype (K4190). In this aircraft an extra bay was incorporated in the fuselage and the tail assembly was re-designed. It flew for the first time on 17 April 1934. On 10 November 1934 the twin-float seaplane conversion made its first flight at Hamble. Catapult-launching trials later took place aboard HMS *Repulse*.

Following successful tests at Martlesham, the T.R.S.II was adopted by the Air Ministry and named the Swordfish. The first contract for 86 aircraft was placed in April 1935 and three more (a development batch) added in May. Successive contracts followed, and by early 1940, when Faireys handed over Swordfish production to Blackburn, to make way for Albacores at Hayes, the parent company had delivered 692 Swordfish. Peak output from Hayes was in 1937, when 201 were delivered. The first pre-production Swordfish (K5660) was flown on 31 December 1935, and the first delivered to the Service (K5661) reached Gosport on 19 February 1936. Serial numbers allocated to Fairey-built Swordfish Mk.I were K5660 to 5662, K5926 to 6011, K8346 to 8449, K8860 to 8886, L2717 to 2866, L7632 to 7661, L7670 to 7701, L9714 to 9743, L9756 to 9785, P3991 to 4039, P4061 to 4095, P4123 to 4169, P4191 to 4232 and P4253 to 4279.

The production Swordfish, designated Mk.I, was built to Spec S.38/34 (the prototype K4190 was to Spec S.15/33) and mounted the 690 hp Pegasus IIIM.3 engine driving a three-bladed Fairey-Reed fixed-pitch metal airscrew. Twin metal floats were readily interchangeable with the land undercarriage.

The Swordfish I was followed in production by the Mk.II, which first appeared in 1943. This variant was distinguished by a strengthened lower mainplane stressed for carrying and launching rocket projectiles which eventually became an important part of the Swordfish's armament. Initial batches of Swordfish IIs retained the Pegasus IIIM.3 engine, but later the Pegasus XXX was substituted. The final production version, which also appeared in 1943, was the Swordfish III, which mounted a radome containing an ASV Mk.XI radar scanner below the fuselage between the undercarriage legs. Also produced in small quantities were some Swordfish IIs with enclosed cockpits for use in Canada.

From December 1940 all Swordfish aircraft came from the Blackburn factory, which produced one in 1940, 415 in 1941, 271 in 1942, 592 in 1943 and 420 in 1944. The last of the 2,391 Swordfish to be built (including the 692 by Fairey) was the Mk.III NS204, which was completed at Sherburn-in-Elmet on 18 August 1944.

The Blackburn-built Swordfish Mk.Is were serialled V4288–4719, the Mk.IIs W5836–5995, DK670–792, HS154–678, LS151–461, NE858–999 and NF113–250. The Mk.IIIs were NF251–414, NR857–999 and NS112–204.

The first FAA squadron to be equipped with the Swordfish was No.825, which received its aircraft in July 1936 in exchange for Fairey IIIFs. No.825's Swordfish were embarked in HMS *Glorious*, where they were still serving at the outbreak of war, protecting merchant shipping in the Indian Ocean. By the close of 1936 Swordfish had also replaced the Baffins of Nos.811 and 812 Squadrons and the Seals of No.823 Squadron. By September 1937, when the Blackburn Sharks of Nos.810, 820 and 821 Squadrons were superseded, the Swordfish had become the only torpedo-bomber in FAA service. When the FAA went to war in September 1939 it had 13 squadrons of Swordfish in the first line, forming the spearhead of its offensive force. During the war years a further 17 squadrons of Swordfish were formed, so that, from first to last, the FAA had the astonishing total of 30 first-line squadrons equipped with this veteran biplane. This figure excludes second-line squadrons and the various seaplane units for catapult operations. The last squadron to be formed with Swordfish was No.860, which received six at Donibristle as late as 15 June 1943 for use aboard merchant aircraft carriers.

At the outbreak of war in 1939 Swordfish squadrons were embarked in five aircraft-carriers. These were: *Ark Royal* (Nos.810,814,820 and 821 Squadrons), *Courageous* (Nos.811 and 822 Squadrons), *Eagle* (Nos.813 and 824 Squadrons), *Glorious* (Nos.823 and 825 Squadrons) and the recently rc-fitted *Furious* (Nos.816 and 818 Squadrons). Also at sea were Swordfish spotter-reconnaissance seaplanes of Nos.701 and 702 Catapult Flights, serving in battleships and cruisers.

The opening months of the war saw the Swordfish engaged on convoy escort and Fleet protection duties, and they saw no actual fighting until the Norwegian campaign opened in April 1940. It was during the Second Battle of Narvik, on 13 April 1940, that a catapult Swordfish in HMS *Warspite* covered itself with glory during a naval battle in Ofot Fiord. This Swordfish not only spotted for the guns of *Warspite* and other vessels, leading to the destruction of seven enemy destroyers, but itself bombed and sank an enemy submarine and finished off one of the destroyers in another bombing attack. It was piloted by P/O F C Rice, and

Swordfish I seaplane (L2742) of No.810 Squadron, *Courageous*. *(Charles E Brown)*

This Swordfish I (L7673) was still flying with the FAA in 1944, five years after it first entered service with No.821 Squadron in May 1939. *(Imperial War Museum)*

Swordfish (P4221) of No.821 Squadron from *Ark Royal*. *(FAA Museum)*

Swordfish II (HS158) of No.816 Squadron carrying rocket projectiles, aboard escort-carrier *Tracker. (Imperial War Museum)*

the submarine it sank, *U-64*, was the first to be destroyed by a FAA aircraft in the Second World War.

The Norwegian campaign gave the FAA its first chance to show its paces, and on 11 April torpedo-carrying Swordfish went into action for the first time, flying from *Furious*; later they joined Sea Gladiators in providing air cover for the military landings at Namsos, Aandalsnes and Narvik.

In May 1940 Swordfish began another type of operation for which they became famous: mine-laying and bombing of enemy-held Channel ports under the direction of RAF Coastal Command. For this hazardous task they carried auxiliary fuel-tanks in the rear cockpit and operated with a crew of two. The pioneer squadron in this field was No.812, which operated in turn from North Coates, Thorney Island, Detling and St Eval during the period May 1940 to March 1941; targets attacked included oil-tanks at Calais and invasion barges at Rotterdam. From May to July 1940 Swordfish of No.825 Squadron were also detached to Coastal Command, and these aircraft, flying from Detling, spotted for the bombardment of Calais by HMS *Arethusa*.

With the entry of Italy into the war, Swordfish based in the Mediterranean area came into prominence. Swordfish of No.767 Training Squadron, based in the south of France, attacked Genoa on 14 June 1940, using French bombs borrowed for the occasion. This was the first British air raid on Italy. Shortly afterwards this intrepid squadron divided up, one half going to Malta, where it became No.830 Squadron on 22 June 1940. On the night of 30 June/1 July it made its first operation from Malta, bombing oil-tanks at Augusta. From then onwards Malta-based Swordfish never ceased to be a thorn in the side of the enemy. Although the force never at any time exceeded 27 aircraft, it sank an average of 50,000 tons of shipping every month for nine months, the peak being 98,000 tons in one month. In 1942, joined by Albacores, the FAA torpedo force at Malta sank 30 ships in 36 night attacks, expending 67 torpedoes and losing only three aircraft.

In July 1940, after the defeat of France, Swordfish played an important part in the destruction of the French Fleet to prevent its use by the enemy. It was during

143

these operations that Swordfish mounted the first successful air-torpedo attack against a capital ship in naval history. This was at Oran on 6 July 1940, when 12 Swordfish from Nos.810 and 820 Squadrons aboard *Ark Royal* immobilised the battle-cruiser *Dunkerque*.

A few weeks later Swordfish were also to aid General Wavell in his first offensive against the Italians in the Western Desert: on 22 August Swordfish of No.824 Squadron led by Captain Patch, DSO, DSC, of the Royal Marines, sank four enemy ships (including a submarine) in Bomba harbour, Libya, for the expenditure of only three torpedoes.

In November 1940 came the crowning achievement of the Swordfish's career: the epic attack on Taranto. This magnificent victory is a landmark in the history of naval air warfare, for it was the first time that aircraft had shown themselves capable of knocking out an entire enemy fleet and, unaided, altering the balance of power at sea. Taranto was indeed a suitable reward for all those whose years of work and faith in the FAA had made such a triumph possible.

The attack took place on the night of 11 November 1940, when the moon was three-quarters full. Preliminary reconnaissance of Taranto harbour showed that the Italians had six battleships at anchor, as well as several cruisers and destroyers. The Swordfish, each specially fitted with long-range tanks in the rear cockpit displacing the third crew member, took off from *Illustrious*, 180 miles from the target. The first strike force, of 12 aircraft, was airborne at 8.30 p.m., and was followed by a second force of eight (later joined by a ninth aircraft) after an hour's interval. Eleven of the Swordfish carried torpedoes, six carried bombs and four were equipped with flares to illuminate the target. The first flare-droppers arrived over the target about 11 p.m. and the strike force (led by Lt-Cdr K Williamson) dived to the attack through the middle of a balloon barrage. Despite intense anti-aircraft fire, they all hit the target and only one aircraft was lost. The second wave, which arrived at midnight, was equally successful and again only one Swordfish was lost. Next day, when the smoke cleared, air reconnaissance showed that the Italians had suffered a crippling blow: the three battleships *Cavour*, *Duilio* and *Italia* had all been severely damaged and two of them were under water. As well as this, the cruiser *Trento* and the destroyers *Libeccio* and *Pessango* had been hit, two auxiliary vessels sunk and seaplane hangers and oil-storage tanks knocked out. The Swordfish responsible for this holocaust had been drawn from Nos.815 and 819 Squadrons (embarked in *Illustrious*), and Nos.813 and 824 Squadrons from *Eagle*, temporarily embarked in *Illustrious* for the operation.

One of the Taranto squadrons, No.815, struck again in the Battle of Cape Matapan, disabling the Italian cruiser *Pola* on 28 March 1941, and the same squadron fought gallantly in the Greek campaign until 23 April 1941. In May, flying from Cyprus, No.815's Swordfish struck Vichy shipping and shore targets in Syria. The same month Swordfish of No.814 Squadron assisted the RAF in quelling the Iraqi rebellion, dive-bombing barracks at Samawa Nasariya. Before this they had wrought much execution among Italian shipping, whilst based at Port Sudan, in the East African campaign.

Meanwhile, out in the Atlantic, another great drama was being enacted: the hunting and destruction of the German battleship *Bismarck*. Swordfish participating in this historic engagement were from Nos.810 and 818 Squadrons in *Ark Royal*, and Nos.820 and 825 Squadrons in *Victorious*. The first attack on

Bismarck was made by No.825 Squadron, led by Lt-Cdr Eugene Esmonde, on 25 May, but it was not until the next day that No.818 Squadron, led by Lt-Cdr T P Coode, succeeded in making the two torpedo hits on *Bismarck* which crippled her steering and finally enabled the Fleet to intercept and sink her with gunfire and surface torpedoes.

The name of the Swordfish will always be linked with that of the celebrated carrier *Ark Royal*, and it was one of her squadrons, No.825, that figured in the tragic but heroic attack on the German battleships *Scharnhorst*, *Gneisenau* and *Prinz Eugen* as they escaped through the English Channel in February 1942. No.825 Squadron had been aboard *Ark Royal* when she was sunk on 13 November 1941: all its Swordfish had been lost, but the crews survived, and it was six aircraft of the re-formed squadron, commanded by Lt-Cdr Esmonde, which made the disastrous sortie of 12 February 1942. Flying from Manston, Kent, the gallant little Swordfish force sighted the enemy about 10 miles off Ramsgate. From the moment they spotted the enemy's enormous fighter screen above the battleships the Swordfish crews knew that they had little chance of survival, but they never faltered in their mission. The Swordfish attacked in line astern, through devastating anti-aircraft fire. As they made their torpedo runs the enemy fighters attacked from astern. The outcome was utter disaster: every Swordfish was shot down and only five out of 18 members of the aircrews survived. All the survivors were decorated and a posthumous VC was awarded to Lt-Cdr Esmonde, the first to be won by a member of the FAA.

The English Channel episode was the last of the classic torpedo attacks by the Swordfish: henceforth it was to be used primarily in the anti-submarine rôle using depth charges and later rocket projectiles. The introduction of ASV radar and the rocket projectile—inventions which sealed the fate of many a U-boat—was pioneered by Swordfish, and the new devices gave the old biplane a new lease of life for operations from the new 'flat-tops' converted from merchant-ships. The first air trials of ASV radar in a Swordfish from St Athan were a failure, but shortly afterwards, on 26 December 1939, a second experiment from Lee-on-Solent proved successful. By the end of 1941 Swordfish were taking ASV radar on operations, and on the night of 21 December 1941 a Swordfish so equipped from No.812 Squadron, based at Gibraltar, sank the first U-boat ever destroyed by an aircraft at night, *U-451*.

About two months previously, on 25 October 1941, the first experimental

The last Swordfish to be built, the Mk.III NS204, leaves the Blackburn factory. *(Blackburn)*

145

A Swordfish (HS553) as used in Canada with enclosed cockpits. *(Crown Copyright Photo.)*

rocket projectile (then a very secret weapon) had been fired from a Hurricane, and it fell to the lot of the Swordfish to test the suitability of this new armament for FAA work. The first air test from a Swordfish took place at Thorney Island on 12 October 1942: just over seven months later, on 23 May 1943, a Swordfish of No.819 Squadron from HMS *Archer*, flown by Sub-Lt H Horrocks, scored the first operational success with the new weapon by sinking the submarine *U-752* about 750 miles west of Ireland. Five days later the feat was repeated by a Hudson of the RAF.

Swordfish had also been singularly successful against submarines during the Allied invasion of Madagascar. Using depth charges, Swordfish of No.829 Squadron from *Illustrious* sank the submarine *Bevezieres* on 5 May 1942 and another, *Le Heros*, on 8 May.

During the last three years of the war the Swordfish (succeeded in the big carriers by Albacores, Avengers and Barracudas) operated mainly from the smaller escort carriers, which carried both fighter and strike aircraft. They made a valuable contribution to the winning of the Battle of the Atlantic, and from August 1942 did valiant service in the escort of the North Russian convoys. In one of the Russian convoys, Swordfish embarked in the escort carriers *Vindex* and *Striker* flew 1,000 hours on anti-submarine patrol in the space of 10 days. In May 1944, *Fencer's* No.842 Squadron sank *U-277*, *U-674* and *U-959* in a single voyage. Such feats were accomplished in the face of the most appalling weather conditions, frequently at night, and with all the arctic rigours of snow and ice on the decks. Yet, just as in earlier days, the Swordfish never failed its crews, and it is on record that an aircraft of No.768 Squadron, in the escort carrier *Speaker*, completed 324 deck landings in four days without once becoming unserviceable. On another occasion Swordfish aboard the escort carrier *Nabob*, torpedoed and sinking, succeeded in flying ashore to safety even although the carrier's deck was sloping upwards towards the bows at about 20 degrees.

At the beginning of 1945, nine years after the first Swordfish had been delivered to the FAA, nine squadrons were still equipped with the type for

Swordfish, with D-Day invasion stripes, of No.816 Squadron in 1944.

first-line duties. Swordfish also served with No.119 Squadron of the RAF from bases in Belgium until VE-Day: one of them attacked a midget submarine only 3½ hr before Germany's surrender! At long last, on 21 May 1945, the only remaining squadron to use the Swordfish officially in the FAA was disbanded. This was No.836 Squadron, the operational pool for all merchant aircraft carriers which, with No.860 Squadron, had kept 19 'flat-tops' supplied with Swordfish. Another noteworthy date was 28 June 1945, when the last operational flight of a biplane in the FAA was that of a Swordfish from the merchant aircraft carrier *Empire Mackay*.

So ended the fighting career of one of the greatest aircraft in the history of air warfare. A few examples of this grand old warrior remained at Royal Naval air stations for odd duties after the war and on 24 March 1953 the Swordfish NF389 was transferred from the Torpedo Development Unit at Gosport to the Headquarters of the FAA at Lee-on-Solent, and retained as a permanent exhibit. The only other Swordfish to have survived in Great Britain are LS326, maintained by the FAA at Yeovilton, in flying trim, HS618 (repainted as 'P4139') in the FAA Museum at Yeovilton, NF370 which is preserved in the Imperial War Museum at Lambeth and W5856 of the FAA Historic Flight.

UNITS ALLOCATED

No.810 Squadron (equipped 1937; embarked in *Courageous, Ark Royal, Furious* and *Illustrious*); No.811 Squadron (equipped 1936; embarked in *Furious* and then *Courageous* until latter was sunk 17 September 1939. Re-equipped with Swordfish from Chesapeakes November 1941; embarked in *Biter* and *Vindex*. Also shore-based with Coastal Command); No.812 Squadron (equipped in December 1936; embarked in *Argus, Furious* and *Ark Royal*. Also shore-based with Coastal Command); No.813 Squadron (formed January 1937; embarked in *Eagle, Illustrious, Campania* and *Vindex*); No.814 Squadron (formed November 1938; embarked in *Ark Royal* and *Hermes*); No.815 Squadron (formed October 1939; embarked in *Illustrious*); No.816 Squadron (formed September 1939; embarked in *Furious* and *Ark Royal* until latter sunk 13 November 1941. Re-formed February 1942; embarked in *Avenger* and *Dasher* until latter blown up 27 March 1943. Re-formed again July 1943; embarked in *Tracker, Chaser* and *Activity*); No.818 Squadron (formed September 1939; embarked in *Furious* and *Ark Royal*); No.819 Squadron (formed January 1940; embarked in *Illustrious*. Re-formed October 1941; embarked in *Avenger, Archer* and *Activity*. Also shore-based with Coastal Command); No.820 Squadron (equipped 1937; embarked in *Courageous, Ark Royal* and *Victorious*); No.821 Squadron (equipped 1937; embarked in *Courageous* and *Ark Royal*. No.821X Flight embarked in *Argus*; shore-based in Malta from January 1941); No.822 Squadron (equipped 1937; embarked in *Courageous* until latter sunk 17 September 1939. Re-formed October 1941); No.823 Squadron (equipped 1936; embarked in *Glorious* until latter sunk 8 June 1940); No.824 Squadron (equipped 1937; embarked in *Eagle* and *Illustrious*, then *Eagle* again until latter sunk August 1942. Re-formed March 1943; embarked in *Unicorn* and *Striker*); No.825 Squadron (equipped July 1936; embarked in *Glorious, Furious, Victorious* and *Ark Royal* until latter sunk 13 November 1941. Re-formed early 1942; embarked in *Avenger, Furious, Vindex* and *Campania*); No.826 Squadron (equipped July 1940; embarked in *Formidable*); No.828 Squadron (Malta, with Albacores); No.829 Squadron (*Formidable*); No.830 Squadron (formed June 1940; shore-based in Malta); No.833 Squadron (formed December 1941; embarked in *Biter, Avenger, Argus Stalker* and *Activity*); No.834 Squadron (formed December 1941; embarked in *Archer, Hunter* and *Battler*); No.835 Squadron (formed March 1942; embarked in *Furious, Activity, Battler, Chaser* and *Nairana*); No.836 Squadron (formed March 1942; embarked in *Biter*. Later became operational pool for MAC ships); No.837 Squadron (formed May 1942; embarked in *Dasher* and *Argus*); No.838 Squadron (formed May 1942; embarked in *Attacker, Rapana* and *Nairana*); No.840 Squadron (formed June 1942; embarked in *Battler, Attacker* and *Empire MacAlpine*); No.841 Squadron (shore-based, mixed with Albacores); No.842 Squadron (formed February 1943; embarked in *Fencer, Indefatigable, Furious, Hunter, Fencer* and *Campania*); No.860 Squadron (formed June 1943; became pool for MAC ships); No.886 Squadron (embarked *Attacker* and shore-based at Gibraltar). *Catapult Flights:* Nos.444, 701, 702 and 705. *Catapult Squadrons:* Nos.700 (pool for catapult aircraft from January 1940), 701, 702 and 705. *Second-line Squadrons:* Nos.705, 707, 710, 722, 726, 727, 728, 730, 731, 733, 735, 737, 739, 740, 741, 742, 743, 744, 747, 753, 759, 763, 764, 765, 766, 767, 768, 769, 770, 771, 772, 773, 774, 775, 776, 777, 778, 779, 780, 781, 782, 783, 785, 786, 787, 788, 789, 791, 794, 796 and 797.

The RAF also used Swordfish for maritime operations, both shore-based with No.119 Squadron and as seaplanes with No.202 Squadron at Gibraltar. Pre-war, they trained torpedo-bomber pilots at the Torpedo Development Squadron at Gosport.

TECHNICAL DATA (SWORDFISH I)

Description: Carrier-based torpedo-spotter-reconnaissance aircraft, or twin-float seaplane for catapult operations aboard warships. Crew of three for reconnaissance or two for torpedo strikes. Metal structure, fabric covered.

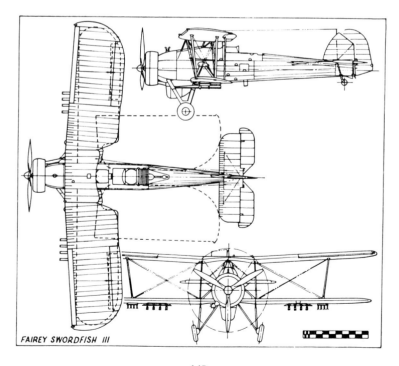

FAIREY SWORDFISH III

Manufacturers: Fairey Aviation Co Ltd, Hayes, Middlesex. Sub-contracted by Blackburn Aircraft Co Ltd, Sherburn-in-Elmet.

Power Plant: One 690 hp Bristol Pegasus IIIM.3 or 750 hp Pegasus XXX.

Dimensions: Span, 45 ft 6 in (17 ft 3 in folded). Length, 36 ft 4 in (40 ft 11 in with floats). Height, 12 ft 10 in (14 ft 7 in on floats). Wing area, 607 sq ft.

Weights (landplane): Empty, 5,200 lb. Loaded, 8,700 lb.

Performance: Maximum speed, 139 mph at 4,750 ft. Cruising speed, 104–129 mph at 5,000 ft. Initial climb, 560 ft/min; 10 min to 5,000 ft. Range 546 miles. Service ceiling, 10,700 ft.

Armament: One fixed, synchronised Browning gun forward and one Lewis or Vickers 'K' gun aft. Provision for one 18 in 1,610 lb torpedo or one 1,500 lb mine below the fuselage or 1,500 lb of bombs comprising (*a*) two 500 lb bombs below the fuselage and two 250 lb bombs below the wings or (*b*) one 500 lb bomb below the fuselage and two 500 lb bombs below the wings. Alternatively, three Mk.VII depth charges. The Swordfish II could carry eight 60 lb rocket projectiles below the wings instead of torpedo or bombs.

Swordfish (K5972) of No.823 Squadron from *HMS Glorious*. (*RAF Museum*)

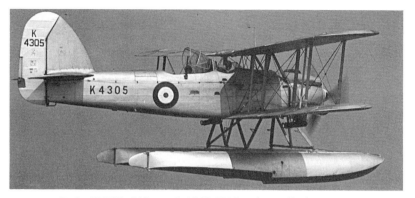

Seafox (K4305) which served with No.765 Squadron. *(Charles E Brown)*

Fairey Seafox

The Seafox was built to Spec 11/32 as a light reconnaissance seaplane suitable for catapulting from cruisers of the Royal Navy. Though orthodox in configuration, it was unusual in providing an enclosed canopy for the observer whilst leaving the pilot in an open cockpit (this latter being necessary to facilitate catapult operations), and in combining a metal monocoque fuselage with fabric-covered wings. The prototype (K4303) first flew at Hamble on 27 May 1936; it was followed by a second prototype (K4304) with a land undercarriage, which flew on 5 November 1936.

Fairey's first contract for Seafoxes was received in January 1936; it was for 49 aircraft. These Seafoxes (K8569 to 8617) were followed by a second batch of 15 (L4519 to 4533), which were ordered in September 1936. All production Seafoxes, with the exception of L4523 from the second contract, were delivered as seaplanes. The first production aircraft (K8569) was delivered on 23 April 1937, and Seafoxes first entered service with No.718 (Catapult) Flight, replacing Osprey seaplanes, in August 1937.

At the outbreak of war in 1939, Seafox seaplanes were serving in a number of cruisers and formed the equipment of catapult reconnaissance flights; these flights were pooled on 21 January 1940 to form No.700 Squadron, which had 11 Seafoxes on strength, as well as 12 Swordfish seaplanes and 42 Walrus amphibians. They also equipped some passenger liners converted to Armed Merchant Cruisers, such as HMS *Canton*, *Pretoria Castle* and *Carnarvon Castle*.

The Seafox will always be associated with the Battle of the River Plate, on 13 December 1939, when the three cruisers *Ajax*, *Achilles* and *Exeter* engaged and defeated the German battleship *Admiral Graf Spee*. This was the fisrt occasion in the Second World War in which a British naval aircraft had been employed to spot for the ships' guns in a sea battle. *Exeter*'s two Walruses were both put out of action by gunfire and only one of the two Seafoxes (K8581 and K8582) in *Ajax* was able to get away. Flown by Lt E D G Lewin, with Lt R E N Kearney as observer, the Seafox (belonging to No.718 Catapult Flight) spotted throughout the action and did reconnaissances every day until it was able to signal, at

8.54 p.m. on 17 December, that the *Graf Spee* had blown herself up. The pilot of the Seafox received the DSC for his part in this action, being the first FAA officer to be decorated in the Second World War.

With the introduction of escort-carriers, catapult spotting aircraft were gradually discarded and the last Seafox unit (No.702) disbanded in July 1943.

UNITS ALLOCATED

Catapult Flights: Nos.713, 714, 716 and 718. *Catapult Squadrons:* Nos.700, 702, 703, 713, 714, 716 and 718. *Second-line Squadrons:* Nos.754, 764, 765 and 773.

TECHNICAL DATA (SEAFOX)

Description: Two-seat spotter-reconnaissance seaplane. All-metal structure with monocoque fuselage and fabric-covered wings.
Manufacturers: Fairey Aviation Co Ltd, Hamble, Hants.
Power Plant: One 395 hp Napier Rapier VI.
Dimensions: Span, 40 ft. Length, 33 ft 5½ in. Height, 12 ft 1 in. Wing area, 434 sq ft.
Weights: Empty, 3,805 lbs. Loaded, 5,650 lbs.
Performance: Maximum speed, 124 mph at 5,860 ft. Crusing speed, 106 mph. Climb, 10.4 min to 5,000 ft. Range, 333 nautical miles. Endurance, 4¼ hr. Service ceiling, 9,700 ft.
Armament: One Lewis gun in rear cockpit and provision for two 100 lb or eight 20 lb light bombs below the wings.

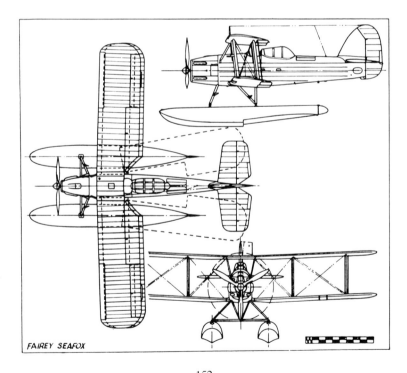

FAIREY SEAFOX

Albacore I (X9053) of No.817 Squadron from *Victorious*. *(Imperial War Museum)*

Fairey Albacore

The Albacore was designed to Spec. S.41/36, which sought a replacement type for the Swordfish, but such were the qualities of the Swordfish that it outlived its intended successor. As events turned out, the Albacore merely supplemented the Swordfish and there were some FAA pilots who preferred the older biplane. There is no denying, however, that the Albacore possessed many advantages, particularly in terms of crew comfort. In place of the Swordfish's draughty cockpits was a comfortable, enclosed cabin with heating circuits and such added refinements as a windscreen wiper and an automatic device to launch the dinghy without the invervention of the crew if the aircraft were to ditch. Also new was the all-metal monocoque fuselage (something of an innovation in British biplanes of the period) and the smooth-running sleeve-valve engine with its variable-pitch airscrew, which bestowed a very rapid take-off and ensured the greatest economy of fuel when cruising. Yet another advance was the introduction of hydraulic flaps to be used as air-brakes during dive-bombing.

The prototype Albacore (L7074) was flown for the first time by C S Staniland at Fairey's Great West Aerodrome (now London Airport) on 12 December 1938. It was followed by a second prototype (L7075) and production began in 1939 with L7076, which was later flown experimentally as a floatplane. The two prototypes and 98 production aircraft had all been ordered from Faireys under an Air Ministry contract placed in May 1937. All the Albacores were built at the Hayes factory, and afterwards test-flown at Heathrow. When production finally ceased in 1943 a total of 800 had been delivered. The serial numbers allocated to production Albacores were L7076 to 7173, N4152 to 4200, N4219 to 4268, N4281 to 4330, N4347 to 4391, N4420 to 4425, T9131 to 9175, T9191 to 9215, T9231 to 9260, X8940 to 8984, X9010 to 9059, X9073 to 9117, X9137 to 9186, X9214 to 9233, X9251 to 9290, BF584 to 618, BF631 to 680, BF695 to 739, and BF758 to 777. Modifications to the Albacore in the course of production were remarkably few; the most notable was a change from the 1,065 hp Taurus II originally fitted to the 1,130 hp Taurus XII.

The first FAA unit to be equipped with Albacores was No.826 Squadron, which was formed specially for the new type. It received 12 Albacores at Ford, Sussex, on 15 March 1940. Albacores made their first operation with No.826 Squadron on 31 May 1940, when they bombed road and rail communications at Westende and attacked E-boats off Zeebrugge. In June 1940 No.826's Albacores moved to Bircham Newton, Norfolk, and they remained under Coastal Command's direction (with periods at Jersey and Detling) until November 1940. During this period they made repeated night attacks on targets from Borkum to Boulogne, laying mines and bombing shipping and harbour installations. Altogether, they made 22 night raids and dropped seven tons of mines and 56 tons of bombs. During the month of September they also escorted 57 convoys.

These shore-based operations were typical of the Albacore's operational life during 1940, and it was not until 1941 that it figured in carrier-borne actions. By the end of 1940 No.826 had been joined by three more squadrons, all formed for Albacores: No.829 formed in June at Lee-on-Solent, No.828 in September at Ford and No.827 in October at Yeovilton. No.827's Albacores did anti-submarine patrols from Stornoway in the Hebrides; those of No.829 Squadron made night attacks on Brest from bases at St Eval and St Merryn under the direction of Coastal Command. On 26 November 1940, Nos.826 and 829 Squadrons became the first Albacore units aboard a carrier, embarking in HMS *Formidable* to escort a convoy to Cape Town.

The first big naval action in which Albacores took part was the Battle of Cape Matapan in March 1941. During this engagement Albacore strikes by Nos.826 and 829 Squadrons from *Formidable*, led by Lt-Cdr W G H Saunt, DSC, succeeded in severely damaging the Italian battleship *Vittorio Veneto*. The Albacores pressed home their attacks with great gallantry, despite intense anti-aircraft fire and a splash barrage from the battleship's 15 in shells. This was the first occasion on which Albacores had used their torpedoes in action, and the operation confirmed the effectiveness of this weapon, which had already been used with such striking success by Swordfish the previous November at Taranto.

In July 1941 Albacores were prominent again in the FAA attack on Kirkenes and Petsamo. The object of this operation was to attack German shipping in the two harbours and to damage oil-tanks and dock installations. Albacores of Nos.817, 822, 827 and 828 Squadrons from *Furious* and *Victorious* took part in this raid, but the element of surprise it had been hoped to achieve was lost, and casualties were very heavy.

Another phase of the Albacore's operational career was spent in Malta. From October 1941 until July 1943 No.828 Squadron flew its Albacores from Hal Far, using mines and bombs against targets in Italy, Sicily and North Africa. On one occasion it attacked an enemy convoy, sinking one ship and damaging two others.

In March 1942 Albacores of No.817 Squadron in *Victorious* joined in the hunt for the German battleship *Tirpitz* and made one attack with torpedoes, but without success.

By the middle of 1942 the Albacore had reached the peak of its operational career, and at this period no fewer than 15 squadrons of the FAA were equipped with the type. They were engaged in a wide range of activities, both ashore and afloat. Those embarked in carriers were joining in the gruelling convoys to North Russia as well as flying anti-submarine patrols in the Mediterranean and the Indian Ocean. Ashore they were continuing their work with Coastal Command on mine-laying and anti-shipping strikes and, in the Western Desert, had adopted a new rôle of flare-dropping. Each Albacore carried 28 flares, and they did invaluable work illuminating targets for RAF night bombers, as well as joining in the bombing themselves. During the two months prior to the Battle of El Alamein, Albacores dropped about 12,000 flares and laid bare most of Rommel's troop dispositions. The first Albacore squadron to join in the Western Desert fighting was No.826, which began operations from Dekheila in July 1941. On 9 July 1942 nine Albacores of this squadron flew 250 miles behind the enemy lines, were refuelled at a secret rendezvous by Bombay transports, and flew on to deliver a night attack on an enemy convoy off Tobruk. Another Albacore squadron on Western Desert flare-dropping was No.821, which operated during May and June 1942 and again during the Tunisian fighting from March to May 1943.

From February to March 1943 a special flight of Albacores from No.815 Squadron was based at Dekheila to spot for the guns during Naval bombardments of ports along the North African coast. The same squadron was also active on anti-submarine patrols in the Eastern Mediterranean from bases at Nicosia and Haifa, no fewer than 17 U-boats being attacked.

During the Allied invasion of North Africa in November 1942 Albacores of Nos.817, 820, 822 and 832 Squadrons were in action. Their share of the operation was to fly anti-submarine patrols over the approaches to the landing beaches, and they also took part in bombing raids on land targets, silencing the guns of enemy naval forts which were holding up the advance of the Commandos. One striking force of Albacores, led by Lt J G A McI. Nares, bombed La Senia airfield, destroying 47 aircraft in their hangars and at dispersals. One of the Vichy-French Dewoitine fighters that attacked them was shot down by one of the Albacores' air-gunners.

On 21 November 1942, Albacores of No.817 Squadron flying from *Victorious* sank the submarine *U-517* in the Atlantic Ocean.

Albacores of Nos.817 and 832 Squadrons aboard *Victorious*. *(Imperial War Museum)*

155

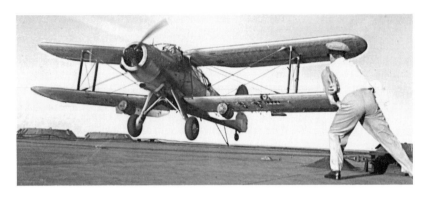

An Albacore lands aboard its carrier. *(Imperial War Museum)*

During 1943 Albacore squadrons progressively re-equipped with the Fairey Barracuda (except for No.832, which received Grumman Avengers), and by November only two squadrons—Nos.820 and 841—remained. No.820 Squadron's Albacores were the last to serve in an aircraft-carrier (*Formidable*) and had taken part in the invasion of Sicily and the landing at Salerno, providing air cover at the beach-heads. No.841 Squadron was unique in that its Albacores had spent their entire service, since July 1942, in shore-based operations under the direction of RAF Fighter Command, flying chiefly from Manston. Its rôle was to attack enemy shipping in the English Channel and North Sea at night. Between 23 August 1942 and 21 November 1943 a total of 99 such attacks was made. With its disbandment in November 1943, No.841 Squadron handed over its Albacores to No.415 Squadron of the RCAF, which continued to fly from Manston. So it came about that the Albacore, though no longer serving the FAA, nevertheless played a useful rôle in the D-Day operations of June 1944, preventing enemy shipping from interfering with the invasion fleets and spotting for Naval bombardments of the enemy coast.

UNITS ALLOCATED

No.815 Squadron (August 1941 to July 1943; shore-based at Dekheila, Haifa and Nicosia); No.817 Squadron (March 1941 to August 1943; shore-based at Crail, Hatston; embarked in *Furious, Victorious* and *Indomitable*); No.818 Squadron (November 1941 to June 1942; embarked in *Formidable*, aircraft handed over to No.796 Pool Squadron, E. Africa, after a brief period in Ceylon); No.820 Squadron (June 1941 to November 1943; shore-based at Hatston and Crail; embarked in *Victorious* and *Formidable*; detachments to Algeria, Malta, Gibraltar and Alexandria); No.821 Squadron (March 1942 to October 1943; shore-based at Dekheila, Nicosia, Hal Far, Castel Benito and Monastir); No.822 Squadron (March 1942 to August 1943; shore-based at Crail, Donibristle, Macrihanish, Twatt, Gibraltar and Lee-on-Solent; embarked in *Furious*); No.823 Squadron (April 1942 to June 1943; shore-based at Tangmere and Manston; embarked in *Furious*); No.826 Squadron (March 1940 to August 1943; shore-based at Ford, Bircham Newton, Jersey, Detling, St Merryn, Nicosia, Dekeila, Haifa, Benghazi, Blida and Hal Far; embarked in *Formidable*); No.827 Squadron (October 1940 to August 1942; shore-based at Yeovilton, Stornoway, Thorney Island, St Eval, Macrihanish, Hatston and Aden; embarked in

Victorious and *Indomitable*); No.828 Squadron (September 1940 to September 1943; shore-based at Ford, St Merryn, Campbeltown, Hatston, Crail, Hal Far and Monastir; embarked in *Victorious* and *Ark Royal*); No.829 Squadron (June 1940 to June 1941; shore-based at Lee-on-Solent, St Eval, St Merryn, Dekheila and Lydda; embarked in *Formidable* and *Illustrious*); No.830 (September 1940 to July 1942; shore-based in Malta); No.831 Squadron (April 1941 to May 1943; shore-based at Norfolk, USA, Wingfield, Aden, Crail and Lee-on-Solent; embarked in *Indomitable*); No.832 Squadron (April 1941 to November 1942; shore-based at Lee-on-Solent, Campbeltown, Hatston and Crail; embarked in *Victorious*); No.841 Squadron (July 1942 to November 1943; shore-based at Lee-on-Solent, Macrihanish, Middle Wallop and Manston); No.415 Squadron RCAF (Manston); No.119 Squadron, RAF. *Second-line squadrons:* Nos.733, 747, 750, 753, 754, 756, 763, 766, 767, 768, 769, 774, 775, 778, 781, 782, 783, 785, 787, 788, 789, 791, 793, 796, 797 and 799.

TECHNICAL DATA (ALBACORE)

Description: Carrier-borne or shore-based torpedo-bomber with a crew of three. Metal monocoque fuselage and metal wings, fabric covered.

Manufacturers: Fairey Aviation Co Ltd, Hayes, Middlesex.

Power Plant: One 1,085 hp Bristol Taurus II or 1,130 hp Bristol Taurus XII.

Dimensions: Span, 50 ft. Length, 39 ft 9½ in. Height, 15 ft 3 in. Wing area, 623 sq ft.

Weights: Empty, 7,200 lb. Loaded, 10,365 lb (normal) or 12,830 lb (maximum).

Performance: Maximum speed, 159 mph at 4,500 ft. Cruising speed, 113 mph at

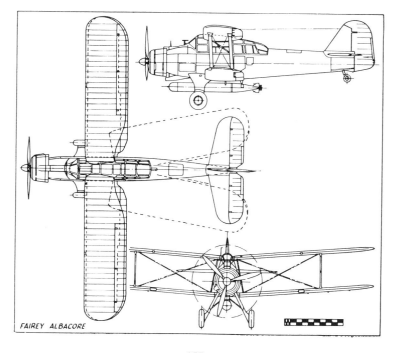

FAIREY ALBACORE

6,000 ft. Climb, 8 min to 6,000 ft. Range, 710 miles (normal) or 930 miles (maximum). Service ceiling, 18,800 ft.

Armament: One fixed Browning gun in starboard wing firing forward and one Vickers 'K' gun in rear cockpit. Provision for one 18 in 1,610 lb torpedo beneath the fuselage or six 250 lb or three 500 lb bombs in external racks below the wings. Alternatively, four Mk. VII depth charges.

Albacores of No.817 Squadron from *Victorious. (Imperial War Museum)*

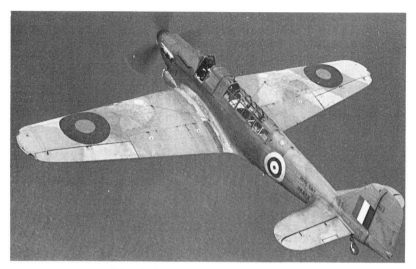

Fulmar II (DR673). *(Crown Copyright Photo.)*

Fairey Fulmar

The Fulmar was a welcome arrival in the FAA, for until it entered squadron service in the summer of 1940 there were no carrier-borne fighters with the same weight of fire-power as the Hurricane and Spitfire of the RAF. It was the first Fairey fighter to be used by the FAA since the Flycatcher had been retired in 1934, and the first with eight-gun armament. The existence of the Fulmar was kept a closely-guarded secret by the Admiralty for nine months after the prototype had flown and it was not until September 1940 that its name was first made known to the public.

The Fulmar was designed to Spec O.8/38 and was developed from the two P.4/34 light bomber prototypes. The first P.4/34 (K5099) flew on 13 January 1937 and the second (K7555) on 19 April 1937. The Fairey P.4/34 was designed, like the Fulmar, by M. Lobelle and was of exceptionally clean aerodynamic form. It attained a maximum speed of 284 mph with a 1,030 hp Rolls-Royce Merlin II engine. The Fulmar bore a close resemblance to its forerunner, but had the 1,080 hp Merlin VIII engine, a non-continuous canopy, deck-arrester gear, the eight-gun armament previously mentioned, folding wings, catapult points and a dinghy. A notable point of exterior difference between the two types was that the Fulmar had a longer and more prominent radiator beneath the nose.

The prototype Fulmar (N1854) made its first flight at Ringway on 4 January 1940, the pilot being Duncan Menzies. Production of 150 Fulmar Is followed at the Stockport factory, the serial numbers allotted to these aircraft being N1855 to 1893, N1910 to 1959, N1980 to 2016 and N3994 to 4016.

The second version of the Fulmar to be built was the Mk.II, which differed from its predecessor in having the 1,300 hp Merlin XXX engine and tropical equipment. The prototype Fulmar II flew for the first time at Ringway on 20

January 1941. Production of 413 Fulmar II fighters ensued, the serial numbers allocated being N4017 to 4043, N4060 to 4100, N4116 to 4147, X8525 to 8574, X8611 to 8655, X8680 to 8714, X8729 to 8778, X8798 to 8817, BP775 to 796, BP812 to 839, DR633 to 682 and DR700 to 749. The last of 563 Fulmars (DR749) was delivered to the FAA in February 1943.

Fulmars first entered first-line service with the FAA in June 1940, going to No.806 Squadron, stationed at Worthy Down. This squadron later embarked in *Illustrious* and took part in some of the Mediterranean convoys taking supplies to Malta. In July 1940, No.808 Squadron at Worthy Down became the second Fulmar squadron to be equipped and a third squadron (No.807) formed at Worthy Down in September 1940. On 1 December 1940 three Fulmars of No.807 Squadron went on board HMS *Pegasus* to become the first aircraft to be used for the Catapult Fighter Ship scheme.

The year 1941 saw five more Fulmar squadrons formed. No.809 Squadron took delivery at St Merryn in January; No.804 Squadron exchanged its Martlets for Fulmars and Sea Hurricanes in February; No.800 Squadron converted from Skuas in April and No.884 Squadron formed at Donibristle in November. No.805 Squadron, formed on 1 January 1941 at Aboukir, Egypt, was the first Fulmar squadron to serve from a FAA shore station overseas.

In 1942 the Fulmar went to more squadrons (Nos.879, 886, 887, 889 and 893) and had reached the peak of its operational career. By 1943 it was being steadily superseded by the much faster Seafire: No.809 was the last day fighter squadron to relinquish Fulmars in April 1943. The last operational squadron with Fulmars was No.813, which used a night-fighter version until its disbandment at Macrihanish on 1 March 1945. No.813 Squadron received its first Fulmar night fighters in April 1944: they were taken over from No.784 Squadron at Drem, which had pioneered FAA night-fighter tactics with Fulmars since forming at Lee in June 1942.

Operationally, the Fulmar first saw action against the Italian Air Force during its defence of Malta convoys with Nos.806, 807 and 808 Squadrons in the period September–October 1940. Fulmars of No.806 Squadron, embarked in *Illustrious*, shot down 10 Italian bombers between 2 September and 14 October 1940, and in November, whilst giving fighter cover to the Swordfish action at Taranto, shot down a further six enemy aircraft. In March 1941 Fulmars of No.805

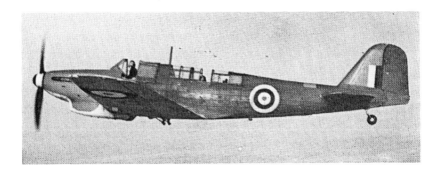

Fulmar I (N1952) of No.807 Squadron. *(Charles E Brown)*

Squadron fought in the defence of Crete, alongside Brewster Buffaloes and RAF Gladiators and Hurricanes.

Little publicity has ever been given to the fact that Fulmars played an important rôle in the shadowing of the German battleship *Bismarck* in May 1941. Six Fulmars of No.800Z Squadron were aboard *Victorious* on 22 May when it was reported that *Bismarck* had put to sea from Bergen. *Victorious*, with other units of the Home Fleet, went in pursuit. Largely due to excellent night reconnaissance work by the Fulmars, Swordfish were able to attack with torpedoes shortly before midnight on 25 May.

Fulmars were next in action during the FAA attack on Petsamo, up on the North Cape, in July 1941. Fulmars of No.800 Squadron, in *Furious*, and No.809 Squadron, in *Victorious*, provided fighter cover for four squadrons of Albacores. The raid met with stiff enemy fighter opposition, but Fulmars of No.809 Squadron succeeded in shooting down four Messerschmitt Bf 109s.

Another rôle in which Fulmars were active during 1941 was night-intrusion operations from shore-bases. From May to November, Fulmars of No.800X Squadron made night-intruder raids from Malta.

Early in 1942, when the threat of invasion by a Japanese fleet hung over Ceylon, Fulmars of Nos.803 and 806 Squadrons were based in the island. Fulmars of No.806 Squadron destroyed four Aichi Val dive-bombers when flying to protect the carrier *Hermes* from enemy attack when she was sunk by the Japanese on 9 April 1942.

Fulmars played a major rôle in the defence of the Malta reinforcement convoys during the island's prolonged siege. One of the most fiercely contested of these perilous voyages through the Mediterranean was that of August 1942. In this action, Fulmars of Nos.804, 809 and 884 Squadrons took part and were aided by Sea Hurricanes and Grumman Martlets. During the desperate air battles which raged above the convoy, Lt-Cdr Parker, the CO of No.884 Squadron, shot down two Cant Z.1007 bombers in his Fulmar.

From February 1942 twelve Fulmars of No.889 Squadron provided fighter defence for the Suez Canal zone and in November, with the Allied invasion of North Africa, those of No.809 Squadron operated from *Victorious* on tactical reconnaissance sorties over the landing beaches. Also present during the North African invasion were the Fulmars of No.893 Squadron (which also had Martlets), embarked in *Formidable*. This squadron later took part in the invasion of Sicily in July 1943 and on convoys to North Russia from October to November 1943.

North Russian convoys also fell to the lot of No.813 Squadron, embarked in *Campania* and *Vindex*. Equipped with 12 Swordfish and four Wildcats, No.813 Squadron also had a flight of Fulmar night-fighters which took part in several of the Russian convoys, between September 1944 and March 1945.

The Fulmar fought well with the FAA and shot down 112 enemy aircraft between September 1940 and August 1942: this was nearly one-third of all FAA victories in the Second World War. It wrought much execution among the slower Italian fighters, bombers and reconnaissance seaplanes, but was less effective against the faster German aircraft. This lack of speed was, of course, entirely due to the presence of the second seat for the navigator, but it must be remembered that at the time the Fulmar was designed navigational aids were not sufficiently developed to ensure a single-seat fighter's return to its carrier in

A Fulmar I of No.809 Squadron. *(Imperial War Museum)*

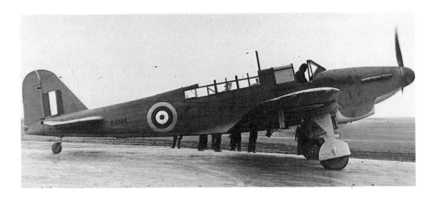

A Fulmar I (N2005) of the third production batch, N1980 to 2016.

bad weather. Perhaps the best summary of the Fulmar's qualities appears in Terence Horsley's book *Find, Fix and Strike:*

'There was never anything wrong with the eight-gun Fulmar. It was a fine aeroplane, manoeuvrable, with a good take-off, moderate climb, and plenty of endurance. It satisfied the demands for a navigator's seat and several wireless sets considered essential for Fleet work. It merely lacked the fighter's first essential quality—speed. Unless the pilot's first burst made a kill, he rarely got a second chance.'

The first prototype Fulmar survives to the present day and for some years was operated for communications work by its makers under the civil registration G-AIBE. It is converted to Mk.II standard, with a Merlin XXX, and later joined the FAA Museum at Yeovilton in its original livery, serialled N1854.

UNITS ALLOCATED

No.800X Squadron (*Furious*); No.800Y Squadron (*Argus*); No.800Z Squadron (*Victo-*

162

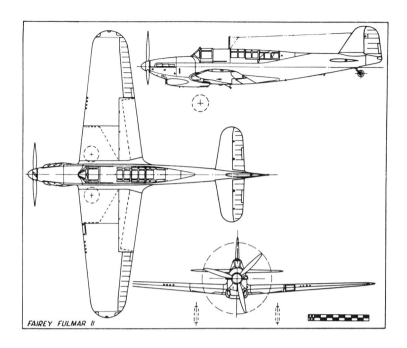

FAIREY FULMAR II

rious and *Indomitable*); No.803 Squadron (India and Ceylon; *Formidable*); No.804 Squadron (*Pegasus, Eagle, Argus, Furious* and in catapult armed merchant ships); No.805 Squadron (with Buffaloes, Egypt and Crete); No.806 Squadron (*Illustrious, Formidable, Indomitable* and Ceylon); No.806B Squadron (with Wildcats, *Illustrious*); No.807 Squadron (*Pegasus, Furious, Ark Royal, Argus, Eagle,* and catapult armed merchant ships); No.808 Squadron (*Ark Royal* and *Biter*); No.809 Squadron (*Victorious*); No.813 Squadron (with Swordfish and Wildcat, night-fighters in *Campania* and *Vindex*); No.879 Squadron (St Merryn); No.884 Squadron (*Victorious*); No.886 Squadron (Donibristle); No.887 Squadron (Lee-on-Solent); No.889 Squadron (Egypt); No.893 Squadron (with Martlets, *Formidable*); Fulmars also equipped No.273 Squadron of the RAF in Ceylon. *Second-line Squadrons:* Nos.700, 740, 746, 748, 759, 760, 761, 762, 766, 767, 768, 769, 772, 775, 778, 780, 781, 784, 787, and 790.

TECHNICAL DATA (FULMAR I and II)

Description: Two-seat carrier-borne day and night fighter. All-metal stressed-skin construction.
Manufacturers: Fairey Aviation Co Ltd, Stockport, Cheshire.
Power Plant: (Mk.I) One 1,080 hp Rolls-Royce Merlin VIII. (Mk.II) One 1,300 hp Rolls-Royce Merlin XXX.
Dimensions: Span, 46 ft 4½ in. Length, 40 ft 2 in. Height, 14 ft. Wing area, 342 sq ft.
Weights: (Mk.I) Empty, 7,560 lb. Loaded, 9,800 lb. (Mk.II) Empty, 7,676 lb. Loaded, 10,350 lb.
Performance:(Mk.I) Maximum speed, 246 mph at 9,000 ft. Initial climb, 1,105 ft/min; 15 min to 15,000 ft. Maximum range, 830 miles. Service

163

ceiling, 22,400 ft. (Mk.II): Maximum speed, 259 mph at 9,000 ft. Climb, 12 min to 15,000 ft. Service ceiling, 23,900 ft.

Armament: Eight fixed Browning guns mounted in the wings. Mk.II had capacity for 500 lb of bombs.

Fulmars of No.808 Squadron from *Ark Royal. (FAA Museum)*

164

Barracuda IIs of No.713 Squadron from Ronaldsway. *(Charles E Brown)*

Fairey Barracuda (Mks.I to III)

The Barracuda was a beast of burden if ever there was one: few aeroplanes in the course of their career can have been cluttered up with such a remarkable variety of extraneous equipment. Radomes, radar masts, rockets, bombs, mines, torpedoes, lifeboats, even containers below the wings for dropping secret agents in France; all were to be seen festooned about the Barracuda at one time or another. Add to this propensity such intrinsic features as the shoulder wing with its Fairey-Youngman flaps below the trailing-edge, the curious undercarriage design and the high-mounted tailplane, and it will be evident why the sight of a Barracuda caused many a raised eyebrow among spectators new to the experience. Perhaps the most amazing sight of all was that of a Barracuda using rocket-assisted take-off gear being shot off the deck of a carrier amidst a cloud of smoke.

Yet, though it might not have been handsome, the Barracuda acquitted itself well in its exacting range of duties and it proved a valuable addition to the FAA's strike force in the later years of the war. Its high power loading, fully laden, was apt to cause difficulty for the inexperienced pilot, but it retained its excellent manoeuvrability even when carrying a torpedo or bombs, and it proved especially useful as a dive-bomber, for which purpose the Fairey-Youngman flaps were inclined 30 degrees to act as dive brakes. It was, in fact, as a dive-bomber that the Barracuda figured most prominently: it used the torpedo only rarely.

Design work on the Barracuda, then known as the Fairey Type 100, began in 1937. It was to meet the requirements of Spec S.24/37 and was intended as a replacement for the Albacore biplane. At the outset the Rolls-Royce Exe engine was chosen as the power plant, but when this engine was abandoned the design was modified to take the Rolls-Royce Merlin. When the prototype (P1767) made its maiden flight on 7 December 1940 it was the first all-metal monoplane torpedo-bomber for carrier-borne duties ever built in Great Britain.

It was due to no intrinsic fault that the Barracuda got off to a bad start. It made its appearance at a critical period of the war, when the resources of the aircraft industry were being concentrated on achieving maximum output of a few selected aircraft and, as a result, series production of the new monoplane was delayed for almost two years. A second prototype (P1770) flew on 29 June 1941, but it was not until 18 May 1942 that the first production Barracuda Mk.I (P9642) took the air. The initial production batch consisted of 25 aircraft, P9642 to 9666 inclusive. These were the only Mk.Is to be built, and all were fitted with the 1,260 hp Merlin 30 engine.

Production Barracudas differed from the original version of the prototype in having the characteristic high-mounted tailplane. On its first appearance the prototype P1767 had an orthodox low-set tailplane, but it was found that this suffered from buffeting caused by turbulence when the large Fairey-Youngman flaps were lowered, so it was raised. The prototype Barracuda made its first deck-landing on 18 May 1941.

With the Barracuda Mk.II, the 1,640 hp Merlin 32 engine was installed, driving a four-blade airscrew instead of the three-blade type used on the Barracuda I. This increased the all-up weight from 13,500 lb to 14,100 lb. The prototype for the Barracuda II (P1767) flew for the first time on 17 August 1942, and by 1943 production of this major variant was in full swing, not only at Fairey's Stockport factory, but also by Blackburn at Brough and Boulton Paul at Wolverhampton. Later, the Westland Company at Yeovil also joined the Barracuda production group.

The last variant of the Barracuda produced during the war years was the Mk.III. The Barracuda III was generally similar to the Mk.II, but was intended chiefly for anti-submarine reconnaissance duties, and for this purpose mounted an ASV Mk.X scanner in a radome under the rear fuselage. The prototype for the Barracuda III was a converted Mk.II, DP855, which first flew in 1943.

The Barracuda III followed the Mk.II through the shops, and the grand total of Mks.I, II and III built amounted to 2,150. Of this total, 1,190 were built by the parent company at Heaton Chapel, 550 by Blackburn, 392 by Boulton Paul

Barracuda II (MD717) built by Blackburn. *(Blackburn)*

166

and 18 by Westland. Serial numbers allocated to Fairey-built aircraft were P9642 to 9666, P9667 to 9691, P9709 to 9748, P9787 to 9836, P9847 to 9891, P9909 to 9943, P9957 to 9986, DT813 to 831, DT845 to 865, DT878 to 887, LS464 to 506, LS519 to 556, LS568 to 595, LS615 to 653, LS668 to 713, LS726 to 763, LS778 to 820, LS833 to 878, LS891 to 936, LS949 to 974, PM682 to 723, PM738 to 780, PM796 to 838, PM852 to 897, PM913 to 958, PM970 to 999, PN115 to 164, RK328 to 369, RK382 to 428, RK441 to 485 and RK498 to 523.

The Barracuda first entered an operational unit on 10 January 1943, when No.827 Squadron re-formed with 12 Mk.IIs at Stretton, Cheshire. No.827 Squadron had until the previous August flown Albacores. During 1943 the Barracuda force was steadily built up. No.810 Squadron, also at Stretton, became the second Barracuda unit in February 1943, and thereafter Albacore and Swordfish squadrons were re-equipped one by one, until in January 1944 the FAA had 12 squadrons of Barracudas in the front line.

Barracudas were first in action in September 1943, when they served with No.810 Squadron in *Illustrious* during the Allied landings at Salerno, but they did not spring into prominence until the following year, when they made their memorable attack on *Tirpitz*. *Tirpitz* was lying in Kaafiord, in the northern tip of Norway, where she had undergone repairs after the attack by British midget submarines in September 1943. The objective of the FAA attack was to render the great battleship incapable of interfering with the convoys to North Russia.

Under the command of Admiral Sir Michael Denny, six aircraft-carriers gathered for the strike: they were *Furious*, *Victorious*, *Emperor*, *Fencer*, *Pursuer* and *Searcher*. Just before dawn on 3 April 1944, the force reached its flying-off position, and the aircraft took off whilst it was still dark. Forty-two

Barracuda II (P9926), a Fairey-built aircraft, with torpedo. *(Imperial War Museum)*

Barracudas were flown off, in two groups of 21 each, and they had a strong escort of 80 fighters. The enemy was taken completely by surprise. Before anybody aboard *Tirpitz* realised what was happening, the Barracudas had dived between the high, steep sides of the fiord, shattering its customary silence, and delivered their heavy armour-piercing bombs with deadly accuracy. The second wave of Barracudas bombed blind through the smoke a minute later. The ship's anti-aircraft guns were manned too late to be fully effective, and only three Barracudas and a single fighter were lost. *Tirpitz* had received 15 direct hits from the 500 lb and 1,000 lb bombs of the Barracudas of Nos.827, 829 and 830 Squadrons from *Victorious* and No.831 Squadron from *Furious*. The fighter cover was provided by Hellcats of No.800 Squadron, Seafires of No.801 Squadron, Wildcats of No.898 Squadron and Corsairs of No.1834 Squadron.

After this initial success, further Barracuda strikes were made on *Tirpitz* from May to August 1944. These took place on 15 May, 14 July, 22 August, 24 August and 25 August. By using smoke-screens, *Tirpitz* escaped further serious damage, though a direct hit by a 1,000 lb bomb was secured in the raid of 24 August.

Only a fortnight after the initial *Tirpitz* attack, Barracudas made their operational début in the Pacific war theatre. Between 16 and 21 April 1944, Barracudas of Nos.810 and 847 Squadrons, embarked in *Illustrious*, joined US Navy dive-bombers in a shattering attack on the Japanese submarine base and oil-tanks at Sabang, Sumatra. Other Barracuda squadrons which made their mark in the Pacific were Nos.815 and 817 in *Indomitable*, and Nos.822 and 831 in *Victorious*, all of which were engaged in dive-bombing over Sumatra in the period August–September 1944.

Back in home waters, No.841 Squadron in *Implacable* was active in a series of anti-shipping strikes off the Norwegian coast from August to October 1944, and other Barracudas did invaluable work on anti-submarine patrol with the smaller escort carriers. To get off these small carrier decks, the Barracuda was equipped with RATOG, and some of the squadrons so engaged were No.821, in *Puncher*, No.823, in *Atheling*, and No.815 in *Activity*, *Smiter* and *Fencer*.

Barracudas were last in action at Hong Kong on 1 September 1945 in a final operation with Corsairs, Hellcats and Avengers against Japanese boats defying the cease-fire.

With the arrival of VJ-Day, those Barracuda squadrons still operational were rapidly disbanded, and at the beginning of 1946 only five remained. These were Nos.812, 814, 826, 827 and 860. They were very quickly re-armed with Fireflies and changed their rôle to fighter reconnaissance.

After being absent from first-line squadrons of the FAA for almost two years, the Barracuda was revived in December 1947, when No.815 Squadron re-formed at Eglinton, Northern Ireland. No.815 Squadron was equipped with 12 Barracuda IIIs taken over from No.744 Squadron. These aircraft, the last Barracudas in first-line service, were eventually superseded by Grumman Avengers in May 1953.

UNITS ALLOCATED

No.810 Squadron (formed April 1943 at Lee-on-Solent; embarked in *Illustrious* and *Activity*); No.812 Squadron (formed June 1944 at Stretton; shore-based at Crail and Fearn; embarked in *Vengeance*); No.814 Squadron (formed July 1944 at Stretton; shore-based at Fearn and Macrihanish; embarked in *Venerable*); No.815 Squadron (formed October 1943 at Lee-on-Solent; embarked in *Indomitable*, *Activity*, *Smiter* and *Fencer*; also post-war from December 1947 at Eglinton); No.816 Squadron (formed February 1945 at Lee-on-Solent); No.817 Squadron (formed December 1943 at Lee-on-Solent; embarked in *Begum*, *Indomitable* and *Unicorn*); No.818 Squadron (formed May 1945 at Crimond); No.820 Squadron (formed January 1944 at Lee-on-Solent; embarked in *Indefatigable*); No.821 Squadron (formed May 1944 at Stretton; embarked in *Puncher* and *Trumpeter*); No.822 Squadron (formed August 1943 at Lee-on-Solent; embarked in *Victorious* and *Rajah*); No.823 Squadron (formed June 1943 at Lee-on-Solent; embarked in *Atheling*); No.824 Squadron (formed July 1945 at Lee-on-Solent; embarked in *Activity*); No.825 Squadron (formed July 1945 at Rattray); No.826 Squadron (formed December 1943 at Lee-on-Solent; embarked in *Indefatigable* and *Formidable*); No.827 Squadron (formed January 1943 at Stretton; embarked in *Furious, Victorious, Formidable* and *Colossus*); No.828 Squadron (formed March 1944 at Lee-on-Solent; embarked in *Implacable*); No.829 Squadron (formed October 1943 at Lee-on-Solent; embarked in *Victorious*); No.830 Squadron (formed May 1943 at Lee-on-Solent; embarked in *Furious* and *Formidable*); No.831 Squadron (formed June 1943 at Stretton; embarked in *Victorious* and *Furious*); No. 837 Squadron (formed August 1944 at Stretton; embarked in *Glory*); No.841 Squadron (formed February 1944 at Lee-on-Solent; embarked in *Formidable* and *Implacable*); No.847 Squadron (formed June 1943 at Lee-on-Solent; embarked in *Illustrious*); No.860 Squadron (formed September 1945 at Ayr; embarked in *Nairana*). *Second-line Squadrons:* Nos.700, 703, 706, 707, 710, 711, 713, 714, 716, 717, 719, 731, 733, 735, 736, 737, 744, 747, 750, 753, 756, 764, 767, 768, 769, 774, 778, 780, 781, 783, 785, 786, 787, 796, 797, 798 and 799.

TECHNICAL DATA (BARRACUDA I, II AND III)

Description (Mks.I and II): Three-seat carrier-borne or shore-based torpedo-bomber and dive-bomber. (T.R.III): Three-seat carrier-borne or shore-based torpedo-reconnaissance aircraft. All-metal stressed skin construction.

Manufacturers: Fairey Aviation Co Ltd, Stockport, Cheshire. Sub-contracted by Blackburn, (serials in ranges BV640–981, MD612–807 and MX635–907); Boulton Paul (serials in ranges DP855–999, DR113–335, MD811–992, ME114–293 and RJ759–966); and Westland (serials DN625–642).

Power Plant (Mk.I): One 1,260 hp Rolls-Royce Merlin 30. (Mks.II and III): One 1,640 hp Rolls-Royce Merlin 32.

Dimensions (All marks): Span, 49 ft 2 in. Length, 39 ft 9 in. Height, 15 ft 1 in. Wing area, 367 sq ft.

Weights: (Mk.I): Empty, 10,012 lb. Loaded, 11,404 lb or 13,068 lb (maximum): (Mk.II): Empty, 10,818 lb. Loaded, 12,600 lb or 14,100 lb (maximum). (Mk.III): Empty, 11,113 lb. Loaded, 12,895 lb or 14,250 lb (maximum).

Performance: (Mk.I): Maximum speed, 235 mph at 11,000 ft. Cruising speed 138 mph (economical) or 191 mph (maximum) at 6,000 ft. Climb, 6.7 min to 6,000 ft. Range, 524 miles with 2,000 lb of bombs; 853 miles with a 1,610 lb torpedo; 1,320 miles with maximum fuel and no bombs. Service ceiling, 18,400 ft. (Mk.II): Maximum speed, 210 mph at 2,000 ft. Cruising speed, 172 mph (economical) or 193 mph (maximum) at 5,000 ft. Initial climb, 1,200 ft/min. Range, 524 miles with 1,800 lb of bombs; 686 miles with a 1,620 lb torpedo; 1,150 miles with maximum fuel and no bombs. Service ceiling, 17,500 ft. (Mk.III): Maximum speed 239 mph at 1,750 ft. Cruising speed, 170 mph (economical) or 205 mph (maximum) at 5,000 ft. Climb, 4½ min to 5,000 ft. Range, 684 miles with a 1,572 lb torpedo; 818 miles with no bombs and 226 gallons of fuel; 1,125 miles with no bombs and 342 gallons of fuel. Service ceiling, 15,000 ft.

Armament: All marks had twin Vickers 'K' guns in rear cockpit. (Mk.I): One 1,610 lb torpedo or one 1,500 lb mine below fuselage or four 500 lb or six 250 lb bombs below wings. (Mk.II): One 1,620 lb torpedo or four 450 lb depth charges or six 250 lb bombs. (Mk.III): One 1,572 lb torpedo or four 450 lb depth charges.

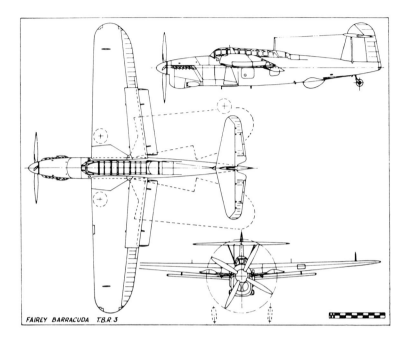

FAIREY BARRACUDA T.B.R 3

Firefly I (Z1832). *(Charles E Brown)*

Fairey Firefly (Mks.I and II)

The Firefly was designed to the Naval Spec N.5/40 (a combination of two earlier project tenders by Fairey to Specs N.8/39 and N.9/39) and it carried on the tradition, peculiar to the FAA, of the fast two-seater combining the fighter and reconnaissance rôles. This class of aircraft had first been conceived as early as 1926 and embodied in a specification which brought forth the Fairey Fleetwing and Hawker Osprey biplanes. The Osprey served until 1939, and in 1940 the fighter-reconnaissance philosophy was perpetuated by the Fairey Fulmar, the first monoplane of the class and the Firefly's immediate predecessor.

The prototype Firefly (Z1826) was first flown by C S Staniland on 22 December 1941, less than 18 months after the Admiralty had approved the original mock-up.

Designed by Mr H E Chaplin, the Firefly was generally similar to its predecessor but of improved aerodynamic form, with aesthetically pleasing elliptical wings and the much more powerful Griffon engine in place of the Merlin. Fire-power was also vastly improved by the substitution of four 20-mm guns for the eight machine-guns. It at once commended itself by proving 40 mph faster than the Fulmar, yet had excellent handling qualities at the lower end of the speed range, so essential in a carrier-borne aircraft. A great feature of the design was the incorporation of fully-retractable Fairey-Youngman flaps which could be extended beneath the trailing edge, almost horizontal with the line of flight, to improve cruising and manoeuvrability characteristics, as well as being lowered at an angle, in the usual way, for take-off and landing requirements.

Three further Firefly prototypes were built: these were Z1827, flown in March 1942, Z1828, flown in August 1942, and Z1829, flown in September 1942. After tests with these aircraft two changes were incorporated: the horn-balanced rudder was modified and metal ailerons replaced the original fabric-covered type.

Following an initial order for 200 aircraft, production of the Firefly I began with Z1830, which was delivered on 4 March 1943. The parent firm built over 700 of these aircraft at its Hayes factory, and the type was also sub-contracted by the General Aircraft Company, which built another 132 at Hanworth. A total of 975 Firefly Mk.Is was built, the last aircraft (TW679) being delivered on 23 November 1946. Early production Fireflies in the Mk.I range differed from later aircraft in having a low raked front screen-panel with a windscreen wiper and a shallow hood; this was later made taller, the wiper deleted and the bubble hood increased in height to give more headroom. This improved the forward view, which was somewhat deficient in early Fireflies. Other modifications introduced

Firefly Is of Nos.816 and 1792 Squadrons from HMS *Ocean*.

on the Mk.I production line included the addition of fairing to the 20-mm gun barrels, the deletion of the two-man dinghy stowed inside the rear fuselage in favour of individual K-type seat dinghies and (from the 470th aircraft) the installation of the Griffon XII engine in place of the Griffon IIB.

The next Firefly development was the production of a night-fighter version. There were two prototypes (Z1833 and Z1836), which had two small radomes containing AIX radar mounted well inboard on the wings at either side of the fuselage. The additional equipment for the AI observer in the rear cockpit upset the centre of gravity position: this was rectified by lengthening the nose 18 in, inserting an extra bay between the firewall and the front cockpit. Production of the Firefly N.F.II ceased after only 37 had been built, because it had been found possible to fit a more compact form of radar in a container beneath the centre section without the need for structural alterations. This enabled the F.R.I to be modified for night-fighter duties by conversion on the production line. This variant, the N.F.I, had shrouded exhausts.

The final operational variant of the Mk.I was the Firefly F.IA, which was the F.I converted to F.R.I standard by the addition of ASH radar.

Production Fireflies first went aboard an aircraft-carrier in July 1943, and the first operational unit of the FAA, No.1770 Squadron, formed with 12 aircraft at Yeovilton on 1 October 1943. After periods of shore-based service at Grimsetter and Hatston, No.1770 Squadron's Fireflies embarked in HMS *Indefatigable*, and were operational for the first time over Norway, between 14 and 19 July 1944, during FAA attacks on the German battleship *Tirpitz*. The Fireflies were used in attacks on gun positions and two auxiliary vessels during these operations. Between 18 August and 2 September 1944 Fireflies of No.1770 Squadron made photographic reconnaissance flights over *Tirpitz* and obtained vital information which led to the final destruction of the battleship, by RAF Lancasters, on 12 November 1944.

The second Firefly squadron, No.1771, formed at Yeovilton on 1 February 1944 and eventually embarked in HMS *Implacable*. No.1771 Squadron made its first operational sorties in October 1944, and until December its Fireflies were active in armed reconnaissance and anti-shipping strikes along the Norwegian coast.

The first major naval action in which Fireflies took part, however, was with the British carriers operating in the Far East, attached to the East Indies Fleet based on Ceylon. This was the spectacularly successful attack on the Japanese oil refineries in Sumatra, which produced vast quantities of fuel for enemy air and naval operations. Fireflies of No.1770 Squadron made rocket attacks on refineries at Pangkalan Brandan between 1 and 7 January 1945, before the main Fleet action of 24 January, in which 48 Avengers, 16 Hellcats and 32 Corsairs took part as well as the 12 Fireflies of No.1770 Squadron. First victory in air combat by a Firefly was on 2 January 1945, when Lt D Levitt of No.1770 Squadron shot down an Oscar fighter during the Sumatra strike. The Fireflies were flown off *Indefatigable*, the other carriers engaged being *Indomitable*, *Illustrious* and *Victorious*. The plan of campaign, which worked admirably, was for the fighters to attack enemy airfields and eliminate the fighter defences, thus leaving the way clear for the Avengers and Fireflies to make their strike. The target was the refinery at Pladjoe, Palembang, one of the most important in the Far East. In order to reach it, the Avengers and Fireflies had to dive through a

Firefly Is of No.816 Squadron in echelon formation.

balloon barrage and run the gauntlet of intense anti-aircraft fire, but they pressed home their attack and succeeded in devastating the main buildings of the refinery. On 29 January a similar force repeated the operation, this time against the other Palembang refinery at Songei Gerong. Once again the Avengers and Fireflies (the former with bombs and the latter with rockets) knocked out the target. As some wag remarked at the time, the Fireflies had helped to put the 'bang' into Palembang.

This, the first major action by the FAA against the Japanese, resulted in the loss of only 16 aircraft by enemy action: a small enough price to pay for an operation which altered the whole course of the war in the Pacific. Months later the Japanese were still feeling the effects of this curtailment of their oil supplies.

After Sumatra the carriers sailed to Australia, where they joined the British Pacific Fleet, based on Sydney. On 14–15 June 1945 Fireflies of No.1771 Squadron, in *Implacable*, joined in the attacks on Truk in the Carolina Islands, and on 10 July aircraft of this squadron became the first in the FAA to fly over the Japanese mainland. On 24 July they were joined in the operations against shipping and shore targets among the Japanese islands by Fireflies of No.1772

Firefly N.F.II (Z1875). *(Imperial War Museum)*

174

Firefly F.R.I. (MB745) from No.795 Squadron, Eglinton. *(MoD)*

Squadron (HMS *Indefatigable*), which had first formed at Burscough on 1 May 1944. During these operations (in preparation for an amphibious landing which was forestalled by the dropping of the atomic bombs) Fireflies had the honour of being the first British aircraft to fly over Tokyo.

One of the first activities in which Fireflies engaged after the Second World War was the dropping of supplies to prisoner-of-war camps in Japan. This operation was carried out by No.1772 Squadron between 21 and 30 August 1945.

When VJ-Day arrived a total of 658 Fireflies had left the factories (574 of them from Fairey) and the FAA had eight squadrons in being, of which four were with the British Pacific Fleet (Nos.1770, 1771, 1772 and 1790, the latter night-fighters), and the remainder working up in the United Kingdom. There were also two Fireflies embarked in the escort carrier *Vindex*, with Wildcat VIs of No.882 Squadron. In Nos.816 and 822 Squadrons the Fireflies were displacing Barracudas. The remaining home-based squadrons (Nos.1791 and 1792) were equipped with Firefly night-fighters. Both the home-based night-fighter squadrons and the Fireflies in the Far East had a relatively short post-war existence; most of them had gone by 1946.

During the post-war period, the Firefly I was nevertheless destined to play a part in Fleet Air Arm history. With No.827 Squadron it served in the Korean War until September 1950, mounting strikes on coastal targets and shipping from the aircraft carrier HMS *Glory*. Later, Firefly Is equipped some of the squadrons of the Royal Navy Volunteer Reserve at shore stations in the United Kingdom and remained with No.1841 Squadron based at Stretton in Cheshire until replaced by Firefly Mk.6s in March 1955.

UNITS ALLOCATED

No.805 Squadron (formed September 1946; shore-based at Malta; embarked in *Ocean*); No.812 Squadron (formed January 1946; embarked in *Theseus*); No.814 Squadron (formed January 1946; embarked in *Vengeance*); No.816 Squadron (formed July 1945 at

Firefly N.F.I (DT933), the night-fighter conversion of the F.R.I with shrouded exhausts and radome beneath the nose. *(Imperial War Museum)*

A Firefly F.R.I (DT934) of No.1770 Squadron with the East Indies Fleet in *Implacable*. *(Imperial War Museum)*

Woodvale; embarked in *Nairana* and *Theseus*; augmented by four Firefly night-fighters in May 1946; embarked in *Ocean* and *Sydney*); No.822 Squadron (formed August 1945 at Woodvale; disbanded February 1946); No.824 Squadron (formed October 1945 at Ayr; disbanded January 1946); No.825 Squadron (formed November 1945; embarked in *Warrior* of Royal Canadian Navy); No.826 Squadron (formed January 1946; disbanded February 1946); No.827 Squadron (formed August 1946; embarked in *Triumph*); No.837 Squadron (formed November 1945; embarked in *Glory*); No.860 Squadron (formed February 1946; shore-based at St Merryn and Dale, transferred to Royal Netherlands Navy in September 1946); No.861 Squadron (formed September 1946; transferred to Royal Netherlands Navy in February 1947); No.882 Squadron (two Fireflies added to Wildcats aboard *Vindex* in February 1945; subsequently embarked in *Searcher* and disbanded October 1945); No.1770 Squadron (formed October 1943 at Yeovilton; embarked in *Indefatigable*; disbanded September 1945); No.1771 Squadron (formed February 1944 at Yeovilton; embarked in *Implacable*; disbanded September 1945); No.1772 Squadron (formed May 1944 at Burscough; embarked in *Ruler* and *Indefatigable*;

176

disbanded March 1946); No.1790 Squadron (formed January 1945 at Burscough; embarked in *Vindex* and *Implacable*; disbanded June 1946); No.1791 Squadron (formed March 1945 at Lee-on-Solent; shore-based at Inskip, Drem and Burscough; disbanded September 1945); No.1792 Squadron (formed May 1945 at Lee-on-Solent; shore based at Inskip and Drem, embarked in *Ocean*; disbanded April 1946); No.1830 Squadron, RNVR (formed May 1947 at Abbotsinch). No.1841 Squadron (formed August 1952 at Stretton). *Second-line squadrons:* Nos.700, 703, 706, 730, 731, 732 (night-fighter), 736, 737, 741, 744, 746 (night-fighter), 748, 759, 764, 766, 767, 768, 771, 772 (night-fighter), 778, 780, 781, 783, 784 (night-fighter), 790, 792 (night-fighter), 794 (night-fighter), 795, 796, 798 and 799.

TECHNICAL DATA (FIREFLY F.I)

Description: Two-seat carrier-borne fighter-reconnaissance aircraft. All-metal stressed-skin construction.

Manufacturers: Fairey Aviation Co Ltd, Hayes, Middlesex. Serials in the ranges Z1830 to 2120, DT931 to 991, DV117 to 150, MB378 to 758, PP391 to 660 and TW677 to 679. General Aircraft Ltd, Hanworth, Middlesex. Serials in the range DK414 to 570.

Power Plant: One 1,735 hp Rolls-Royce Griffon IIB or 1,990 hp Griffon XII.

Dimensions: Span, 44 ft 6 in (13 ft 3 in folded). Length, 37 ft 7¼ in. Height, 12 ft 7 in. Wing area, 328 sq ft.

Weights: Empty, 8,925 lb. Loaded, 13,284 lb.

Performance: Maximum speed, 319 mph at 17,000 ft. Initial climb, 1,800 ft/min,

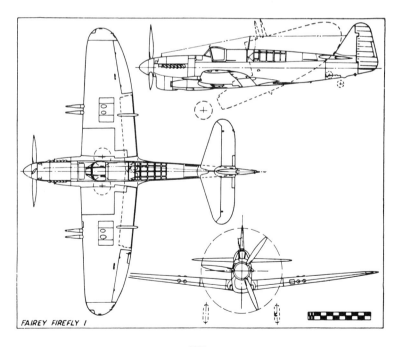

FAIREY FIREFLY I

9.6 min to 15,000 ft. Maximum range, 1,088 miles. Service ceiling, 28,200 ft.

Armament: Four fixed 20-mm guns in wings. Provision for eight 60 lb rocket projectiles or two 1,000 lb bombs below the wings.

Firefly I (PP617) from the penultimate Mk.I production batch by Fairey at Hayes, Middlesex.

Barracuda V (RK558) of No.783 Squadron from Lee-on-Solent. *(Crown Copyright)*

Fairey Barracuda V

The Barracuda V appeared too late to see action in the Pacific against the Japanese, where it was intended to serve as an interim replacement type prior to the introduction of the Fairey Spearfish. Though superficially similar to the wartime Barracudas (described separately), it was in fact extensively re-engineered and had an improved performance. This resulted from the installation of the Griffon engine in place of the Merlin: it also had increased range due to additional internal fuel capacity.

The installation of the Griffon in a Barracuda had first been planned for the Mk.IV, but this did not get beyond the project stage. The first prototype Barracuda V was a rebuilt Mk.II (P9976), and it first flew at Ringway on 16 November 1944. A Griffon VII (later VIII) of 1,850 hp was installed and the wing-span was increased by 4 ft, the tips being squared and the entire structure re-stressed to give a greater margin of safety in a dive. Another change was the deletion of the third crew position, the rear cockpit being occupied by a navigator/radar operator with no gunnery duties. The prototype was followed by four more conversions (DT845, PM944, PM941 and PM940) and a small initial production batch, converted from earlier marks (including LS479 and LS486), which retained the original type of fin and rudder. Barracudas from RK530 were built as Mk.Vs and had a large dorsal fillet, giving additional fin area. Late production aircraft underwent a further tail revision and introduced a tall, pointed rudder.

The first true-built Barracuda V (RK530) flew on 22 November 1945, but, with the end of the war, contracts for 140 had been curtailed and output was limited to 30 (RK530–542 and RK558–574) deliveries ending on 27 October 1947. The production Barracuda Vs mounted an easily-detachable radome under the port wing and had the up-rated Griffon 37 engine. They were used mostly for training by the FAA and did not enter first-line squadrons.

The first Barracuda Vs in service went to No.778 Squadron in September 1946 and the type was finally withdrawn in October 1948.

Second-line squadrons: No.778 (RNAS Ford) and No.783 (RNAS Lee-on-Solent). Also served at sea with the Ship's Flight in HMS *Illustrious* and *Implacable*.

TECHNICAL DATA (BARRACUDA B.R.V)

Description: Two-seat carrier-borne or shore-based bomber-reconnaissance aircraft. All-metal stressed-skin construction.

Manufacturers: Fairey Aviation Co Ltd, Stockport, Cheshire.

Power Plant: One 1,890 hp Rolls-Royce Griffon VIII.

Dimensions: Span, 53 ft 0½ in (19 ft 6 in folded). Length, 41 ft 1 in. Height, 13 ft 2½ in. Wing area, 480 sq ft.

Weights: Empty, 10,607 lb. Loaded, 14,400 lb (normal); 16,000 lb (overload).

Performance: Maximum speed, 256 mph at 11,000 ft. Cruising speed, 203 mph. climb, 1,300 ft/min; 3.9 min to 5,000 ft. Range, 1,120 miles at 170 mph without bombs or 600 miles at 163 mph with 2,000 lb of bombs. Service ceiling, 24,000 ft.

Armament: Two machine-guns. Bomb-load: one 2,000 lb bomb or four 250 lb depth charges or one 1,672 lb torpedo.

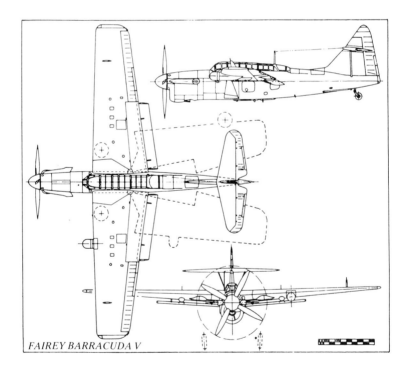

FAIREY BARRACUDA V

Firefly Mk.4s of No.816 Squadron from Eglinton. *(Charles E Brown)*

Fairey Firefly (Mks.4 to 6)

From 1945, when the fully modified Mk.4 made its first appearance, the Firefly assumed notably different external characteristics. The wings were clipped, which improved the rate of roll but detracted rather from the appearance, and the beard radiator disappeared, to be replaced by coolant radiators in extensions of the leading edges of the centre section. A four-bladed Rotol airscrew replaced the earlier three-bladed type, and an extension was made to the leading edge of the fin, increasing its area and improving stability. To complete the transformation, two large fairings appeared beneath the wings: the port fairing housed auxiliary fuel formerly carried in the centre section and the starboard fairing carried the radar scanner previously mounted below the centre section.

These changes came about as a result of installing the two-speed two-stage supercharged Griffon 74 (Griffon 72 in the prototypes), which improved the high-altitude performance considerably, raising the maximum speed by as much as 50 mph. The original testing of a two-stage Griffon engine was in a converted Firefly Mk.I (Z1835), which, fitted with a Griffon 61 series engine, was re-designated Firefly Mk.III. This experimental prototype was flown in 1943: it retained similar cowling arrangements to that of the earlier Griffon, resulting in a somewhat bulky nose, which produced unsatisfactory flight characteristics, and the type was abandoned.

In its original form, as flown in 1944, the first prototype Firefly Mk.4 (a converted Mk.I, Z2118) retained the elliptical wing and the original tail unit. In 1945 it was modified to full Mk.4 standard, and three more conversions were made from the Mk.I airframes (MB649, Z1835 and PP482) for trial installations and further test flying before genuine Mk.4 production began. The prototypes had the 2,330 hp Griffon 72 engine, which was replaced by a 2,245 hp Griffon 74 in production aircraft.

The first production Firefly F.R.4 (TW687) flew on 25 May 1945, and a total of 160 went to the FAA. This figure included a small number of N.F.4 night-fighters. Some 43 production aircraft were converted on the line from Mk.I airframes. The last Firefly Mk.4 (VH144) was delivered from the Fairey factory on 9 February 1948. Retrospectively, a number of Firefly Mk.4s were converted for target-towing duties, being fitted with an ML type G winch under the centre section and designated T.T.4. They served with Nos.700 and 771 Squadrons from 1951 to 1957.

The first FAA squadrons to be equipped with the Firefly Mk.4 were Nos.825 and 810, which were re-armed at Eglinton in August and October 1947, respectively. At that time No.825 Squadron was on detachment to the Royal Canadian Navy.

The Firefly Mk.4 was followed on the production line by the Mk.5, the most prolific of the later Fireflies. With this mark the Firefly began to be fitted with varying equipment for specialised rôles, resulting in the subvariants F.R.5 for day-fighter-reconnaissance, the N.F.5 for night-fighting and the A.S.5 for anti-submarine patrol. The differences between these Fireflies were mainly internal. Altogether 322 Firefly Mk.5s reached the FAA and served in ten first-line squadrons. The first production Firefly 5 (VT362) made its original flight on 12 December 1947 and was delivered to the FAA on 9 January 1948. The final Firefly 5 (WB424) left the Fairey factory in May 1950.

One important change introduced during the life of the Firefly 5 was that of power-folding wings. The first aircraft so modified (VX414) left the factory on 24 January 1949.

First-line Firefly squadrons of the FAA re-equipped with the Mk.5 version during 1948 and 1949, the first being No.812 at Eglinton in July 1948. The following year war started in Korea, and in this conflict, which was to last two years, Fireflies found themselves in action once again in the Far East. The Far Eastern Fleet of the Royal Navy was at its station off the Korean coast only three days after the fighting started, and within six days was engaged in operations. The first air sortie was flown from the light fleet-carrier *Triumph*, and, from that time onwards, an aircraft-carrier of the Royal Navy, or one of the Commonwealth navies, was constantly in West Korean waters. Though strikes against enemy mine-layers and supply shipping were flown, the major part of the flying was in support of the armies ashore, disrupting enemy supplies and communications. In these bombing and rocket strikes Fireflies shared honours with Hawker Sea Furies, and some remarkable records of intensive operational flying and high serviceability factors were achieved. During the first spell of operations from *Theseus* no aircraft was ever unserviceable for longer than two hours, and no fewer than 1,300 deck landings were made without a failure or accident of any kind. As the war progressed the light fleet-carriers slowly increased their average daily sorties flown from 60 to 120. The Firefly Mk.5 squadrons engaged in Korea were No.810 (in *Theseus* and *Ocean*), No.812 (in *Glory*), No.817 (in the Australian light fleet-carrier *Sydney*), No.821 (in *Glory*) and No.825 (in *Ocean*. During the severe Korean winters the aircraft frequently operated in arctic weather conditions, with rough seas, snowstorms and temperatures well below freezing. Undaunted, the Fireflies and Sea Furies carried on, and even amidst the most appalling weather of November 1951, *Sydney*'s aircraft flew 270 sorties during air strikes against Hungnam. Her

Firefly A.S.5 (VT406). *(Flight)*

Fireflies (No.817 Squadron) and Sea Furies (No.805 Squadron) started many fires in industrial areas and severely damaged harbour and rail communications. In another close-support operation for United Nations troops No.817's Fireflies demolished four important bridges with 16 bombs. It was during *Sydney*'s period of operations (from November 1951 to January 1952) that one of her Fireflies, flown by Sub-Lt N D MacMillan, RAN, completed the 2,000th operational sortie flown from this carrier.

A particularly distinguished record was put up by the 14th Carrier Air Group, comprising Fireflies of No.812 Squadron and the Sea Furies of No.804 Squadron, embarked in the light fleet-carrier *Glory*. This Group flew 4,834 operational sorties in the Korean War for the loss of only 27 aircraft.

Another Firefly 5 squadron, No.825, was awarded (jointly with its companion Sea Fury squadron, No.802) the Boyd Trophy for 1952 for its work in Korea from the light fleet-carrier *Ocean*. The Fireflies and Sea Furies of *Ocean* surpassed all previous Korean records by achieving 123 sorties in a single day. They expended 6,000 rockets and dropped 4,000 bombs during ground-attack sorties in the close-support rôle.

In 1954 the Fireflies of No.825 Squadron went into action again in the ground-attack rôle, this time against bandits in Malaya. During these operations they were embarked in the light fleet-carrier *Warrior*.

By the time of the Coronation Naval Review at Spithead on 15 June 1953 the Firefly squadrons had been once more re-armed, the Mk.5 having given way to the Mk.6. The first Mk.6s went to No.814 Squadron at Culdrose in January 1951. In this version the Firefly was equipped exclusively for anti-submarine duties and was designated A.S.6. Generally similar to the A.S.5, the A.S.6 differed in carrying no armament, and it became the FAA's leading type of anti-submarine aircraft until the introduction of the Gannet in 1955. Total production of the Firefly A.S.6, all built at Hayes, was 161. The first Firefly A.S.6 (WB425) made its maiden flight on 23 March 1949 and the last A.S.6 to be built (WJ121) was delivered on 18 September 1951.

As well as being standard equipment in first-line squadrons (Nos.812, 814, 817, 820 and 826 all flew A.S.6s in the Coronation fly-past), the type was widely employed by the anti-submarine squadrons of the RNVR air divisions. The first of these squadrons to be formed, No.1830, received A.S.6s in October 1951 at Donibristle in place of its older Fireflies and, until 1955, other RNVR units were supplied with the A.S.6. Nos.1830, 1840 and 1841 Squadrons joined the first-line squadrons in the fly-past at Spithead, making the Firefly by far the most predominant FAA aircraft on this historic and impressive occasion.

The Firefly A.S.6 outlasted the A.S.7 (described separately) in the FAA squadrons to become the last representative of the prolific Firefly family to remain on operational duties. By 1956 the FAA's anti-submarine force had completed its transition to Gannets and Avengers and the Firefly disappeared from the scene after 13 years of valuable service.

Firefly A.S.6s of No.812 Squadron from *Glory*. *(MoD)*

Firefly T.T.4 (VH132) of No.771 Squadron from Ford. *(MoD)*

184

Firefly A.S.6 (WD917) of No.1840 Squadron from Ford. *(Crown Copyright)*

A Firefly Mk.5 (WB271) is preserved at the FAA Museum at Yeovilton, Somerset.

UNITS ALLOCATED

(Firefly Mk.4): No.810 Squadron (*Implacable* and *Theseus*), No.812 Squadron (*Ocean*), No.814 Squadron (*Vengeance*), No.816 Squadron (*Sydney*), No.825 Squadron (*Magnificent*), No.1840 Squadron (Culham and Ford). *Second-line Squadrons:* Nos.703, 727, 736, 767, 778, 781, 782, 787 and 799. (T.T.4): Nos.700 and 771. (Firefly Mk.5): No.804 Squadron (*Ocean*), No.810 Squadron (*Ocean, Glory* and *Theseus*), No.812 Squadron (*Ocean, Triumph* and *Glory*), No.814 Squadron (*Vengeance*), No.816 Squadron (*Sydney* and *Vengeance*), No.817 Squadron (*Sydney*), No.820 Squadron (*Indomitable* and *Theseus*), No.821 Squadron (*Glory*), No.825 Squadron (*Magnificent, Theseus, Ocean* and *Warrior*), No.880 Squadron (*Magnificent*), No.1830 Squadron (Culdrose) and No.1844 Squadron (Bramcote). *Second-line Squadrons:* Nos.703, 719, 737, 778, 781, 782 and 796. (T.T.5): Nos.723, 725 and 771. (Firefly Mk.6): No.812 Squadron (*Glory, Theseus* and *Eagle*), No.814 Squadron (*Vengeance, Illustrious, Theseus* and *Eagle*), No.816 Squadron (*Sydney* and *Vengeance*), No.817 Squadron (*Sydney* and *Vengeance*), No.820 Squadron (*Indomitable* and *Theseus*), No.821 Squadron (*Illustrious*), No.824 Squadron (*Illustrious* and *Theseus*), No.826 Squadron (*Illustrious, Indomitable* and *Theseus*), No.851 Squadron (*Sydney*), No.1830 Squadron (Donibristle), No.1840 Squadron (Ford), No.1841 Squadron (Stretton) and No.1844 Squadron (Bramcote). *Second-line Squadrons:* Nos.703, 719, 723, 724, 737, 744, 751, 767, 771, 782 and 796. (T.T.6) Nos.724 and 725.

TECHNICAL DATA (FIREFLY A.S.5)

Description: Two-seat carrier-borne anti-submarine reconnaissance and strike aircraft. All-metal stressed-skin construction.

Manufacturers: Fairey Aviation Co Ltd, Hayes, Middlesex. Mk.4 serial numbers were TW687–699, TW715–754, VG957–999 and VH121–144.

185

Mk.5 serial numbers were VT362–381, VT392–441, VT458–504, VX371–396, VX413–438, WB243–272, WB281–316, WB330–382 and WB391–424. Mk.6 serial numbers were WB425–440, WB505–523, WD824–925, WH627–632 and WJ104–121.

Power Plant: One 2,245 hp Rolls-Royce Griffon 74.

Dimensions: Span, 41 ft 2 in. Length, 27 ft 11 in. Height, 14 ft 4 in. Wing area, 330 sq ft.

Weights: Empty, 9,674 lb. Loaded (normal), 13,927 lb; (maximum), 16,096 lb.

Performance: Maximum speed, 386 mph at 14,000 ft. Cruising speed, 220 mph. Initial climb, 2,050 ft/min; 6 min 50 sec to 10,000 ft; 15½ min to 20,000 ft. Range, 660 miles (with 192 gals) or 1,300 miles (with 418 gals). Endurance, 6½ hr. Service ceiling, 29,200 ft.

Armament: Four fixed 20-mm guns in wings and provision for eight 60 lb rocket projectiles or two 1,000 lb bombs below the wings.

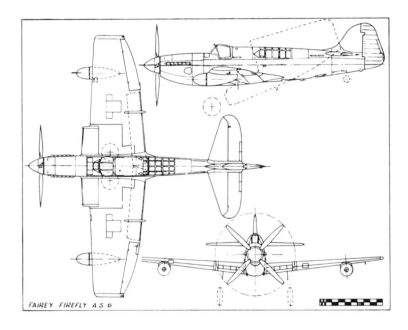

FAIREY FIREFLY A.S. 6

Firefly T.1 (Z1980). *(Flight)*

Fairey Firefly Trainer (Mks.1 to 3)

In 1946, with the Firefly I firmly established as the Royal Navy's standard fighter-reconnaissance aircraft, the Fairey concern turned its attentions to the provision of a dual-control trainer version. This differed fundamentally from the fighter in having the rear (instructor's) cockpit raised 12 in above the normal position to improve forward vision for landing when flown from the back seat, and in mounting two instead of four 20-mm guns in the wings. The original Firefly Trainer (MB750) first flew at Ringway in July 1946. It was flown by Mr Duncan Menzies, and tested at the Admiralty Flying School at Hinstock, the Operational Flying School at Lossiemouth, the Deck-Landing Training School at Milltown and the School of Naval Air Warfare at St Merryn.

The initial production version, designated Firefly T.1, was like the prototype in being a conversion of Mk.I airframes. The first of 34 such conversions (MB473) flew for the first time on 1 September 1947. Only nine of these aircraft carried the two wing-mounted guns; the rest were unarmed. The Firefly T.1s were used principally as deck-landing conversion trainers.

The next Firefly Trainer was the T.2, equipped to operate primarily as a tactical weapons trainer. All the Firefly T.2s mounted two 20-mm guns in the wings and had gyro gunsights in both cockpits. Fifty-four Firefly T.2s were delivered, all conversions of Mk.I fighters. The first T.2 conversion (MB543) made its maiden flight on 12 August 1949.

The last trainer variant based on the Firefly I airframe was the Firefly T.3, which first flew in 1951. Firefly T.3s were conversions of F.R.Is, and differed from the earlier trainers in having no raised rear cockpit. They carried special equipment for the training of naval air observers in the techniques of anti-submarine warfare and were unarmed. Firefly T.3s were eventually retired in July 1954, being superseded in this rôle by the Firefly T.7.

UNITS ALLOCATED

Second-line squadrons: (T.1): Nos. 736 (St Merryn), 737 (Eglinton), 764 (Yeovilton), 766 (Lossiemouth and Culdrose), 767 (Yeovilton, Henstridge and Stretton), 771 (Ford), 778 (Ford), 781 (Lee-on-Solent), 782 (Donibristle) and 799 (Yeovilton and Machrihanish).

(T.2): No.737 (Eglinton), 744 (Malta), 764 (Yeovilton), 765 (Culdrose), 766 (Lossiemouth and Culdrose), 771 (Ford), 781 (Lee-on-Solent), 782 (Donibristle) and 799 (Machrihanish). (T.3): No.796 (St Merryn). *RNVR Squadrons:* Nos.1830 (Abbotsinch and Donibristle), 1831 (Stretton), 1833 (Bramcote and Honiley), 1840 (Ford), 1841 (Stretton), 1842 (Ford) and 1844 (Bramcote).

TECHNICAL DATA (FIREFLY T.1)

Description: Two-seat dual-control deck-landing conversion trainer. All-metal stressed-skin construction.
Manufacturers: Fairey Aviation Co Ltd, Stockport, Cheshire.
Power Plant: One 1,735 hp Rolls-Royce Griffon II or XII.
Dimensions: Span, 44 ft 6 in (13 ft 6 in folded). Length, 37 ft 7¼ in. Height, 13 ft 7 in. Wing area, 328 sq ft.
Weights: Empty, 9,647 lb. Loaded, 12,300 lb.
Performance: Maximum speed, 305 mph at 16,500 ft; 283 mph at sea level. Climb, 5.75 min to 10,000 ft. Range, 805 miles. Service ceiling, 28,000 ft.
Armament: A few aircraft with two 20-mm guns in wings; rest unarmed.

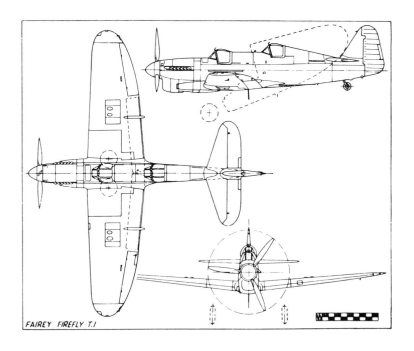

FAIREY FIREFLY T.1

Firefly A.S.7s of No.719 Squadron from Eglinton. *(Flight)*

Fairey Firefly (Mk.7)

The Firefly A.S.7 was produced as an interim anti-submarine aircraft pending the availability of the Gannet A.S.1 and subsequently, in its trainer version, became the last variant of the Firefly to be built, excluding radio-controlled target drones. Many airframe changes were incorporated in the Mk.7, making it readily distinguishable from earlier Fireflies. The full-span wing (though of modified plan-form) was revived and a deep beard radiator, larger than on the original Fireflies, mounted below the nose. Provision was made for a crew of three, with two radar operators in the rear cockpit, which had a large, bulged canopy similar to that of the Gannet. Most noticeable of all the changes was a completely revised tail.

In the event, the Firefly A.S.7 saw no service in first-line squadrons, and production was switched to the T.7 version, equipped for the training of observers. This variant flew from shore bases with second-line squadrons and had the deck-arrester gear deleted.

The prototype Firefly A.S.7 (WJ215) flew on 22 May 1951 and the first production aircraft (WJ146) on 16 October 1951.

Deliveries of Firefly Mk.7s totalled 137 when production ended in December 1953. Serial numbers were WJ146–174, WJ187–209, WK348–373, WM761–779, WM796–809, WM824–832, WM855 and WM864–879. They first entered service with No.719 Squadron at Eglinton in Northern Ireland in March 1953 which, together with No.750 Squadron, flew their Mk.7s in the massed fly-past of FAA aircraft in the Coronation Naval Review at Spithead on 15 June 1953.

The Firefly T.7s were last in service with No.796 Squadron at Culdrose where they remained until December 1957.

UNITS ALLOCATED

No.719 Squadron (Eglinton), No.750 Squadron (St Merryn and Culdrose), No.765

189

Squadron (Culdrose), No.796 Squadron (St Merryn and Culdrose) and No.1840 Squadron of the RNVR at Ford.

TECHNICAL DATA (FIREFLY A.S.7)

Description: Anti-submarine search aircraft with a crew of three. All-metal stressed-skin construction.

Manufacturers: Fairey Aviation Co Ltd, Hayes, Middlesex, and Stockport, Cheshire.

Power Plant: One 1,965 hp Rolls-Royce Griffon 59.

Dimensions: Span, 44 ft 6 in. Length, 38 ft 3 in. Height, 13 ft 3 in. Wing area, 342½ sq ft.

Weights: Empty, 11,016 lb. Loaded, 13,970 lb.

Performance: Maximum speed, 300 mph at 10,750 ft. Cruising speed, 257 mph. Climb, 1,550 ft/min. Range, 860 miles at 166 mph. Service ceiling, 25,500 ft.

Armament: None carried. Intended for search rôle only.

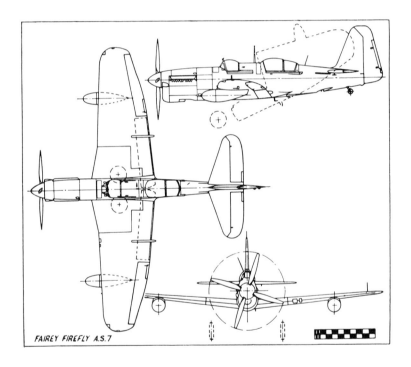

FAIREY FIREFLY A.S.7

Firefly U.8 (WP354) converted at Stockport. (*Fairey*)

Fairey Firefly U.8

The U.8 was a pilotless target drone version of the Mk.7 developed for duties in connection with guided missile tests. The first U.8 (WM810) flew on 30 December 1953 and the last (WP354) on 20 April 1956. This aircraft was to be the last of over 1,700 Fireflies of all variants built since 1941.

There were 52 Firefly U.8s, of which six (WJ147 and WJ149–153) were conversions of Mk.7s and the remainder (WM856–863, WM810–823, WM880–899 and WP351–354) new build.

Firefly U.8s served with No.728B Squadron in Malta in 1960–61.

Fairey Firefly U.9

Forty of these pilotless target drones (converted from Firefly 5 aircraft) were supplied to the Royal Navy. Equipped No.728B Squadron at RNAS Hal Far, Malta, to provide targets for Firestreak and Seaslug missiles, from July 1958 to November 1961. WB257 is illustrated.

Gannet A.S.1 (XA391) of No.820 Squadron from *Bulwark*. *(Flight)*

Fairey Gannet (Mks.1 to 5)

The Gannet, which from 1955 became the mainstay of the FAA's carrier-borne anti-submarine force, was the first aircraft in the world to fly with a double airscrew-turbine unit, providing all the qualities of a twin-engined aircraft with a single-engine configuration. This unusual characteristic offered special advantages for naval aviation. Each half of the Double Mamba engine could be controlled independently, shut down and its airscrew feathered, permitting all the economies of single-engined operation and extending the cruising range during normal patrol. When extra speed was needed, in combat, the thrust of both airscrews was immediately available again. Another advantage derived from the use of contra-rotating co-axial airscrews was that no asymmetric problems were encountered as with a normal twin-engined aircraft. Making the Gannet even more suitable for carrier operation was the fact that its Double Mamba engine was designed from the outset to run on kerosene, wide cut turbine fuel or naval diesel fuel. This assisted the Admiralty policy of eliminating petrol stowage in aircraft-carriers.

The Gannet was the first aircraft in FAA squadrons to combine the search and strike rôle: it was provided with an exceptionally capacious weapons bay, aft of which was installed a large retractable radar scanner. It is of interest to note that the Gannet was the first British-built naval aircraft to enter squadron service capable of carrying all its strike weapons (except wing-mounted rocket projectiles) internally. This included two homing torpedoes: all previous FAA torpedo-carriers had their weapon mounted externally, with the exception of the American-built Grumman Avenger.

The prototype Gannet, then known as the Fairey Type 'Q', was ordered by the Ministry of Supply on 12 August 1946. Like its unsuccessful competitor, the Blackburn Y.B.1 (also with a Double Mamba), it was built to the requirements of Spec G.R.17/45, and the first aircraft (VR546) was flown by Gp Capt Slade at Aldermaston on 19 September 1949. This and the second prototype (VR557, flown 6 July 1950) were two-seaters: meanwhile in June 1949 a third prototype equipped as a three-seater had been ordered. The first prototype reappeared on 13 March 1951—with a mock-up third cockpit and the radar scanner moved further aft; in June 1951 it was again modified and mounted auxiliary fins.

The third prototype (WE488) made its first flight on 10 May 1951, and was generally similar in appearance to subsequent production aircraft. All three prototypes underwent an intensive development and test programme, and on 19 June 1950, VR546 was landed aboard HMS *Illustrious* at sea. This was the first occasion on which a turbo-prop aircraft had ever landed aboard a carrier (the Blackburn Y.B.1 did not achieve this feat until 30 October 1950, also aboard *Illustrious*). During the carrier trials the three Gannet prototypes completed over 250 deck landings.

On 14 March 1951 the Gannet was ordered into quantity production under the 'Super-Priority' scheme, and the first production aircraft (WN339) was flown by Peter Twiss on 9 June 1953. First production Gannets, designated A.S.1, mounted the same Double Mamba (100) ASM.D.1 as the prototypes and were built at Hayes, assembled at Northolt and flown to White Waltham for collection by FAA pilots. From October 1954 Gannet A.S.1s (beginning WN370) also came off the Fairey assembly line at Stockport, being test-flown at Ringway. Total production of Gannet A.S.1s was 160, serials being in the ranges WN339–464, XA319–436 and XG784–795.

In October 1953 the first production Gannet A.S.1 successfully completed its carrier trials (some of them at night) and in April 1954 four Gannets (WN347, 348, 349 and 350) joined No.703X Flight of No.703 Squadron Service Trials Unit at Ford, Sussex, commanded by Lt-Cdr F E Cowtan. With Service trials completed, the first operational Gannet unit, No.826 Squadron, formed up at Lee-on-Solent on 17 January 1955. In February 1955 No.824 Squadron at Eglinton, Northern Ireland, also received Gannets. No.826 Squadron embarked in the new carrier *Eagle* in May 1955 and No.824 Squadron in *Ark Royal* in October 1955. In July 1955 the third Gannet squadron, No.825, was formed.

On 13 April 1956, the Gannet A.S.4 (beginning XA410) made its first flight. This aircraft, which succeeded the A.S.1 in production, differed from the earlier version in having the Double Mamba (101) ASM.D.3 and in detail changes. Prototype development of the A.S.4 took place with the converted A.S.1, WN372. With the Gannet A.S.4, the FAA completed its anti-submarine re-equipment programme, and this type supplanted all remaining Firefly A.S.6s and Avengers. A total of 56 A.S.4s was built, serialled between XA410 and XA473 and XG783 and XG832. Gannet A.S.4s first entered service with No.824 Squadron at Culdrose in October 1956.

When equipment of first-line squadrons had been fully completed, Gannets were also issued to the RNVR in place of Fireflies. One squadron (No.1840) had been so equipped when these units disbanded at the beginning of 1957.

From 1955 dual-control trainer versions of the Gannet were also supplied to the FAA. The first prototype Gannet T.2 (WN365, a converted A.S.1) made its initial flight on 16 August 1954, and 34 production aircraft were numbered XA508 to 530 and XG869 to 881. The Gannet T.2 differed from the A.S.1 in having no retractable radome, as well as in the installation of dual controls in the observer's cockpit and an additional periscope, retractable when the front hood opened. The second trainer variant, the Gannet T.5, made its maiden flight on 1 March 1957. Aircraft serialled XG869 to XG881 were converted T.2s. Gannet T.5s serialled XG882 to 889 were built as Mk.5s from the outset, all at Fairey's Hayes factory.

At the SBAC Show at Farnborough, Hampshire, in September 1957, FAA

Gannet T.2 (XA508) of No.737 Squadron from Eglinton. *(Flight)*

aircraft participated in strength for the first time, and it fell to 12 Gannets to provide a most effective fly-past in Royal Navy 'anchor' formation. The Gannets were drawn from Nos.737, 796 and 825 Squadrons.

From 1958, Gannets were gradually superseded in first-line anti-submarine duties by Whirlwind helicopters. The last on operational service were those of No.810 Squadron which made a final cruise in *Centaur* ending July 1960.

Gannets were also employed in the electronic counter-measures (ECM) rôle with No.831 Squadron, shore based at Culdrose and Watton from February 1961 to May 1966 and as ship to shore communications (COD) aircraft with the four flights of No.849 Squadron.

UNITS ALLOCATED

(A.S.1): No.812 Squadron (Eglinton and *Eagle*), No.815 Squadron (Eglinton, *Bulwark* and *Ark Royal*), No.816 Squadron (Culdrose and *Melbourne*), No.817 Squadron (Culdrose and *Melbourne*), No.820 Squadron (Eglinton and *Centaur*), No.824 Squadron (Brawdy and *Ark Royal*), No.825 Squadron (Culdrose and *Albion*), No.826 Squadron (Lee-on-Solent and *Eagle*), No.847 Squadron (Eglinton and Cyprus) and No.1840 Squadron of the RNVR at Ford. (A.S.4): No.810 Squadron (Culdrose and *Centaur*), No.814 Squadron (Culdrose, Eglinton and Eagle), No.815 Squadron (Culdrose and *Ark Royal*), No.824 Squadron (Culdrose, *Ark Royal* and *Albion*), No.825 Squadron (Culdrose), No.847 Squadron (Cyprus) and No.849 Squadron. *Second-line squadrons:*

Gannet C.O.D.4 (XG786) of HMS *Eagle. (Aviation Photo News)*

194

(A.S.1): Nos.700, 703, 719, 724, 725, 737, 744 and 796. (A.S.4): No.700. (T.2): Nos.700, 719, 724, 725, 728, 737 and 796. Some T.2s also issued to Nos.812, 816, 820, 824, 825 and 1840 Squadrons and T.5s to No.849 Squadron.

TECHNICAL DATA (GANNET A.S.1 AND A.S.4)

Description: Carrier-borne anti-submarine search and strike aircraft with a crew of three. All-metal stressed-skin construction.

Manufacturers: Fairey Aviation Co Ltd, Hayes, Middlesex, and Stockport, Cheshire.

Power Plant (A.S.1): One 2,950 ehp Armstrong Siddeley Double Mamba 100. (A.S.4): One 3,035 ehp Armstrong Siddeley Double Mamba 101.

Dimensions: Span, 54 ft 4 in. Length, 43 ft 0 in. Height, 13 ft 8½ in (or 13 ft 9 in with power-operated double-hinged wings in folded position).

Weights: Empty, 15,069 lb. Loaded, 22,506 lb.

Performance: (A.S.4). Maximum speed, 299 mph. Initial climb, 2,000 ft/min. Service ceiling, 25,000 ft. Range, 662 miles. Endurance, 4.9 hr cruising at 150 mph.

Armament: Provision in bomb-bay for two homing torpedoes; parachute mines, depth charges or four 1,000 lb bombs. Also provision for 16 60 lb rocket projectiles below the wings.

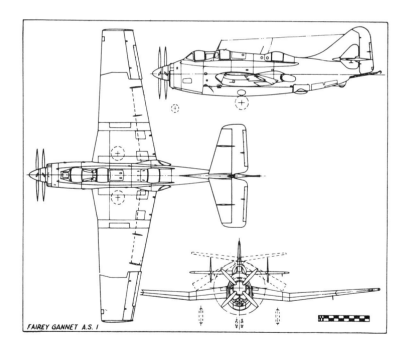

FAIREY GANNET A.S. I

Gannet A.E.W.3 (XL450) of No.849 Squadron from HMS *Ark Royal.*

Fairey Gannet A.E.W.3

Derived from earlier anti-submarine versions of the Gannet, the A.E.W.3 was designed as a replacement for the Douglas Skyraider, which had been the standard airborne early warning aircraft of the Royal Navy since 1953.

The Gannet A.E.W.3 introduced a completely new fuselage incorporating a large 'guppy' radome, a new fin and rudder and a more powerful Double Mamba engine with shortened jet pipes. The first prototype (XJ440) made its maiden flight at Northolt on 20 August 1958, and the first production aircraft (XL449) first flew on 2 December 1958. The second, fully-equipped, production aircraft followed from the Hayes factory in January 1959.

Initial deck-landing trials began on 18 November 1958 with XJ440 on HMS *Centaur* and proving was undertaken by No.700G Flight (Lt-Cdr W Hawley, RN) which received its first aircraft at RNAS Culdrose, Cornwall, on 17 August 1959. Trials were completed on 31 January 1960, and on the following day the unit was re-designated No.849A Flight, signifying the entry of the A.E.W.3 into first-line service. No.849 Squadron, 'A' Flight, embarked in *Ark Royal* in February 1960.

The A.E.W.3 was used by aircraft-carrier task forces to extend the range of their defensive radar system. By carrying radar search equipment into the air, the A.E.W.3 overcame the line of sight limitations of radar beams which cannot 'bend' over the horizon. When acting in the air defence rôle, the A.E.W.3 provided early warning of low-flying reconnaissance or strike aircraft and was also employed for Strike Direction, Anti-Submarine Warfare and Surface Search and Shadowing. It was one of the most highly utilised aircraft in the Royal Navy, and the 18 A.E.W.3s of No.849 Squadron's 'A', 'B', 'C' and 'D' Flights (plus a Headquarters Flight) averaged well over 40 hours flying per aircraft per month during their operational heyday.

The A.E.W.3 accommodated two observers who sat side-by-side in the fuselage behind the pilot.

Deliveries were completed in June 1963 after 44 had been supplied to the Royal Navy. Serials allocated were XL449 to 456, XL471 to 482, XL493 to 503, XP197 to 199, XP224 to 229 and XR431 to 433.

In the summer of 1970, Gannets XL482, XL494, XP229 and XR433 went to sea with the freshly-commissioned HMS *Ark Royal*, the last Fairey aircraft to serve on first-line duties with the Fleet Air Arm. These aircraft served with *Ark Royal* until the carrier was phased out in 1978. The last A.E.W.3 was refurbished by Westland at Weston-super-Mare early in 1976.

UNITS ALLOCATED

No.849 Squadron with four operational flights (disposed one per carrier) and a permanent shore base at Culdrose (to December 1964), Brawdy (to November 1970) and Lossiemouth (to December 1978).

TECHNICAL DATA (GANNET A.E.W.3)

Description: Three-seat, carrier-borne airborne early warning reconnaissance aircraft. All-metal stressed-skin construction.
Manufacturers: Fairey Aviation Co Ltd, Hayes, Middlesex.
Power Plant: One 3,875 ehp Armstrong Siddeley Double Mamba 102.
Dimensions: Span, 54 ft 4 in. Length, 44 ft 0 in. Height, 16 ft 10 in.
Weights: Empty, 16,960 lb. Loaded, 25,000 lb.
Performance: Maximum speed, 250 mph. Initial climb, 2,200 ft/min. Range, 800 miles. Endurance, 5 to 6 hr cruising at 130 to 140 mph. Service ceiling, 25,000 ft.

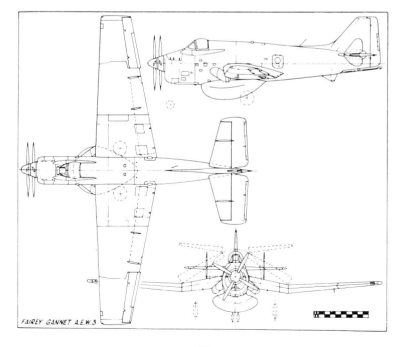

FAIREY GANNET A.E.W.3

F.2A (N4545) from Felixstowe. *(Imperial War Museum)*

Felixstowe F.2A

Though it saw action only during the last year of the First World War, the F.2A earned a reputation comparable with that of the Sunderland in the Second World War. By virtue of its great endurance and heavy defensive armament, it bore the brunt of the long-range anti-submarine and anti-Zeppelin patrols over the North Sea in 1918 and figured in innumerable fights with German seaplanes; the exploits of Great Yarmouth's boats were typical, and are related at length in C F Snowden Gamble's classic, *The Story of a North Sea Air Station*. It established the trend of British flying-boat design for two decades and was a triumphant justification of the pioneer work of John Porte, who had from 1914 devoted himself unceasingly to the development of the flying-boat as a weapon of war.

The F.2A was the first of the Felixstowe boats to be widely used by the RNAS. The first of the series was the F.1 (No.3580), which combined the Porte I type of hull with the wings and tail assembly of a Curtiss H.4. This was an experimental design only and was not put into quantity production. The success of the Porte I hull was such that it was decided to build a larger one on the same principles which could be married to the wings and tail assembly of the Curtiss H.12 Large America. The outcome of this idea was the Felixstowe F.2, the immediate forerunner of the F.2A. The Porte-type hulls offered greater seaworthiness than had been the case with the Curtiss hulls, yet their method of construction was such that they could be produced by firms with no previous boat-building experience. This was an obvious asset at a period of the war when the need for greater numbers of flying-boats for anti-submarine patrol was becoming urgent.

The first F.2A flying-boats were delivered late in 1917, and by March 1918 some 160 had been ordered; by the Armistice just under 100 had been completed, and in the immediate post-war period some aircraft ordered under these contracts were converted on the production line to F.5 flying-boats. The total production of 180 would undoubtedly have been greater if a decision had not been taken by the Admiralty to issue extensive contracts for the F.3, a flying-boat in some respects inferior to the F.2A. As the F.2A had originally been intended for operation from sheltered harbours, it was necessary to make some structural modifications to the hull when its use became more widespread and indiscriminate. Nevertheless, the F.2A stood up well to harsh operational conditions, and such setbacks as it had were due not to lack of seaworthiness, but rather to the inadequacies of the fuel system, for the windmill-driven piston pumps failed all too frequently.

One of the great advantages of the F.2A in view of its considerable range (some boats stayed airborne for as long as 9¼ hours by carrying extra petrol in cans) was the provision of dual control; this had not been available on earlier types, such as the H.12. Modifications to the boats to suit the ideas of individual air stations were quite common; one of the most noteworthy was the removal of the cabin for the pilot and second pilot, leaving an open cockpit. This improved both visibility and performance, and from about September 1918 was incorporated in aircraft as they left the works.

F.2As of the Felixstowe air station inherited from the Curtiss H.12s the historic 'Spider's Web' patrol system. This patrol began in April 1917, and was centred on the North Hinder Light Vessel, which was used as a navigation mark. Flying-boats operated within an imaginary octagonal figure, 60 sea-miles across, and followed a pre-arranged pattern which enabled about 4,000 square miles of sea to be searched systematically. One flying-boat could search a quarter of the whole web in about three hours, and stood a good chance of sighting a U-boat on the surface, as submarines had to economise on battery power. Moreover, flying-boats had the advantage over other heavier-than-air anti-submarine aircraft in that they could carry bombs of 230 lb, which could seriously damage a submarine, even if a direct hit were not secured.

F.2A on ocean patrol. *(Imperial War Museum)*

The F.2A, despite its five-and-a-half tons, could be thrown about the sky in a 'dog-fight' with enemy seaplanes, and on 4 June 1918 there occurred one of the greatest air battles of the war, waged near the enemy coastline, over three hours' flying time from the RNAS bases at Great Yarmouth and Felixstowe. The formation of flying-boats, led by Capt R Leckie, consisted of four F.2As (N4295 and N4298 from Great Yarmouth and N4302 and N4533 from Felixstowe) and a Curtiss H.12. One F.2A (N4533) was forced down before the engagement, due to the old trouble of a blocked fuel line, but the remaining F.2As fought with a force of 14 enemy seaplanes and shot six of them down. During the action another F.2A (N4302) was forced down with a broken fuel pipe, but a repair was effected, and finally three F.2As returned triumphantly to base having suffered only one casualty. Following this action, in which the danger of being forced down on the sea with fuel-pipe trouble became only too evident, it was decided to paint the hulls of the F.2As in distinctive colours for ready recognition. Great Yarmouth boats were painted to the crews' own liking, and some bizarre schemes resulted; Felixstowe, on the other hand, imposed a standardised scheme of coloured squares and stripes. The scheme of each individual F.2A was charted, and copies were held by all air and naval units operating off the East Coast.

The F.2a was also successful against Zeppelins. The most remarkable of these engagements was on 10 May 1918, when N4291 from Killingholme, flown by Capts T C Pattinson and A H Munday, attacked the Zeppelin L62 at 8,000 ft over the Heligoland minefields and shot it down in flames. Some F.2As, operating as far afield as Heligoland, were towed to the scene of action on lighters behind destroyers. This technique was first employed on 10 March 1918, and was originally part of a scheme to extend the flying-boats' range so as to mount a bombing offensive on enemy naval bases.

One variation of the F.2A was built with the designation F.2C (N65); it had a

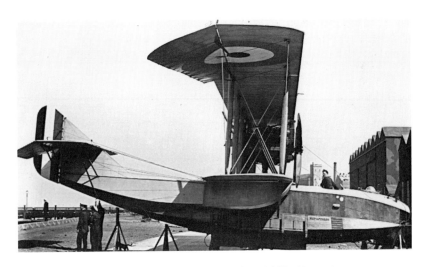

The Felixstowe F.2C flying-boat. *(Imperial War Museum)*

F.2A flying-boats on the slipway at a coastal air station of the RNAS. *(Imperial War Museum)*

modified hull of lighter construction and alterations to the front gun position. Although only one F.2C was produced, it saw active service with the RNAS at Felixstowe. The F.2C, flown by Wg Cdr J C Porte, the famous flying-boat pioneer, shared the credit with two other flying-boats in the same formation for the destruction of a U-boat.

UNITS ALLOCATED

No.228 Squadron (ex-324, 325 and 326 Flights) at Great Yarmouth; Nos.230, 231, 232 and 247 Squadrons (ex-327, 328, 329, 330, 333, 334, 335, 336, 337 and 338 Flights) at Felixstowe; No.238 Squadron (ex-347, 348 and 349 Flights) at Cattewater; No.240 Squadron (ex-345, 346, 410 and 411 Flights) at Calshot; No.257 Squadron (ex-318 and 319 Flights) at Dundee and No.267 Squadron (ex-360, 361, 362 and 363 Flights) at Kalafrana. Also Nos.320, 321 and 322 Flights at Killingholme.

TECHNICAL DATA (F.2A)

Description: Fighting and reconnaissance flying-boat with a crew of four. Wooden structure, with wood and fabric covering.

Manufacturers: Aircraft Manufacturing Co Ltd, Hendon (with hulls from May, Harden & May, Southampton); S E Saunders Ltd, Isle of Wight; Norman Thompson Flight Co, Bognor Regis. Serial numbers allocated were N4080 to N4099, N4280 to N4309, N4430 to N4504, N4510 to N4519, N4530 to N4554 and N4560 to N4568, but some aircraft were eventually delivered as F.5s.

Power Plant: Two 345 hp Rolls-Royce Eagle VIII

Dimensions: Span, 95 ft 7½ in. Length, 46 ft 3 in. Height, 17 ft 6 in. Wing area, 1,133 sq ft.

Weights: Empty, 7,549 lb. Loaded, 10,978 lb.

Performance: Maximum speed, 95½ mph at 2,000 ft; 80½ mph at 10,000 ft. Climb, 3 min 50 sec to 2,000 ft; 39 min 30 sec to 10,000 ft. Endurance (normal) 6 hr. Service ceiling, 9,600 ft.

Armament: From four to seven free-mounted Lewis machine-guns (in bows, waist positions, rear cockpit and above pilot's cockpit) and two 230 lb bombs mounted in racks below the bottom wings.

F.2A flying-boat N4297 from Felixstowe. *(Imperial War Museum)*

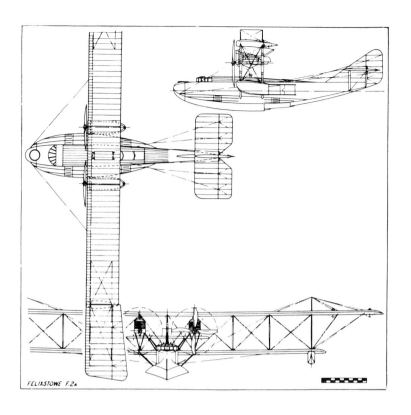

FELIXSTOWE F.2A

203

F.3 (N4230) built by Dick, Kerr & Co Ltd. *(Imperial War Museum)*

Felixstowe F.3

It is generally conceded that the F.3, though the subject of large-scale production contracts (263 ordered and 176 delivered), was in many respects the inferior of the F.2A. Admittedly it could carry twice as many bombs, but it was slower and less manoeuvrable, and hence lacked the qualities which had enabled the F.2A to take on German seaplane fighters in air combat. On the other hand, it was capable of a greater range. It first entered service in February 1918 and was not declared obsolete until September 1921.

The prototype F.3 (N64) differed from production aircraft in having twin 320 hp Sunbeam Cossack engines instead of Rolls-Royce Eagles. It is recorded that it served operationally during 1917–18 with the Royal Naval air station at Felixstowe. It made its maiden flight in February 1917 and was finally written off in May 1918.

The F.3 operated extensively in the Mediterranean, and in October 1918 accompanied the Naval attack on Durazzo in Albania. The operational requirements for anti-submarine flying-boats in the Mediterranean area were, in fact, so pressing that manufacture of F.3 flying-boats was undertaken locally in Malta dockyards. Twenty-three were built in Malta between November 1917 and the Armistice.

UNITS ALLOCATED

No.234 Squadron (ex-350, 351, 352 and 353 Flights) at Tresco; No.238 Squadron (ex-347, 348 and 349 Flights) at Cattewater; No.263 Squadron (ex-359, 435, 436 and 441 Flights) at Otranto; No.267 Squadron (ex-360, 361, 362 and 363 Flights) at Kalafrana and No.271 Squadron (ex-357, 350, 359 and 367 Flights) at Taranto. Also No.300 Flight at Catforth, Nos.306 and 307 Flights at Houton and Nos.309, 310 and 311 Flights at Stenness.

TECHNICAL DATA (FELIXSTOWE F.3)

Description: Anti-submarine patrol flying-boat with a crew of four. Wooden structure, with wood and fabric covering.

Manufacturers: Short Bros Ltd, Rochester (N4000 to N4036); Dick, Kerr & Co
　　Ltd, Preston (N4100 to N4117 and N4230 to N4279); Phoenix Dynamo
　　Manufacturing Co Ltd, Bradford (N4160 to N4176 and N4400 to N4429);
　　Malta Dockyard (N4310 to N4321 and N4360 to N4370).
Power Plant: Two 345 hp Rolls-Royce Eagle VIII.
Dimensions: Span, 102 ft. Length, 49 ft 2 in. Height, 18 ft 8 in. Wing area,
　　1,432 sq ft.
Weights: Empty, 7,958 lb. Loaded (normal), 12,235 lb.
Performance: Maximum speed, 91 mph at 2,000 ft; 86 mph at 6,500 ft. Climb,
　　5¼ min to 2,000 ft; 24 min to 6,500 ft. Endurance, 6 hr. Service ceiling,
　　8,000 ft.
Armament: Four Lewis machine-guns on free mountings and four 230 lb bombs
　　on racks beneath the wings.

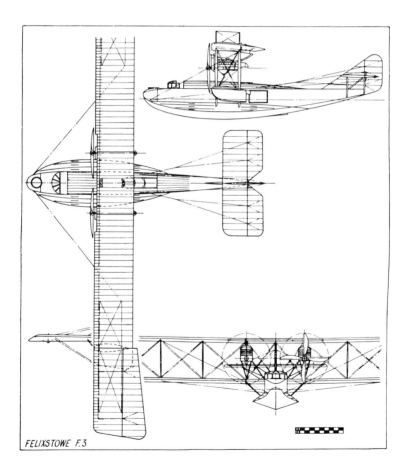

FELIXSTOWE F.3

Sea Gladiator (N5567) of No.805 Squadron which fought at Crete. (*RAF Museum*)

Gloster Sea Gladiator

Just as the Gladiator was the last biplane fighter of the RAF, so was the Sea Gladiator the last of its kind in the FAA. It differed little from its RAF counterpart, except in the installation of catapult points, a deck-arrester hook and a collapsible dinghy in a fairing beneath the fuselage between the undercarriage legs.

First production orders were placed in June 1938 at a time when the FAA was badly in need of a new carrier fighter to replace the Hawker Nimrods which had served since 1932.

Sixty Sea Gladiators (N5500 to N5549 and N5565 to N5574) were specially built for the FAA. There were also 38 interim versions (N2265 to N2302) converted from RAF Gladiators. First deliveries were made to RNAS Worthy Down in December 1938 and to Donibristle in February 1939. In May 1939, Sea Gladiators replaced Nimrods and Ospreys in No.802 Squadron in HMS *Glorious*. By September 1939, the FAA had a total of 54 Sea Gladiators in service.

During 1940 Sea Gladiators fought both in the North Sea and in the Mediterranean. In August, during the naval bombardment of Bardia, Sea Gladiators of No.813 Squadron in *Eagle* provided effective fighter protection for the spotting Swordfish, and in the Norwegian campaign Sea Gladiators of No.804 Squadron in *Glorious* went into action against the *Luftwaffe*, providing fighter patrols whilst ferrying the RAF Gladiators of No.263 Squadron to Norway. By May 1941, however, the Sea Gladiator had completed first-line service in aircraft-carriers.

As is now well known, six Sea Gladiators borrowed from the FAA and flown by the RAF (N5519, N5520, N5523, N5524, N5529 and N5531) operated alongside Hurricanes in Malta from 11 to 28 June 1940.

Although Sea Gladiators served with eight first-line squadrons, they only ever formed the sole equipment of one, namely No.802. In July 1940, four Sea Gladiators were added to No.813's Swordfish in *Eagle* to form what was then the only fighter defence of the Mediterranean Fleet. The average number of Sea Gladiators embarked in carriers was only 15 at any one time throughout 1940. By mid-1941 they had been wholly superseded by Martlets and Sea Hurricanes.

UNITS ALLOCATED

No.801 Squadron (Donibristle and *Courageous*), No.802 Squadron (*Glorious* and *Eagle*), No.804 Squadron (Wick, Hatston, *Glorious* and *Furious*), No.805 Squadron (Egypt), No.806 Squadron (Egypt and *Illustrious*), No.813 Squadron (*Eagle* and *Illustrious*), No.880 Squadron (Arbroath) and No.885 Squadron (Egypt). *Second-line squadrons:* Nos.759, 760, 767, 769, 770 , 771, 775, 778, 787, 791 and 797.

TECHNICAL DATA (SEA GLADIATOR)

Description: Single-seat carrier-borne fighter. Metal structure, with fabric and metal covering.
Manufacturers: Gloster Aircraft Co Ltd, Hucclecote, Gloucester.
Power Plant: One 840 hp Bristol Mercury VIIIA.
Dimensions: Span 32 ft 3in. Length 27 ft 5 in. Height, 10 ft 4 in. Wing area, 323 sq ft.

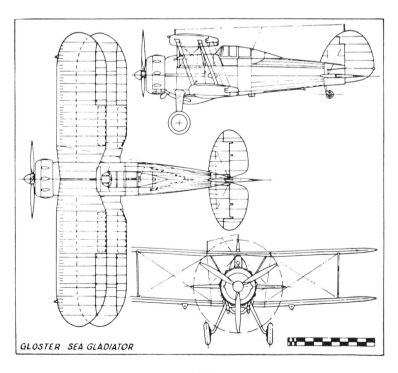

GLOSTER SEA GLADIATOR

Weights: Empty, 3,745 lb. Loaded, 5,020 lb.

Performance Maximum speed, 245 mph at 15,000 ft. Cruising speed, 212 mph at 15,000 ft. Initial climb, 2,300 ft/min; 2 min 30 sec to 5,000 ft; 4 min 30 sec to 10,000 ft; 6 min 45 sec to 15,000 ft. Range, 320 nautical miles. Endurance, 2 hr 20 min. Service ceiling, 32,000 ft.

Armament: Four fixed Browning guns: two mounted in wings and two in fuselage.

Sea Gladiator (N5517) which did trials with No.801 Squadron in HMS *Courageous* in 1939.

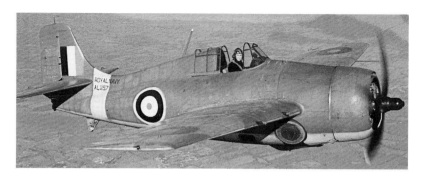

Martlet I (AL257) of No.804 Squadron, Hatston. *(Imperial War Museum)*

Grumman Martlet (Mks.I to III)

One of the Grumman Martlet's chief claims to fame is that it was the first type of American fighter in service with British forces to shoot down a German aircraft in the Second World War. This notable event occurred on 25 December 1940 and two Martlets (BJ515 and BJ562) of No.804 Squadron were involved. Flown by Lt L V Carver, RN, and Sub-Lt (A) Parke, RNVR, the Martlets were on patrol over the Home Fleet base at Scapa Flow, when they intercepted and forced down a Junkers Ju 88 attempting to bomb the Fleet. The crew of four from the Ju 88 was captured. So began the Martlet's long and fruitful career with the FAA.

The Martlet was the British version of the US Navy and Marine Corps F4F-3, and was ordered for the FAA at the same time that it was accepted for service in the US Services. It was known to its manufacturers as the G-36, and was the latest of a long line of successful Grumman fighters for the US Navy, though it differed from all its predecessors in being a monoplane. Grumman's association with US Navy fighters began with their two-seat FF-1 biplane of 1931 and developed through the F2F-1 single-seater of 1935 and the F3F-1, a 1936 derivative. All these biplanes were characterised by the tubby fuselage later to be seen on the F4F monoplane, and were unusual in their day in employing a retractable undercarriage: the 27 FF-1 fighters which went aboard *Ranger* in 1934 were the first aircraft with retractable undercarriage ever seen aboard a carrier.

Grumman's new monoplane fighter made its first flight on 2 September 1937, and in 1940 the US Navy placed an initial contract for 78 F4F-3s, as the production version was designated, to supersede the Grumman F3F-3, which was the last biplane fighter in US Navy squadrons. The F4F-3 was a notable advance in US naval fighters, offering as it did about 310 mph against the F3F-3 biplane's 270 mph and four 0.50-calibre guns in place of two of 0.30 calibre. In 1941 the US Navy named the type the Wildcat, but Martlet was retained as the British nomenclature until January 1944.

With the entry of the USA into the war in December 1941, the Wildcat was the most widely-used fighter aboard US aircraft-carriers, and it also equipped numbers of shore-based units of the US Marine Corps. It was one of the latter units—Marine Fighting Squadron 211—which defended Wake Island so heroically against the Japanese in an action strongly reminiscent of the *Faith, Hope* and *Charity* epic with Sea Gladiators in Malta. The first six British Martlets (AX824 to 829) arrived at Prestwick in August 1940.

With the FAA, Martlets first entered service with No.804 Squadron at Hatston on 8 September 1940, superseding Sea Gladiators. These aircraft were drawn from a batch of 91 ex-French Martlet I (AL231 to 262, AX725 to 747, AX824 to 829, BJ507 to 527 and BJ554 to 570). The Martlet I had fixed wings, a single-row Wright Cyclone engine and mounted four machine-guns. It was followed from March 1941 by 100 Martlet IIs powered by the two-row Pratt & Whitney Twin Wasp engine. By virtue of its folding wings, the Martlet II was the first of the series to be embarked in British aircraft-carriers. The first ten (AM954–963) had fixed wings but the remaining 90 (AM964–999 and AJ100–153) were folding. A further batch of Martlet fighters comprised 30 Mk.III aircraft from a former Greek contract. The Martlet III was similar to the Martlet II except that it had fixed wings, as on the Martlet I. Total production of Martlets I to III was 221.

First to go to sea with Martlets was No.802 Squadron, whose aircraft were embarked in *Argus* in August 1941 on a convoy to Murmansk and then on board the small escort carrier HMS *Audacity*, a converted German merchant-ship of 5,600 tons, during her first trip in September 1941, escorting a Gibraltar-bound convoy. On 19 September the Martlets attacked a U-boat with machine-gun fire, forcing it to submerge, and the next day succeeded in shooting down a Focke-Wulf Fw 200 four-engined bomber which had been shadowing the convoy. The two Martlets responsible were flown by Sub-Lts N H Patterson and G R P Fletcher. During the second voyage by *Audacity*, in November 1941, No.802 Squadron's Martlets destroyed four Focke-Wulf Fw 200 bombers, and in one day alone flew a total of 30 hr. On this hectic day the last two Martlets to return to *Audacity* had to land in the dark whilst the ship was rolling 14 degrees.

In May 1942 Martlets of Nos.881 and 882 Squadrons, both embarked in *Illustrious*, added to their growing reputation as formidable fighting aircraft during operations over Madagascar. On 6 May Martlets patrolled the beaches, carried out tactical reconnaissances for the Army and ground-straffed enemy positions holding up the advance. They also shot down three Potez 63 bombers without loss to themselves. The next day there were numerous air combats between the Martlets and Vichy French Moranes, and in the whole three days of fighting the Martlets shot down seven enemy aircraft for the loss of only one, as well as having given the landing parties complete air cover.

In August 1942 Martlets of No.806 Squadron in *Indomitable* sailed with one of the famous Malta convoys and were in action against Italian bombers over the Mediterranean. The following November, with the Allied invasion of North Africa, Martlets were in the thick of the fighting once more. Again they covered the troops going ashore in assault craft and attacked machine-gun posts along the beaches. It was during these operations that a Martlet of No.882 Squadron, from *Victorious*, took the surrender of the French fighter airfield at Blida, about 30 miles from Algiers. Whilst on patrol over the airfield, Lt B H C Nation noticed some French officers signalling. He landed, was greeted by the Commandant, and handed a formal surrender.

Martlet II (AJ132) of No.881 Squadron. *(Imperial War Museum)*

As well as operating with great success from carriers, Martlets from an ex-Greek contract (delivered via Gibraltar) also took part in the air operations over the Western Desert from the formation of the Royal Naval Fighter Unit in September 1941. First Martlet victory in North Africa was on 28 September 1941 whhen Sub Lt W M Walsh shot down a Fiat G.50 while escorting Maryland bombers.

In all these operations the Martlet proved itself a sturdy and reliable aircraft. In the words of one pilot:

'It was manoeuvrable and could turn inside any aircraft it met. It dived at 390 to 400 mph with no trouble at all. The Twin Wasp was a most reliable engine and one Martlet was, apart from routine inspections, never once unserviceable in twelve months of operations. On completion of 190 hours' flying in *Illustrious* its engine was running as well as ever. The heavy calibre guns meant that fifty rounds per gun frequently sufficed to shoot down an enemy aircraft.'

The only surviving Martlet in the United Kingdom (AL246) is preserved in the FAA Museum at Yeovilton, Somerset.

UNITS ALLOCATED

(Mk.I): No.802 Squadron (Donibristle, *Audacity, Victorious* and *Argus*), No.804 Squadron (Hatston, Yeovilton and *Furious*), No.805 Squadron (North Africa), No.806 Squadron (*Indomitable*), No.880 Squadron (Arbroath), No.881 Squadron (Lee-on-Solent), No.882 Squadron (Donibristle, *Illustrious* and *Archer*), No.888 Squadron (Lee-on-Solent and St Merryn), No.893 Squadron (Donibristle and *Archer*), No.1832 Squadron (Eglinton and Speke). *Second-line squadrons:* Nos.738, 748, 759, 760, 762, 767, 768, 778, 781, 787 and 795. (Mk.II): No.802 Squadron (*Argus, Victorious* and *Audacity*), No.806 Squadron (*Indomitable*), No.881 Squadron (Lee-on-Solent and *Illustrious*), No.882 Squadron (*Archer* and *Illustrious*), No.888 Squadron (St Merryn, Lee-on-Solent and *Formidable*), and No.1832 Squadron (Eglinton, Speke and Stretton). *Second-line squadrons:* Nos.768, 778, 787 and 795. (Mk.III): No.802 Squadron (Macrihanish, *Audacity, Argus* and *Victorious*).

TECHNICAL DATA (MARTLET I AND II)

Description: Single-seat carrier-borne or shore-based fighter. All-metal stressed-skin construction.

Manufacturers: Grumman Aircraft Engineering Corporation, Bethpage, Long Island, New York.

Power Plant: (Mk.I): One 1,240 hp Wright Cyclone G-205A. (Mk.II): One 1,200 hp Pratt & Whitney Twin Wasp S3C4-G.

Dimensions: Span, 38 ft. Length, 28 ft 10 in. Height 9 ft 2½ in. Wing area, 260 sq ft.

Weights: (Mk.I): Empty, 5,000 lb. Loaded, 6,607 lb. (Mk.II): Empty, 5,168 lb. Loaded, 7,255 lb.

Performance: (Mk.I): Maximum speed, 304 mph. Cruising speed, 247 mph. Climb, 2,140 ft/min. Range, 830 miles. Service ceiling, 30,800 ft. (Mk.II): Maximum speed, 300 mph. Cruising speed, 246 mph. Climb, 2,030 ft/min. Range, 830 miles. Service ceiling, 30,500 ft.

Armament: (Mk.I): Four fixed 0.50-calibre guns in wings. (Mk.II): Six fixed 0.50-calibre guns in wings.

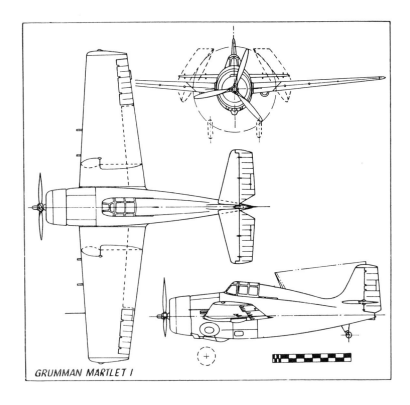

GRUMMAN MARTLET I

Wildcat V (JV579) of No.846 Squadron from *Trumpeter*.

Grumman Wildcat (Mks.IV to VI)

Unlike the earlier Martlets delivered to the FAA in 1940 and 1941, the Martlet IV and subsequent fighters in the series were not bought by the British Government, but were supplied under Lend-Lease arrangements. Both the Martlet IV and V were known as such until January 1944, when the name was changed to Wildcat to conform with US Navy nomenclature. The Wildcat VI, which entered service after this date, was known from the outset under this name. For the sake of simplicity, the name Wildcat is used throughout the following narrative.

The Wildcat IV was the FAA equivalent of the US Navy's F4F-4B. It was generally similar to the Mk.II, but had two additional wing guns, making a total of six, and reverted to the Cyclone engine. The total of aircraft supplied was 220, the serial numbers allocated being FN100 to 319. Deliveries began in 1942.

The Wildcat V, which followed in 1943, was the British equivalent of the US Navy's FM-1, the new designation signifying that the aircraft were built by the Eastern Aircraft Division of the General Motors Corporation, instead of the parent company. Grumman had by this time tapered off Wildcat production (after building about 1,600) in favour of the new Hellcat. Thereafter all Wildcats came from the General Motors plant, where about 5,500 were built before VJ-Day. Total deliveries of the Wildcat V to the FAA amounted to 312 aircraft, with serial numbers JV325 to 636. The Mk.V re-introduced the Twin Wasp engine.

Wildcat IV and V fighters served for the most part in MAC-ships, the light escort carriers built in the USA, which made such an invaluable contribution to victory in the Battle of the Atlantic. Some of the later Wildcats, however, also saw action from the larger carriers, notably in *Illustrious* during the Salerno landings, and in *Victorious* for operations in the South West Pacific.

In the escort carriers the Wildcats worked mainly in conjunction with Swordfish. Their rôle was to provide fighter protection for convoys and to assist the Swordfish in their rocket strikes on submarines, by diverting the attention of the U-boat's gun-team whilst the strike aircraft made its run. The first squadron equipped with the Wildcat IV was No.892, which took delivery of six aircraft at Norfolk, Virginia, on 15 July 1942. It subsequently embarked in the escort carriers *Battler* and *Archer*. The Wildcat IVs were joined in 1943 by Wildcat Vs, and by the middle of 1944 there were about 15 squadrons in the escort carrier force flying these fighters. Some of them saw action in the North Russian convoy escorts: Wildcats of No.813 Squadron (also equipped with 12 Swordfish) shot down two enemy aircraft during the convoy of September 1944. Wildcats from escort carriers were also active in the invasion of the South of France by the Allies: No.882 Squadron, in *Searcher* flew 167 sorties over the landing-beaches between 15 and 23 August 1944, and others, from No.881 Squadron, were flown off from *Pursuer*. Wildcats were also called upon to provide fighter escorts for Barracudas during the series of dive-bombing raids on *Tirpitz* in 1944, the squadrons engaged being Nos. 881, 896 and 898. In subsequent operations over Norway from *Searcher* No.898 Squadron Wildcats shot down four Blohm und Voss Bv 138 flying-boats and a Focke-Wulf Fw 200, which were engaged on reconnaissance sorties.

During the Allied landings at Salerno in September 1943 Wildcats of Nos.878 and 890 Squadrons (both embarked in *Illustrious*) maintained constant patrols

Wildcat IV (FN142) of No.893 Squadron. *(Imperial War Museum)*

Wildcat VI (JV642). *(Crown Copyright)*

214

over the beaches, sharing this task with Seafires from the light escort carriers *Attacker, Battler, Hunter* and *Stalker*.

In June 1944 Wildcats of No.846 Squadron participated in the widespread fighter activities over the landing-zones during the D-Day operations. A few weeks previously a Wildcat V of this same squadron had shared, with an Avenger and a Swordfish, in the sinking of *U-288*.

Shortly after D-Day a new version of the Wildcat, the Mk.VI, began to enter FAA squadrons. This was the last variant to be supplied for British service, and was the equivalent of the US Navy's FM-2. It could be easily distinguished from earlier Wildcats by reason of its modified tail design, with much taller fin and rudder. The Wildcat VI also marked a return to the Wright Cyclone engine. This Cyclone was a much-improved version incorporating a turbo-supercharger and developing 1,350 hp.

A total of 370 Wildcat VI fighters was supplied under Lend-Lease, the serial numbers allocated being JV637 to 924 and JW785 to 836. The Wildcat VI first entered service in the FAA with No.881 Squadron in June 1944, embarked in *Fencer*. This variant served chiefly in the Far East. Production ended in August 1945 after 1,123 Wildcats of all variants had been supplied to the Royal Navy.

The FAA's last victory over German fighters was on 26 March 1945 when Wildcat VIs of No.882 destroyed five Bf 109s over Norway. No.882's Wildcats also took part in the last FAA combat in Europe (against Ju 88s) off Denmark on 8 May 1945.

UNITS ALLOCATED

(Mk.IV): No.805 (Eastleigh), No.811 (Hatston and *Biter*), No.819 (St Merryn, *Archer* and *Activity*), No.878 (Lee-on-Solent and *Illustrious*), No.881 (*Illustrious*), No.882 (*Illustrious* and *Victorious*), No.888 (Hatston and *Formidable*), No.890 (*Battler* and *Illustrious*), No.892 (*Battler* and *Archer*), No.893 (Hatston and *Formidable*), No.894 (*Battler*), No.896 (*Victorious*), No.898 (*Victorious*) and No.1832 (Speke and Stretton). *Second-line squadrons:* Nos.700, 719, 738, 748, 759, 768, 771, 772, 778, 787, 794 and 795. (Mk.V): No.813 (Maydown and *Campania*), No.816 (Donibristle and *Chaser*), No.819 (Macrihanish, Lee-on-Solent and Manston), No.824 (Hatston and *Striker*), No.832 (Macrihanish, *Illustrious* and *Begum*), No.883 (*Activity*), No.842 (*Fencer, Furious* and *Indefatigable*), No.845 (*Illustrious, Ameer, Begum* and *Empress*), No.846 (*Tracker* and *Trumpeter*), No.850 (Limavady), No.851 (*Unicorn* and *Shah*), No.852 (*Nabob* and *Trumpeter*), No.853 (*Arbiter, Formidable* and *Tracker*), No.856 (*Trumpeter* and *Premier*), No.878 (*Illustrious*), No.881 (Stretton, *Formidable, Furious* and *Pursuer*), No.882 (*Searcher, Fencer* and *Furious*), No.890 (*Atheling* and *Illustrious*), No.896 (*Victorious* and *Pursuer*), No.898 (Eglinton, *Searcher* and *Fencer*) and No.1832 (*Fencer* and *Tracker*). *Second-line squadrons:* Nos.700, 718, 733, 738, 748, 757, 759, 768, 771, 772, 778, 787 and 790. (Mk.VI): No.811 (*Biter* and *Vindex*), No.813 (*Campania* and *Vindex*), No.815 (Stretton and *Campania*), No.819 (Macrihanish, Lee-on-Solent and Manston), No.821 (*Campania, Puncher* and *Trumpeter*), No.825 (*Vindex, Trouncer* and *Campania*), No.834 (*Battler*), No.835 (*Nairana*), No.838 (Hatston and Skeabrae), No.846 (*Trumpeter* and *Premier*), No.850 (Limavady), No.852 (*Trumpeter* and *Fencer*) No.853 (*Tracker* and *Queen*), No.856 (*Trumpeter* and *Premier*), No.881 (*Fencer, Pursuer, Trumpeter, Implacable, Premier* and *Puncher*) and No.882 (*Searcher, Vindex* and *Campania*). *Second-line squadrons:* Nos.700, 722, 748, 757, 771, 787, 790 and 794.

Description: Single-seat carrier-borne fighter. All-metal stressed-skin construction.

Manufacturers: Grumman Aircraft Engineering Corporation, Bethpage, Long Island, New York.

Power Plant: One 1,200 hp Pratt & Whitney Twin Wasp R-1830-86.

Dimensions: Span, 38 ft. Length, 28 ft 11 in. Height, 9 ft 2½ in. Wing area, 260 sq ft.

Weights: Empty, 5,895 lb. Loaded, 7,975 lb.

Performance: Maximum speed, 320 mph at 18,800 ft. Cruising speed, 238 mph at 15,000 ft. Initial climb, 1,760 ft/min. Normal range, 838 miles. Service ceiling, 34,000 ft.

Armament: Four fixed 0.50-calibre machine-guns in the wings or six 60 lb rocket projectiles below wings.

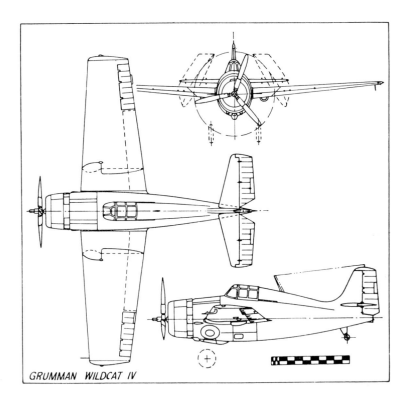

GRUMMAN WILDCAT IV

Avenger I (FN908) of No.846 Squadron. from *Tracker. (Charles E Brown)*

Grumman Avenger (Mks.I to III)

Despite a far from encouraging start when first used on operations in the Pacific in 1942, the Grumman Avenger later redeemed itself and, in fact, became one of the outstanding naval aircraft of the Second World War. It was produced in vast quantities, almost 10,000 being built (about 2,200 by the parent firm and the rest by General Motors), of which nearly 1,000 reached the FAA. No fewer than 15 first-line squadrons of the FAA received Avengers, and they gave excellent service in a great variety of rôles from shore bases and aboard both escort-carriers and large fleet carriers.

The Avenger first flew on 7 August 1941 as the XTBF-1. It was designed by William T Schwendler as a replacement for the Douglas Devastator, which had been the US Navy's standard torpedo-bomber for a number of years. In general appearance it had many features of the same company's Wildcat fighter: both aircraft were the work of the same designer. Two features made the Avenger outstanding: it was the first single-engined American aircraft to mount a power-operated gun turret, and the first to carry a 22-in torpedo. The Devastator had been armed with only a 21-in torpedo.

The first production Avenger, designated TBF-1, left the Grumman factory in February 1942 and less than four months later, in June 1942, six Avengers made their operational debut in the now historic Battle of Midway. Operating from a shore base, the Avengers met with a serious reverse; they failed to sink any enemy ships, and five out of six were shot down.

By July 1943 over 1,000 Avengers had been built, and by this time the manufacturing resources of the great General Motors organisation were being devoted to the type, the latter aircraft being distinguished by the designation TBM-1. The Trenton-built Avengers eventually superseded the old Grumman-built TBFs in the US Navy. The final production total was 9,857, comprising 2,311 TBF-1 and TBF-1C built at Grumman, and 2,882 TBM-1 and TBM-1C, followed by 4,664 TBM-3 and TBM-3E, by General Motors.

217

Avengers delivered to the FAA were supplied under Lend-Lease arrangements, beginning in 1943. Until January 1944 the British name Tarpon was used: thereafter the original American name was revived as part of an inter-Allied standardisation in designations. The Tarpon I (afterwards Avenger I) was the British equivalent of the US Navy TBF-1, and 402 were delivered, numbered FN750 to 949, JT773, and JZ100 to 300. Next came 334 Avenger IIs, equivalent to the US Navy's TBM-1, and numbered JZ301 to 634. The Avenger III, of which 222 were supplied, introduced the R-2600-20 engine, in place of the R-2600-8 used in previous Marks, and there were other detailed changes, including anti-submarine radar in some aircraft. The Avenger III (JZ635 to 746 and KE430 to 539) was the FAA equivalent of the US Navy TBM-3 and 3E. A final batch of 70 Avenger IV (KE540 to 609) was also reserved for Britain, but never delivered.

No.832 Squadron of the FAA, formerly flying Fairey Albacores, was the first to be equipped with Avengers. The squadron took delivery at Norfolk in the USA on 1 January 1943. In April 1943 No.832 Squadron's Avengers went aboard the US Navy carrier USS *Saratoga*, and on 27 June went into action during the landings in the Middle Solomons in the Coral Sea. This is believed to have been the first occasion on which FAA aircraft went into action from an American carrier. Afterwards No.832's Avengers transferred to the East Indies Fleet, embarking first in *Victorious* and later in *Illustrious*. No.832 Squadron's last commission (from June 1944 until disbandment on 21 February 1945) was in the escort carrier *Begum*, which protected shipping in the Indian Ocean.

By the end of 1943 there were eight Avenger squadrons with the FAA. The squadrons formed up at the US Navy bases at Norfolk, Quonset and Squantum, and the crews familiarised themselves with their aircraft before embarking in escort carriers to be ferried to the United Kingdom. Another five squadrons came into being in this way in 1944: all of them started life with Avengers, having had no previous existence. In the case of the last two squadrons to be formed (No.820 in October 1944 and No.828 in February 1945) the Avengers superseded Barracudas.

Although designed primarily as a torpedo-bomber, and widely employed as such by the US Navy, the Avenger in FAA service was rarely engaged in this rôle. Instead it operated as a bomber (with bombs, mines or depth charges) and as a strike aircraft armed with rocket projectiles beneath the wings. In home waters Avengers so equipped operated chiefly with escort-carriers or from shore bases on anti-submarine patrol, or occasionally on mine-laying sorties. Shore-based Avengers operated both from Royal Naval air stations and under the control of Coastal Command at RAF stations. The first Avengers to operate in home waters were those of No.846 Squadron. This unit formed at Quonset on 1 April 1943 and served in turn at RNAS Hatston, Grimsetter and Machrihanish before embarking in the escort-carrier *Tracker*, together with four Wildcat fighters, on 4 January 1944. On 1 April 1944, whilst escorting a Russian convoy, an Avenger of No.846 Squadron shared honours with HMS *Beagle* for the sinking of *U-355* in the Arctic. A few days later, on 4 April, an Avenger and a Wildcat V of No.846 Squadron shared with a Swordfish of No.819 Squadron (*Activity*) the destruction of *U-288*. On 4 May 1945, Avengers of No.846 Squadron sank *U-711*.

Another Avenger squadron engaged on convoy escort, No.853, took part in the last trip to North Russia before VE-Day, and on 7–10 May 1945 escorted naval forces to Copenhagen.

With the gradual build-up for D-Day in 1944 a number of Avenger squadrons were added to the anti-shipping strike forces of Coastal Command, starting in April 1944. They joined Albacores and Beaufighters in Operation 'Channel Stop', which was designed to prevent enemy shipping from entering the English Channel, escorted assault convoys and participated in many night attacks on E boats, R boats and minesweepers. On 24 July 1944 an Avenger of No.850 Squadron, flying from Perranporth, sank a large enemy merchant-ship off Guernsey.

The most spectacular exploits of the FAA's Avengers were, however, in the Far East with the East Indies and Pacific Fleets. One of the first big operations in which they took part was the attack on the Japanese naval base at Sourabaya, Java, on 19 May 1944. Avengers of Nos.832 and 845 Squadrons, flying from *Illustrious*, joined the US Navy Dauntlesses from *Saratoga* in this remarkably successful raid, which took the Japanese completely by surprise. It was the first time that FAA Avengers had bombed a land target.

During the final phases of the war against Japan, Avengers operated first with the East Indies Fleet based on Ceylon, and, afterwards, with the British Pacific Fleet based on Australia to deal the enemy some smashing blows. In January 1945 Avengers played a major rôle in one of the most important FAA actions of the Second World War: a carefully planned attack on the Japanese oil refineries at Palembang, in Sumatra. These refineries produced a large proportion of the oil needed by the Japanese Navy and aviation fuel by their Air Force. Forty-eight Avengers took part, drawn from Nos.820, 849, 854 and 857 Squadrons, respectively aboard *Indefatigable, Victorious, Illustrious* and *Indomitable*; an escort of 32 Corsairs, 16 Hellcats and 12 Fireflies was provided. The attacks were made on 24 and 29 January, and on both occasions the Avengers dived through a balloon barrage to be sure of hitting their targets. Despite intense anti-aircraft fire and strong fighter opposition, the operation was a major success; the Avengers hit their targets fairly and squarely, and both refineries were completely destroyed. This significant victory, the first large-scale action by the FAA against the Japanese, made a vital contribution to ultimate success in the Pacific by depriving the enemy of fuel both for ships and aircraft. As late as May 1945 the refinery at Songei Gerong was still inactive, and the other, at Pladjoe, was producing less than half its normal output.

Between March and May 1945 Avengers from the carriers *Illustrious, Indefatigable, Indomitable, Formidable* and *Victorious*, all of the 1st Aircraft Carrier Squadron of the British Pacific Fleet based on Sydney, made intensive bombing raids on enemy fighter bases in Formosa and islands south of Japan to assist the American landings in Okinawa. On 24 July 1945 Avengers of No.848 Squadron (*Formidable*) became the first FAA bombers to attack Japan proper, during a raid on Yokushima airfield. They were supported in this operation by Avengers of No.828 Squadron (*Implacable*), which had the previous June seen action in the Battle of Truk, one of the bloodiest operations of the Pacific War. The mainland of Japan remained under attack by Avengers until 15 August 1945, one of the last raids being a strike in the Tokyo area by No.820 Squadron. With the end of the war Avengers disappeared from front-line squadrons of the FAA.

Avenger of No.857 Squadron from *Indomitable*

By an unusual turn of events Avengers made their appearance in first-line squadrons once again in 1953, and details of this post-war version, the Avenger A.S.4, can be found on page 227.

UNITS ALLOCATED

No.820 (October 1944 to May 1946; embarked *Indefatigable*); No.828 (February 1945 to June 1946; shore-based Fearn and *Implacable*); No.832 (January 1943 to February 1945; embarked *Saratoga, Victorious, Illustrious* and *Begum*); No.845 (February 1943 to October 1945; shore-based Machrihanish and Trincomalee; embarked *Chaser, Engadine, Illustrious, Ameer, Empress, Emperor* and *Shah*); No.846 (August 1943 to October 1945; shore-based Hatston, Grimsetter, Machrihanish, Burscough, Limavady, Ayr and Crail; embarked *Ravager, Tracker, Trumpeter* and *Premier*); No.848 (June 1943 to October 1945; shore-based Hatston, Eglinton, Manston, Thorney Island, Dekheila and Nowra; embarked *Trumpeter, Formidable, Illustrious* and *Victorious); No.849* (August 1943 to October 1945; shore-based Hatston, Eglinton, Perranporth, St Eval and Ceylon;

An Avenger of No.854 Squadron from *Illustrious. (Imperial War Museum)*

embarked *Khedive, Rajah* and *Victorious*); No.850 (September 1943 to December 1944; shore-based Perranporth, Limavady and Maydown; embarked USS *Charger* and *Empress*); No.851 (October 1943 to October 1945; embarked *Emperor* and *Shah*); No.852 (November 1943 to October 1944; embarked *Nabob, Trumpeter* and *Fencer*); No.853 (February 1944 to May 1945; embarked *Arbiter, Tracker* and *Queen*); No.854 (January 1944 to December 1945; shore-based Thorney Island; embarked *Indomitable, Activity* and *Illustrious*); No.855 (February 1944 to October 1944; shore-based Hawkinge, Manston, Bircham Newton and Docking; embarked *Queen*); No.856 (March 1944 to June 1945; embarked *Smiter* and *Premier*) and No.857 (April 1944 to November 1945; embarked *Rajah* and *Indomitable*). Avengers also served with the following second-line squadrons: Nos.700, 703, 706, 711, 733, 736, 738, 744, 751, 756, 763, 764, 768, 774, 778, 782, 783, 785, 787, 797 and 798.

TECHNICAL DATA (AVENGER T.R.I AND T.R.III)

Description: Three-seat carrier-borne or shore-based torpedo-bomber and anti-submarine strike aircraft. All-metal stressed-skin construction.

Manufacturers: Grumman Aircraft Engineering Corporation, Bethpage, Long Island, New York. Sub-contracted by General Motors, Eastern Aircraft Division, Trenton, New Jersey.

Power Plant (Mk.I): One 1,850 hp Wright Cyclone GR-2600-8. (Mk.III): One 1,750 hp Wright Cyclone R-2600-20.

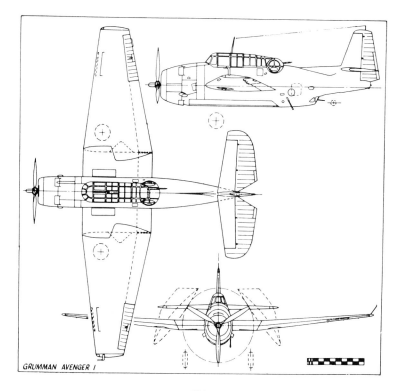

GRUMMAN AVENGER I

Dimensions: Span, 54 ft 2 in. Length, 40 ft. Height, 15 ft 8 in. Wing area, 490 sq ft.

Weights: (Mk.I): Empty, 10,627 lb. Loaded, 16,300 lb. (Mk.III): Empty, 10,700 lb. Loaded, 16,400 lb.

Performance (Mk.I): Maximum speed, 259 mph at 11,200 ft; 247 mph at sea level. Cruising speed, 171 mph at 5,000 ft. Climb, 4.3 min to 5,000 ft. Range, 1,020 miles (normal) and 1,910 miles (maximum, with no bombs and extra fuel). Service ceiling, 21,400 ft. (Mk.III): Maximum speed, 262 mph at 16,600 ft; 257 mph at 5,300 ft. Cruising speed, 174 mph at 5,000 ft. Initial climb, 1,300 ft/min, 3.8 min to 5,000 ft. Range 1,000 miles with 2,000 lb of bombs or 2,230 miles with no bombs and extra fuel. Service ceiling, 26,400 ft.

Armament: Two fixed 0.50 calibre guns in the wings, one 0.30-calibre gun in ventral position and one 0.50-calibre gun in dorsal turret. Provision inside bomb-bay for one 22 in torpedo of 1.921 lb or one 1,600 lb torpedo, or one 1,000 lb bomb or four 500 lb bombs. Eight 60 lb rocket projectiles below the wings.

Avengers of No.846 Squadron over the carrier *Tracker*. *(FAA Museum)*

Hellcat I (FN376) of No.800 Squadron. *(Charles E Brown)*

Grumman Hellcat

The Hellcat was designed as a replacement for the Wildcat in US Navy fighter squadrons and it succeeded the earlier type on the Grumman production lines in 1942. It was originally created as a private venture as a result of close collaboration between Grumman's engineering staff and US Navy pilots with extensive experience of air combat with the Japanese. The outcome was a fighter which, whilst following the general lines of its predecessor, was nearly 50 mph faster and possessed a much superior rate of climb. Fire-power remained unchanged, but more ammunition could be carried, range and ceiling were improved and the protective armour plating for the pilot was much augmented. The most notable change in external appearance was the re-positioning of the wings lower down the fuselage, enabling the undercarriage to be retracted into the centre section instead of the fuselage, as on the mid-wing Wildcat. By this method a much wider undercarriage track was obtained, improving ground handling. The high-placed cockpit was designed to give good vision, and an unusual feature was the three degrees of down-thrust in the engine installation, which gave a tail-down attitude in flight.

The prototype Hellcat, designated XF6F-1, was first flown on 26 June 1942 and differed from production aircraft in having a Curtiss Electric airscrew with a large spinner. This was replaced in production Hellcats by the Hamilton Standard hydromatic airscrew. The transition from the prototype to the production stage was achieved remarkably quickly, and the first production Hellcat was delivered in November 1942, less than a year after design had first begun. Hellcats remained in production for three years and over 10,000 were built.

Early in 1943 Hellcats were made available to Great Britain under

Lend-Lease arrangements, and deliveries continued until the end of the war, a total of 1,182 being allocated. These comprised 252 Hellcat I (originally known as the Gannet I in British service until standardisation of names was introduced), and 930 Hellcat II. The Hellcat I was the British equivalent of the US Navy's F6F-3, with the Double Wasp R-2800-10 engine, and the Hellcat II the equivalent of the F6F-5 with R-2800-10W engine. Some 74 of the Hellcat IIs were equipped for night-fighter duties, and could be distinguished by means of a radome mounted on the starboard wing. These aircraft were the British equivalent of the US Navy's F6F-5N. The Hellcat Is were allocated the serial numbers FN320 to 449 and JV100 to 221; the Hellcat IIs JV222 to 324, JW700 to 784, JW857 to 899, JX670 to 999, JZ775 to 827, JZ890 to 999, KD108 to 160 and KE118 to 265.

Hellcats first entered service with the FAA on 1 July 1943, when No.800 Squadron re-equipped from Sea Hurricanes. No.800 Squadron's Hellcats first saw operational service during anti-shipping strikes off the Norwegian coast after embarkation in the light escort-carrier *Emperor*, in December 1943. In April 1944 they joined the fighter forces covering the attack on *Tirpitz* in Kaafiord. A later strike on *Tirpitz*, in August 1944, was escorted by Hellcats of No.1840 Squadron embarked in *Indefatigable*.

Most of the Hellcat's FAA service, however, was with Royal Navy carriers in the Far East. By the end of 1944 Hellcats were with No.800 Squadron in *Emperor*, No.804 Squadron in *Ameer*, No.808 Squadron in *Khedive*, No.888 Squadron in *Empress*, No.1839 Squadron in *Indomitable*, No.1840 Squadron in *Indefatigable* and No.1844 Squadron in *Indomitable*. Hellcats of No.808 Squadron were in action off the Malayan coast from October 1944 and on 2 May 1945 those of No.800 Squadron provided fighter cover during the capture of Rangoon. No.888 Squadron specialised in photographic reconnaissance work, and, between 22 February and 7 March 1945, their Hellcats completed 22 reconnaissance sorties over the Kra Isthmus, Penang and Northern Sumatra. Earlier, No.1839 Squadron's Hellcats had also been active over Sumatra.

During the FAA's first major action against the Japanese, the attack on the

Hellcat II of No.804 Squadron from *Ameer*. *(Imperial War Museum)*

Hellcat II (JX 715) of No.896 Squadron from *Empress. (FAA Museum)*

oil refineries in Sumatra in January 1945, Hellcats played an important part. Flying from the carrier *Indomitable*, Hellcats of Nos.1839 and 1844 Squadrons provided close escort during the early strike on Pangkalan Brandan, and again in the large operations against Palembang on 24 and 29 January 1945. For these latter the 16 Hellcats were joined by 32 Corsairs of Nos.1830 and 1833 Squadrons from *Illustrious*.

No.1844 Squadron's Hellcats were in action again in air operations over the Sakashima Islands between 26 March and 20 April 1945, and during May were fighting over Formosa.

Meanwhile, from Janaury 1945, Hellcats had been replacing Wildcats in the light escort-carrier force building up in readiness for the invasion of Japan. Nos.896 and 898 Squadrons re-equipped with Hellcats at Wingfield, South Africa, in January 1945, and No.881 Squadron followed in April. Also formed in April 1945 was the first Hellcat night-fighter squadron (No.892) at Eglinton, Northern Ireland. It was joined by a second (No.891) at Nutt's Corner in August 1945 but they were too late to see any operational service before the war ended, though No.892 served briefly in the post-war light fleet carrier *Ocean*.

Only two of the 12 squadrons of Hellcats which were serving with the FAA on VJ-Day survived into 1946; these were No.892 and No.888, which disbanded in April and June 1946 respectively. One remaining Hellcat (KE209) is now in the FAA Museum.

UNITS ALLOCATED

No.800 Squadron (equipped July 1943; embarked in *Emperor*); No.804 Squadron (*Ameer, Emperor, Empress* and *Shah*); No.808 Squadron (equipped October 1944; embarked in *Khedive* and *Emperor*); No.881 Squadron (formed April 1945); No.885 Squadron (equipped August 1944; embarked in *Ruler*); No.888 Squadron (equipped June 1944; embarked in *Indefatigable, Empress, Emperor* and *Ameer*); No.889 Squadron (equipped June 1945); No.891 Squadron (equipped June 1945); No.892 Squadron (equipped April 1945; embarked in *Ocean*); No.896 Squadron (equipped January 1945; embarked in *Ameer* and *Empress*); No.898 Squadron (equipped January 1945; embarked in *Attacker*);

No.1839 Squadron (formed November 1943; embarked in *Indomitable*); No.1840 Squadron (formed March 1944; embarked in *Indefatigable, Furious, Formidable* and *Speaker*); No.1844 Squadron (formed December 1943; embarked in *Begum* and *Indomitable*); No.1847 Squadron (formed February 1944.) *Second-line squadrons:* Nos.700, 703, 706, 709, 721, 723, 732, 735, 746, 748, 756, 757, 759, 760, 768, 771, 778, 781, 784 and 787.

TECHNICAL DATA (HELLCAT II)

Description: Single-seat carrier-borne day- or night-fighter. All-metal stressed-skin construction.

Manufacturers: Grumman Aircraft Engineering Corporation, Bethpage, Long Island, New York.

Power Plant: One 2,250 hp Pratt & Whitney Double Wasp R-2800-10W.

Dimensions: Span, 42 ft 10 in (16 ft 2 in folded). Length, 33 ft 7 in. Height, 14 ft 5 in. Wing area, 334 sq ft.

Weights: Empty, 9,328 lb. Loaded (maximum), 12,740 lb.

Performance: Maximum speed, 380 mph at 23,400 ft; 331 mph at sea level. Economical cruising speed, 237 mph. Initial climb, 2,980 ft/min. Range, 945 miles (normal) or 1,115 miles (maximum). Service ceiling, 37,300 ft.

Armament: Six fixed 0.50-calibre machine-guns in wings. Provision for six 60 lb rocket projectiles or two 1,000 lb bombs below the wings.

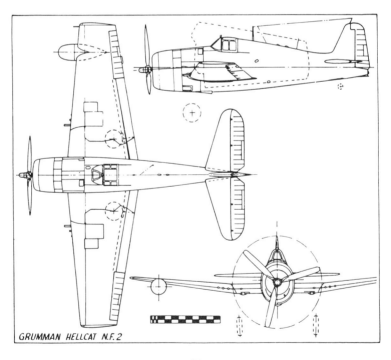

GRUMMAN HELLCAT N.F. 2

Avenger A.S.5 (XB520) from No.815 Squadron at RNAS Ford. (*Flight*)

Grumman Avenger (A.S.4 to 6)

As related in the earlier narrative on the Grumman Avenger in wartime service with the FAA, the last first-line squadron relinquished its Avenger IIIs in June 1946 and the intended deliveries of Avenger IVs (KE540 to KE609) never materialised. However, early in 1953 it was announced in the House of Commons, during the presentation of the Navy Estimates, that the Avenger was to enter service again in the Royal Navy. The Avengers were to strengthen the anti-submarine force, which at that time was at a low ebb, as the new Fairey Gannet was then some distance away from squadron service and did not in fact reach a first-line unit until January 1955.

The 100 post-war Avengers were supplied under the Mutual Defence Assistance Programme and were of the TBM-3E type as used by the US Navy. Avengers remained in first-line service with the US Navy until superseded by the Grumman S2F-1 Tracker in June 1954. The first shipment of TBM-3Es for the Royal Navy arrived at Glasgow in the carrier *Perseus* on 30 March 1953, and in May 1953 entered service with No.815 Squadron, replacing Barracudas. In July 1953 they also entered service in No.824 Squadron, superseding Fireflies.

At the close of 1953 the six unmodified TBM-3E Avengers were followed by 94 Avenger A.S.4 and A.S.5 aircraft which were fully modified to British requirements. No.815 Squadron was the first with Avenger A.S.4s in January 1954 and No.814 with A.S.5s in March 1954. Avengers of No.815 Squadron and No.881 (RCN) Squadron participated in the Coronation Naval Review fly-past at Spithead on 15 June 1953, and the type remained in first-line squadrons until supplanted by Gannets in 1955. Later, Avengers superseded Fireflies in several squadrons of the RNVR air divisions and remained with this force until its disbandment in March 1957.

227

Last variant of the Avenger to enter Fleet Air Arm service was the A.S.6 which had its radome re-positioned below the fuselage. This served with No.831 Squadron on electronic counter-measures duties from May 1958 until June 1959.

Serial numbers allocated to the post-war Avengers were XB296–332, XB355–404 and XB437–449. The sole survivor is XB446, which remains on exhibition at the FAA Museum at Yeovilton.

UNITS ALLOCATED

(TBM-3E): No.815 (Eglinton and Lee-on-Solent), (A.S.4): No.814 (Eglinton and *Centaur*), No.815 (Eglinton and *Eagle*), No.820 (Eglinton and *Centaur*), No.824 (Culdrose and *Bulwark*). *Second-line squadrons:* Nos.703, 751 and 767. (A.S.5): No.814 (*Centaur*), No.815 (*Eagle*), No.1830 (Abbotsinch), No.1841 (Stretton) and No.1844 (Bramcote). *Second-line squadrons:* Nos.703, 745, 751 and 767. (A.S.6): No.831 (Culdrose and Watton).

TECHNICAL DATA (AVENGER A.S.4)

Description: Three-seat carrier-borne or shore-based anti-submarine strike aircraft. All-metal stressed-skin construction.

Manufacturers: General Motors, Eastern Aircraft Division, Trenton, New Jersey.

Power Plant: One 1,750 hp Wright Cyclone R-2600-20.

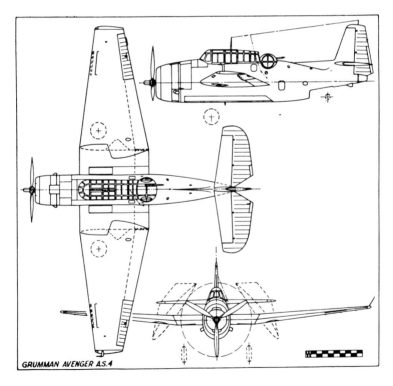

GRUMMAN AVENGER A.S.4

Dimensions: Span, 54 ft 2 in. Length, 40 ft. Height, 15 ft 8 in. Wing area, 490 sq ft.

Weights: Empty, 10,700 lb. Loaded, 16,761 lb.

Performance: Maximum speed, 261 mph. Cruising speed, 151 mph. Range, 1,130 miles. Service ceiling, 22,600 ft.

Armament: Provision for 2,000 lb of bombs or depth charges and eight 60 lb rocket projectiles below the wings.

Avenger A.S.4 (XB 381) from the second batch delivered to the Royal Navy in 1953.

O/100 of the RNAS at Manston. *(H H Russell.)*

Handley Page O/100

It is not always appreciated that the Admiralty was the first of the British Service Departments to recognise the potentialities of the large aeroplane for long-range bombing work, and that it made its requirements known to the industry as early as December 1914. The O/100, the forerunner of the much better known O/400, was the outcome of this policy and the answer to Commodore Murray F Sueter's classic request, when Director of the Air Department of the Admiralty, for a 'bloody paralyser' of an aeroplane.

The prototype O/100, with an enclosed cabin for the crew, flew for the first time at Hendon on 18 December 1915. Later the cabin was removed and, also, most of the armour plating. Deliveries of production aircraft to the RNAS began in September 1916, and the first front-line unit to receive the type was the Fifth Naval Wing at Dunkirk in November 1916. The third O/100 for the RNAS was delivered to the enemy intact on 1 January 1917, due to a navigational error.

Apart from a solitary night raid by an O/100 of the Third Wing on 16/17 March 1917, the O/100s were at first employed in their original intended rôle of oversea patrols off the Belgian coast and in September/October 1917 flew anti-submarine patrols from Redcar with No.7 (Naval) Squadron. Later they concentrated almost exclusively on night-bombing raids against U-boat bases, rail centres and Gotha aerodromes. By the end of 1917 the RNAS had four squadrons of O/100s in action, including Naval 'A' Squadron—later No.16 (Naval) Squadron—which joined the 41st Wing at Ochey, the nucleus of the Independent Force for strategic raids against targets in southern Germany. These O/100s first operated on the night of 24/25 October 1917 with F.E.2bs of No.100 Squadron, RFC.

In June 1917 an O/100 flown by Sqn Cdr K S Savory went overseas to Mudros in the Aegean, and on 9 July succeeded in bombing Constantinople. During this raid the enemy battle-cruiser *Goeben* was attacked with eight 112 lb bombs.

Forty-six O/100s were built, the airframe numbers being 1455 to 1466 and 3115 to 3142 for Eagle-engined aircraft and B9446 to B9451 for Cossack-engined versions.

One O/100 (No.3127) based in Northern France made an historic bombing raid on Cologne on 24/25 March 1918. Flt Cdr F K Digby, its pilot, had also attacked Mannheim in the same aircraft on 24/25 January 1918 and later bombed Freseaty on 10/11 November 1918, achieving 400 hours operational flying.

UNITS ALLOCATED

Nos.7 and 7A (later No.14 Naval) of the RNAS 5th Wing at Dunkirk; RNAS 3rd Wing at Luxeuil; 'A' Squadron (later No.16 Naval) at Ochey; RNAS Mudros (one aircraft).

TECHNICAL DATA (O/100)

Description: Heavy night-bomber with a crew of four. Wooden structure, fabric covered.
Manufacturers: Handley Page Ltd, Cricklewood, London.
Power Plant: Two 266 hp Rolls-Royce Eagle II or two 320 hp Sunbeam Cossack.
Dimensions: Span, 100 ft. Length, 62 ft 10¼ in. Height, 22 ft. Wing area, 1,648 sq ft.
Weights: Empty, 8,000 lb (approx). Loaded, 14,000 lb (approx).
Performance: Maximum speed, 85 mph (approx).
Armament: Up to five free-mounted Lewis machine-guns in nose, amidships and ventral positions and a bomb-load comprising 16 112 lb bombs.

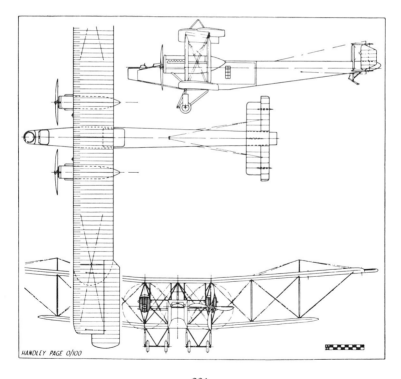

HANDLEY PAGE O/100

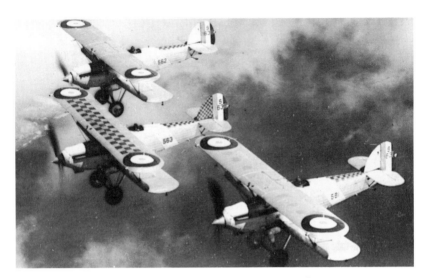

Nimrods of No.408 Flight from *Glorious*. *(MoD)*

Hawker Nimrod

The Nimrod was introduced in the FAA in 1931 as a replacement for the well-tried Fairey Flycatcher, which had by then been the standard carrier-borne fighter for almost a decade. Although a naval counterpart of the RAF's Fury interceptor, it was quite a distinct type and differed in having wings of greater span and special equipment, such as flotation boxes in the wings and fuselage, producing a slightly reduced performance.

Originally named the Norn, the Nimrod started its life like the radial-engined Hoopoe as a private venture, but later the Air Ministry Specification 16/30 was drafted round it. The original prototype flew in 1930, but the first to 16/30 standard (S1577) made its maiden flight on 14 October 1931. The first production Nimrod (S1578) flew on 31 October 1931, and a total of 56 Mark Is was built, serialled S1578 to 1588, S1614 to 1639 and K2823 to 2841. Early Nimrods had no arrester gear, which was not incorporated until K2823. This aircraft became the Nimrod II prototype, to Spec 11/33, which first appeared on 28 February 1933 and incorporated sweep-back on both upper and lower wings. The first production Nimrod II (K2909) flew in February 1934, and 28 of this version were built, ending in November 1935. Nimrod IIs all had arrester hooks and slightly enlarged tail surfaces. The first three production aircraft (K2909 to 2911) were built of stainless steel but subsequent aircraft reverted to normal steel and duralumin. Serials allocated were K2912 to 2914, K3654 to 3662, K4620 to 4629 and K5056 to 5058.

First in service with No.408 Flight in *Glorious* in November 1931, Nimrods superseded Flycatchers in Nos.402, 404 and 409 Fleet Fighter Flights in 1932, and afterwards served with Nos.800, 801 802 and 803 Squadrons, each of which had two flights of Nimrods and one flight of Osprey two-seaters. Nimrods were still serving with No.802 Squadron in *Glorious* as late as May 1939, but by the outbreak of war the type had disappeared from front-line squadrons, where it had been supplanted by the Skua and the Sea Gladiator. The Nimrod was declared obsolete in July 1941.

No.401 Flight (*Furious*), No.402 Flight (*Courageous*), No.404 Flight (*Courageous*), No.408 Flight (*Glorious*), No.409 Flight (*Glorious*), No.800 Squadron (*Courageous*), No.801 Squadron (*Furious*), No.802 Squadron (*Glorious*) and No.803 Squadron (*Ark Royal*). *Second-line squadrons:* No.757 Squadron (Worthy Down), No.759 Squadron (Eastleigh), No.780 Squadron (Eastleigh) and No.781 Squadron (Lee-on-Solent). Also No.1 FTS Leuchars for catapult training, and Base Training Squadron, Gosport.

TECHNICAL DATA (NIMROD I AND II)

Description: Single-seat carrier-borne fighter. All-metal structure with metal and fabric covering.

Manufacturers: Hawker Aircraft Ltd, Kingston-on-Thames, Surrey.

Power Plant: One 590 hp Rolls-Royce Kestrel II.S. (Mk.I) or 608 hp Kestrel V (Mk.II).

Dimensions: Span, 33 ft 6¾ in. Length, 26 ft 11¾ in. Height, 9 ft 9 in. Wing area, 298½ sq ft (Mk.I), 301 sq ft (Mk.II).

Weights: Empty, 3,065 lb. Loaded, 4,258 lb.

Performance: (Mk.II). Maximum speed, 195 mph at 14,000 ft. Climb, 1,640 ft/min; 2.2 min to 3,280 ft; 12 min to 16,400 ft. Endurance, 1.65 hr at 10,000 ft. Service ceiling, 28,800 ft.

Armament: Two fixed synchronised Vickers guns. Provision for four 20 lb bombs below wings.

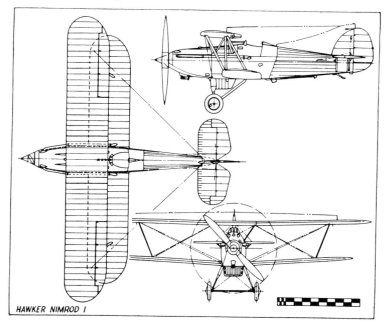

HAWKER NIMROD I

233

Nimrod II (K5056) from final production batch. *(FAA Museum)*

Nimrod II (K3656) of No.802 Squadron from *HMS Glorious*. *(RAF Museum)*

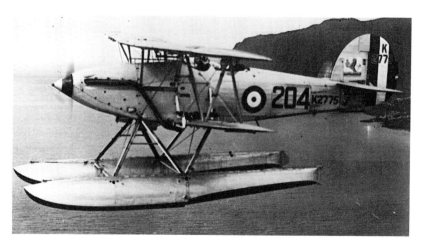

Osprey seaplane (K2775) from No.407 Flight, 2nd Cruiser Squadron. *(FAA Museum)*

Hawker Osprey

The advent of the Osprey in the FAA in 1932 saw the introduction of a hitherto unknown class aboard aircraft-carriers—the fast, two-seat fighter-reconnaissance aircraft. The Osprey inherited its performance from the Hart day-bomber, of which it was the deck-landing variant, and was available both with land undercarriage and as a twin-float seaplane.

The original Osprey, first flown in the summer of 1930, was the Hart prototype (J9052) converted to the requirements of Spec O.22/26, to which the Fairey Fleetwing was also designed. It incorporated folding wings, flotation gear and other naval equipment and was included in the composite flight of new types aboard HMS *Eagle* when it visited the Argentine for the British Empire Trade Exhibition in March 1931. Two prototype Ospreys (S1677 and S1678) were followed by 37 Mark I production aircraft (S1679 to 1698 and K2774 to 2790) fitted with Kestrel IIMS engines and Watts wooden propellers. Fourteen Mark IIs (K4322 to 4335) were followed by 49 Mark IIIs with Fairey Reed metal airscrews (S1702 to 1704, K3615 to 3653 and K3914 to 3920). There were also three special Osprey IIIs (S1699, S1700 and S1701) with stainless-steel construction. Final production version for the Fleet Air Arm was the Osprey IV fitted with the Kestrel V, of which 26 were built, beginning K5742. The last of 129 Ospreys for the FAA (K5767) was delivered in October 1935.

The first units equipped with Ospreys were Nos.405 and 409 Flights in October 1932, formerly with Flycatchers. From April 1933 Ospreys joined Nimrod single-seat fighters in Nos.800 and 802 Squadrons, each of which had three Ospreys and nine Nimrods. No.801 Squadron received Ospreys in place of Flycatchers in February 1934 and No.803 Squadron was, from the outset, an all-Osprey unit. In January 1939 No.800 Squadron embarked its six Ospreys in the new carrier *Ark Royal* for its shake-down cruise, returning to Portsmouth for disembarkation in March.

As a seaplane, the Osprey first replaced Fairey IIIFs in No.407 Flight of the Home Fleet's 2nd Cruiser Squadron in November 1932.

The Osprey was finally declared obsolete in 1940, its latter years having been spent in target-towing and training duties.

UNITS ALLOCATED

Catapult Flights: No.403 (5th Cruiser Squadron, China), No.406 (East Indies Squadron), No.407 (2nd Cruiser Squadron, Home Fleet), No.443 (West Indies Squadron and South Africa), No.444 (Capital Ships, Home Fleet), No.445 (3rd Cruiser Squadron, Mediterranean Fleet), No.447 (1st Cruiser Squadron, Mediterranean Fleet), No.404 Flight (*Courageous*), No.405 Flight (*Glorious*). *Embarked in carriers:* No.800 Squadron (*Courageous* and *Ark Royal*), No.801 Squadron (*Furious*), No.802 Squadron (*Glorious*) and No.803 Squadron (*Eagle* and *Hermes*). *Catapult Squadrons (formerly Flights):* Nos.711, 712, 713, 714, 715, 716 and 718.

TECHNICAL DATA (OSPREY IV)

Description: Two-seat carrier-borne or seaplane fighter-reconnaissance aircraft. Metal structure, metal and fabric covered.

Manufacturers: Hawker Aircraft Ltd, Kingston-on-Thames, Surrey.

Power Plant: One 640 hp Rolls-Royce Kestrel V.

Dimensions: Span, 37 ft (15 ft 7¼ in folded). Length, 29 ft 4 in (31 ft 9¾ in as seaplane). Height, 10 ft 5 in (12 ft 5 in as seaplane). Wing area, 339 sq ft.

Performance (Landplane): Maximum speed 176 mph at 13,120 ft; 161 mph at 6,560 ft. Cruising speed, 109 mph. Climb, 1,625 ft/min. Endurance, 2¼ hr. Service ceiling, 25,000 ft. (Seaplane): Maximum speed, 169 mph. Climb, 1,300 ft/min. Service ceiling, 22,000 ft.

Armament: One fixed Vickers gun and one movable Lewis gun.

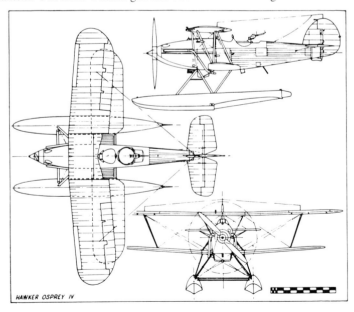

HAWKER OSPREY IV

236

Sea Hurricane IA (P3090) of No.760 Squadron from Yeovilton. *(Charles E Brown)*

Hawker Sea Hurricane

The Sea Hurricane arrived on the FAA scene when it equipped No.880 Squadron at Arbroath in March 1941 and on embarking in *Furious* in July 1941 it was the first British single-seat monoplane fighter to be used aboard aircraft-carriers of the Royal Navy. Until the introduction of the Seafire in 1942, the Sea Hurricane was the fastest of the FAA's fighters, and it proved a most welcome addition to its contemporaries, the American Grumman Martlet and the two-seat Fairey Fulmar. Its contribution to the war at sea was twofold, for it was used not only from carriers but also as a catapult fighter from the decks of merchant ships. In this way it effectively countered the threat of the Focke-Wulf Fw 200 Condor four-engined bombers, which were being used against shipping increasingly until the 'Catafighter' scheme was initiated.

First victory by a Sea Hurricane was on 21 July 1941, when an aircraft of No.880 Squadron shot down a Dornier Do 18 flying-boat off Norway.

The Sea Hurricane IA, the first version to appear, was specifically produced for the 'Catafighter' scheme, and had catapult spools only. The second version, with both catapult spools and a deck-arrester hook, was the Sea Hurricane IB. These aircraft, and all other variants of the Sea Hurricane, were conversions from existing Hurricane land-fighters, and no Sea Hurricanes were built as such. Many of the earlier Sea Hurricanes were converted from Battle of Britain veterans which had already seen a good deal of operational flying with the RAF. The Sea Hurricane IA and IB were followed into service in January 1942 by the Mk.IC, with four 20-mm guns in the wings, and the Mk.IIC, which introduced the Merlin XX engine. The Sea Hurricane IIC was equipped for carrier operations, but had no catapult points. The final variant was the Sea Hurricane XIIA, which was the conversion from the Canadian-built Hurricane with a Packard-Merlin XXIX engine. No precise records exist of the number of Sea Hurricanes supplied to the FAA, but contracts for at least 800 conversions were issued. The last delivered, in August 1943, was the Austin-built Mk.IIC NF717. The great majority of the Sea Hurricane conversion work was undertaken by General Aircraft Ltd in 1941–42 and in 1943 at Hawker's Langley factory. The

237

Sea Hurricane differed little from its land counterpart, and the modifications were for the most part limited to the local reinforcement of the airframe to withstand the extra loads imposed by catapult accelerations and, in the case of deck-landing aircraft, the sudden decelerations when the hook picked up the arrester wires on deck. Although a scheme was prepared for a Hurricane with folding wings, this modification was never incorporated, and all Sea Hurricanes had fixed wings.

For the catapult rôle which began in the summer of 1941 about 250 Hurricanes were converted to Sea Hurricane IAs. They served with No.804 Squadron which provided aircraft for Fighter Catapult Ships such as HMS *Ariguana, Maplin, Patia* and *Springbok* escorting convoys to Gibraltar and in the North Atlantic. On 2 August 1941 came the first victory over an FW 200 Condor by Lt R W H Everett, RNVR, flying from *Maplin*, earning a well deserved DSO.

Sea Hurricanes also served in Catapult Aircraft Merchantmen (35 converted freighters) using RAF pilots. CAM-ship Sea Hurricanes defended convoys to the USSR during 1942 and escorted Gibraltar convoys until July 1943.

Although the catapulted Sea Hurricanes were successful in reducing the number of bombing attacks on convoys, there was a major disadvantage in the scheme in that the aircraft could not return to the ship, and if, as was frequently the case, they were not within flying distance of a shore base, the pilot had to face the perils of parachuting into the sea as near to the convoy as possible, in the hope of being rescued by a passing vessel. This situation was slightly improved by the fitting of two 45-gallon auxiliary tanks beneath the wings of the Sea Hurricanes in the later stages of the scheme.

An advancement on the naval catapult ship for the protection of convoys was the small escort-carrier, about 40 of which entered service between 1942 and 1945. These small aircraft-carriers were to prove the most effective way of providing close air cover for convoys, particularly in the middle stretches of the Atlantic beyond the range of Coastal Command's land-based anti-submarine aircraft. Each escort-carrier carried its quota of fighters and anti-submarine aircraft, usually a mixture of Swordfish and Sea Hurricanes.

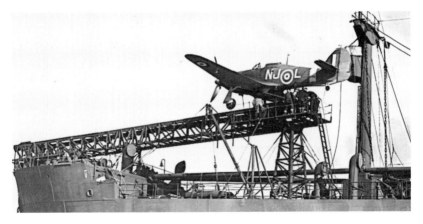

Sea Hurricane IA (V6756) on CAM-ship *Empire Tide*'s catapult. *(Imperial War Museum)*

Sea Hurricanes did particularly valuable service aboard escort-carriers on the arduous Russian convoys. No.802 Squadron, which had flown Martlets in the first of the merchant carriers, *Audacity*, re-formed at Yeovilton in February 1942 with six Sea Hurricanes and embarked in *Avenger*, joining six more Sea Hurricanes of No.883 Squadron, which had also formed at Yeovilton the previous October. *Avenger*'s Sea Hurricanes, together with three Swordfish, played a vital rôle in protecting convoy P.Q.18, which sailed from Loch Ewe for North Russia on 2 September 1942. This operation was typical of many which were to follow. It was the first in which an escort-carrier had been provided: the previous Russian convoy P.Q.17 had been badly mauled by German aircraft from Norway and Finland through lack of air cover. With convoy P.Q.18 it was a different story: the Sea Hurricanes of Nos.802 and 883 Squadrons together shot down five enemy aircraft and damaged 17 others. Four Sea Hurricanes were lost, but three of the pilots were saved.

Meanwhile aboard the larger aircraft-carriers Sea Hurricanes were playing their part in the hard-fought battles over the Mediterranean as convoys made the bitterly-contested voyage to the relief of Malta. One of the largest of these convoys was that of August 1942, for which a fighter cover of 70 Sea Hurricanes, Fulmars and Martlets was provided by the carriers *Victorious*, *Indomitable* and *Eagle*. The Sea Hurricanes were those of No.880 Squadron (*Indomitable*), No.801 Squadron (*Eagle*) and No.885 Squadron (*Victorious*). It was during this voyage that *Eagle* met her end, being torpedoed by U-boats. Yet, in spite of this loss, the FAA enjoyed one of their greatest victories during three days of air fighting against a force of about 500 German and Italian bombers, torpedo-carriers and escorting fighters. Sea Hurricanes, aided by the Fulmars and Martlets, shot down 39 enemy aircraft and damaged many more for the loss of only eight of their own number. Time and time again they drove off attacking forces of Cant Z.1007 and Junkers Ju 88 aircraft, and one pilot alone (Lt R J Cork, DSC, of No.880 Squadron) shot down three German and three Italian aircraft in his Sea Hurricane. Faced with such skill and determination, the enemy aircraft could make little impression and, against all the odds, the convoy got through.

Sea Hurricane IC (V6741) used by No.804 Squadron. *(Imperial War Museum)*

Sea Hurricane IIC (NF717). *(Imperial War Museum)*

The Malta convoy of August 1942 was one of the last major actions in which Sea Hurricanes operated from large aircraft-carriers: during the North African invasion in November 1942 the Seafire was predominant. But Sea Hurricanes continued to give good service in the escort-carriers, and No.891 Squadron, in *Dasher*, did in fact contribute to the North African landings as well as No.800 Squadron in *Biter*.

By mid-1944, the Sea Hurricane had largely disappeared from front-line units of the FAA, the last to serve afloat being the Mk.IICs of No.835 Squadron in *Nairana* and No.825 in *Vindex* in September 1944.

UNITS ALLOCATED

(Mk.IA): No.801 (Yeovilton and Arbroath), No.802 (Yeovilton and *Avenger*), No.804 (Yeovilton, *Pegasus* and *Maplin*), No.880 (Arbroath and *Furious*). (Mk.IB): No.800 (Lee-on-Solent, *Indomitable* and *Biter*), No.801 (Yeovilton, *Argus* and *Eagle*), No.802 (Yeovilton and *Avenger*), No.804 (*Pegasus* and *Maplin*), No.806 (unconverted Hurricanes shore-based in Western Desert), No.813 (*Eagle*), No.880 (*Indomitable*), No.882 (*Illustrious*), No.883 (Yeovilton and *Avenger*), No.885 (Yeovilton, *Victorious* and *Formidable*), No.891 (Lee-on-Solent, *Argus* and *Dasher*), No.895 (Stretton, Lee-on-Solent and Machrihanish), No.897 (Stretton and Lee-on-Solent). (Mk.IC): No.801 (*Argus* and *Eagle*), No.802 (*Avenger*), No.880 (*Indomitable*), No.883 (*Avenger*), No.885 (*Victorious*). (Mk.IIB): No.800 (Hatston, Lee-on-Solent and *Biter*), No.802 (*Avenger*), No.804 (*Maplin*, *Eagle* and *Argus*), No.877 (shore-based East Africa), No.883 (Lee-on-Solent and Machrihanish). (Mk.IIC): No.800 (*Biter* and *Unicorn*), No.804 (*Dasher*), No.824 (*Striker*), No.825 (*Pretoria Castle* and *Vindex*), No.835 (*Nairana*) and No.891 (*Argus* and *Dasher*). Sea Hurricanes also used by second-line squadrons Nos.702, 731, 748, 759, 760, 761, 762, 766, 768, 769, 771, 774, 778, 779, 781, 787, 788, 789, 791, 792, 794 and 795.

TECHNICAL DATA (SEA HURRICANE IB)

Description: Single-seat carrier-borne fighter. Metal structure with metal and fabric covering.
Manufacturers: Hawker Aircraft Ltd, Kingston-on-Thames, Surrey.
Power Plant: One 1,030 hp Rolls-Royce Merlin III.
Dimensions: Span, 40 ft. Length, 32 ft 3 in. Height, 13 ft 3 in. Wing area, 258 sq ft.

Sea Hurricane IB of No.768 Squadron, Machrihanish. *(Imperial War Museum)*

Sea Hurricane IBs of No.801 Squadron. *(Imperial War Museum)*

Weights: Empty, 5,334 lb. Loaded, 7,015 lb.

Performance: Maximum speed, 315 mph at 17,500 ft. Cruising speed, 208 mph at 20,000 ft. Range, 500 miles (normal) or 1,030 miles with auxiliary tanks. Initial climb, 2,010 ft/min, 10 min to 20,000 ft. Service ceiling, 32,700 ft.

Armament: Eight fixed 0.303 machine-guns in wings and capacity for two 250 lb bombs below wings.

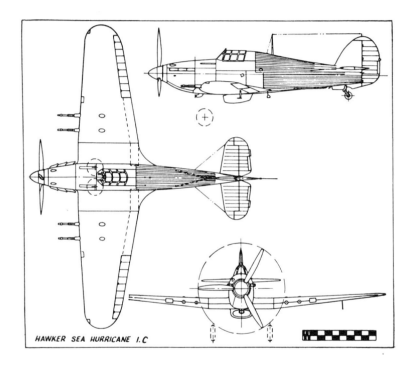

HAWKER SEA HURRICANE I.C

Sea Fury F.B.11 (VW714) of No.738 Squadron from RNAS Lossiemouth. *(Flight)*

Hawker Sea Fury

The Sea Fury was the FAA's last piston-engined fighter in first-line squadrons, where it served from 1947 until 1955. It was also the first British naval aircraft in regular service with power-folding wings.

The prototype Sea Fury (SR661) first flown on 21 February 1945, was a navalised version of the Fury I, which had been designed to Spec F.2/43 as an intended replacement for the Tempest in the RAF. Deck-landing trials with SR661 (which had a sting type arrester hook but fixed wings) took place aboard HMS *Ocean* in October 1945. Two subsequent prototypes (SR666 and VB857) incorporated folding wings, and were followed by the first production Sea Fury F.10 (TF895), which flew on 30 September 1946. Fifty Sea Fury F.10s (TF895 to 928 and TF940 to 955) were built to Spec 22/43 and were followed by 565 Sea Fury F.B.11s, the last of which (WZ656) was delivered in November 1952.

F.B.11 serials were in the ranges VR918 to 952, VW224 to 243, VW541 to 718, VX608 to 764, WF590 to 627, WG564 to 630, WE673 to 806, WH581 to 623, WJ221 to 301, WM472 to 495, WN474 to 487 and WZ627 to 656.

Sea Furies first entered service with Nos.803 and 807 Squadrons at Eglinton in August and September 1947, and in May 1948 they converted to F.B.11s. By the time that the Korean War began in 1950 the Sea Fury was the FAA's leading single-seat fighter, and it fought with distinction throughout the campaign. Sea Fury squadrons engaged were No.802 (in *Ocean*), No.807 (in *Theseus*), Nos.801 and 804 (in *Glory*) and Nos.805 and 808 (in *Sydney*). Although used chiefly in conjunction with Fireflies for ground-attack duties, using bombs and rockets, the Sea Furies also fought the much faster MiG-15 jet fighters, the first victory being claimed by Lt P Carmichael of No.802 Squadron flying from HMS *Ocean* on 9 August 1952.

Sea Furies first entered RNVR service in August 1951, when they equipped No.1831 Squadron at Stretton. No.1831 took its Sea Furies to Malta in May 1952, being the first of the reserve units to do their annual training overseas.

From 1953, the Sea Fury was superseded in first-line squadrons by the Sea Hawk. Last in service was No.810, disbanded at Ford in March 1955. In the RNVR, Sea Furies stayed until June 1956 with No.1832 at Benson.

243

(F.10): No.802 (Lee-on-Solent and Eglinton), No.803 (Eglinton and *Magnificent*), No.805 (Eglinton and *Sydney*), No.807 (Eglinton, *Implacable* and *Theseus*). (F.B.11): No.801 (*Vengeance, Indomitable, Illustrious, Glory* and *Ocean*), No.802 (*Vengeance, Indomitable, Illustrious, Theseus* and *Ocean*), No.803 (*Magnificent*), No.804 (*Glory, Theseus, Illustrious* and *Indomitable*), No.805 (*Sydney*), No.806 (*Magnificent*), No.807 (*Implacable, Theseus, Ocean* and *Glory*), No.808 (*Sydney* and *Vengeance*), No.810 (*Centaur*), No.811 (*Warrior*), No.850 (*Vengeance* and *Sydney*), No.870 (*Magnificent*), No.871 (*Magnificent*), No.883 (*Magnificent*), No.898 (*Ocean, Theseus* and *Glory*). *RNVR Squadrons:* Nos.1831 (Stretton), 1832 (Culham and Benson), 1833 (Bramcote) and 1834 (Benson and Yeovilton). *Second-line squadrons:* Nos.700, 703, 723, 724, 725, 736, 738, 767, 773, 778, 781, 782, 787 and 799.

TECHNICAL DATA (SEA FURY F.B.11)

Description: Single-seat carrier-borne fighter-bomber. All-metal stressed-skin construction.

Manufacturers: Hawker Aircraft Ltd, Langley, Bucks.

Power Plant: One 2,480 hp Bristol Centaurus 18.

Dimensions: Span, 38 ft 4¾ in (16 ft 1 in folded). Length, 34 ft 8 in. Height, 15 ft 10½ in. Wing area, 280 sq ft.

Weights: Empty, 9,240 lb. Loaded, 12,500 lb.

Performance: Maximum speed, 460 mph at 18,000 ft. Initial climb, 4,300 ft/min; 7.2 min to 20,000 ft. Range, 680 miles at 30,000 ft or 1,045 miles with two 45-gallon drop-tanks. Service ceiling, 35,800 ft.

Armament: Four fixed 20-mm guns in wings and provision for eight 60 lb rocket projectiles or two 1,000 lb bombs below the wings.

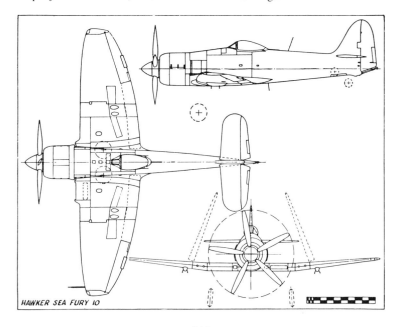

HAWKER SEA FURY 10

Sea Fury T.20 (VZ346) of Midlands Air Division, RNVR, Bramcote. (*A J Jackson*)

Hawker Sea Fury T.20

The Sea Fury T.20 was a straightforward two-seat dual-control trainer adaptation of the Sea Fury single-seat fighter. Basically similar to the fighter, the T.20 had a second cockpit for the instructor connected to the front cockpit by a long Perspex fairing, each cockpit being provided with an individual sliding canopy. Whereas the fighter had four 20-mm guns in the wings, the T.20 mounted only two, so as to permit the installation in the wing of equipment displaced from the fuselage by the second cockpit. Another feature peculiar to the trainer was the installation of a mirror on a tripod between the cockpits; this enabled the instructor to see the reflector gunsight over the head of his pupil. All Sea Fury T.20s were shore-based since they had no arrester hooks.

The prototype Sea Fury T.20 (VX818) made its first flight on 15 January 1948, some 15 months after the first production Sea Fury fighter had flown. Deliveries of the production version of the Sea Fury Trainer proceeded concurrently with fighters. Total production of the type amounted to 60 aircraft, the last (WG656) being delivered to the Royal Navy in March 1952. Serial numbers allocated were VX280 to 292, VX297 to 310, VZ345 to 355, VZ363 to 372, WE820 to 826 and WG652 to 656.

The Sea Fury T.20s were used by second-line squadrons of the FAA, providing operational training at Culdrose, Cornwall, for pilots who had previously graduated through the RAF Flying Training School at Syerston and more advanced instruction at Lossiemouth. Later, with the introduction of Sea Fury fighters in the squadrons of the RNVR, the T.20 was issued to reserve units as a conversion trainer. Sea Fury Trainers were on the strength of the Northern Air Division at Stretton, the Scottish Air Division at Abbotsinch, and the Southern Air Division at Benson and Yeovilton. They also served at Bramcote and Culham with the Midland Air Division.

The Sea Fury T.20 was finally withdrawn in June 1956.

Second-line squadrons: Nos.703 (Ford), 736 (Culdrose), 738 (Culdrose and Lossiemouth), 759 (Culdrose and Lossiemouth), 771 (Arbroath), 781 (Ford), 782 (Eglinton), 787 (West Raynham), 799 (Yeovilton). *RNVR Squadrons:* Nos. 1830 (Abbotsinch), 1831 (Stretton), 1832 (Culham and Benson), 1833 (Bramcote) and 1834 (Benson and Yeovilton).

TECHNICAL DATA (SEA FURY T.20)

Description: Two-seat dual-control advanced trainer. All-metal stressed-skin construction.

Manufacturers: Hawker Aircraft Ltd, Langley, Bucks.

Power Plant: One 2,480 hp Bristol Centaurus 18.

Dimensions: Span, 38 ft 4¾ in. Length, 34 ft 7 in. Height, 12 ft 3½ in. Wing area, 280 sq ft.

Weights: Empty, 8,697 lb. Loaded, 11,930 lb.

Performance: Maximum speed, 445 mph at 20,000 ft; 415 mph at 7,500 ft; 370 mph at sea level. Climb, 4,300 ft/min; 1.3 min to 5,500 ft; 4.05 min to 15,000 ft; 5.65 min to 20,000 ft. Range (without external tanks), 940 miles, (with two 90-gallon drop-tanks), 1,310 miles. Service ceiling, 35,600 ft.

Armament: Two 20-mm guns mounted in wings.

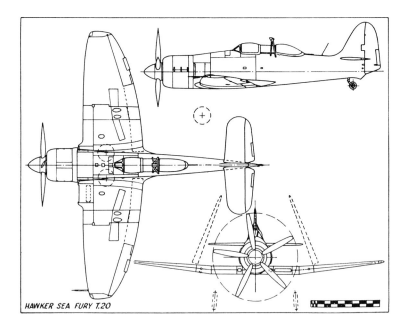

HAWKER SEA FURY T.20

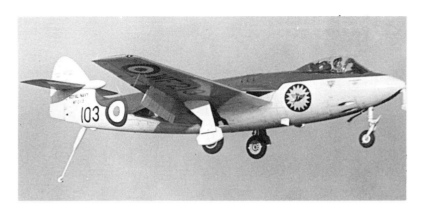

Sea Hawk F.G.A.4 (WF213) of No.898 Squadron. (*Flight*)

Hawker Sea Hawk (Mks.1 to 6)

The Sea Hawk first entered FAA squadrons in 1953, superseding the Attacker jet fighter and the Sea Fury piston-engined fighters. Its basic design stemmed from that of Hawker's first jet fighter, the P.1040, which was adapted for carrier-borne interceptor duties to Spec N.7/46. Two naval prototypes were ordered in February 1946, and the first (VP413) flew on 3 September 1948. The first production Sea Hawk F.1 (WF143) flew on 14 November 1951, with its wing-span increased from 36 ft 6 in to 39 ft, an increase in tailplane area, a revised cockpit canopy and a Nene 101 engine in place of the Nene 2 or 4. The initial 35 aircraft were built by Hawker, but the second production batch of 60 Mk.1s was by Armstrong Whitworth, which built all subsequent Sea Hawks. Serials were WF143 to 192, WF196 to 235 and WM901 to 905.

The Sea Hawk F.1 was succeeded by the F.2 (40 built serialled WF240 to 279) which introduced power-boosted ailerons, and the F.B.3 (116 built, serialled in ranges WF280 to 303, WM906 to 999 and WN105 to 119) which had a strengthened wing for external loads. The first Sea Hawk F.2 (WF240) flew on 24 February 1954, and the first F.B.3 (WF280) on 13 March 1954. The next production version was the F.G.A.4, equipped for the close-support rôle, the first example of which (WV792) flew on 26 August 1954. Ninety-seven Mk.4s were built, serialled WV792 to 807, WV824 to 871 and WV902 to 922. The Sea Hawk F.B.5 was a retrospective conversion of the F.B.3. Final production version for the Royal Navy was the F.G.A.6, of which 95 were built, terminating with XE490, the 443rd and last Sea Hawk for the Fleet Air Arm, delivered early in 1956. Serials allotted to the F.G.A.6 were XE339 to 344, XE362 to 411, XE435 to 463 and XE489 to 490.

Sea Hawks first entered service with No.806 Squadron at Brawdy in March 1953, subsequently embarking in *Eagle*. Sea Hawks with a carrier task force provided close support for the Anglo-French landings in Egypt in November 1956, being flown by Nos.800, 802, 804, 810, 897 and 899 Squadrons from the carriers *Albion, Eagle* and *Bulwark*.

247

The last Sea Hawk squadron of the FAA (No.806) disbanded at Brawdy on 15 December 1960. Sea Hawks were superseded by Scimitars in first-line fighter squadrons from 1958.

UNITS ALLOCATED

(F.1): Nos.802 (Lossiemouth), 804 (Lossiemouth and Ford), 806 (Brawdy and *Eagle*), 807 (Brawdy) and 1832 (Benson). (F.2): Nos.802 (Lossiemouth) and 807 (Brawdy and *Bulwark*). (F.B.3): Nos.800 (Brawdy), 802 (Lossiemouth and *Albion*), 803 (Lee-on-Solent, *Albion* and *Centaur*), 806 (Yeovilton and *Centaur*), 807 (Brawdy and *Bulwark*), 811 (Lossiemouth, Ford, *Bulwark*, *Albion* and *Centaur*), 895 (*Bulwark*) and 897 (Brawdy and *Eagle*). (F.G.A.4): Nos.800 (*Ark Royal* and *Albion*), 801 (Lossiemouth, Ford, *Bulwark*, *Albion* and Centaur), 802 (Lossiemouth and *Eagle*), 804 (Lossiemouth and *Eagle*), 806 (*Centaur*), 807 (Brawdy and *Albion*), 810 (Lossiemouth, *Albion* and *Bulwark*), 811 (Lossiemouth), 895 (Brawdy and *Bulwark*), and 898 (Brawdy and *Ark Royal*). (F.B.5): Nos.802 (Lossiemouth, *Ark Royal* and *Eagle*) and 806 (Lossiemouth and *Eagle*). (F.G.A.6): Nos.800 (*Ark Royal*, *Albion* and *Centaur*), 801 (*Bulwark* and *Centaur*), 803 (*Eagle*), 804 (*Bulwark*, *Ark Royal* and *Albion*), 806 (*Eagle* and *Albion*), 810 (*Albion* and *Bulwark*), 895 (*Bulwark*), 897 (*Eagle*), 898 (*Ark Royal*, *Bulwark* and *Eagle*) and 899 (*Bulwark* and *Eagle*). *Second-line squadrons:* Nos.700 ,703, 736, 738, 764, 767, 781 and 787.

TECHNICAL DATA (SEA HAWK F.G.A.6)

Description: Single-seat carrier-borne ground-attack fighter. All-metal stressed-skin construction.
Manufacturers: Sir W G Armstrong Whitworth Aircraft Ltd, Baginton, Coventry.
Power Plant: One 5,200 lb thrust Rolls-Royce Nene 103.
Dimensions: Span, 39 ft (13 ft 4 in folded). Length, 39 ft 10 in. Height, 8 ft 9 in. Wing area, 278 sq ft.

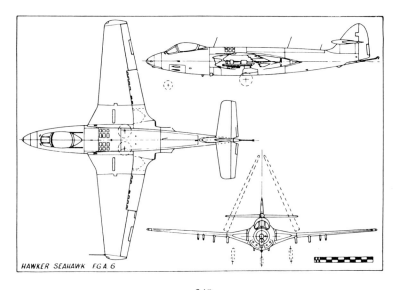

HAWKER SEAHAWK FGA 6

Weights: Empty, 9,560 lb. Loaded (clean), 13,200 lb; (with two 100 gallon drop-tanks), 15,200 lb; (with two drop-tanks and two 500 lb bombs), 16,200 lb.

Performance: (As fighter-bomber with drop-tanks and two 500 lb bombs): Maximum speed, 518 mph at sea level; 524 mph at 10,000 ft. Initial climb, 4,720 ft/min. Range: 576 miles. (As fighter, without bombs or drop tanks); Maximum speed, 560 mph at 36,000 ft; (with two drop tanks), 530 mph at 36,000 ft. Initial climb, 5,700 ft/min, 11 min 50 sec to 44,500 ft. Service ceiling, 44,500 ft.

Armament: Four fixed 20-mm guns in fuselage and provision for 20 3-in rocket projectiles or four 500 lb or two 1,000 lb bombs below wings.

Sea Hawk F.G.A.4s from No.898 Squadron. *(Flight)*

Hunter G.A.11 (WT809) of No.764 Squadron at Lossiemouth.

Hawker Hunter G.A.11

From 1962, the Fleet Air Arm took delivery of 40 Hunter G.A.11s, all converted from former Royal Air Force Hunter F.4 single-seat fighters. The Hunter G.A.11s were used primarily by No.738 Training Squadron, based at RNAS Lossiemouth and Brawdy, for instruction in ground attack tactics.

The serial numbers of the Hunter G.A.11s were WT711, 712, 713, 718, 722, 723, 741 and 744, WT804, 805, 806, 808, 809 and 810, WV256, 257, 267, 374, 380, 381 and 382, WW654 and 659, XE668, 673, 674, 680, 682, 685, 689, 707, 712, 716 and 717, XF291, 297, 300, 310, 368 and 977. WT723 was later converted to Hunter P.R.11.

Three Hunter G.A.11s, together with one Hunter T.8, from No.738 Squadron formed a Fleet Air Arm aerobatic team in 1967, lead by Lt Cdr Chris Comins. They made many successful public appearances, including one on BBC television.

The Hunter G.A.11 achieved great popularity in the Fleet Air Arm, being pleasant both to fly and maintain. The first G.A.11s began to arrive at RNAS Lossiemouth in June 1962 and by the end of 1962 No.738 Squadron had twelve G.A.11s on charge as well as six Hunter T.8s. The G.A.11 was a natural progression for students who had first converted to Hunter T.8s on arrival from their No.1 FTS course on Vampire T.11s. The introduction of the G.A.11 became necessary with front-line squadrons of the FAA going over to swept-wing fighters such as the Scimitar and Sea Vixen in the early 1960s, and the modified RAF fighters were bought very economically by the Royal Navy at about £33,000 each. Although with the Avon 113 engine they lacked the performance of the more powerful Hunter T.8s, they nevertheless had better all-round handling characteristics than the T.8 and a much lower loaded weight resulting from the removal of the Aden guns and radar.

Reviving the earlier success of the FAA's Hunter aerobatic team, came in July 1975 the *Blue Herons*, four G.A.11s (serialled WT806, WV382, WW654 and XF977) flown by civil pilots of Airwork Services and based at RNAS Yeovilton. They performed magnificently at the International Air Tattoo at Greenham Common, both in 1976 and again in 1977. The *Blue Herons* formed part of the Fleet Requirements and Air Directions Unit (FRADU) which, among other tasks, helped to train fighter controllers at RNAS Yeovilton. The name of the *Blue Herons* derived from its home base, HMS *Heron*, otherwise known as Yeovilton.

UNITS ALLOCATED

Second-line squadrons: Nos.738 (Lossiemouth and Brawdy) and 764 (Lossiemouth).

TECHNICAL DATA (HUNTER G.A.11)

Description: Single-seat shore-based advanced fighter trainer. All-metal stressed-skin construction.
Manufacturers: Hawker Aircraft Ltd, Kingston-on-Thames, Surrey.
Power Plant: One Rolls-Royce Avon 113 turbojet of 7,500 lb static thrust.
Dimensions: Span, 33 ft 8 in. Length, 45 ft 10½ in.
Weights: Empty, 12,543 lb. Loaded, 17,000 lb.
Performance: Maximum speed, Mach 0.94 at 36,000 ft. Climb, 9.85 min to 45,000 ft. Service ceiling, 50,000 ft.
Armament: Fixed gun armament deleted, but provision for rocket projectiles below wings on some aircraft.

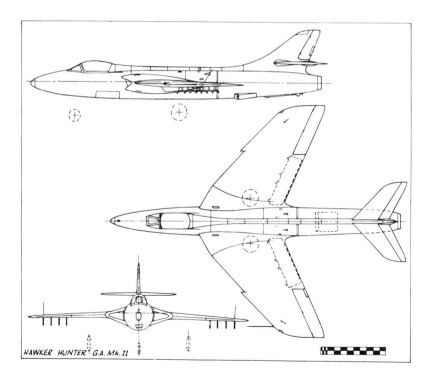

HAWKER HUNTER G.A. Mk. 11

Hunter T.8 (XL602) of No.764 Squadron. *(Aviation Photo News)*

Hawker Hunter T.8

The Hunter T.8 was the Fleet Air Arm version of the Hunter T.7 of the Royal Air Force. This dual-control training version of the famous fighter first entered service with the Royal Navy at RNAS Lossiemouth in July 1958 when the type was issued to No.736 Squadron.

Altogether 41 Hunter T.8s were delivered to the Fleet Air Arm. Thirty-one of these were conversions from ex-RAF Hunter F.4 single-seat fighters and the remaining ten were diverted RAF Hunter T.7s.

Serial numbers allocated to the diverted T.7s were XL580 to 582, XL584, XL585, XL598, XL599, XL602, XL603 and XL604.

The converted F.4s were numbered WT701, 702, 722, 745, 755, 772 and 799, WV319, 322, 363, 396 and 397, WW661 and 664, XE664 and 665, XF289, 322, 357, 358, 938, 939, 942, 967, 978, 983, 985, 991, 992, 994 and 995.

The prototype Hunter T.8 (a converted Mk.4, WW664) made its first flight on 3 March 1958, and the first of the diverted RAF trainers (XL580) on 30 May 1958. Although the Hunter T.8 had an arrester hook installed below the rear fuselage, this was used only for naval airfield emergency purposes and not for deck-landing: Hunter T.8s in fact operated only from shore bases. Based mainly at Brawdy and Lossiemouth, the T.8s played a vital rôle in training naval pilots in weapon delivery and provision was made both for two-inch rocket batteries and Bullpup missiles. With the introduction of TACAN equipment in the Fleet Air Arm, the Hunter T.8s were modified to carry this by the removal of the Aden gun and radar ranging. The Hunter T.8B had full TACAN equipment and the Hunter T.8C partial installation.

During Sea Harrier development, two Hunter T.8Ms (XL602 and XL603) fitted with Blue Fox radar in the nose were produced to develop nav-attack systems and subsequently joined No.899 Squadron for training from August 1981.

UNITS ALLOCATED

Second-line squadrons: Nos.700B (Lossiemouth), 700Y (Yeovilton), 700Z (Lossiemouth), 738 (Lossiemouth and Brawdy), 759 (Brawdy), 764 (Lossiemouth).

Also issued to operational squadrons for continuation training and as communications aircraft to Flag Officers.

Description: Two-seat shore-based advanced operational trainer. All-metal stressed-skin construction.

Manufacturers: Hawker Aircraft Ltd, Kingston-on-Thames, Surrey.

Power Plant: One Rolls-Royce Avon Mk.122 turbojet of 7,550 lb static thrust.

Dimensions: Span, 33 ft 8 in. Length, 48 ft 10½ in. Height, 13 ft 2 in. Wing area, 349 sq ft.

Weights: Empty, 13,360 lb. Loaded, 17,200 lb.

Performance: Maximum speed, 703 mph at 36,000 ft. Climb 12.5 min to 45,000 ft. Range, 552 miles. Service ceiling, 47,000 ft.

Armament: One Aden gun and underwing pylons to carry various combinations of 500 lb or 1,000 lb bombs, napalm weapons, Bullpup missiles or 2-in rocket batteries. Aden gun deleted in Mk.8B and 8C.

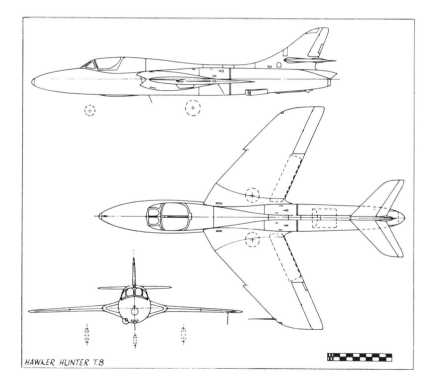

HAWKER HUNTER T.8

Sea Vixen F.A.W.2 (XP924) of No.899 Squadron from Yeovilton. *(Flight)*

Hawker Siddeley Sea Vixen F.A.W.2

In 1961, with the Sea Vixen F.A.W.1 firmly established as the Fleet Air Arm's standard all-weather fighter, it was decided to seek further development of the type by installing additional fuel tanks in forward extensions of the tail booms, increasing the range, and also to incorporate a launching system for the new Red Top air-to-air guided missiles. Two Sea Vixen F.A.W.1s from Christchurch (XN684 and XN685) were converted at Hatfield to become F.A.W.2 interim prototypes and made their first flights on 1 June 1962 and 17 August 1962 respectively. After a period of trials, both these aircraft were converted to full production F.A.W.2 standard at Hawker Siddeley's Hawarden factory and eventually went on the strength of No.893 Squadron at Yeovilton.

Full-scale production of the F.A.W.2 began at Hawarden in 1962, the first 14 aircraft (XP919 to 925 and XP953 to 959) being airframes started as Mk.1s and completed as Mk.2s. The first production F.A.W.2 (XP919) made its maiden flight on 8 March 1963. Fifteen more Sea Vixens (XS576 to 590) were built from the outset as F.A.W.2s, the last being completed in 1966. In addition, from 1963 to 1968, there were 67 conversions from F.A.W.1 to F.A.W.2.

No.899 Squadron at Yeovilton was the first to receive Sea Vixen F.A.W.2s, the first aircraft arriving in February 1964. In December 1964, No.899 Squadron's F.A.W.2s embarked in HMS *Eagle* and the following year formed part of the Royal Navy force off the East coast of Africa mounting the blockade on Rhodesia. Other squadrons equipped with the F.A.W.2 were No.766 (from July 1965), No.893 (from November 1965), No.892 (from December 1965) and No.890 (from August 1967).

The Sea Vixen F.A.W.2 was in its heyday in the summer of 1968, the year in which the famous aerobatic team 'Simon's Sircus' formed from No.892 Squadron, commanded by Lt Cdr Simon Idiens, RN, thrilled the crowds at Farnborough. In October 1968, No.892 Squadron disbanded (to be re-formed the following year with Phantoms) and this began the slow decline of the Sea Vixen force: No.893 disbanding in July 1970, No.766 in December 1970. The last Sea Vixens in front-line squadron service with an aircraft-carrier were those of No.899 Squadron, retained in HMS *Eagle* to the end of its service in January 1972.

No.890 Squadron (Yeovilton and Lossiemouth), No.892 Squadron (*Centaur* and *Hermes*), No.893 Squadron (Yeovilton, *Victorious* and *Hermes*), No.899 Squadron (*Centaur* and *Eagle*). *Second-line squadrons:* No.766 (Yeovilton).

TECHNICAL DATA (SEA VIXEN F.A.W.2)

Description: Two-seat carrier-borne all-weather interceptor or strike fighter. All-metal stressed-skin construction.

Manufacturers: Hawker Siddeley Aviation Ltd, Hawarden, Chester.

Power Plant: Two Rolls-Royce Avon 208 turbojets, each of 11,230 lb static thrust.

Dimensions: Span, 51 ft 0 in. Length, 55 ft 7 in. Height, 10 ft 9 in. Wing area, 648 sq ft.

Weights: Empty, 31,715 lb. Loaded, 45,700 lb.

Performance: Maximum speed, 640 mph at sea level. Mach 0.95 at high level. Initial climb, 8,000 ft/min. Service ceiling, 48,000 ft. Maximum range, nearly 2,000 miles.

Armament: Four Red Top air-to-air missiles plus two retractable pods each containing 14 2-in rockets, in front fuselage. Up to four 500 lb bombs below wings.

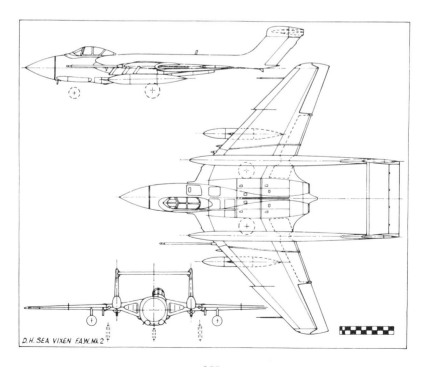

D.H. SEA VIXEN F.A.W.Mk2

Buccaneer S.2 of No.809 Squadron from *Hermes*. *(FAA Museum)*

Hawker Siddeley Buccaneer S.2

The Spey-engined Buccaneer S.2 was a natural development of the Gyron-engined S.1 as the original airframe design had built-in potential for more powerful engines. The Buccaneer S.2 had a 30 per cent increase in thrust and a lower fuel consumption bestowing greater range. The main external modification visible was the enlargement of the circular engine intakes to an oval shape to take the Spey's greater mass flow.

The Buccaneer S.2 was ordered by the Royal Navy in January 1962 and the pre-production protoype (XK526, a converted S.1) flew on 17 May 1963. A second prototype (XK527) flew on 19 August 1963, introducing the non-retractable refuelling probe.

The first full production Buccaneer S.2 (XN974) made its maiden flight on 6 June 1964 and the type stayed in production for the Fleet Air Arm until December 1968. Total production for the Royal Navy was 84, the serial numbers allocated being XN974 to 983, XT269 to 288, XV152 to 168, XV332 to 361 and XV863 to 869. Some of these aircraft were transferred to the RAF to equip No.12 Squadron, prior to the delivery of 26 Buccaneer S.2B aircraft specially built for the RAF. The first production S.2 (XN974) made the first non-stop crossing of the Atlantic by a FAA aircraft on 4 October 1965. Crewed by Cdr G Higgs, RN, and Lt Cdr A Taylor, RN, it flew from Goose Bay, Labrador, to Lossiemouth, a distance of 1,950 miles in 4 hours 16 minutes. There was no flight refuelling.

Buccaneer S.2s were first delivered to the Fleet Air Arm in March 1965 and No.700B Flight, an Intensive Flying Trials Unit, was commissioned at Lossiemouth in April 1965. The first operational unit to be equipped was No.801 Squadron at Lossiemouth on 14 October 1965, and one of its aircraft (XN980) made a low-level pass over Nelson's Column on 18 October to mark the 160th Anniversary of the Battle of Trafalgar.

In June 1966, No.801 Squadron's S.2s embarked in HMS *Victorious* and other units equipped were No.809 Squadron (from January 1966), No.800 Squadron (from June 1966) and No.803 Squadron (from January 1968). Buccaneers of Nos.800 and 736 Squadrons took part in the *Torrey Canyon* operation in March

1967, flying from RNAS Brawdy. No.800 Squadron's Buccaneers, land-based at Luqa, Malta, during the NATO Exercise *Eden Apple* in 1968, claimed a very high success rate in strikes.

The Buccaneer S.2 continued in service with HMS *Eagle* until it retired in 1972 and with *Ark Royal* until 1978. The aircraft were then transferred to the RAF.

UNITS ALLOCATED

No.800 Squadron (*Eagle*), No.801 Squadron (*Victorious* and *Hermes*), No.803 Squadron (*Hermes*), No.809 Squadron (*Victorious, Hermes* and *Ark Royal*). *Second-line squadrons:* Nos.700 and 736.

TECHNICAL DATA (BUCCANEER S.2)

Description: Two-seat carrier-borne low-level strike aircraft. All-metal stressed-skin construction.

Manufacturers: Hawker Siddeley Aviation Ltd, Brough and Holme-on-Spalding Moor, E Yorks.

Power Plant: Two Rolls-Royce Spey Mk.101 turbojets, each of 11,150 lb static thrust.

Dimensions: Span, 44 ft 0 in. Length 63 ft 5 in. Height 16 ft 3 in. Wing area, 515 sq ft.

Weights: Empty, 33,500 lb. Loaded, 62,000 lb.

Performance: Maximum speed, 646 mph. Initial climb, 7,000 ft/min. Range 2,300 miles. Service ceiling, over 40,000 ft.

Armament: Maximum weapon load of 16,000 lb comprising a variety of armaments including 1,000 lb bombs, 500 lb bombs, rocket-pods and (S.2D) Martel missiles. Additionally, nuclear strike capacity.

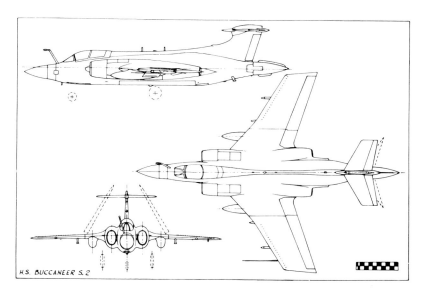

H.S. BUCCANEER S.2

Henry Farman F.22. *(Imperial War Museum)*

Henry Farman F.20 and F.22

The name of the Henry Farman pusher biplane appears in some of the earliest annals of British naval aviation. It is recorded that on 27 August 1914 seaplanes Nos.97 and 156 of the RNAS led the Battle Fleet to sea. The seaplanes in question were Henry Farmans and, indeed, many of the aircraft of this type supplied to the RNAS before the outbreak of war were fitted with twin floats as shown in the three-view drawing. Both landplanes and seaplanes were built in England by the Aircraft Manufacturing Company at Hendon, and all were powered by the 80 hp Gnome, with the exception of No.115, which had a 100 hp Renault.

The first RNAS unit to go overseas, the Eastchurch squadron commanded by Wg Cdr C R Samson, flew to Ostend with nine assorted types, one of which was a Henry Farman F.20. In March 1915 this unit became No.3 Squadron, RNAS, and was sent to the Eastern Mediterranean to participate in the Dardanelles campaign with eight Henry Farmans, two B.E.2cs, two B.E.2s, two Sopwith Tabloids, a Breguet and three Maurice Farmans. Of all these types, the Henry Farmans were the least useful, as they were too slow and difficult to maintain in the field. They were used briefly as single-seaters for reconnaissance; a further six which arrived in May were promptly returned to England as being valueless for first-line duties. Re-engined with the 140 hp Canton Unné, the Henry Farman was distinctly better, and served as a bomber with the RNAS in the Aegean from July 1915 onwards. This version, the F.27, was of steel construction, and it was with this type that Wg Cdr Samson dropped a 500 lb bomb (the biggest of the war at that date) on a Turkish barracks during a flight from Imbros on 18 December 1915. The Farman F.27 is described and illustrated separately in Appendix A.

Some of the earliest bombing attacks on submarines and Zeppelin sheds were made by Henry Farmans of the RNAS in Belgium. On the night of 6/7 June 1915, F/Sub-Lt J S Mills of No.1 Wing destroyed LZ38 in its shed at Evère with four 20 lb bombs. On 26 August 1915 Sqn Cdr A W Bigsworth of No.2 Wing attacked a U-boat six miles off Ostend and, on 28 November 1915, F/Sub-Lt Viney claimed to have blown a U-boat in half with two well-aimed 65 lb bombs, but this feat was never officially recognised.

Eastchurch squadron, which became No.3 Squadron, RNAS, in March 1915 and No.3 Wing, RNAS, in June 1915. Also Nos.1 and 2 Squadrons (later Nos.1 and 2 Wings), RNAS.

TECHNICAL DATA (HENRY FARMAN F.20)

Description: Two-seat reconnaissance, bombing and training aircraft. Wooden structure, fabric covered.

Manufacturers: Henry and Maurice Farman, Billancourt (Seine), France. Sub-contracted by Aircraft Manufacturing Co Ltd, Hendon.

Power Plant: One 80 hp Gnome.

Dimensions: Span, 44 ft 9 in. Length, 26 ft 6 in. Height, 12 ft. Wing area, 375 sq ft.

Weights: Empty, 820 lb. Loaded, 1,440 lb.

Performance: Maximum speed, 60 mph at sea level. Climb, 18½ min to 3,000 ft. Endurance, 3 hr.

Armament: None standardised, but some aircraft fitted with a Lewis gun in front cockpit.

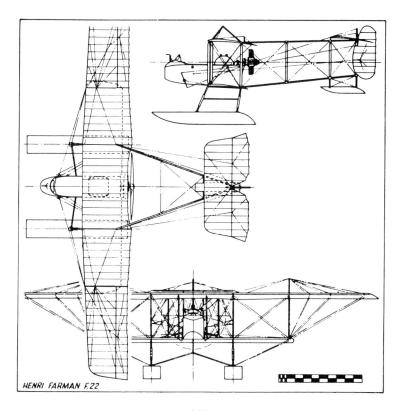

HENRI FARMAN F.22

Sea Prince C.1 (WF137). *(Crown Copyright)*

Hunting Percival Sea Prince

The Royal Navy was the first of the Services to order a military version of the Percival Prince civil feeder liner and executive transport, which first made its appearance in August 1948. The first Sea Prince, as the naval version was named, emerged almost three years before the RAF's Pembroke.

The first Sea Prince C. Mk.1 (WF136) made its maiden flight on 24 March 1950, and was equipped for special communications duties. It was followed by two further C. Mk.1s; one was fitted out as an 'Admiral's Barge' VIP transport, and another was a standard eight-seater for the use of the naval staff of the Joint Services Mission in Washington, DC. This latter aircraft was delivered by air across the North Atlantic, via Iceland, Greenland, Newfoundland and Canada. The three Sea Prince C. Mk.1s were similar in most respects to the Prince Series II. The maker's designation was P.66 and the serial numbers WF136 to WF138. First recipients were No.781 Squadron in July 1950.

The next production version was the Sea Prince T.Mk.1 (to spec T.14/49) which met the Royal Navy's requirement for a 'flying classroom'. This version introduced a number of changes, such as a lengthened nose to accommodate radar, a long-stroke twin-wheel undercarriage leg and longer engine nacelles. The interior of the fuselage was fitted out to accommodate three pupils, and a comprehensive range of wireless and radar equipments for the training of observers in navigation and the techniques of anti-submarine warfare. The first Sea Prince T.Mk.1 (WF118) made its initial flight at Luton, on 28 June 1951, and a total of 41 aircraft of this type was built, serialled WF118 to 133, WF934, WF949, WM735 to 742 and WP307 to 321.

The last version of the Sea Prince was the C.Mk.2 which was a communications version of the T.Mk.1, and four of these were delivered. The first C.Mk.2 (WM756) flew on 1 April 1953 and the last (WJ350) was delivered to the Royal Navy on 3 September 1953.

Jetstreams replaced No.750 Squadron's Sea Princes from October 1978 and the type was finally phased out of Fleet Air Arm service in May 1979.

(T.1): Nos.831, 1830, 1840, 1841 and 1844 Squadrons. *Second-line squadrons:* Nos.702, 727, 744, 750 and 781. (C.1): No.781 (C.2): No.781.

TECHNICAL DATA (SEA PRINCE T.1)

Description: Navigation and anti-submarine trainer with a crew of two and three pupils. All-metal stressed-skin construction.

Manufacturers: Hunting Percival Aircraft Ltd, Luton, Bedfordshire.

Power Plant: Two 550 hp Alvis Leonides 125.

Dimensions: Span, 56 ft. Length, 46 ft 4 in. Height, 16 ft 1 in. Wing area, 365 sq ft.

Weights: Empty, 8,850 lb. Loaded, 11,850 lb.

Performance: Maximum speed, 223 mph at 2,000 ft. Cruising speed, 183 mph at 11,000 ft. Climb, 1,400 ft/min. Range, 400 nautical miles. Service ceiling, 22,000 ft.

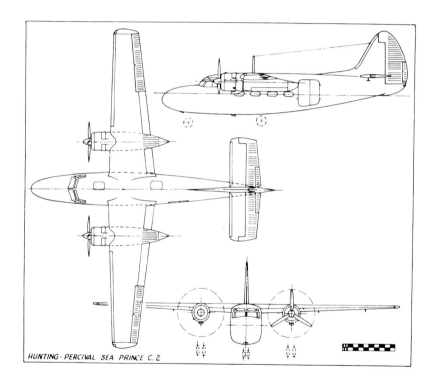

HUNTING-PERCIVAL SEA PRINCE C.2

Maurice Farman Shorthorn (N6310) of the RNAS *(F Cheesman)*

Maurice Farman Shorthorn

Both the Maurice Farman Shorthorn and the Longhorn (see Appendix) were being supplied to the RNAS by the Aircraft Manufacturing Company at Hendon before the First World War. Among the first 200 official serial numbers allotted by the Admiralty for naval aircraft, the S.7 Longhorn made its first appearance as No.23, and the S.11 Shorthorn as No.29. The latter was a twin-float seaplane (as shown in the three-view drawing), and was stationed at Great Yarmouth from July 1913. Another of the early Shorthorn seaplanes appeared on strength at Cromarty in July 1913.

The Longhorn and the Shorthorn (the latter distinguished by the absence of a forward elevator) had been introduced to the British flying services as trainers at the Central Flying School as early as 1912, and they continued to serve in this rôle with both the RFC and the RNAS.

Whereas the Longhorn was used only as a trainer, the Shorthorn also saw operational service for reconnaissance and bombing. Of the RNAS's first-line strength of 40 landplanes and 31 seaplanes on 4 August 1914, four were Maurice Farman landplanes fitted with 70 hp or 100 hp Renault engines.

The Maurice Farmans, with 100 hp Renaults, accompanied Samson's No.3 Squadron, RNAS, to the Dardanelles and were flown over the Turkish lines.

The last Shorthorns delivered to the RNAS were 20 built as trainers by the Eastbourne Aviation Company. The RNAS used 90 Shorthorns in all.

UNITS ALLOCATED

With Wg Cdr Samson's unit in Belgium, later No.3 Squadron RNAS, at Dardanelles. RNAS stations at Calshot, Cromarty, Grain and Great Yarmouth.

TECHNICAL DATA (S.11 SHORTHORN)

Description: Two-seat reconnaissance and bombing aircraft, also used for training. Wooden structure, fabric covered.

Manufacturers: Henry and Maurice Farman, Billancourt (Seine), France. Sub-contracted by Aircraft Manufacturing Co Ltd, Hendon, Eastbourne Aviation and others.

Power Plant: One 70 hp or 100 hp Renault.

Dimensions: Span, 53 ft. Length, 30 ft 8 in. Height, 10 ft 4 in. Wing area, 561 sq ft.

Weights: Empty, 1,441 lb. Loaded, 2,046 lb.

Performance: Maximum speed, 66 mph at sea level. Climb, 15 min to 3,000 ft. Endurance, 3¾ hr.

Armament: No defensive armament normally carried. Light bomb-load below wings.

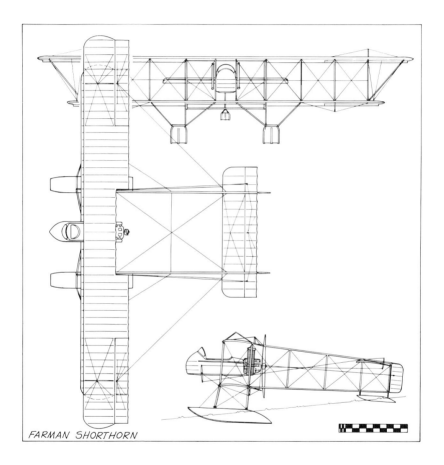

FARMAN SHORTHORN

Phantom F.G.1 of No.892 Squadron. *(MoD (Royal Navy))*

McDonnell Douglas Phantom

This classic American multi-mission fighter was first ordered for the Fleet Air Arm in July 1964 and in April 1968, when the first entered service at Yeovilton, it became the first truly supersonic fighter of the Royal Navy. Sadly, with the decision not to proceed with large aircraft-carriers after *Ark Royal* retired in 1978, it was also the last Fleet Air Arm air superiority fighter and No.892 Squadron, the only Phantom first-line unit of the FAA, symbolised this fact with its 'omega' tail insignia.

Revisions in British defence policy resulted in the original Royal Navy requirement for 140 being reduced to 52 F.G.1s, serialled XT595–598, XT857–876 and XV565–592. The main modifications in the British version were the introduction of Rolls-Royce Spey turbofans in place of the American J79 turbojets, folding nose radome to fit RN hangar lifts, larger flaps, drooping ailerons, slotted tailplane (with reduced anhedral) and a new nose landing gear extending 40 inches compared with the American F-4K's 20 inches. Net result was a 10 mph reduction in approach speed, improved catapult performance, 10 per cent increase in radius of action, 15 per cent increase in ferry range and better take-off, climb and acceleration.

The first F.4K Phantom for the Royal Navy (XT595) flew at St Louis on 27 June 1966. The first F.G.1s arrived at Yeovilton on 29 April 1968 and the following day a trials squadron, No.700P, was commissioned. Then on 14 January 1969 the Phantom Training Unit, No.767 Squadron, was formed to train crews for the first operational unit, No.892 Squadron (formerly Sea Vixens), which commissioned on 31 March 1969, commanded by Lt Cdr Brian Davies, RN.

No.892's Phantom XT858, flown by the CO, established the fastest overall west-east time in the *Daily Mail* Transatlantic Air Race of May 1969 with a new record crossing time of 4 hr 46 min 57 sec, averaging a true air speed of 1,100 mph.

Before embarkation in HMS *Ark Royal*, Phantoms of No.892 operated from the US carrier *Saratoga* in the Mediterranean in 1969. *Ark Royal* finally embarked No.892's twelve Phantoms on 14 June 1970.

From early 1974, FAA Phantoms began to appear with new fin-top housings for passive ECM equipment. No.892's Phantoms served with HMS *Ark Royal* until the demise of the fleet carrier in 1978. The last Phantom catapulted from *Ark Royal* was XT870 on 27 November 1978.

UNITS ALLOCATED

No.892 Squadron (Yeovilton, Leuchars and *Ark Royal*). *Second-line squadrons:* Nos.700P and 767 (Yeovilton).

TECHNICAL DATA (PHANTOM F.G.1)

Description: Two-seat carrier-borne interceptor fighter. All-metal stressed-skin construction.

Manufacturers: McDonnell Douglas Aircraft Corporation, St Louis, Missouri. Sub-assemblies by British Aircraft Corporation (Preston) and Short Bros and Harland (Belfast).

Power Plant: Two Rolls-Royce Spey 203 turbofans, each of 12,250 lb static thrust (20,515 lb with re-heat).

Dimensions: Span, 38 ft 5 in. Length, 57 ft 7 in. Height, 16 ft 1 in. Wing area, 530 sq ft.

Weights: Empty, 31,000 lb. Loaded, 58,000 lb.

Performance: Maximum speed, 1,386 mph at 40,000 ft. Initial climb 32,000 ft/min. Combat radius, 500 miles. Ferry range, 2,500 miles. Service ceiling, 57,200 ft.

Armament: Four fuselage-mounted Sparrow III air-to-air missiles and four Sidewinder air-to-air missiles below wings for interception duties. Could be adapted to carry up to 10,000 lb of conventional bombs, rockets or missiles for attack duties.

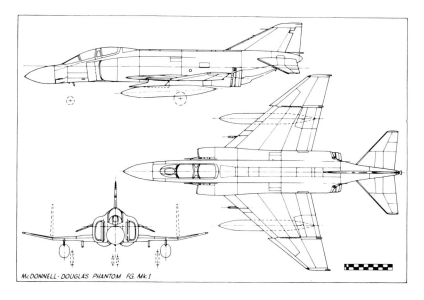

McDONNELL-DOUGLAS PHANTOM FG Mk.1

Morane Parasol (No.3253) flown by Warneford with French roundels.

Morane-Saulnier Type L

The Morane-Saulnier Company was one of the pioneer firms of the French aircraft industry. The type L two-seat monoplane, more generally known as the Morane Parasol, made its first appearance in 1913, and was at once ordered by the French Army. At the end of 1914, when French aircraft were eagerly sought by the British Government, the Morane Parasol was also acquired for the RNAS, and 25 (Nos.3239 to 3263) were delivered. The first deliveries were to No.1 (Naval) Squadron at Dunkirk in May 1915. The RNAS thus became the first of the British flying services to use the type, though the later version, Type LA, was subsequently adopted by the RFC for artillery observation duties during 1916–17.

The name of the Morane Parasol will forever be associated with the remarkable feat of F/Sub-Lt R A J Warneford, who was flying an aircraft of this type, No.3253, when he destroyed the Zeppelin LZ37 over Ghent on 7 June 1915. Warneford, a member of No.1 Squadron, RNAS, had set off from Dunkirk to bomb Berchem St Agathe, but was diverted from his task by the sight of a Zeppelin, which he chased, though under heavy machine-gun fire from its gondolas. Eventually he outclimbed the Zeppelin and reached 11,000 ft, from which height he dived to drop six 20 lb bombs on the LZ37's envelope. The Zeppelin exploded and went down in flames; meanwhile a broken petrol pipe forced Warneford to land inside enemy lines, where he stayed for 35 min before he effected a repair and flew back. This was the first time that a Zeppelin had been destroyed in the air, and for his achievement Warneford was awarded the VC, being the second airman to be so decorated.

Apart from this outstanding incident, the career of the Morane Parasol with the RNAS was not particularly distinguished. In addition to its service in Belgium, Wg Cdr E L Gerrard's No.2 Wing had six Moranes on strength during the Dardanelles operations. The Moranes had scant success, chiefly because their Le Rhône engines picked up the fine sand so easily.

266

No.1 Squadron, later No.1 Wing, RNAS, at Dunkirk, No.2 Squadron, later No.2 Wing, RNAS, at Dunkirk and Imbros and No.3 Squadron, later No.3 Wing, RNAS, at Mudros.

TECHNICAL DATA (MORANE TYPE L)

Description: Two-seat reconnaissance aircraft, frequently used as a single-seater by the RNAS. Wooden structure, fabric covered. Maker's designation: M.S.3.

Manufacturers: Morane-Saulnier Soc. de Constructions Aéronautiques, Paris.

Power Plant: One 80 hp Le Rhône 9C

Dimensions: Span, 36 ft 9 in. Length, 22 ft 7 in. Height, 12 ft 10 in. Wing area, 197 sq ft.

Weights: Empty, 847 lb. Loaded, 1,441 lb.

Performance: Maximum speed, 72 mph. Climb, 468 ft/min.

Armament: No standard armament, though rifles could be carried and bomb racks improvised in the field.

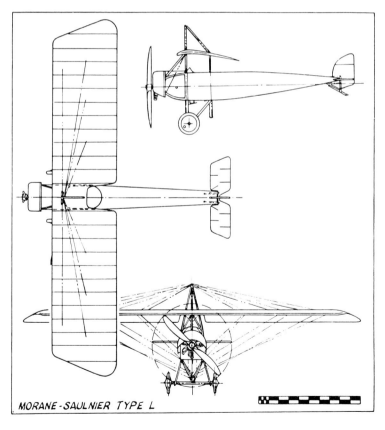

MORANE-SAULNIER TYPE L

Nieuport 17bis (N5875) of the RNAS at Chingford. *(J M Bruce.)*

Nieuport Scout

In its various guises, the Nieuport V-strutter sesquiplane scout was one of the most famous aircraft of the First World War, and will always be associated with the brilliant exploits of such pilots as Ball and Bishop of the RFC, and Navarre and Nungesser of the French Air Force.

The first RNAS Nieuport Scouts were the Type 11 with 80 hp Le Rhône engines, described and illustrated in the Appendix and in the drawing opposite. These arrived early in 1916 and saw extensive service with No.1 Wing of the RNAS in Belgium and No.2 Wing in the Aegean. 'A' Squadron at Furnes in Belgium commanded by Squadron Commander F K Haskins became the first homogenous fighter unit of the RNAS in June 1916. From November 1916, the improved Nieuport 17bis was introduced. This had a 130 hp Clerget engine and a round-sided, streamlined fuselage. Around 80 of these were supplied to the RNAS. Those serialled between N3100 and N3209 were from the original French manufacturers but the remainder (N5860–5909) were built under licence by the British Nieuport Co. Ten additional Nieuport Scouts were of the Type 21 model which reverted to the 80 hp Le Rhône engine. These were serialled 3956–3958 and 8745–8751 and for some reason were known to the RNAS as Nieuport 17Bs.

The RNAS Nieuport Scouts played a significant rôle in support of the RFC on the Western Front from late 1916 until replaced the following year by Sopwith Triplanes and Camels. For the most part they flew in squadrons with mixed equipment, usually alongside Sopwith Pups as in the case of the famous Naval Eight, but one unit, No.6 (Naval) Squadron, had a full complement of Nieuport 17bis.

UNITS ALLOCATED

No.1 Wing, RNAS (Dunkirk), No.2 Wing, RNAS (Aegean) and No.3 Wing, RNAS (Aegean). No.6 (Naval) Squadron and partial equipment of Nos.1, 4, 8, 9, 10 and 11 (Naval) Squadrons on the Western Front.

Description: Single-seat fighting scout. Wooden structure, fabric covered.

Manufacturers: Soc Anonyme des Établissements Nieuport, Issy-le-Moulineaux (Seine), France, and British Nieuport Company, Cricklewood.

Power Plant: One 130 hp Clerget.

Dimensions: Span, 27 ft 3 in. Length, 19 ft 6 in. Height, 7ft. Wing area, 158 sq ft.

Weights: Empty, 825 lb. Loaded, 1,233 lb.

Performance: Maximum speed, 115 mph at sea level. Climb, 5½ min to 6,500 ft; 9 min to 10,000 ft. Endurance, 2 hr. Service ceiling, 18,000 ft.

Armament: One fixed Lewis gun mounted above the top wing firing clear of the airscrew disc. Later a synchronised Vickers gun was mounted above the cowling. Provision for four Le Prieur rockets on each V strut.

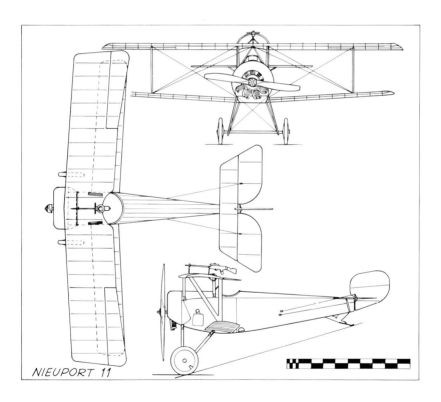

NIEUPORT 11

Nieuport 12 (9233) built by Beardmore. *(Imperial War Museum)*

Nieuport Two-Seater

In common with the Nieuport Scout, which it closely resembled in general configuration, the Nieuport two-seater was widely used by the RNAS as well as the RFC.

The early Nieuport 10 two-seater (see Appendix) was followed by the larger, improved Nieuport 12. Both types were, as might be expected, of somewhat larger overall dimensions than the Scout and accommodated pilot and observer in closely-coupled cockpits, the pilot being seated immediately beneath the centre section and the observer-gunner level with the trailing edge. Some Nieuport 10s in RNAS service, however, dispensed with the rear gunner and were flown as single-seaters from the rear cockpit, a single Lewis gun being mounted above the top wing to fire above the airscrew disc, as on the normal Scouts. It was a Nieuport of this type (No.3172) that was being flown by Squadron Commander Bell Davies on 19 November 1915 when he won his VC.

The original batches of Nieuport two-seaters in British service were purchased from the French industry, but later the type was built in Britain. The British-built Nieuports differed from the earlier model (shown in the three-view drawing) in having a fixed fin and a fully circular cowling instead of the cutaway type. Fifty were built for the Admiralty by Beardmore in 1916, the serial numbers being 9201 to 9250. Later, some of these aircraft (Nos.9213 to 9232) were transferred to the RFC as A5183 to 5202. Altogether the RNAS received 194 Nieuport two-seaters: 72 had the 130 hp Clerget engine and the remainder the 110 hp Clerget.

The Nieuport two-seaters did some good work with the Dunkirk Wing in combat with German aircraft along the Belgian coast. A typical engagement was that of 14 December 1915 when F/Sub-Lt C W Graham, with Sub-Lt A S Ince as observer, shot down in flames a German seaplane which was attempting to bomb an Allied merchant steamer stranded on a sandbank. The Nieuport crew were forced down in the sea, but were rescued by the mine-sweeper *Balmoral*.

No.1 Wing, RNAS, Dunkirk; No.2 Wing, RNAS, Imbros; No.3 Wing, RNAS, Dardanelles; No.5 Wing, RNAS, Petite Synthe; No.7 (Naval) Squadron, Petite Synthe; No.10 (Naval) Squadron, St Pol.

TECHNICAL DATA (NIEUPORT 12)

Description: Two-seat fighting, reconnaissance and bombing aircraft. Wooden structure, fabric covered.

Manufacturers: Soc Anonyme des Établissements Nieuport, Issy-le-Moulineaux (Seine), France. Sub-contracted by Wm Beardmore & Co Ltd, Dalmuir, Dumbartonshire.

Power Plant: One 110 hp or 130 hp Clerget.

Dimensions: Span, 29 ft 7½ in. Length, 23 ft 11¼ in. Height, 8 ft 9 in. Wing area, 236½ sq ft.

Weights: Empty, 1,210 lb. Loaded, 2,026 lb.

Performance: Maximum speed, 78 mph at 5,000 ft. Climb, 14 min to 6,500 ft. Endurance, 3 hr. Service ceiling, 13,000 ft.

Armament: Single free-mounted Lewis gun in rear cockpit for observer or single fixed Lewis gun above top wing when flown as single-seaters.

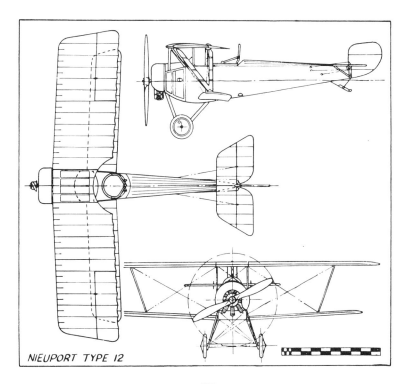

NIEUPORT TYPE 12

Nightjar (H8539) as flown from HMS *Argus*. *(MoD)*

Nieuport Nightjar

The Nightjar was the first new type of single-seat fighter to be used aboard British aircraft-carriers after the end of the First World War. It remained in service for only a brief period, from 1922 to 1924, and was followed by the Parnall Plover and Fairey Flycatcher.

Like its FAA contemporary, the Parnall Panther spotter-reconnaissance aircraft, the Nightjar was powered by the Bentley B.R.2 rotary engine, and it was this feature that distinguished it from the closely related Nieuport Nighthawk, as used by the RAF, which had an Armstrong Siddeley Jaguar or Bristol Jupiter radial engine. Nightjars were, in fact, straight conversions from Nighthawk airframes and contracts for 22 were placed (H8535–8545 and J6930–6941) with Glosters.

The Nightjar was but one of a series of fighters produced by the Gloucestershire company after the original Nieuport Nighthawk design had been taken over in 1920. Differing only in detail, these fighters were known as the Mars series. The Mars II, III and IV were supplied in quantity to the Japanese Navy, where they were known as the Sparrowhawk I, II and III respectively. The Mars IV (the only version with a radial instead of a B.R.2 engine) was the Nighthawk, and the Mars X became the Nightjar. The Nightjar differed from earlier Mars fighters in having an undercarriage of wider track and longer stroke, with arrester hooks on the axle to engage fore-and-aft wires on the carrier deck.

Nightjars first entered service in August 1922 and operated with No.203 Squadron during the Chanak (Turkish) crisis of 1922, being ferried out from Leuchars in crates aboard HMS *Argus* in September. The six Nightjars involved superseded Sopwith Camels and from April 1923 went on to serve with No.401 Flight until replaced by Flycatchers in 1924.

No.203 Squadron (Leuchars and *Argus*), No.401 Flight (Leuchars and *Argus*), No.403 Flight (*Hermes*) and No.404 Flight (*Furious*).

TECHNICAL DATA (NIGHTJAR)

Description: Single-seat carrier-borne fighter. Wooden structure, fabric covered.
Manufacturers: Gloucestershire Aircraft Co Ltd, Cheltenham.
Power Plant: One 230 hp Bentley B.R.2.
Dimensions: Span, 28 ft. Length, 19 ft 2 in. Height, 9 ft 7 in. Wing area, 270 sq ft.
Weight: Empty, 1,489 lb. Loaded, 2,165 lb.
Performance: Maximum speed, 120 mph at sea level. 110 mph at 15,000 ft. Climb, 20 min to 15,000 ft. Endurance, 2 hr at 3,000 ft. Service ceiling, 19,000 ft.
Armament: Two fixed, synchronised Vickers guns.

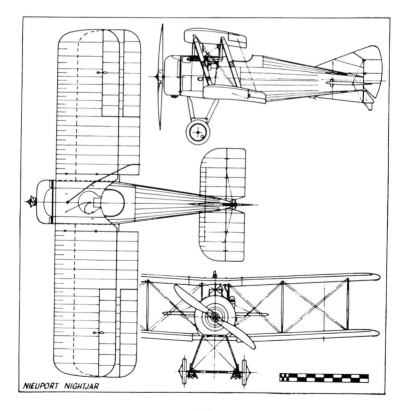

NIEUPORT NIGHTJAR

273

N.T.4A (N2142) of the RNAS. *(Imperial War Museum)*

Norman Thompson N.T.4

The Norman Thompson N.T.4 is perhaps the least known of all the large flying-boats employed on coastal patrol by the RNAS in the First World War. It never enjoyed the fame that attended the American Curtiss boats, or the Felixstowe series, but nevertheless was responsible for a good deal of routine anti-submarine reconnaissance from a string of bases between Calshot and Scapa Flow.

The N.T.4 was the first new design to appear after the old White and Thompson Company changed its name to the Norman Thompson Flight Company in October 1915, and its emergence coincided with the Curtiss H.4. For this reason, in the somewhat haphazard custom of those days, it was known by the name of 'America', and later changed to 'Small America', in the same way as the Curtiss. This may account for the obscurity in which its operational record is shrouded, as there may have been some confusion between the two types in official archives.

A feature of the N.T.4 was the completely enclosed accommodation for the crew. In the earlier version the view was poor and the cabin was progressively improved, so that in the late production models the cabin-top was glazed as well as the sides.

The first batch of aircraft (Nos.8338 to 8343) were fitted with two 150 hp Hispano-Suiza engines. Subsequent machines had 200 hp geared Hispanos, were designated N.T.4A and were allotted the serial numbers 9061 to 9064 and N2140 to 2159. Production ceased in the summer of 1918 after 30 had been built.

One of the N.T.4 flying-boats (No.8338) was the subject of an interesting experiment in armament. It was fitted with a Davis two-pounder recoil-less gun mounted above the cabin. The installation was never embodied in production aircraft.

RNAS coastal air stations at Calshot, Cattewater, Dundee, Felixstowe, Invergordon, Killingholme and Scapa Flow.

TECHNICAL DATA (N.T.4A)

Description: Anti-submarine reconnaissance flying-boat with a crew of four. Wooden structure, with wood and fabric covering.
Manufacturers: Norman Thompson Flight Co Ltd, Bognor Regis, Sussex.
Power Plant: Two 200 hp Hispano-Suiza.
Dimensions: Span, 78 ft 7 in. Length, 41 ft 6 in. Height, 14 ft 10 in. Wing area, 936 sq ft.
Weights: Empty, 4,572 lb. Loaded, 6,469 lb.
Performance: Maximum speed, 95 mph at 2,000 ft; 91 mph at 10,000 ft. Climb, 3 min 50 sec to 2,000 ft; 31 min 5 sec to 10,000 ft. Service ceiling, 11,700 ft.
Armament: Possibly provision for free-mounted Lewis gun firing through a side window and racks for bombs beneath lower wings.

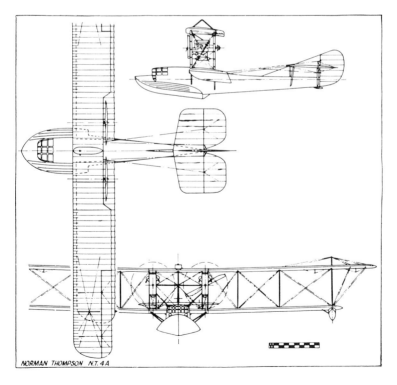

NORMAN THOMPSON N.T. 4A

Panther (N7511) with non-standard oleo undercarriage. *(MoD)*

Parnall Panther

The Panther was one of the first British aircraft designed specifically for operation from aircraft-carriers. It was the work of Mr Harold Bolas, formerly with the Air Department of the Admiralty, and met the requirements of the Admiralty Spec N.2A for a two-seat deck-landing reconnaissance aircraft. The first prototype (N91) emerged in April 1918 and was followed by five other prototypes (N92 to 96). It was unorthodox in a number of respects: it had a monocoque fuselage, a form of construction not then very common, and to conserve space aboard ship the fuselage was made to fold, being hinged just aft of the rear cockpit so that the rear fuselage and tail assembly could be swung to starboard. The pilot and observer were mounted unusually high; this gave the pilot an excellent forward view for deck-landing, but restricted entry to the cockpit which had to be reached through a hole in the top wing.

Two other features of the Panther, which added to its somewhat singular appearance, were the flotation air bags fitted beneath the bottom wings at either side of the undercarriage, and the hydrovane to prevent the aircraft nosing over in the event of a forced descent in the sea. The wheels could be jettisoned.

The original order for 312 Panthers was reduced to 150 with the Armistice, and these aircraft (N7400 to 7549) were built mostly by Bristol at Filton during 1919 and 1920 following a small initial batch by Parnall. The Panthers equipped Fleet Spotter Reconnaissance Flights aboard *Argus* and *Hermes* at a period when longitudinal arrester wires supporting hinged wooden flaps were in vogue. The aircraft itself carried hooks on the axle. This system was far from satisfactory and caused a lot of accidents; during training only five landings out of six escaped mishap. Although the Panthers handled well in the air, their Bentley engines needed careful nursing and demanded frequent attention. Be that as it may, the Panther was a great pioneer of early deck-flying, and remained in first-line service with the FAA as late as October 1924 with No.442 Flight at Leuchars. Panthers were finally superseded by the Fairey IIID.

No.205 Squadron (April 1920–April 1923, Leuchars), No.441 Flight (April 1923–June 1924, embarked *Argus* and *Hermes*), No.442 Flight (April 1923–October 1924, embarked *Argus*).

TECHNICAL DATA (PANTHER)

Description: Two-seat carrier-borne spotter-reconnaissance aircraft. Wooden structure with wood and fabric covering.
Manufacturers: Parnall & Sons, Bristol. Sub-contracted by the British & Colonial Aeroplane Co Ltd, Filton, Bristol.
Power Plant: One 230 hp Bentley B.R.2.
Dimensions: Span, 29 ft 6 in. Length, 24 ft 11 in (14 ft 6 in folded). Height, 10 ft 6 in. Wing area, 336 sq ft.
Weights: Empty, 1,328 lb. Loaded, 2,595 lb.
Performance: Maximum speed, 108½ mph at 6,500 ft; 103 mph at 10,000 ft. Climb, 2 min 20 sec to 2,000 ft; 17 min 5 sec to 10,000 ft. Endurance, 4½ hr. Service ceiling, 14,500 ft.
Armament: One free-mounted Lewis machine-gun in rear cockpit.

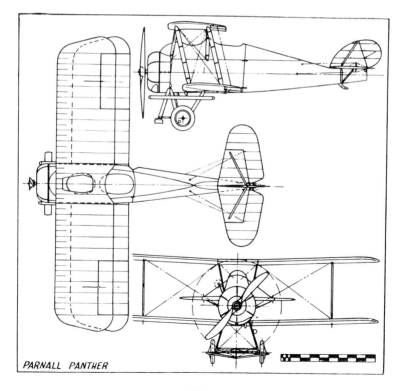

PARNALL PANTHER

Plover (N9702) which served with No.405 Flight. *(MoD)*

Parnall Plover

Having established themselves as designers of naval aircraft with their Panther two-seat spotter, the Parnall concern produced in 1922 the Plover single-seat fighter. Like its more successful competitor, the Flycatcher, the Plover met an Air Ministry specification (6/22) for a decklanding fighter, capable of superseding the Nieuport Nightjar and utilising either the Bristol Jupiter or Armstrong Siddeley Jaguar radial engine. As might be expected, the Plover bore many points of resemblance to its Fairey rival, but it never earned the same favour and disappeared into obscurity after a very short life with the FAA.

The Plover was designed by Harold Bolas (who was also responsible for the Panther), and three prototypes were built, numbered N160, N161 and N162. The first two Plovers had the 436 hp Jupiter engine, and the third aircraft a 385 hp Jaguar. Like the Flycatcher, the Plover was also available as an amphibian, with wheels projecting from the bottom of twin floats, and N161 appeared in this guise. One of the Plovers was exhibited in the New Types Park at the RAF Display at Hendon in 1923.

Small-scale production of the Plover (with the Jupiter engine and parallel interplane struts instead of N struts) took place in 1923, when it entered service alongside Nightjars with Nos.403 and 404 Fleet Fighter Flights. The Plovers were contemporaries of the Flycatchers then with No.402 Flight and in 1924 briefly served alongside the Flycatchers of No.405 Flight. The Flycatcher soon proved its superiority and the following year superseded the Plovers as well as the Nightjars. The Plover's rapid eclipse was possibly due to structural weakness: R R Money recalls in his book *Flying and Soldiering* an incident at Leuchars in 1924 when a Plover on test had its centre section collapse during aerobatics. The unfortunate pilot had no parachute, but by skilful flying

278

contrived to crash-land the Plover on a moor near the mouth of the River Eden.

Fourteen production Plovers were built, the serial numbers being N9608–9610 and N9698–9708.

UNITS ALLOCATED

No.403 Flight (Leuchars and *Hermes*), No.404 Flight (Leuchars and *Furious*) and No.405 Flight (*Furious*).

TECHNICAL DATA (PLOVER)

Description: Single-seat carrier-borne fighter available either as a landplane or an amphibian. Wooden structure, fabric covered.
Manufacturers: George Parnall & Co Ltd, Park Row, Bristol.
Power Plant: One 436 hp Bristol Jupiter IV.
Dimensions: Span, 29 ft. Length, 23 ft. Height, 12 ft. Wing area, 306 sq ft.
Weights: Empty, 2,035 lb. Loaded, 2,984 lb.
Performance: Maximum speed, 142 mph. Climb, 25 min 13 sec to 20,000 ft. Service ceiling, 23,000 ft.
Armament: Twin, synchronised Vickers machine-guns.

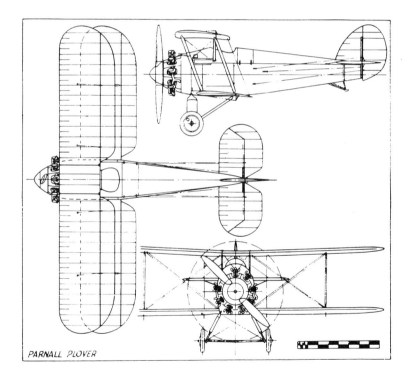

PARNALL PLOVER

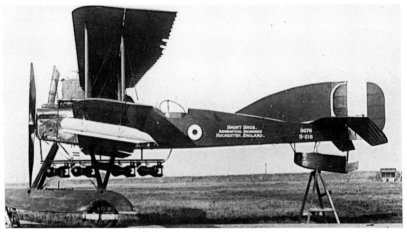

Short Type 184 (No.8076) with 240 hp Sunbeam, built by Short Brothers. *(Imperial War Museum)*

Short Type 184 Seaplane

In any history of the development of British naval aviation the Short Type 184 must occupy an honoured place. It was to the First World War what the Swordfish became in the Second World War; both types made history as torpedo-carrying aircraft and earned reputations in every theatre of war for solid reliability. More than 900 Short Type 184 seaplanes were built for the RNAS. They served at practically every coastal air station round Great Britain, as well as in the Mediterranean, the Aegean, the Red Sea, in Mesopotamia and on the French coast. The most important fact about the Short Type 184, however, is that it was the first aircraft in the world to sink an enemy ship at sea by means of a torpedo attack. It was also the only aircraft to play an active part in the Battle of Jutland.

As was the case with a number of key types of British naval aircraft, the Short Type 184 owed its existence to the fertile brain of Commodore Murray F Sueter (later Rear-Adm Sir Murray Sueter), who was Director of the Air Department of the Admiralty in the formative years of the RNAS. Commodore Sueter, from the earliest days a keen advocate of the torpedo as a RNAS weapon, had had his hand strengthened by the success of the experiment, on 28 July 1914, when a 14-in Whitehead torpedo of 810 lb had been dropped from a Short seaplane with 160 hp Gnome engine. With the outbreak of war, Commodore Sueter pressed his theories about the value of a powerful torpedo-carrying seaplane, and talked over his plans with Shorts. The outcome, early in 1915, was the Short Type 184. It took its designation from the curious Admiralty custom of those days whereby types were referred to by the number allocated to the first aircraft. Later, the type became known in general service by the more colloquial '225', which was the horse-power of the engine, though more powerful engines were subsequently fitted.

280

Some of the first Short 184s delivered to the RNAS (including the original No.184) went aboard the seaplane carrier *Ben-my-Chree* to serve in the Dardanelles campaign from June 1915. Within a few weeks it seemed that the optimism about the torpedo had been justified, for, on 12 August, F/Cdr C H K Edmonds made his historic flight, during which he sank an enemy ship. Flying from the Gulf of Xeros, he spotted a 5,000-ton Turkish merchant vessel, glided down from 800 ft to 15 ft, and launched his Whitehead torpedo at a range of 300 yards, striking the ship abreast the mainmast. On 17 August F/Cdr Edmonds took his Short seaplane out again and repeated his success; his torpedo hit one of three steamers making for Ak Bashi Liman. The steamer was set on fire and had to be towed back to Constantinople, a burnt-out hulk. Meanwhile, F/Lt G B Dacre in another Short 184 had succeeded in sinking a large steam tug whilst taxying on the water after a forced alighting due to engine failure. Afterwards he coaxed his Short into the air again under heavy Turkish fire.

These early successes with air-launched torpedoes were not to be repeated,

Short Type 184 (N1091) with 240 hp Renault, built by Short Brothers *(Short Bros)*

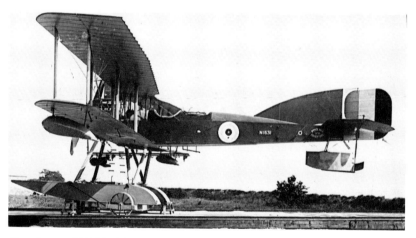

Short Improved 184 (N1631) with 260 hp Sunbeam, built by Phoenix. *(Imperial War Museum)*

but the Shorts from *Ben-my-Chree* were far from inactive. They performed a vital reconnaissance function, spotting for a naval monitor which shelled enemy transports, and bombing Turkish harbours. On 8 November 1915 Short seaplanes bombed the railway bridge over the River Maritza, and they were still hammering away at enemy communications as late as 27 August 1916, when Cdr C R Samson (who had taken over command of *Ben-my-Chree* the previous May) led a raid on Chikaldir Bridge, with F/Cdr England and Lt Clemson in the other Shorts. As Cdr Samson recalls in his book *Fights and Flights*, these raids were not without their difficulties; engines gave a lot of trouble due to overheating, as the coolant water boiled readily in the hot climate.

In February 1916 five Short 184s were sent to Mesopotamia, where they operated from the River Tigris. During the siege of Kut they dropped supplies to the garrison, each seaplane carrying about 250 lb of food.

In home waters Short 184s did a vast amount of routine anti-submarine patrol, and on one occasion (9 November 1916) even participated in a night-bombing raid on Ostend and Zeebrugge. For these operations they flew from coastal air stations, but they were also embarked in seaplane carriers, and it was one of these latter aircraft that achieved immortality in the Battle of Jutland. The Short 184 in question (No.8359, a Westland-built aircraft) was serving in *Engadine* and operating with the Battle Cruiser Fleet under Sir David Beatty. Piloted by F/Lt F J Rutland (who later pioneered the flying of Pups from gun-turret launching platforms), and with Assistant Paymaster G S Trewin as observer, the Short took off just after 3 p.m. on 31 May 1916. Within 40 min it had reported the presence and course of three enemy cruisers and ten destroyers. To make this observation, the Short had to fly low, under enemy gun-fire, as the clouds were at 900 ft and the visibility was poor. Continued bad weather made further air activity impracticable during the Battle of Jutland, and *Engadine* returned to Rosyth on 2 June. Limited as it was, the reconnaissance of 31 May was a milestone in naval air warfare equal in significance to the torpedo attack of the previous August.

The Short 184 was progressively improved throughout its career, some of the changes being introduced by the sub-contracting firms, of which there were many. In 1915, after only 12 Short 184s had been completed by the parent company, contracts were issued to S E Saunders Ltd, Mann, Egerton & Co Ltd, Westland, the Phoenix Dynamo Company and Frederick Sage & Co Ltd. Some of these firms had never previously built aircraft; nevertheless the first sub-contracted aircraft (from Sage) was ready in September 1915, and was followed by deliveries from Mann, Egerton in November 1915 and from Westlands and Phoenix early in 1916. Meanwhile the type continued in production at Shorts, and still more contractors were brought in later. As mentioned earlier, total production reached over 900, of which more than 300 were still in service in October 1918.

The power of the Short 184 was progressively increased from the 225 hp of the original Sunbeam to the 275 hp of the Sunbeam Maori III. This latter engine was fitted in some late production models, which could be distinguished by their twin exhaust stacks. Other standard installations were the 240 hp Sunbeam, the 240 hp Renault and the 260 hp Sunbeam.

The late production 260 hp Short became known as the Dover type; it differed from its fore-runners in having a car-type radiator immediately behind the

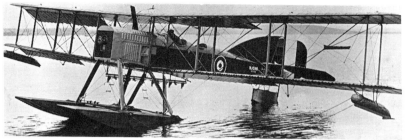

Short 184 Dover Type (N1098) with 260 hp Sunbeam and nose radiator, built by Short Brothers.
(Short Bros)

airscrew and dispensed with the ugly box-type radiator above or at the sides of the engine which had characterised other Short 184s. Most of the later Short 184s had a bomb-beam below the fuselage, between the float struts, and a Scarff ring for the observer in the aft cockpit.

By late 1918 the 184s were being steadily replaced in the Grand Fleet at sea by Fairey Campania seaplanes and at shore stations by the Fairey IIIB, but they continued to form the sole equipment of Nos.235, 237 and 239 Squadrons based at Newlyn, Cattewater and Torquay. The 184 saw only brief post-war service and was mostly withdrawn during 1919. The last Short 184s in service were most probably those with No.202 Squadron at Alexandria which were retained until May 1921.

It is interesting to note that the unique historic remains of Short 184 No.8359 (built by Westlands), which served from the seaplane-carrier *Engadine* at the Battle of Jutland arrived on public display at the FAA Museum at Yeovilton on 27 January 1976.

UNITS ALLOCATED

Seaplane carriers: Embarked in *Anne, Ben-my-Chree, Campania, City of Oxford, Empress, Engadine, Furious, Nairana, Pegasus, Raven II, Riviera* and *Vindex*. Units at RNAS coastal air stations re-designated after formation of RAF as follows:- No.202 Squadron (Alexandria), No.219 Squadron (Westgate), No.229 Squadron (Great Yarmouth), No.233 Squadron (Dover), No.234 Squadron (Tresco), No.235 Squadron (Newlyn), No.237 Squadron (Cattewater), No.238 Squadron (Cattewater), No.239 Squadron (Torquay), No.240 Squadron (Calshot), No.241 Squadron (Portland), No.242 Squadron (Newhaven), No.243 Squadron (Cherbourg), No.245 Squadron (Fishguard), No.246 Squadron (Seaton Carew), No.248 Squadron (Hornsea), No.249 Squadron (Dundee), No.253 Squadron (Bembridge), No.263 Squadron (Otranto), No.264 Squadron (Suda Bay), No.266 Squadron (Mudros and Petrovsk), No.267 Squadron (Kalafrana), No.286 Squadron (Kalafrana), No.269 Squadron (Port Said), No.270 Squadron (Alexandria) and No.271 Squadron (Taranto).

TECHNICAL DATA (SHORT 184)

Description: Two-seat reconnaissance, bombing and torpedo-carrying seaplane. Wooden structure, fabric covered.

Manufacturers: Short Bros, Rochester, Kent (Nos.184, 185, 841 to 850, 8031 to 8105, N1080 to 1099, N1580 to 1589). Sub-contracted by Brush Electrical

Engineering Co Ltd, Loughborough (N1660 to 1689, N2630 to 2659, N2790 to 2819, N9060 to 9099 and N9260 to 9289); Mann, Egerton & Co Ltd, Norwich (Nos.8344 to 8355); Phoenix Dynamo Manufacturing Co Ltd, Bradford (Nos.8368 to 8379, N1630 to 1659 and N1740 to 1759); Robey & Co Ltd, Lincoln (Nos.9041 to 9060, N1220 to 1229, N1260 to 1279, N1820 to 1839, N2900 to 2949, N9000 to 9059 and N9290 to 9317); Frederick Sage & Co Ltd, Peterborough (Nos.8380 to 8391, 9065 to 9084, N1130 to 1139, N1230 to 1239, N1590 to 1599 and N1780 to 1799); S E Saunders Ltd, Isle of Wight (Nos.8001 to 8030, N1140 to 1149, N1600 to 1624 and N1760 to 1774); Supermarine Aviation Works Ltd, Southampton (N9170 to 9199); Westland Aircraft Works, Yeovil (Nos.8356 to 8367) and J Samuel White & Co Ltd, Isle of Wight (N1240 to 1259, N2950 to 2999 and N9100 to 9139).

Power Plant: One 225 hp or 240 hp or 260 hp Sunbeam; 240 hp Renault or 275 hp Sunbeam Maori III.

Dimensions: Span, 63 ft 6¼ in. Length, 40 ft 7½ in. Height, 13 ft 6 in. Wing area, 688 sq ft.

Weights (with 260 hp Sunbeam): Empty, 3,703 lb. Loaded, 5,363 lb.

Performance (with 260 hp Sunbeam): Maximum speed, 88½ mph at 2,000 ft; 84 mph at 6,500 ft. Climb, 8 min 35 sec to 2,000 ft; 33 min 50 sec to 6,500 ft. Endurance, 2¾ hr. Service ceiling, 9,000 ft.

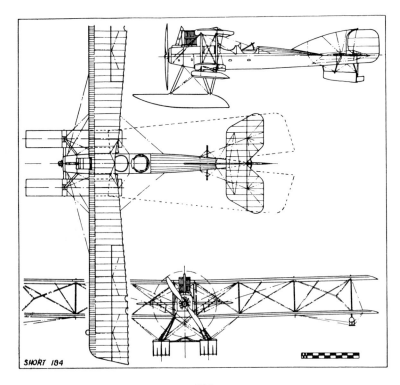

SHORT 184

Armament One free-mounted Lewis machine-gun aft and provision for one 14-in torpedo or various loads of bombs up to a maximum of 520 lb.

A particularly good flying picture of a Short Type 184. *(Imperial War Museum)*

Short Bomber (No.9834) built by Phoenix. *(Imperial War Museum)*

Short Bomber

As will be evident from its appearance, the Short Bomber was a landplane adaptation of the famous Short Type 184 seaplane. The prototype (No.3706) was produced to meet the requirements of an Admiralty competition of 1915 for a bomber offering good range and load-carrying properties, for even at this early stage the RNAS was turning its attention to the possibilities of strategic bombing. The prototype originally had standard Short 184 three-bay wings, then two-bay wings with overhung top surfaces, but all production aircraft had three-bay wings of increased span. The fuselage, too, was lengthened on later production aircraft, though early batches had a short fuselage, as in the drawing. Contracts for over 80 Short Bombers were placed, of which 36 were by Short Bros (Nos.9306 to 9340), 15 by Sunbeam (Nos.9356 to 9370), 20 by Mann, Egerton (Nos.9476 to 9495), six by Parnall (Nos.9771 to 9776) and six by Phoenix (Nos.9831 to 9836). The Sunbeam Company fitted the 225 hp Sunbeam engine in their aircraft: otherwise the 250 hp Rolls-Royce was standard.

The Short Bomber first entered service with No.7 Squadron, RNAS. Four of the new Shorts (250 hp engines) joined 18 other bombers of the 4th and 5th Naval Wings in a raid on the Ateliers de la Marine and the Slyken Electric Power Station at Ostend on the night of 15 November 1916. Each Short carried eight 65 lb bombs, twice the bomb-load of the accompanying Caudrons, but well below the aircraft's total capacity of 900 lb. No.7's Short Bombers continued to raid enemy naval installations throughout the winter of 1916–17, until superseded by Handley Page O/100s when the Squadron moved to Coude-kerque in April 1917.

Early in 1916 15 Short Bombers (together with 20 Sopwith 1½ Strutter bombers) were reserved for the initial equipment of the new RNAS bombing unit known as No.3 Wing, based at Luxeuil in the Nancy area, but ambitious plans for raids on German industry were seriously hampered by the need to transfer aircraft to the hard-pressed RFC, at the request of Gen Trenchard. It is not known to what extent the Shorts eventually participated in the No.3 Wing raids which began on 12 October 1916.

No.7 Squadron of No.5 Wing, RNAS, Coudekerque, and No.3 Wing, RNAS, Luxeuil.

TECHNICAL DATA (SHORT BOMBER)

Description: Two-seat long-range bomber. Wooden structure, fabric covered.
Manufacturers: Short Bros, Rochester. Sub-contracted by Mann, Egerton & Co Ltd of Norwich; Parnall & Sons Ltd of Bristol; the Phoenix Dynamo Manufacturing Co Ltd of Bradford, and the Sunbeam Motor Car Co Ltd of Wolverhampton.
Power Plant: One 225 hp Sunbeam or 250 hp Rolls-Royce Eagle.
Dimensions: Span, 85 ft. Length, 45 ft. Height, 15 ft. Wing area, 870 sq ft.
Weight: Loaded, 6,800 lb.
Performance: Maximum speed, 77½ mph at 6,500 ft. Climb, 45 min to 10,000 ft. Endurance, 6 hr. Service ceiling, 9,500 ft.
Armament: One free-mounted Lewis gun in rear cockpit. Bomb-load of four 230 lb or eight 112 lb bombs on racks below wings.

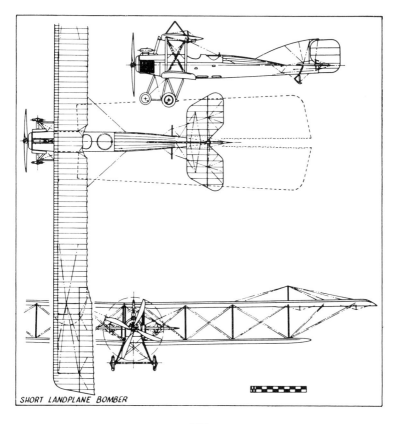

SHORT LANDPLANE BOMBER

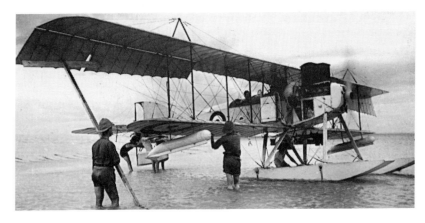

Short Admiralty Type 827 of the RNAS. *(Imperial War Museum)*

Short 827/830 Seaplane

Very similar in appearance to the Short 166 Seaplane (see Appendix), the Short 827/830 was of somewhat smaller dimensions and had two alternative power plants. The Type 827 could be more readily distinguished from the Type 166 in that it had an in-line Sunbeam engine, whereas the Type 830 had a Salmson water-cooled radial as in the Type 166.

The Admiralty's first contract for 12 aircraft was placed in the summer of 1914: it covered six Type 827s (Nos.822 to 827) and six Type 830s (Nos.819 to 821 and 828 to 830). Ultimately, the Type 827 predominated and 108 were ordered, against 28 of the Type 830. The Short 827 enjoyed a remarkably long operational life, for it served from 1915 until the Armistice.

Unlike the Short 830, which was built by the parent firm only, the Short 827 was manufactured by four firms in addition to Short Bros and, indeed, 12 aircraft of this type (Nos.8550 to 8561) were the first aircraft ever built by Fairey before they turned to their own designs.

Both the Short 827 and 830 were used from seaplane carriers, from RNAS coastal air stations and overseas. In March 1916 four Short 827s accompanied four Voisins to Zanzibar to form a unit which became No.8 Squadron, RNAS. They did much useful work in the East African campaign and a number of successful attacks were planned after photographic reconnaissance by a Short 827 operating from the seaplane carrier *Manica*. Short 827s operated in Mesopotamia from September 1915 and in December two were converted as landplanes to bomb the Turks advancing on Kut al Imara.

The following year, on 25 April 1916, a Short 827 (No.3108) from Great Yarmouth bombed the German warships that were shelling Lowestoft.

UNITS ALLOCATED

No.8 Squadron, RNAS (East Africa). *Seaplane carriers: Ben-my-Chree, Engadine, Manica* and *Raven II. Armed merchant vessels: Himalaya* and *Laconia. RNAS coastal air*

288

stations: Calshot, Dundee, Great Yarmouth, Isle of Grain and Killingholme. *Overseas:* Basra and Otranto.

TECHNICAL DATA (SHORT 827)

Description: Two-seat reconnaissance and bombing seaplane. Wooden structure, fabric covered.

Manufacturers: Short Bros (827s serialled 822–827, 3063–3072, 3093–3112 and 830s serialled 819–821, 828–830, 1335–1346 and 9781–9790). Subcontracted 827s by Brush Electrical (serialled 3321–3332 and 8230–8237), by Parnall (8218–8229 and 8250–8257), by Fairey (8550–8561) and by Sunbeam (8630–8649).

Power Plant: One 150 hp Sunbeam Nubian.

Dimensions: Span, 53 ft 11 in. Length, 35 ft 3 in. Height, 13 ft 6 in. Wing area, 506 sq ft.

Weights: Empty, 2,700 lb. Loaded, 3,400 lb.

Performance: Maximum speed, 61 mph. Endurance, 3½ hr.

Armament: One free-mounted Lewis machine-gun. Bomb-racks below fuselage.

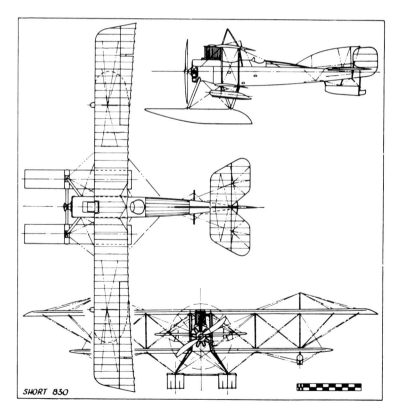

SHORT 830

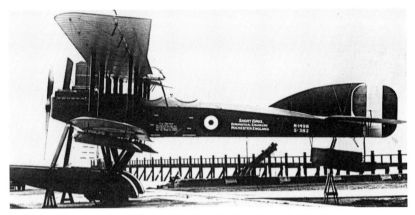

Short Type 320 (N1498) built by Short Brothers. *(Imperial War Museum)*

Short 320 Seaplane

The Short 320 was the last of many types of Short seaplane to enter service during the First World War. It was also the largest, since it was designed to combine long range with weight-lifting capacity to carry the new Mk.IX 18-in torpedo of 1,000 lb.

The designation of the Short 320 derived from its 320 hp Sunbeam Cossack engine, though the original version had a Sunbeam of only 310 hp. The prototypes (Nos.8317 and 8318) made their first flights in 1916 and were followed by 75 production aircraft from Shorts and 45 from Sunbeam. At this time the Admiralty was giving increasing attention to the claims of the Mediterranean, where U-boats based in the Adriatic called for more air patrols. As an immediate step, six Short 225s were transferred from Dundee air station to this theatre, and plans were finalised for attacks by torpedo-carrying seaplanes on the Austrian fleet at Pola. It was decided that the new Otranto base should have 12 Short 320s on its strength when these became available and two more were to be established at a torpedo school based in Malta.

The first attack by the Italian-based Short 320s was launched on 2 September 1917, when six aircraft, carrying their 18-in torpedoes, were towed by motor launches to a point 50 miles south of Traste Bay, where they were to take off for a raid on submarines lying off Cattaro. The operation proved abortive; by a great misfortune it was robbed of success by gales and heavy seas which sprang up on 3 September.

For some unexplained reason, no further attacks of this kind were made, though a series of experiments with torpedo drops at Calshot in February 1918 proved very successful. By 31 March 1918 the RNAS had received 110 Short 320s and when the war ended there were 50 still in service: 30 of these were in the Mediterranean. Thereafter, with more interest being shown in the carrier-borne landplane for torpedo work, the Short 320 soon disappeared from the scene. Some of the last remained with No.268 Squadron, which served at Malta until disbanded in October 1919.

RNAS coastal air stations which, following the formation of the RAF, were designated No.229 Squadron (Great Yarmouth), No.240 Squadron (Calshot), No.248 Squadron (Hornsea), No.263 Squadron (Otranto), No.264 Squadron (Suda Bay), No.266 Squadron (Mudros), No.268 (Malta) and No.269 Squadron (Kalafrana).

TECHNICAL DATA (SHORT 320)

Description: Two-seat anti-submarine patrol or single-seat torpedo-carrying seaplane. Wooden structure, fabric covered.

Manufacturers: Short Bros (serialled N1300–1319, N1390–1409 and N1480–1504) and Sunbeam (serialled N1360–1389, N1690–1696 and N1702–1709).

Power Plant: One 310 hp or 320 hp Sunbeam Cossack.

Dimensions: Span, 75 ft. Length, 45 ft 9 in. Height, 17 ft 6 in. Wing area, 810 sq ft.

Weights (with torpedo): Empty, 4,933 lb. Loaded, 7,014 lb.

Performance (with torpedo): Maximum speed, 72½ mph at 1,200 ft. Climb, 12 min to 2,000 ft. Service ceiling, 3,000 ft.

Armament: One free-mounted Lewis machine-gun above front cockpit level with wing. One 18-in torpedo or two 230 lb bombs below the fuselage.

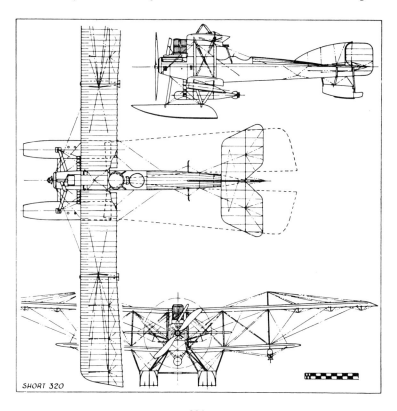

SHORT 320

Sturgeon T.T.2 (TS486) of No.728 Squadron. *(MoD)*

Short Sturgeon

The Sturgeon was the first twin-engined aircraft designed specifically for naval use to enter service with the FAA; the Monitor, Sea Mosquito and Sea Hornet were all conversions of aircraft designed originally for the RAF. It was originally intended as a reconnaissance-bomber for operation from *Ark Royal* and *Hermes* class aircraft-carriers, being designed to Spec S.11/43, and the first prototype (RK787) flew in June 1946 at Rochester. Carrier trials took place in *Implacable* in June 1948 with the second prototype (RK791). With changed operational requirements in the post-war period, the Sturgeon never entered production as a first-line aircraft, but was modified instead for high-speed target-towing duties to a new specification, Q.1/46.

The new variant was known as the Short S.A.2 Sturgeon T.T. Mk.2, and two prototypes were built (VR363 and VR371), the first flight being made on 1 September 1949. The Sturgeon T.T.2 was fully equipped for deck-landing and had power-operated folding wings and a lengthened nose to accommodate photographic equipment. The FAA took delivery of 23 Sturgeon T.T.2s (TS475 to 497); the first production aircraft flew on 8 June 1950. These aircraft were used from carriers for Fleet gunnery practice, for air-to-air firing exercises, photographic marking and radar calibration. Initial deliveries were to No.771 Squadron at Lee-on-Solent in September 1950.

After some years of useful service, it was decided to use Sturgeons from shore-based units only, and accordingly five T.T.2 airframes were converted to T.T.3 standard. The new variant, the Short S.B.9 Sturgeon T.T. Mk.3 (see three-view), reverted to the short nose of the original Sturgeon and had manually folding wings; the deck-landing gear was deleted. Sturgeon T.T.3s served from July 1954 until October 1958, mainly at the Royal Naval air station, Hal Far, Malta, where they were used by No.728 Squadron, a Fleet Requirements Unit, to replace ageing Sea Mosquitos.

Sturgeons were eventually superseded by Meteor T.T.20s.

No.703 Squadron (Ford), No.728 Squadron (Hal Far, Malta) and No.771 Squadron (Lee-on-Solent and Ford).

TECHNICAL DATA (STURGEON T.T.2)

Description: High-speed carrier-borne target-tug with a crew of two. All-metal stressed-skin construction.

Manufacturers: Short Bros & Harland Ltd, Queens Island, Belfast, Northern Ireland.

Power Plant: Two 1,660 hp Rolls-Royce Merlin 140S.

Dimensions: Span, 59 ft 9 in (22 ft 5 in folded). Length, 48 ft to 10½ in. Height, 13 ft 2½ in. Wing area, 564 sq ft.

Weights: Empty, 17,647 lb. Loaded, 22,350 lb.

Performance: Maximum speed, 370 mph; 356 mph at 24,200 ft; 302 mph at 15,000 ft; 248 mph with 32 ft span winged target; 262 mph with sleeve target. Range, 1,600 miles. Endurance, 3¼ hr including 1 hr with 32 ft winged target. Service ceiling, 35,700 ft; 32,900 ft with 32 ft winged target.

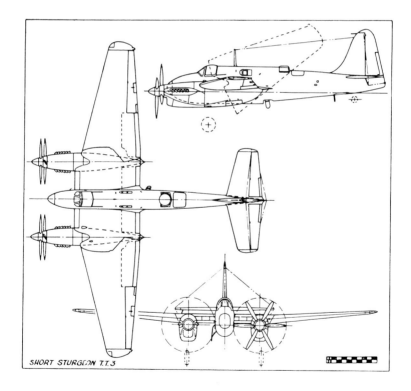

SHORT STURGEON T.T.3

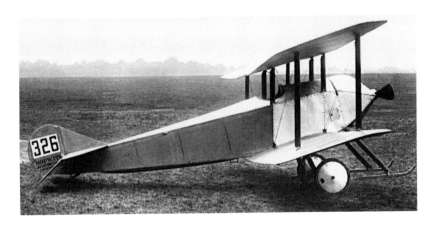

Tabloid single-seat scout (No.326). *(Imperial War Museum)*

Sopwith Tabloid

The Tabloid was one of the most outstanding aircraft produced in Great Britain before the outbreak of war in 1914. By the standards of those days, its top speed of over 90 mph and its climb of 1,200 ft per min were remarkable, and it caused a sensation when demonstrated in public for the first time by Harry Hawker, at Hendon on 29 November 1913. The prototype seated two, side-by-side, but subsequent Tabloids were single-seaters, including the seaplane flown to victory in the 1914 Schneider Trophy contest by Howard Pixton.

The military potential of the Tabloid was immediately apparent and production for the Naval and Military Wings of the RFC began early in 1914. By October 1914 the RNAS possessed only three Tabloids, yet in that month the type struck a telling blow at the enemy. On the 8th Sqn Cdr Spenser Gray and F/Lt R L G Marix took off from Antwerp, then under bombardment by the enemy, in Tabloids Nos.167 and 168 to bomb Zeppelin sheds at Cologne and Düsseldorf. Mist prevented Spenser Gray from finding his target, so he bombed Cologne railway station, but Marix's success was complete. He dived on the sheds at Düsseldorf and bombed from 600 ft. Within 30 seconds flames had risen to 500 ft; the new Zeppelin ZIX had been destroyed, the first to fall a victim to a British aircraft.

Between October 1914 and June 1915, a further 36 Tabloids were built and delivered to the RFC and RNAS. The naval Tabloids served with Wg Cdr Samson's Eastchurch squadron in Belgium, as already mentioned, and later with Samson's No.3 Squadron, RNAS, in the Dardanelles campaign. Others served aboard the seaplane-carrier *Ark Royal* in the same campaign, and at least one Tabloid was on the strength of the RNAS station at Great Yarmouth.

RNAS Tabloids received the serial numbers 167, 168, 169, 326, 362, 378, 386, 387, 392, 394 and 1201 to 1213.

294

Description: Single-seat scouting and bombing aircraft. Wooden structure, fabric covered.

Manufacturers: Sopwith Aviation Co Ltd, Kingston-on-Thames.

Power Plant: One 100 hp Gnome Monosoupape.

Dimensions: Span, 25 ft 6 in. Length, 20 ft 4 in. Height, 8 ft 5 in. Wing area, 241 sq ft.

Weights: Empty, 730 lb. Loaded, 1,120 lb.

Performance: Maximum speed, 92 mph at sea level. Climb, 1 min to 1,200 ft. Endurance, 3½ hr.

Armament: One Lewis machine-gun mounted on the centre section or at the side of the fuselage. A small load of 20 lb bombs could be carried.

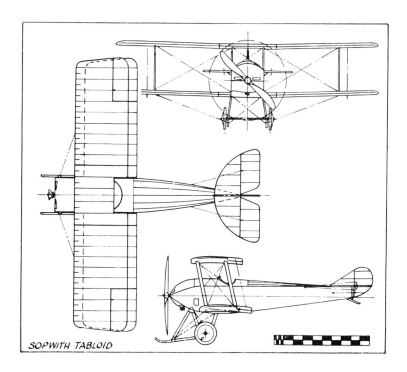

SOPWITH TABLOID

Schneider (No.3734) with wing warping. *(Imperial War Museum)*

Sopwith Schneider

The Schneider was so named because it was directly descended from the Sopwith Tabloid seaplane which had been used by Mr Howard Pixton to win the Schneider Trophy contest for Great Britain at Monaco on 20 April 1914. The little Tabloid performed magnificently; its average speed was over 86 mph, and in an extra two laps after finishing the race Pixton reached 92 mph, which was then a world's record for seaplanes.

It was natural that with the outbreak of war the RNAS should adopt this fine seaplane, and production began in November 1914 with an order for 12 aircraft, Nos.1436 to 1447. The early RNAS Schneider differed little from Pixton's Tabloid. The same 100 hp Monosoupape Gnome engine was used, housed in a curious bull-nosed cowling which became a characteristic feature of the Schneider and in fact distinguished the type from the later Baby. Early aircraft had a triangular fin and employed wing-warping; later an enlarged, curved fin and normal ailerons were introduced, as in the three-view drawing. Subsequent orders were for 24 Schneiders (Nos.1556 to 1579) and 100 (Nos.3707 to 3806), and the final production total was 160, five of which remained in commission in March 1918.

During 1915 repeated attempts were made to use Schneiders to intercept Zeppelins over the North Sea. The seaplanes were carried in light cruisers, paddle-steamers such as *Killingholme* and *Brocklesby*, and in the seaplane-carriers *Ben-my-Chree* and *Engadine*. Scant success attended these sorties; frequently the seaplanes could not take off due to heavy seas, or the floats broke up in the water. A remedy was sought by fitting two-wheeled dollies beneath the floats, enabling the Schneiders to operate from the short flying-off deck of carriers so equipped. The first successful take-off using this device was from *Campania* on 6 August 1915. The Schneider was flown by F/Lt W L Welsh. On 26 March 1916 a Schneider bombed aircraft sheds at Sylt and, on 6 May, the Zeppelin sheds at Tondern.

Overseas, Schneiders did an immense amount of useful work, both reconnaissance and fighting, in the eastern Mediterranean and the Red Sea. They saw service in the Dardanelles campaign, flying from *Ark Royal*, and as late as 21 November 1916 a Schneider, flown by F/Sub Lt A F Brandon, shot down an enemy aircraft over Mudros.

UNITS ALLOCATED

RNAS coastal air stations at Calshot, Dundee, Dunkirk, Felixstowe, Fishguard, Great Yarmouth, Killingholme, Scapa Flow and Westgate. Seaplane carriers: *Anne, Ark Royal, Ben-my-Chree, Campania, Empress, Engadine,* and *Raven II.* RNAS stations in Aegean, Egypt and Mediterranean. Also used experimentally aboard submarine *E.22.*

TECHNICAL DATA (SCHNEIDER)

Description: Single-seat scouting seaplane. Wooden structure, fabric covered.
Manufacturers: Sopwith Aviation Co Ltd, Kingston-on-Thames.
Power Plant: One 100 hp Gnome Monosoupape.
*Dimensions:*Span, 25 ft 8 in. Length, 22 ft 10 in. Height, 10 ft. Wing area, 240 sq ft.
Weights: Empty, 1,220 lb. Loaded, 1,700 lb.
Performance: Maximum speed, 87 mph. Climb, 15 min to 6,500 ft and 30 min to 10,000 ft. Service ceiling, 8,000 ft.
Armament: One Lewis machine-giun firing through aperture in centre section and provision for one 65 lb bomb below fuselage.

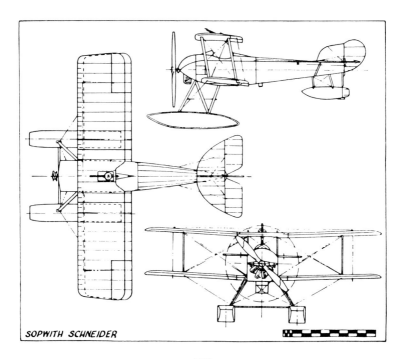

SOPWITH SCHNEIDER

Baby (N2071) of No.229 Squadron, Great Yarmouth. *(Imperial War Museum)*

Sopwith Baby

The Sopwith Baby was a development of the Schneider, from which it differed in having the more powerful 110 hp Clerget engine in place of the Gnome Monosoupape, the bull-nosed cowling of the earlier aircraft being replaced by an open-fronted cowling of more orthodox pattern. Another improvement was the installation of a synchronised Lewis gun above the fuselage, though some Babies retained the original type of gun-mounting with the Lewis inclined upwards through the top wing. The first batch of 100 Babies (Nos.8118 to 8217) were built by Sopwith and delivered between September 1915 and July 1916. The first five aircraft of this batched retained the 100 hp Gnome engine, as did No.8199. The rest had the 110 hp Clerget, and this engine was retained when Baby production was transferred to the Blackburn Company.

The first Blackburn Baby (N300) was followed by 70 production aircraft with 110 hp Clerget engines (N1010 to 1039, N1060 to 1069 and N1100 to 1129) and 115 with the 130 hp Clerget engine (N1410 to 1449 and N2060 to 2134). It had originally been planned to fit the Bentley A.R.1 from N1410, but these engines were not available in time. The first batch of 130 hp Babies differed from the others in having Ranken anti-Zeppelin darts fitted instead of a machine-gun.

In the same way as the Schneiders, Babies operated from seaplane-carriers in the North Sea and in the Mediterranean. They also flew on fighter patrols from Dunkirk until superseded by Sopwith Pups in July 1917. In the various Middle East campaigns, Babies were fequently used in bombing raids. *Ben-my-Chree*'s Babies attacked the Chikaldir railway bridge in December 1916, and, in November, those from the carrier *Empress* took part in the Palestine fighting. Bombing raids on Zeppelin bases from home waters were less successful. In an attack on the Tondern airship base from the carriers *Engadine* and *Vindex* on 4 May 1916 only one out of 11 Babies succeeded in bombing the target.

RNAS coastal air stations at Calshot, Dundee, Dunkirk, Felixstowe, Fishguard, Great Yarmouth, Killingholme, Scapa Flow and Westgate. Seaplane carriers *Ben-my-Chree*, *Campania*, *City of Oxford*, *Empress*, *Engadine*, *Furious*, *Manxman*, *Peony*, *Raven II*, *Riviera* and *Vindex*. RNAS stations at Alexandria, Otranto, Port Said, Santa Maria di Leuca, Suda Bay and Thasos. After April 1918, with Nos.219, 229, 246, 248, 249, 263 and 270 Squadrons.

TECHNICAL DATA (BABY)

Description: Single-seat scouting and bombing seaplane. Wooden structure, fabric covered.

Manufacturers: Sopwith Aviation Co Ltd, Kingston-on-Thames. Sub-contracted by the Blackburn Aeroplane & Motor Co Ltd, Leeds.

Power Plant: One 110 hp or 130 hp Clerget.

Dimensions: Span, 25 ft 8 in. Length, 23 ft. Height, 10 ft. Wing area, 240 sq ft.

Weights (with 130 hp Clerget): Empty, 1,226 lb. Loaded, 1,715 lb.

Performance (with 130 hp Clerget): Maximum speed, 100 mph at sea level. Climb, 35 min to 10,000 ft. Endurance, 2¼ hr.

Armament: One Lewis machine-gun and provision for two 65 lb bombs. Ranken darts replaced the Lewis gun on some aircraft.

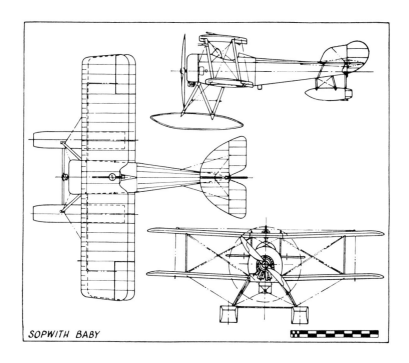

SOPWITH BABY

A 1½ Strutter of the RNAS. *(Imperial War Museum)*

Sopwith 1½ Strutter

The claims of the Sopwith 1½ Strutter to historical fame are many. It was, of course, the first of the Sopwith breed to achieve widespread use as a fighting aeroplane and hence the precursor of a justly renowned series. In addition to this it was the first British aeroplane to enter service already equipped with a synchronising gear, enabling the fixed front gun to fire between the revolving blades of the airscrew, and also the first two-seater which gave the pilot a chance to use his gun effectively as well as the observer. It thus established what came to be a classic formula, that of the two-seat fighter, later exemplified in the Bristol Fighter and the Hawker Demon.

Nor did the 1½ Strutter's pioneering tendencies end here. In 1916, with the 3rd Wing of the RNAS at Luxeuil, 1½ Strutters became the first British aircraft ever to take part in bombing raids of an avowedly strategic nature, attacking German industrial centres and providing, as it were, a prelude to the heavier blows struck later by the squadrons of the RAF's Independent Force. Finally, in the sphere of shipboard flying, it was a 1½ Strutter that became the first two-seater to take off from a British warship, in April 1918.

The Admiralty had from the earliest beginnings of the RNAS shown interest in the products of the Sopwith Company, and it was therefore only logical that the 1½ Strutter should be first ordered for naval service, though it later entered the RFC as well. The prototype (No.3686) was completed at the end of 1915, and first deliveries of RNAS Strutters began early in 1916, against an Admiralty contract for 150. Some of the first to enter service equipped part of No.5 Wing at Coudekerque in April 1916. No.5 Wing was formed in March 1916 for long-range bombing duties and was equipped primarily with Caudrons and Farmans. The 1½ Strutters were able to provide a welcome escort, as well as operating in the bombing rôle themselves. As related in the narrative on the Caudron G.4, a 1½ Strutter was on 2 August 1916 used to control a No.5 Wing bombing formation by firing Very lights, a sort of forerunner of the master bomber technique of the Second World War. A few days later, on 9 August, two of No.5 Wing's 1½ Strutters flown by F/Sub-Lts R H Collet and D E Harkness made bombing attacks on the Zeppelin sheds at Evère and Berchem Ste Agathe; another attack followed on 25 August, this time on the sheds at Cognelee. Subsequently the 1½ Strutters of No.5 Wing participated in many important raids on enemy aerodromes and ammunition dumps, as well as naval targets such as U-boat bases and the Tirpitz battery.

Meanwhile, plans for the establishment of No.3 Wing, RNAS (which was to have received 20 1½ Strutters by 1 July 1916), had been delayed due to the Admiralty's agreement to forgo its Strutters in favour of the RFC, which was desperately short of aircraft with which to fight the Battle of the Somme. Eventually No.3 Wing's 1½ Strutters started their raids in October 1916 and, though severely hampered by winter weather conditions, bombed industrial targets at Hagendingen, Oberndorf, Dillingen and other towns in the Saar where the Admiralty believed steel for U-boats was being manufactured in large quantities. It is interesting to note that No.3 Wing's base at Luxeuil was close to Belfort, from whence the RNAS Avros had taken off in November 1914 to raid Friedrichshafen.

Two distinct versions of the 1½ Strutter were supplied to the RNAS, where the type was officially known as the Sopwith Type 9700. As well as the normal two-seater, the RNAS used a single-seat bomber without the rear cockpit, with provision for 12 bombs stowed internally. It is recorded that, of some 550 1½ Strutters supplied to the RNAS, about 420 were two-seaters and the remainder single-seaters.

Although by 1917 the 1½ Strutter was outclassed as a fighting aircraft on the Western Front, it continued to give extensive service with the RNAS in other theatres of war. The RNAS was, in fact, the only service to operate the type outside France. In Macedonia, particularly, the naval Strutters saw a lot of action in bombing raids between April and September 1917, when they hit targets such as aerodromes, ammunition dumps and railway communications behind the enemy lines on the Struma.

The Sopwith 1½ Strutter's versatility extended also to anti-submarine patrols, both in home waters and in the Mediterranean area. The home-based patrols started in April 1917 and those in the Mediterranean in June 1917. On 17 September 1917 a 1½ Strutter based at Otranto claimed the sinking of a U-boat by attacking it with a 65 lb delayed-action bomb.

Single-seat Type 9700s of No.5 Wing, RNAS. *(H H Russell)*

301

At the Armistice some 170 Sopwith 1½ Strutters remained in service with the RAF and nearly 40 of these were at sea with the Grand Fleet. Indeed, when, in March 1918, HMS *Furious* was made the flagship of the Flying Squadron of the Grand Fleet her complement included 14 1½ Strutters. For deck flying the 1½ Strutter was used both with the normal wheeled undercarriage and with a special skid undercarriage first developed in trials at the Isle of Grain; the latter version usually had a hydrovane mounted at the front end of the skids to prevent the aircraft nosing over if forced into the sea. This device, as well as the inflatable air-bags located either side of the engine nacelle, remained a feature of naval aircraft until about 1923, when flotation equipment was mounted inside the rear fuselage instead.

Numerous experiments in deck-flying were made with 1½ Strutters. One aircraft (N5601) fitted with skids was flown off a railed deck aboard HMS *Vindex*, and the first successful landing aboard HMS *Argus* using the early form of deck arrester gear was made by Wg Cdr Bell-Davies, VC, in F2211 on 1 October 1918. A further development of 1918 was the introduction of 1½ Strutters for

1½ Strutters of No.3 Wing, RNAS. *(Imperial War Museum)*

1½ Strutter takes off from a gun-turret platform. *(Imperial War Museum)*

A 1½ Strutter undergoing flotation tests with inflatable air bags.
(Imperial War Museum.)

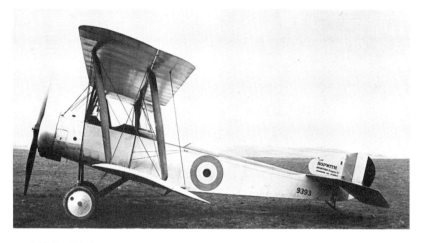

An RNAS 1½ Strutter (No.9393) of the Sopwith-built batch 9376 to 9425. *(Imperial War Museum)*

two-seat reconnaissance duties aboard capital ships. This involved flying off a short platform mounted above the forward gun turret and became standard practice aboard battle cruisers after the first successful take-off had been achieved from the Australian warship HMAS *Australia* by Capt F M Fox on 4 April 1918, carrying an observer and full wireless equipment.

UNITS ALLOCATED

Nos.2, 4, 5, 7 and 8 Squadrons, RNAS (Western Front); Macedonian units: 'A' Squadron (Thasos), 'B' Squadron (later No.23 (Naval)) (Mitylene), 'C' Squadron (later No.20 (Naval)) (Imbros and Mudros), 'D' Squadron (Stavros), 'E' Squadron (Hadzi Junas), 'F' Squadron (Amberkoj), 'G' Squadron (Mudros) and 'Z' Squadron (Thasos). No.225 Squadron (Italy). RNAS coastal air stations at Dover, Great Yarmouth, Mullion, Otranto, Pembroke and Prawle Point. RNAS training schools at Cranwell and Manston.

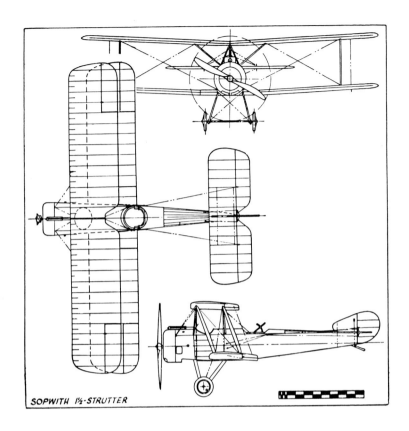

SOPWITH 1½-STRUTTER

Aircraft-carriers: *Argus* and *Furious.* Battleships: *Australia, Barham, Courageous, Glorious, Indomitable, Inflexible, Malaya, Queen Elizabeth, Renown, Repulse, Valiant,* and *Warspite.* Seaplane carriers: *Campania, Vindex* and *Vindictive.*

TECHNICAL DATA (1½ STRUTTER)

Description: Single-seat bomber, or two-seat bomber, fighting and reconnaissance aircraft for shore-based or carrier-borne operations. Wooden structure, fabric covered.

Manufacturers: Sopwith Aviation Co Ltd, Kingston-on-Thames (Nos.9376 to 9425, 9651 to 9750, 9892 to 9897, N5080 to 5179, and N5500 to 5537). Sub-contracted by: Mann, Egerton & Co Ltd, Norwich (N5200 to 5219, N5220 to 5249 and N5630 to 5654) and Westland Aircraft, Yeovil (N5600 to 5624). Also 70 French-built 1½ Strutters converted for ship-board flying in 1918 and serialled F2210–2229 and F7547–7596.

Power Plant: One 110 hp or 130 hp Clerget.

Dimensions: Span, 33 ft 6 in. Length, 25 ft 3 in. Height, 10 ft 3 in. Wing area, 346 sq ft.

Weights (two-seater with 110 hp Clerget): Empty, 1,259 lb. Loaded, 2,149 lb. (single-seater with 130 hp Clerget): Empty, 1,316 lb.

Performance (two-seater with 110 hp Clerget): Maximum speed, 106 mph at sea level; 92 mph at 12,000 ft. Climb, 1 min 20 sec to 1,000 ft; 10 min 50 sec to 6,500 ft; 20 min 25 sec to 1,000 ft. Endurance, 4½ hr. (Single-seater with 130 hp Clerget): Maximum speed, 102 mph at 6,500 ft. Climb, 12 min 40 sec to 6,500 ft; 24 min 35 sec to 10,000 ft. Service ceiling, 13,000 ft.

Armament (single-seat bomber): One Vickers machine-gun forward and four 65 lb bombs. (Two-seater): One Vickers machine-gun forward and one Lewis machine-gun aft. Two 65 lb bombs for anti-submarine patrol.

1½ Strutter (F2211) flies from *HMS Argus*. (*Imperial War Museum*)

305

A Pup takes off from HMS *Yarmouth*. *(Imperial War Museum)*

Sopwith Pup

Although the Sopwith Pup was used both by the RNAS and the RFC it was, like its immediate predecessor the 1½ Strutter, pioneered in service by naval squadrons on the Western Front. As early as May 1916 a Pup was on trial with Naval 'A' Squadron at Furnes and by the following September was in squadron service with the RNAS, fully three months before the first RFC squadron went into action with Pups.

The Pup was known officially as the Sopwith Scout and chronologically occupies a position between the 1½ Strutter and Triplane. It had many qualities to recommend it: it was at once a superior fighting aeroplane and a thoroughly delightful flying machine. As a fighting scout it maintained its ascendancy from the autumn of 1916 until about the middle of 1917: it proved more than a match for the German Albatros and earned the respect of even the most skilful enemy pilots. Due largely to its low wing loading, the Pup could hold its height better than any Allied or enemy aircraft of its day and retained its excellent manoeuvrability to an altitude of about 15,000 ft. These qualities are the most remarkable in view of the low power output of the Le Rhône rotary, even by the standards of 1916.

In keeping with the traditional association of the Sopwith Company and the Admiralty, the Pup prototype (No.3691) which emerged in February 1916, and the five succeeding prototypes (Nos.9496, 9497, 9898, 9899 and 9900), were all delivered to the RNAS. The first production contracts were placed with William Beardmore & Co, and as their first Pup was numbered 9901, the official designation Sopwith Type 9901 was adopted in accordance with the Admiralty custom. Some 175 Pups were built for the Admiralty. The first went to No.5 Wing, RNAS, on 28 May 1916.

RNAS Pups first entered service in quantity with No.1 Wing early in September, and by 24 September 1916 had claimed their first victim when F/Sub-Lt. S J Goble shot down an L.V.G. two-seater. At about this period the

RFC, which had suffered heavy casualties during the Battle of the Somme, began to look for reinforcements, and on 25 October 1916 the famous No.8 (Naval) Squadron under Sqn Cdr G R Bromet was formed for this purpose. Its equipment at first consisted of six Pups, six Nieuports and six 1½ Strutters; later the Pup was standardised throughout. Naval Eight operated from Vert Galand, and was the first complete RNAS squadron to work with the Army on the Western Front. The squadron operated with the RFC until 7 February 1917, when it was relieved by No.3 (Naval) Squadron, also equipped with Sopwith Pups, and returned to the Dunkirk command. During its three months with the RFC, Naval Eight destroyed 14 enemy aircraft and drove down another 13 out of control. Until re-equipped with Camels in July 1917, No.3 (Naval) Squadron's Pups flew and fought with great distinction, and by the middle of June had accounted for no fewer than 80 enemy aircraft. Such was their renown, in fact, as a fighting unit that enemy pilots frequently avoided combat with them. On returning to naval command in June 1917, No.3 (Naval) Squadron was relieved by No.9 (Naval) Squadron, which was attached to the RFC until 28 September 1917. Very shortly after joining the Army command, No.9 (Naval) exchanged its six Pups and nine Triplanes for Sopwith Camels.

Meanwhile another RNAS unit, No.4 (Naval) Squadron at Bray Dunes, had been occupied exclusively on naval work. First equipped with Pups in March 1917, No.4 (Naval) Squadron engaged in offensive patrols, escort duties and the protection of naval units from air attack. Their fighting efficiency was just as high as that of the better-publicised Pup squadrons attached to the RFC. On 12 May 1917, for example, seven of No.4 (Naval)'s Pups shot down five Albatros scouts in a dogfight near Zeebrugge with no losses to themselves.

Another more directly naval use for the Pup was in the protection of merchant shipping and in escorting the slower seaplanes on reconnaissance work. From May 1917 Pups were flown from Walmer for this purpose, and in July 1917 superseded Baby Seaplanes at St Pol. Pups remained with the Seaplane Defence Flight until supplanted by Camels in September 1917; in common with the Walmer Pups, they were provided with airbags to enable them to float if forced down in the sea.

The brilliance of the Pup's fighting record over the Western Front tends to overshadow its other activities. If this were not so it would probably be best remembered for its equally important rôle in the development of deck-flying in the RNAS. At the beginning of 1916 it was decided to introduce Pups in place of Baby seaplanes aboard seaplane-carriers such as *Campania* and *Manxman* which had a short flying-off deck but no provision for landing-on. Until the advent of this scheme, landplanes had never been used from carriers, and the problem at once arose of how to keep the Pup afloat when it alighted alongside its mother ship. This was solved by fitting emergency flotation bags below the lower wings. These were developed after experiments at the Isle of Grain and proved more efficient than the earlier type of air-bag installed inside the rear fuselage.

Having established itself on the early carriers (which had a flying-off deck about 200 ft long), the Pup was then used to initiate two further developments in naval aviation; namely, the take-off from short platforms mounted above the gun turrets of warships and the successful return to a ship's deck instead of the inconvenient ditching. The Pup was the first aeroplane to achieve either of these

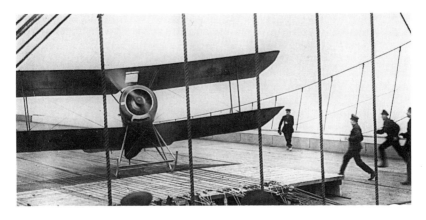

Pup (N6438) lands on *Furious* in April 1918. *(Imperial War Museum)*

feats. The first of them goes to the credit of F/Cdr F J Rutland, who succeeded in flying a Pup off the 20 ft platform of the light cruiser HMS *Yarmouth* in June 1917. The second feat was achieved on 2 August 1917 when Sqn Cdr E H Dunning became the first man in history to land an aircraft on the deck of an aircraft-carrier. The experiment took place aboard HMS *Furious*, and its success was all the more remarkable in view of the fact that at this period the idea of a continuous flying-deck along the full length of a ship was unheard of and Dunning was forced to manoeuvre his Pup round the superstructure and funnels of *Furious* and somehow contrive to get down on the 228 ft flight-deck mounted forward. This he did with great resource, and with the aid of a deck party who seized rope toggles beneath the wings and fuselage to bring the Pup to rest, as at this period there were no arrester devices either. Sad to relate, this great pioneer was killed a few days later when attempting a third landing aboard *Furious*.

Both these successful experiments led rapidly to wider operational uses for the Pup. Many other light cruisers were equipped in the same way as HMS *Yarmouth*, and the value of the scheme was confirmed on 21 August 1917, when F/Sub-Lt B A Smart, flying N6430, took off from *Yarmouth*, then cruising off the Danish coast, and shot down the Zeppelin *L23* in flames.

On 1 October 1917 the Pup was flown from a battle cruiser for the first time, when Sqn Cdr F J Rutland took off from a platform aboard HMS *Repulse*. This marked yet another step forward, for this platform was on a turntable and it enabled the Pups to be launched into wind without the warship diverting from its course: the original platforms had been fixed.

By this time it was clear that the real future of naval aviation lay with the aircraft-carrier proper, and work went ahead to provide HMS *Furious* with an aft landing-on deck at the same time that Pups were being used at the Isle of Grain for early experiments with deck-arrester gear. The original scheme (curiously prophetic of the system re-introduced in the nineteen-thirties) was to utilise transverse cables across the deck which would be engaged by a hook dangling below the rear fuselage. This was first tried out on a Pup (No.9497), but did not work out in practice, and the Pups which eventually went aboard HMS *Furious* in

Pup (No.3691) of Naval 'A' Squadron, Dunkirk, May 1916. *(H H Russell)*

1918 were fitted with a rigid skid undercarriage in place of wheels. In place of the transverse arrester wires were fore-and-aft wires which engaged 'dog-lead' clips on the Pup's undercarriage. Although aircraft with skids eventually gave way once again to those with wheeled undercarriages, the fore-and-aft arrester wires persisted in aircraft-carriers until finally abandoned in the mid nineteen-twenties. The Pups with skids were re-designated Sopwith Type 9901s by the Admiralty. In mid-1918 10 of these aircraft were serving with aircraft-carriers and there were also 13 other Pups with the Grand Fleet being used for gun-turret platform take-offs from battleships and cruisers.

UNITS ALLOCATED

No.1 Wing, RNAS, and Nos.2, 3, 4, 8, 9 and 12 (Naval) Squadrons (Western Front); Naval 'A' Squadron (Dunkirk); Naval 'C' Squadron (Imbros); Seaplane Defence Flight (St Pol); RNAS coastal air stations at Dover, Great Yarmouth, Port Victoria and Walmer; RNAS training schools at Cranwell and Manston. Aircraft-carriers: *Argus, Campania, Furious, Manxman* and *Vindictive.* Warships with flying-off platforms: *Caledon, Cassandra, Cordelia, Dublin, Repulse, Tiger* and *Yarmouth.*

TECHNICAL DATA (PUP)

Description: Single-seat fighting scout for shore-based or shipboard duties. Wooden structure, fabric covered.

Manufacturers: Sopwith Aviation Co Ltd, Kingston-on-Thames (Prototypes and N5180 to 5199, N6160 to 6209, N6460 to 6479). Sub-contracted by Wm Beardmore & Co Ltd, Dalmuir, Dumbartonshire (Nos.9898 to 9950 and N6430 to 6459).

Power Plant: One 80 hp Le Rhône.

Dimensions: Span, 26 ft 6 in. Length, 19 ft 3¾ in. Height, 9 ft 5 in. Wing area, 254 sq ft.

Weights: Empty, 787 lb. Loaded, 1,225 lb.

Performance: Maximum speed, 105 mph at 5,000 ft; 103 mph at 9,000 ft; 85 mph at 15,000 ft. Climb 6½ min to 5,000 ft; 16½ min to 10,000 ft; 35 min to 16,100 ft. Endurance, 3 hr. Service ceiling, 17,500 ft.

The first production Pup built by Sopwith for the RNAS, N5180. *(Imperial War Museum)*

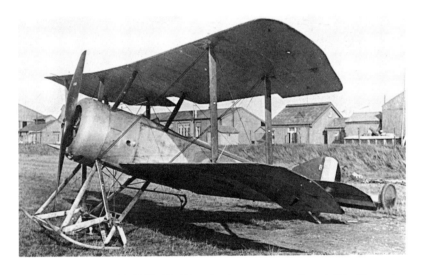

Beardmore-built Pup No.9922 with skids and early arrester gear. *(Imperial War Museum)*

Armament: One fixed, synchronised Vickers maching-gun forward was standard on Pups used over the Western Front. Those flown from ships had a single Lewis machine-gun firing upwards through the centre section or eight Le Prieur rockets mounted on the interplane struts, or both.

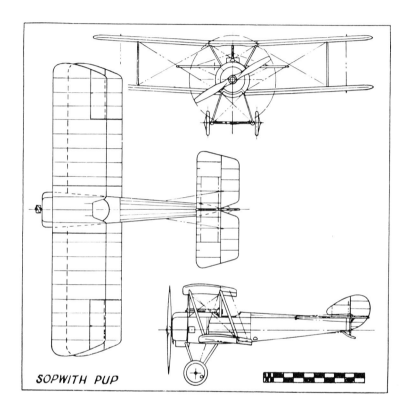

SOPWITH PUP

Triplane (N6290) of No.8 (Naval) Squadron. *(H H Russell)*

Sopwith Triplane

The Sopwith Triplane was one of the great successes of the First World War. Its unusual configuration bestowed such qualities as a remarkable rate of roll and a fast climb, both invaluable in air combat. It was used only by the RNAS, and it gained complete ascendancy over the Western Front during the heavy aerial fighting of 1917.

In the Sopwith chronology the Triplane bridged the gap between the Pup and the Camel, and the first prototype (N500) did Service trials with Naval 'A' Fighting Squadron at Furnes in June 1916. Production Triplanes entered service with No.1 and 8 (Naval) Squadrons in February 1917 and with No.10 (Naval) Squadron in May. Some remarkable engagements were fought by such redoubtable Triplane pilots as Sqn Cdr C D Booker, DSC, and F/Sub-Lt R A Little, of 'Naval Eight' and F/Sub-Lt Raymond Collishaw of 'Naval Ten'. The Triplanes of Collishaw's 'B' Flight (named *Black Death, Black Maria, Black Roger, Black Prince* and *Black Sheep*) became the terror of the enemy: between May and July 1917 they destroyed 87 German aircraft. Collishaw personally accounted for 16 in 27 days and shot down the German ace Allmenroder on 27 June.

The Triplane's career was glorious but brief. It remained in action for only seven months; in November 1917 the Camel had supplanted it in squadrons. Total deliveries to the RNAS amounted to 149. All production aircraft were built by sub-contractors: 104 from Clayton & Shuttleworth and 43 from Oakley. The last Triplane (N5912), delivered by Oakley Ltd on 19 October 1917, survives in the RAF Museum at Hendon.

From February 1917 Triplanes had a smaller tailplane of 8 ft span instead of the original Pup-type of 10 ft span. This accompanied the change to a 130 hp engine and improved diving characteristics.

Nos.1, 8, 9, 10 and 12 (Naval) Squadrons, Western Front. One aircraft (N5431) used by 'E' Squadron of No.2 Wing, RNAS, in Macedonia.

Description: Single-seat fighting scout. Wooden structure, fabric covered.

Manufacturers: Sopwith Aviation Co Ltd, Kingston-on-Thames. Sub-contracted by Clayton & Shuttleworth Ltd, Lincoln (N533–538, N541–543, N5420–5494 and N6290–6309) and Oakley, Ltd, Ilford (N5350–5389 and N5910–5912).

Power Plant: One 110 hp or 130 hp Clerget.

Dimensions: Span, 26 ft 6 in. Length, 18 ft 10 in. Height, 10 ft 6 in. Wing area, 231 sq ft.

Weights: Empty, 1,101 lb. Loaded, 1,541 lb.

Performance (with 130 hp Clerget): Maximum speed, 113 mph at 6,500 ft. Climb, 22 min to 16,000 ft. Endurance, 2¾ hr. Service ceiling, 20,500 ft.

Armament: One fixed, synchronised Vickers machine-gun was standard, but a few aircraft had twin Vickers.

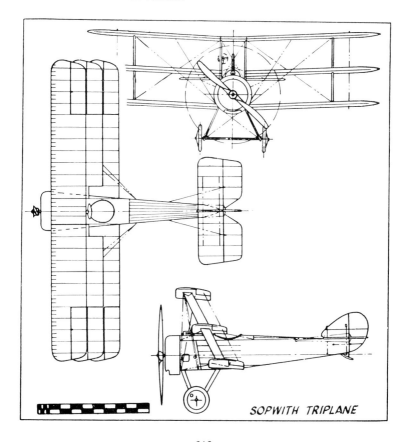

SOPWITH TRIPLANE

F.1 Camel of No.9 (Naval) Squadron. *(H H Russell)*

Sopwith F.1 Camel

The Camel is generally conceded to have been the greatest British fighting scout of the First World War; it destroyed the record total of 1,294 enemy aircraft. The Camels in RNAS service accounted for 386 of these. Its manoeuvrability became a legend and was matched only by that of the Fokker Triplane. The installation of twin Vickers guns contributed to its success; it was the first British fighter to be so equipped.

Five Camels from the RNAS station at Dunkirk were the first to see action, on 4 July 1917, when they attacked a formation of Gothas returning from a raid over England. By the end of July No.6 (Naval) Squadron had gone over completely from Nieuports to Camels and Nos.8 and 9 (Naval) Squadrons were also getting Camels in place of Triplanes. All the original F.1 Camels for the RNAS had 130 hp Clerget engines; later the 150 hp Bentley B.R.1 was substituted, and eventually became the more common installation in naval Camels.

The exploits of naval Camels fighting over the Western Front rivalled those of their RFC counterparts. In August 1917, for example, a Camel of 'Naval Eight' made one of the first successful night ground-attack sorties by a British fighter and destroyed a kite-balloon shed by gun-fire. The RNAS Camels were for long periods placed at the disposal of the Army and attached to the RFC; at other times they reverted to Naval command and flew fleet patrols to protect the ships of the Belgian Coast Barrage from enemy air attack. From 1 April 1918 the naval Camel squadrons became part of the RAF officially, but they retained their naval identity until their disbandment, for the most part in 1919.

It fell to a Bentley-powered Camel of No.209 Squadron (formerly No.9 Naval) to take part in one of the most dramatic air fights of the First World War. This historic event was on 21 April 1918, when the celebrated von Richthofen (80 victories) was shot down by Capt A R Brown.

The F.1 Camel was also used in limited numbers by the RNAS in Italy and the Aegean, at coastal air stations in the United Kingdom and at Cranwell, where a two-seat version of the Camel was also flown.

Clerget-Camel to Nos.6, 8 and 9 (Naval) Squadrons (Western Front) and Bentley-Camel to Nos.1, 3, 4, 8, 9, 10 and 13 (Naval) Squadrons which from April 1918 became Nos.201, 203, 204, 208, 209, 210 and 213 Squadrons, RAF. Also issued as partial equipment of Nos.220 (Imbros), 221 (Stavros), 222 (Thasos and Mudros), 223 (Stavros and Mudros), No.224 (Italy), 225 (Italy), 226 (Italy) and 227 (Italy).

TECHNICAL DATA (F.1. CAMEL)

Description: Single-seat fighting scout. Wooden structure, fabric covered.

Manufacturers: Sopwith Aviation Co Ltd, Kingston-on-Thames and eight sub-contractors.

Power Plant: One 130 hp Clerget or 150 hp Bentley B.R.1.

Dimensions: Span, 28 ft. Length, 18 ft 9 in with Clerget and 18 ft 6 in with B.R.1. Height, 8 ft 6 in. Wing area, 231 sq ft.

Weights (with 130 hp Clerget): Empty, 929 lb. Loaded, 1,453 lb.

Performance (with 130 hp Clerget): Maximum speed, 106 mph at 15,000 ft. Climb, 20 min 40 sec to 15,000 ft. Endurance, 2½ hr. Service ceiling, 19,000 ft.

Armament: Twin fixed, synchronised Vickers machine-guns and capacity for four 25 lb bombs below wings.

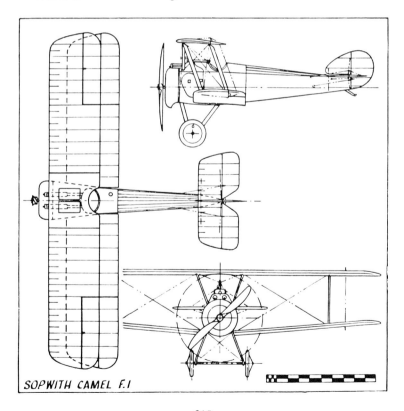

SOPWITH CAMEL F.1

2F.1 Camel (N7136) built by Beardmore. *(Imperial War Museum)*

Sopwith 2F.1 Ship Camel

Unlike the F.1 Camel, which served both the RNAS and RFC, the 2F.1 was designed specifically as a shipboard fighter and, to this end, incorporated a number of features that distinguished it from the earlier Camel. The fuselage was made in two parts, the rear half being detachable just behind the cockpit: this conserved space aboard ship. Another distinguishing feature was the use of steel tubular centre-section struts instead of the wide wooden struts of the F.1.

The prototype 2F.1 Camel (N5) flew in March 1917, and the 230 production aircraft that followed were built by the major sub-contractor Beardmore and six other companies after an initial 50 by Sopwith.

The main operational function of the 2F.1 Camels was to intercept Zeppelins over the North Sea. For this purpose they were carried in numerous warships, where they were flown from platforms mounted above gun turrets in the same way as the Pups they superseded. They were also flown from aircraft-carriers such as *Furious*. Yet another means of getting the Camels to the scene of operations was from lighters towed by destroyers of Harwich Force; the first successful take-off by this method was achieved by Lt S D Culley on 31 July 1918. A few days afterwards, on 11 August, the same officer shot down the Zeppelin *L53* whilst flying from a lighter in Camel N6812. It was the last Zeppelin to be destroyed in air combat.

Another method of attacking Zeppelins was to bomb them in their sheds—a technique much favoured by the RNAS from the earliest days of the war. In June 1918 a specially trained force of 2F.1 Camels joined *Furious* for an audacious strike on the airship sheds at Tondern. Escorted by the First Light Cruiser Squadron, *Furious* flew off seven Camels on 19 July 1918. Six of the Camels, each carrying two 50 lb bombs, succeeded in reaching Tondern and the Zeppelins *L54* and *L60* were destroyed.

By October 1918 there were 129 2F.1 Camels in service and 112 were carried in ships of the Grand Fleet. Camels aboard *Argus* took part in some of the earliest experiments with deck-arrester gear in 1919.

316

Carriers: Argus, Furious, Manxman, Pegasus and *Vindictive*. Turret platform launch from 47 battleships, battle cruisers and cruisers. *RNAS shore stations:* Cranwell, Dover (No.233 Squadron), East Fortune, Felixstowe (No.230 Squadron), Great Yarmouth (Nos.212 and 273 Squadrons), Isle of Grain, Leuchars, Manston (No.219 Squadron), Port Victoria and Turnhouse. Air launch experiments from airship R23.

TECHNICAL DATA (2F.1 CAMEL)

Description: Single-seat ship-board fighting scout.
Manufacturers: Sopwith (N6600–6649) and seven sub-contractors (serials ranging from N6750 to 8204).
Power Plant: One 150 hp Bentley B.R.1.
Dimensions: Span, 26 ft 11 in. Length, 18 ft 9 in. Wing area, 221 sq ft.
Weights: Empty, 1,036 lb. Loaded, 1,530 lb.
Performance: Maximum speed, 117 mph at 15,000 ft. Climb, 25 min to 15,000 ft. Service ceiling, 17,300 ft.
Armament: One fixed, synchronised Vickers gun above the fuselage and one Lewis gun above the wing centre section. Four 25 lb bombs.

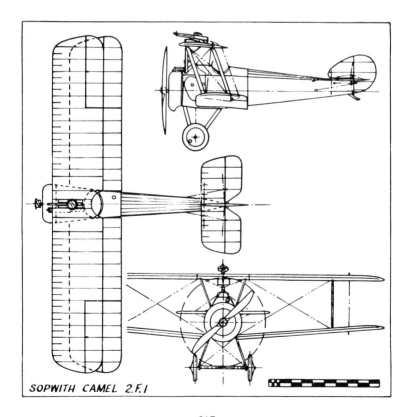

SOPWITH CAMEL 2.F.I

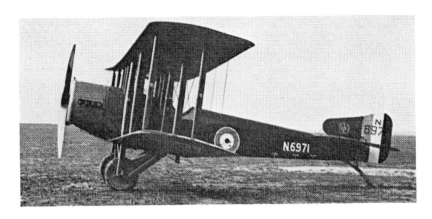

Cuckoo (N6971) built by Blackburn. *(J M Bruce)*

Sopwith Cuckoo

The Cuckoo was something of a landmark in British naval aircraft design; it was the first landplane torpedo-carrier capable of operation from a flying-deck. Before the advent of the Cuckoo the torpedo could be carried only by seaplanes which were severely restricted in their capabilities. They suffered not only the weight handicap of their floats, but also the inability to operate from any but the calmest of seas. The idea of using a landplane first came from that staunch advocate of the torpedo, Commodore Murray Sueter, who made the suggestion to Sopwith in October 1916.

The prototype Sopwith T.1 (N74), later named Cuckoo, first appeared in June 1917 powered by a 200 hp Hispano-Suiza engine. Contracts finally totalled 300 but in the event only 232 were completed as cancellations followed the Armistice in 1918. Blackburn built 162 (N6900–6929, N6950–6999, N7150–7199 and N7980–8011) and the sub-contractors Pegler (N6930–6949) and Fairfield (N7000–7049) twenty and fifty respectively. The first Cuckoo delivered was Blackburn's N6900 in May 1918. Subsequently, about 20 Cuckoos were converted into Mk.IIs which were fitted with the Wolseley Viper engine in place of the Sunbeam Arab of the production Mk.I. Additionally, from N8005, a larger rudder was introduced.

The Cuckoo first entered service with the Torpedo Aeroplane School at East Fortune, and equipped No.185 Squadron in November 1918. The Armistice intervened before the squadron could prove itself in action.

Cuckoos served only briefly in *Argus* and with shore-based torpedo squadrons. They were finally withdrawn when No.210 Squadron disbanded at Gosport in April 1923.

UNITS ALLOCATED

No.185 Squadron (East Fortune), No.186 Squadron (Gosport) and No.210 Squadron (Gosport). Aircraft-carriers *Argus* and *Furious*.

Description: single-seat carrier-borne or shore-based torpedo-carrier. Wooden structure, fabric covered.

Manufacturers: Sopwith Aviation Co Ltd, Kingston-on-Thames. Sub-contracted by Blackburn Aeroplane & Motor Co Ltd, Leeds; Fairfield Shipbuilding & Engineering Co Ltd, Glasgow; Pegler & Co Ltd, Doncaster.

Power Plant: One 200 hp Sunbeam Arab.

Dimensions: Span, 46 ft 9 in. Length, 28 ft 6 in. Height, 10 ft 8 in. Wing area, 566 sq ft.

Weights: Empty, 2,199 lb. Loaded, 3,883 lb.

Performance: Maximum speed, 103½ mph at 2,000 ft; 98 mph at 10,000 ft. Climb, 4 min to 2,000 ft; 31 min to 10,000 ft. Endurance, 4 hr. Service ceiling, 12,100 ft.

Armament: One 18 in Mk.IX torpedo carried below the fuselage.

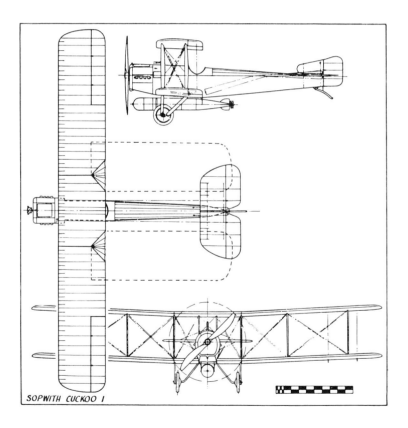

SOPWITH CUCKOO I

Seagull II (N9647) of No.440 Flight from *Eagle. (MoD)*

Supermarine Seagull II

Supermarine began its long association with marine aircraft with the A.D. flying-boat (see Appendix) of 1916, and this was followed by the Baby single-seat flying-boat and the Sea King fighter amphibian which first appeared at Olympia in 1920. In 1921 the Seal deck-landing amphibian fleet spotter was produced, and this was further developed to become the Seagull, ordered in quantity by the Air Ministry in 1922. Both the Seal and the Seagull differed from their predecessors in having a tractor layout: all earlier Supermarine flying-boats and amphibians had featured the pusher arrangement.

The prototype Seagull (N158) was exhibited at the RAF Display at Hendon in 1922 and deliveries of 23 production aircraft (N9562 to 9566, N9603 to 9607 and N9642 to 9654) followed in 1923. Unlike the prototypes, the Seagull II production version had its fuel tanks located under the top mainplane centre-section: those of the earlier marks were inside the hull behind the pilot. The Seagull II was the first single-engined flying-boat to employ gravity feed, and the removal of the tanks from the hull permitted free access between the front and rear crew positions. Two further developments of the Seagull were the Mk.IV and a closely-related type known as the Sheldrake, but neither of these aircraft was produced in quantity. The Seagull IV had twin fins and rudders and was fitted with Handley Page slots. The Seagull V was a much later design which appeared in 1933 and eventually became the Walrus.

The only unit of the FAA to employ the Seagull II was No.440 (Fleet Reconnaissance) Flight, which equipped with the type in May 1923. No.440 Flight's six Seagulls were based in the aircraft-carrier *Eagle* and served on only one cruise, thereafter operating from shore bases. They remained active for only a short period, being superseded in No.440 Flight by Fairey IIIDs in January 1925. With the replacement of the Seagull, the spotter amphibian as a class disappeared from the FAA for a decade until it was revived in the shape of the Walrus.

In 1926, six Seagulls were delivered to the RAAF, where they were known as Mk.IIIs and equipped a special flight which made a photographic survey of the Great Barrier Reef.

No.440 Flight (*Eagle*).

TECHNICAL DATA (SEAGULL II)

Description: Three-seat carrier-borne amphibian for spotter-reconnaissance
duties. Wooden structure, with fabric-covered wings and wooden hull.
Manufacturers: Supermarine Aviation Works (Vickers) Ltd, Southampton.
Power Plant: One 450 hp Napier Lion V.
Dimensions: Span, 46 ft. Length, 37 ft. Height, 12 ft. Wing area, 593 sq ft.
Weights: Empty, 3,897 lb. Loaded, 5,668 lb.
Performance: Maximum speed, 108 mph at sea level. Climb, 11 min to 5,000 ft.
Armament: One Lewis machine-gun mounted amidships, aft of the wings.

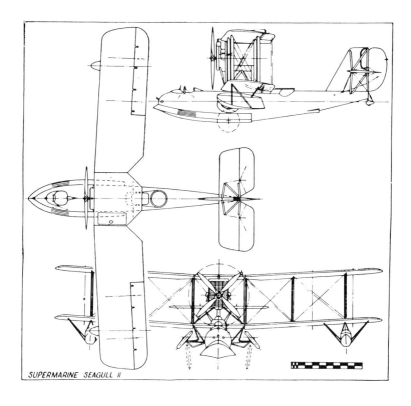

SUPERMARINE SEAGULL II

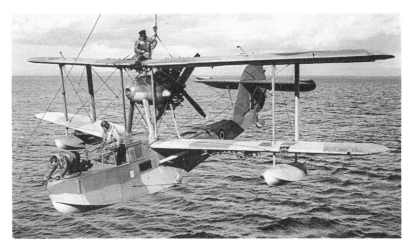

Walrus II (W2743) being hoisted aboard. *(Imperial War Museum)*

Supermarine Walrus

The Walrus amphibian, known universally as the 'Shagbat', enjoyed a reputation in the FAA rivalled only by that of its contemporary, the Swordfish. Both these aircraft, biplanes in a monoplane age, attracted their share of ridicule from the less well-informed who judged only by appearances and knew little of their solid virtues. Naval pilots, who knew better, sang their praises, and their loyalties remained unshaken. They had good reason to praise the Walrus, for it proved its dependability through 10 years of FAA service, flying in every imaginable climate, from the Arctic to the tropics, and performing a remarkable range of duties which on one occasion (during operations in the Red Sea) even included dive-bombing. Predominantly, however, the Walrus was a spotter-reconnaissance aircraft, and its first duty was to be 'the eyes of the Fleet'. Embarked as a catapult aircraft in warships and cruisers, the Walrus performed this rôle all over the world, from the Arctic to the Falkland Islands, from West Africa to Madagascar and from Aden to Ceylon. One of the functions of the Walrus was searching out commerce raiders and one squadron (No.710) was active on these duties only five days after the outbreak of war in 1939 from a base at Freetown, guarding the approaches to West Africa.

When the Walrus first appeared in 1933 it was known as the Seagull V, but it was a very different aircraft from the earlier Seagull amphibians of the 'twenties. Whereas its FAA predecessor, the Seagull II, was a tractor amphibian of wholly wooden construction, the Seagull V had a pusher engine, a metal hull and offered enclosed accommodation for the pilot and navigator. Moreover, it was stressed for catapulting, and in fact became the first amphibian in the world to be catapulted from a warship with full military load. The prototype Seagull V (K4797) was first flown on 21 June 1933 and was designed as a private venture by R J Mitchell, who later achieved fame for his creation of the Spitfire. First ordered by the Australian Government, who retained the name Seagull V, the type was adopted for the FAA under the name Walrus, after trials had taken place aboard *Courageous*, *Renown* and *Nelson* in 1935. Prototype testing was in the hands of No.444 Flight.

The initial Air Ministry contract was placed in May 1935 to Spec 2/35 and was for 12 Walrus I aircraft, K5772 to 5783. In 1936 orders for more aircraft were placed to Spec 37/36, numbered K8338 to 8364, L2169 to 2336, P5646 to 5670, P5696 to 5720, R6543 to 6557 and R6582 to 6591. After 277 Walrus I amphibians had been built by Supermarine, production was transferred to Saunders-Roe to enable the parent firm to concentrate on Spitfires. Saunders-Roe built a further 466 before production ceased in January 1944 with a total of 743. Saro-built aircraft were serialled W2670 to 2689, W2700 to 2792, W2731 to 2760, W2766 to 2798, W3005 to 3051, W3062 to 3101, X1045 and 1046, X9460 to 9484, X9498 to 9532, X9554 to 9593, Z1755 to 1784, Z1804 to 1823, HD804 to 837, HD851 to 878 and HD899 to 936. The Saro-built Walrus differed from the Supermarine version in having a wooden instead of a metal hull and in a number of details such as the substitution of a tailwheel for the original skid, and the prototype (X1045) flew at Anglesey on 2 May 1940. From the total production, about 500 Walruses served with the Fleet Air Arm.

From July 1936, when FAA catapult flights were re-organised in the '700' series, Walruses served in battleships and cruisers as contemporaries of Swordfish and, later, of Seafox floatplanes. In some flights the equipment was mixed: No.702 Flight with the 2nd Battle Squadron had two Seals (later replaced by Swordfish) and one Walrus. The 4th and 8th Cruiser Squadrons also had mixed flights comprised of Walruses and Seafoxes. In January 1940 all catapult units in warships were combined to form No.700 Squadron, which had on its strength 42 Walruses, 11 Seafoxes and 12 Swordfish.

A Walrus being catapulted from a warship. *(Imperial War Museum)*

Mention has already been made of the valuable work done by Walruses of No.710 Squadron off the West African coast from September 1939. During the Norwegian campaign catapult aircraft proved their worth again, spotting for naval bombardments and carrying out anti-submarine and convoy patrols. On 18 April 1940 No.701 Squadron of Walruses commanded by Cdr R S D Armour was established at Harstad, in Northern Norway, where it was used to ferry British and French naval and military officers in a region where communications facilities ashore were otherwise non-existent. Before its re-embarkation in *Ark Royal* on 8 May, Cdr Armour's squadron completed over 200 communications flights, as well as carrying out a bombing attack on German troop concentrations at Solfolla.

This bombing raid was not an isolated instance of the Walrus assuming more offensive capabilities, for on 18 November 1940, HMS *Dorsetshire*'s Walrus was catapulted off armed with bombs for a raid on Italian Somaliland. After hitting enemy fuel supplies, the Walrus went on to spot for the ship's guns during a bombardment of the port of Dante.

Another notable occasion when a Walrus directed a naval bombardment was during an attack by the Royal Navy on Genoa in February 1941. During this action a Walrus circled the town at only 600 ft plotting and reporting the fall of the British shells, and returned to its ship completely unscathed. The following month another Walrus (P5668) made important reconnaissances during the Battle of Matapan.

Perhaps one of the most daring escapades to the credit of the Walrus was during the siege of Tobruk in North Africa, when one of these remarkable aircraft from HMS *Gloucester* alighted in the harbour at night under fire from the enemy to deliver urgent supplies.

In 1942 the hard-worked Walruses of the seaplane-carrier *Albatross*, which had started the war off the West African coast, moved into the Indian Ocean for trade protection duties, and in October played a useful rôle spotting for the guns during the occupation of Madagascar.

In addition to its work with the FAA, the Walrus was also extensively used from 1941 by the RAF, mainly for air-sea rescue duties, and many pilots shot down in the sea owe their life to rescue by a Walrus. Flying near enemy coasts, risking interception, and frequently alighting in mine-infested waters, the Walruses did heroic work which received little publicity at the time.

As a catapult aircraft for spotting, the Walrus last operated from the battleship *King George V* in November 1944 but some remained in service with No.1700 Squadron until after VJ-Day. They operated on air-sea rescue duties with the East Indies Fleet and were based at Trincomalee in Ceylon.

The Walrus will long be remembered by naval pilots, if only for the unforgettable noise made by its 18 open exhaust ports, and its flying characteristics have never been better described than by Terence Horsley in his book *Find, Fix and Strike:*

'Turns are made with slow dignity, as one might imagine a 60-seater bus on a smooth road. Pipes and tobacco come out, the transparent panel is slid over our heads, but the side window is left open for fresh air. The engine makes a steady roar but sufficiently above and behind us to make conversation possible. On a rough day the Walrus behaves more like a cow than a bus—a very friendly cow however. She wallows in the trough of the rough airs as a heifer knee deep in a

Walruses of No.751 Squadron from RNAS Dundee. *(Imperial War Museum)*

boggy meadow. Her driver has a certain amount of heavy work to do in pushing the wheel around but he is reassured by the steady roar of the one and only Pegasus engine.'

The last Supermarine Walrus in existence in Britain (L2301) was added to the Fleet Air Arm Museum's collection on 6 December 1966.

UNITS ALLOCATED

Catapult Flights: No.403 (5th Cruiser Squadron), No.407 Flight (2nd Cruiser Squadron), No.444 Flight (1st Battle Squadron), No.701 Flight (1st Battle Squadron), No.702 Flight (2nd Battle Squadron), No.711 Flight (1st Cruiser Squadron), No.712 Flight (2nd Cruiser Squadron), No.714 Flight (4th Cruiser Squadron), No.715 Flight (5th Cruiser Squadron), No.718 Flight (8th Cruiser Squadron) and No.720 Flight (New Zealand Division). *Catapult Squadrons:* No.700 (Hatston and Twatt), No.701 (Donibristle), No.702 (Mount Batten and Lee-on-Solent), No.710 (Lee-on-Solent), No.711 (Malta and Egypt), No.712 (Mount Batten and Lee-on-Solent), No.714 (Seletar), No.715 (Kai Tak), No.716 (Mount Batten), No.718 (Bermuda) and No.720 (Mount Batten). *Fleet Requirement Units:* No.722 (India), No.771 (Hatston), No.773 (Bermuda), No.777 (West Africa) and No.789 (South Africa). *Communications Squadrons:* No.730 (Abbotsinch), No.742 (Ceylon), and No.781 (Lee-on-Solent). *Air-Sea Rescue Squadrons:* No.733 (Ceylon), No.772 (Machrihanish) and No.1700 (Ceylon). *Training Squadrons:* No.737 (Dunino), No.740 (Arbroath), No.743 (Canada), No.749 (Trinidad), No.751 (Dundee), No.754 (Lee-on-Solent), No.763 (*Pegasus*), No.764 (Pembroke and Lawrenny Ferry), No.765 (Sandbanks) and No.783 (Arbroath). *Service Trials:* No.778 (Lee-on-Solent). *Embarked in the following warships: Achilles, Ajax, Albatross, Anson, Argus, Australia, Barham, Belfast, Bermuda, Berwick, Birmingham, Canberra, Cornwall, Cumberland, Devonshire, Dorsetshire, Duke of York, Edinburgh, Effingham, Emerald, Enterprise, Exeter, Fiji, Gambia, Glasgow, Gloucester, Hobart, Hove, Kent, Kenya, King George V, Leander, Liverpool, London, Malaya, Manchester, Manoora, Mauritius, Nelson, Neptune, Newcastle, Newfoundland, Nigeria, Norfolk, Pegasus, Perth, Prince of Wales, Queen Elizabeth, Renown, Repulse, Resolution, Rodney, Sheffield, Shropshire, Southampton, Suffolk, Sussex, Sydney, Trinidad, Uganda, Valiant, Warspite, Westralia* and *York.*

Ratings fold the wings of a Walrus aboard a carrier. *(Imperial War Museum)*

Walrus I (K8541) of No.718 (Catapult) Flight, HMS *Leander.*

326

Description: Spotter-reconnaissance amphibian for carrier-borne or catapult duties. Crew of three. Metal hull and composite wood and metal wings, fabric covered. Wooden hull on Mk.II.

Manufacturers: Supermarine Aviation Works (Vickers) Ltd, Southampton, Hants. Sub-contracted by Saunders-Roe Ltd, Isle of Wight and Anglesey.

Power Plant: One 775 hp Bristol Pegasus II.M2 or VI.

Dimensions: Span, 45 ft 10 in (17 ft 11 in folded). Length, 37 ft 3 in. Height, 15 ft 3 in. Wing area, 610 sq ft.

Weights: Empty, 4,900 lb. Loaded, 7,200 lb.

Performance: Maximum speed, 135 mph at 4,750 ft. Cruising speed, 95 mph at 3,500 ft. Climb, 5½ min to 5,000 ft; 28 min to 15,000 ft. Range, 444 nautical miles. Service ceiling, 17,100 ft.

Armament: One Vickers K gun in bows and either one or two Vickers K guns amidships, both cockpits with Scarff rings. Provision for six 100 lb or two 250 lb bombs or two Mk.VIII depth charges below the wings.

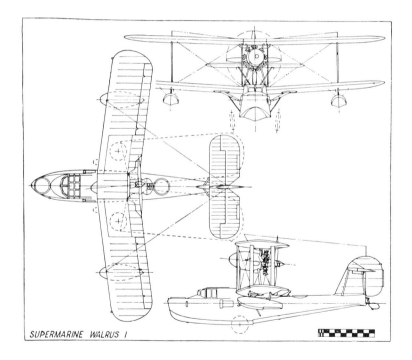

SUPERMARINE WALRUS I

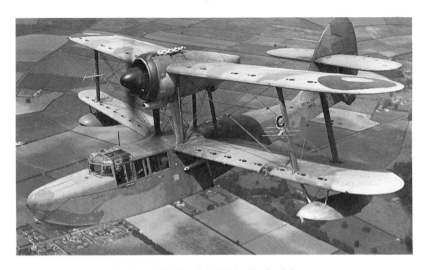

Sea Otter (JM831) of the FAA *(Charles E Brown)*

Supermarine Sea Otter

The Sea Otter first entered service with the FAA in 1944, where it superseded the Walrus for air-sea rescue duties and general communications work. It was employed both in aircraft-carriers and at shore establishments and outlived its more famous predecessor for five or six years to become the last biplane in squadron service with the FAA. With adoption of the helicopter for rescue and communications work from 1950 onwards the Sea Otter gradually disappeared from the Royal Navy and no more amphibians were used after its retirement in December 1952.

As the last of a long line of biplane amphibians designed by Supermarine, the Sea Otter marked a reversion to the tractor layout which had characterised the Seagull II used by the FAA in the 'twenties. Of generally cleaner design than the Walrus, it had more speed, better range and improved handling characteristics on the water. The prototype (K8854) was designed to Spec S.7/38 and first flew in September 1938. After further development to Specs S14/39 and 12/40, it entered production at the Saunders-Roe factory which completed its first Sea Otter in January 1943. Production totalled 290, serials ranging between JM738 and 989, JN104 and 257 and RD869 and 922.

Service trials were conducted by No.778 Squadron at Crail in November 1943 and Sea Otters entered first-line service in November 1944 with No.1700 Squadron of the FAA, which took delivery of six aircraft at Lee-on-Solent, subsequently embarking in the escort-carrier *Khedive*. When the war ended, No.1700's Sea Otters were shore-based at Trincomalee in Ceylon, being attached to the East Indies Fleet. Some served in the Korean War in *Triumph* and *Theseus*. The last Sea Otters with the FAA were those of No.744 Squadron at Eglinton in January 1952.

Air-Sea Rescue and Mine-sweeping: No.1700 Squadron (Ceylon), No.1701 Squadron (Kai Tak), No.1702 Squadron (Malta, Greece and Tunisia) and No.1703 Squadron (Lee-on-Solent). *Second-line squadrons:* Nos.700, 712, 716, 721, 728, 733, 740, 742, 744, 771, 772, 778, 781 and 799. Embarked: *Ameer, Begum, Emperor, Khedive, Ocean, Stalker, Theseus* and *Trouncer.*

TECHNICAL DATA (SEA OTTER II)

Description: Carrier-borne or shore-based air-sea rescue and communications amphibian with a crew of three/four. Metal hull and composite wings, fabric covered.

Manufacturers: Saunders-Roe Ltd, East Cowes, Isle of Wight.

Power Plant: One 965 hp Bristol Mercury 30.

Dimensions: Span, 46 ft. Length, 39 ft 9¾ in. Height, 16 ft 2 in. Wing area, 610 sq ft.

Weights: Empty, 6,470 lb. Loaded, (maximum) 10,130 lb.

Performance: Maximum speed, 154 mph at 5,000 ft. Cruising speed, 120 mph. Climb, 870 ft/min; 7½ min to 5,000 ft. Range (normal) 690 miles; (maximum), 920 miles. Service ceiling, 17,000 ft.

Armament: Two Vickers K guns amidships and one Vickers K gun in bows. Capacity for four 250 lb bombs.

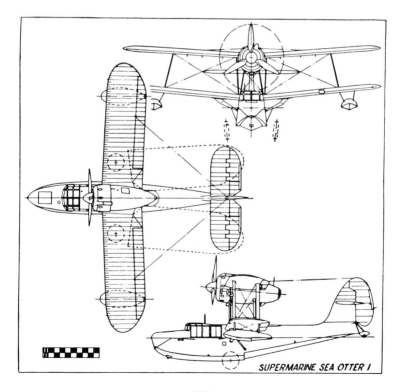

SUPERMARINE SEA OTTER I

Hooked Spitfire (BL676), later Seafire IB MB328

Supermarine Seafire
(Merlin variants)

The decision to adopt the Spitfire for carrier-borne service with the FAA was taken in 1941 after the Sea Hurricane had proved its value both in carriers and with the catapult fighter units. The Sea Hurricane had shown that a high-performance land-fighter could be safely flown from a carrier deck: this caused a revolution in naval thinking, and it was a logical step to seek a fighter of even higher performance, such as the Spitfire. Tests were carried out with a converted Spitfire VB which had been fitted with an arrester hook under the rear fuselage and trials took place aboard *Illustrious* in December 1941. The pilot of this hooked Spitfire (AB205) was Cdr H P Bramwell, DSO, DSC, and trials included catapult take-offs as well as normal carrier operations.

With the success of these trials, work went ahead with the conversion of Spitfires into Seafires prior to the production of Seafires proper, which had been built as such. The original 48 conversions (from Spitfire VBs) were known as Seafire IBs and, apart from the introduction of a retractable V-frame arrester hook, were almost identical to their land-fighter counterparts. Serial numbers ranged from MB328 to 375. Conversion work was undertaken by Air Service Training Ltd, at Hamble, and a further 118 (NX879 to 989 and PA100 to 129) were produced. All the Seafire IBs had fixed wings and the 'B' type Spitfire wing with two 20-mm guns and four machine-guns. Deliveries to the Royal Navy took place over the period from January 1942 to July 1943, the final 30 aircraft being converted by Supermarine's South Marston factory.

The next variant of the Seafire was the Mk.IIC, which began deliveries to the Royal Navy in June 1942. It was generally similar to the Seafire IB, except for the use of the 'C' type Spitfire wing and some reinforcement of the airframe to permit the installation of catapult spools and RATOG (rocket-assisted take-off gear). The 'C' type wing (as fitted to the Spitfire VC) could mount four 20-mm guns or any of the earlier combinations of armament. The L.IIC variant was specially produced for low-altitude operations and mounted the Merlin 32 engine, which drove a four-blade airscrew instead of the three-blade type seen on all earlier Seafires. Total production of the Seafire IIC was 262 by Supermarine (MA970 to MB326 and NM910 to 982) (including 60 conversions by Vickers) and 110 by Westland. Westland-built Seafire IICs were serialled in the range LR631 to 764.

With the introduction of the Seafire III, the major Merlin-engined version, a manually-folding wing appeared on the Seafire for the first time, improving deck-handling and enabling hangar lifts to be utilised. The trial installations aircraft for the folding wing was a converted Seafire IIC (MA970), the Seafire III prototype which flew in November 1942. Large-scale manufacture of the Seafire III began in late 1942 and was undertaken by Cunliffe-Owen Aircraft Ltd and Westland Aircraft Ltd. From a total production of 1,163 aircraft,

Seafire L.IIC of No.801 Squadron (*Furious*). (*Imperial War Museum*)

Seafire F.IIC (MB156) of No.885 Squadron (*Formidable*). (*Imperial War Museum*)

Cunliffe-Owen built 300 between November 1943 and July 1945 serialled in the ranges NN333 to 641 and PX913 to 962. All but the first 20 Cunliffe-Owen Seafire IIIs had four-blade airscrews and the revised tropical filter appeared on the 90th and subsequent aircraft. From the 130th aircraft, provision was made for a 30-gallon flush-fitting drop tank below the fuselage. The Seafire L.F.III was the low-altitude variant corresponding to the earlier L.IIC. All Seafire IIIs could be fitted with rocket-assisted take-off equipment, first tested on the Seafire IIC MB141. They appeared both with clipped and full-span wings and could carry either two 250 lb bombs under the wings or a 500 lb bomb beneath the fuselage.

The 911 Westland-built Seafire IIIs were serialled between LR765 and 881, NF418 and 665, NM984 and 999, NN112 and 330, PP921 and 999, PR115 and 334, RX156 and 353.

Seafires first entered service with No.807 Squadron in June 1942, followed by No.801 Squadron in September 1942. Both these squadrons embarked their Seafires in *Furious* in time to participate in Operation Torch, the Allied invasion of North Africa in November 1942. This operation, the first in which Seafires took part and the largest naval action of the war to that date, was an Anglo-American venture in which the American troops captured Casablanca whilst British forces took Oran and Algiers. The Seafires were in action from daybreak on 8 November, when they escorted a strike force of Albacores and made low-flying attacks on enemy airfields. During these attacks they were engaged by Vichy-French Dewoitine D.520 fighters. In the dogfight which followed, Sub-Lt G C Baldwin, DSC, flying a Seafire IIC (MA986) of No.807 Squadron, shot down one of the Dewoitines: this was the first air victory claimed by a Seafire. Later, another Dewoitine was shot down by a Seafire during tactical reconnaissance of La Senia and Lourmel airfields. An amusing story is told of one Seafire pilot who landed alongside an American tank column to find out his whereabouts, later rejoining his carrier safely.

By the end of 1942 the FAA had six squadrons of Seafires, mostly armed with the Mk.IIC. Nos.801 and 807 had been joined by Nos.808, 884 and 887

Seafire III (LR765) built by Westland Aircraft Ltd.

332

(formerly with Fulmars) and No.880 (formerly with Sea Hurricanes). The following year, as Seafire production mounted, Nos.809, 886, 894, 895, 897 and 899 Squadrons also received the type: additionally six Seafires were allotted to each of Nos.833, 834, 842 and 879 Squadrons in the escort-carriers.

Following the success of the FAA's fighters in providing cover for the landings in North Africa, they were once again allotted this responsible task in the even greater amphibious assault almost a year later, known as Operation Avalanche. This was the Allied landing in the Gulf of Salerno, which took place in September 1943. Naval air support was provided by the escort-carriers *Attacker, Battler, Hunter, Stalker* and *Unicorn* and the Fleet carriers *Formidable* and *Illustrious*. Seafire IICs of Nos.807, 808, 809, 833, 834, 879, 880, 885, 886, 887, 894, 897 and 899 Squadrons were all engaged.

Typical of the work done by Seafires at Salerno was the achievement of No.879 Squadron. This unit, which had equipped with Seafire IBs at Stretton in March 1943, flew no fewer than 75 offensive patrols over the landing beaches in the period 9 to 13 September 1943: it was operating from the escort-carrier *Attacker*.

In November 1943 the Seafire III entered service, initially with No.894 Squadron at Henstridge, and eventually equipped 17 first-line squadrons.

Both the landings in North Africa and at Salerno had been covered in the initial phases exclusively by FAA fighters as land-based fighters were out of range. The same situation obtained during Operation Dragoon, the Allied invasion of the south of France in August 1944. Once again the escort-carriers and the Seafires were active: the British sector of the beach was covered by aircraft from *Attacker, Emperor, Khedive, Hunter, Pursuer* and *Searcher*. Seafire IIIs of No.807 Squadron, which had flown with No.879 Squadron from shore bases in Italy since June 1944, operated from the escort-carrier *Hunter*. Also present were Seafire IIIs of No.809 Squadron (in *Stalker*) and No.899 Squadron. No.899 Squadron completed 201 sorties from *Khedive* during the period 15 to 23 August 1944.

Mention has already been made of the tactical reconnaissance duties performed by Seafires with the Desert Air Force in Italy. With the Allied invasion of northern France in June 1944, Seafires also formed part of the Second Tactical Air Force, operating with the Air Spotting Pool of No.34 (Photographic Reconnaissance) Wing, which contained Nos.808, 885, 886 and 897 Squadrons of the FAA as well as two Spitfire squadrons, Nos.26 and 63. These units were among the first to operate from the hastily improvised airstrips established in the face of enemy fire soon after troops had landed in Normandy. The Seafires remained shore-based with the Second Tactical Air Force until the middle of July, when they returned to naval command.

Seafires played their part in a number of the celebrated attacks on the German battleship *Tirpitz* during 1944. In the first Barracuda strike, during April, Seafires of No.801 Squadron operated from the carrier *Furious*, joining Hellcats and Corsairs to provide fighter protection. Later, during an attack on 22 August, Seafires of No.894 Squadron from *Indefatigable* shot down two enemy aircraft. This squadron's Seafire IIIs had had the unusual task the previous spring of escorting Typhoon fighter-bombers of the RAF on raids from Culmhead, Somerset.

In 1945, when the FAA's striking power was concentrated in the Far East for

Seafire III. showing the wing-folding arrangement. *(Vickers)*

the final phases of the war against Japan, the Seafire III was serving with eight squadrons in this theatre. Nos.807, 809, 879 and 899 Squadrons were in the escort-carriers *Hunter, Stalker, Attacker* and *Chaser*, whilst Nos.801 and 880 were in *Implacable* and Nos.887 and 894 in *Indefatigable*. No.807 Squadron provided fighter cover for the invasion of Rangoon and Penang, and the Seafires of *Indefatigable* joined in the large fighter escort for the brilliant attacks on the Japanese oil refineries in Sumatra by Avengers and Fireflies. In March–April 1945 Pacific Fleet Seafires were in action over the Sakashima Islands, in June at Truk and by August were flying over the Japanese mainland.

At the time of VJ-Day Seafires equipped 12 first-line squadrons of the FAA: all but four were still flying the Mk.III, which had been in action since 1943. If the war had continued, the Seafire IIIs would have been superseded by the Griffon-engined versions of the Seafire, more details of which appear in the following pages. In the event, the Griffon-engined Seafires were almost wholly post-war types in the FAA, with the exception of the Seafire XVs of Nos.802, 803 and 805 Squadrons, which were working up in the United Kingdom preparatory to Pacific service when the war ended.

The Seafire III remained only briefly in FAA squadrons after the war and was last in service with No.1832 Squadron of the RNVR at Culham until November 1947.

Total production of Merlin-engined Seafires was 1,700, of which 226 were converted RAF Spitfires. The RN also received about 60 unconverted Spitfires.

UNITS ALLOCATED

(*Seafire IB*): No.801 Squadron (Stretton. Machrihanish and *Furious*). No.807 Squadron

334

(Lee-on-Solent, Yeovilton and *Furious*), No.809 Squadron (Stretton, Machrihanish and *Unicorn*), No.816 Squadron (Maydown and *Tracker*), No.842 Squadron (Maydown and *Fencer*), No.879 Squadron (Stretton), No.885 Squadron (Machrihanish and *Formidable*), No.887 Squadron (Machrihanish), No.894 Squadron (Machrihanish and Hatston) and No.897 Squadron (Lee-on-Solent). *Second-line squadrons:* 700, 708, 715, 719, 731, 736, 748, 759, 761, 768, 778, 779, 781, 787, 790 and 798. (*Seafire IIC*): No.801 Squadron (Stretton and *Furious*), No.807 Squadron (Lee-on-Solent, *Furious, Indomitable, Battler* and *Hunter*), No.808 Squadron (St Merryn, *Battler* and *Hunter*), No.809 Squadron (Stretton, *Unicorn* and *Stalker*), No.816 Squadron (Fearn, Machrihanish and *Tracker*), No.833 Squadron (Machrihanish and *Stalker*), No.834 Squadron (Machrihanish, *Hunter* and *Battler*), No.842 Squadron (Machrihanish and *Fencer*, No.879 Squadron (Machrihanish, *Attacker* and *Hunter*), No.880 Squadron (Stretton, *Argus, Indomitable* and *Stalker*), No.884 Squadron (Skeabrae and *Victorious*), No.885 Squadron (Machrihanish and *Formidable*), No.886 Squadron (Machrihanish and *Attacker*), No.887 Squadron (Machrihanish and *Unicorn*), No.889 Squadron (Ceylon and *Atheling*), No.894 Squadron (Machrihanish and *Illustrious*), No.895 Squadron (St Merryn, Machrihanish and Turnhouse), No.897 Squadron (Machrihanish, *Unicorn* and *Stalker*) and No.899 Squadron (Hatston, *Indomitable* and *Hunter*). *Second-line squadrons:* Nos.700, 708, 718, 719, 728, 731, 748, 757, 759, 761, 768, 770, 775, 776, 778, 787, 790, 794, 798 and 799. (*Seafire III*) No.801 Squadron (Skeabrae, *Furious* and *Implacable*), No.802 Squadron (Arbroath), No.803 Squadron (Arbroath and Nutts Corner), No.805 Squadron (Machrihanish), No.806 Squadron (Machrihanish), No.807 Squadron (Italy, *Hunter,* Greece and Ceylon), No.808 Squadron (Lee-on-Solent), No.809 Squadron (Dekheila, *Stalker* and *Attacker*), No.879 Squadron (Long Kesh and *Attacker*), No.880 Squadron (Skeabrae, *Furious* and *Implacable*), No.883 Squadron (Arbroath and Nutts Corner), No.885 Squadron (St Merryn, Henstridge and Lee-on-Solent), No.886 Squadron (Henstridge, St Merryn and Lee-on-Solent), No. 887 Squadron (Henstridge, *Indefatigable* and *Implacable*), No.889 Squadron (Ceylon and *Atheling*), No.894 Squadron (Henstridge and *Indefatigable*), No.899 Squadron (Machrihanish, *Indomitable, Hunter, Khedive* and *Chaser*). *RNVR:* No.1832 Squadron (Culham). *Second-line squadrons:* Nos.700, 706, 708, 709, 715, 718, 721, 728, 733, 736, 740, 744, 748, 757, 759, 760, 761, 766, 767, 768, 771, 772, 778, 781, 782, 787, 790, 794 and 799.

TECHNICAL DATA (SEAFIRES II AND III)

Description: Single-seat carrier-borne fighter, fighter-bomber or tactical reconnaissance aircraft. All-metal stressed-skin construction.

Manufacturers: Supermarine Division of Vickers-Armstrongs Ltd, Southampton. Sub-contracted by Cunliffe-Owen Aircraft Ltd, and Westland Aircraft Ltd. Maker's designation, Type 340, 357 and 358.

Power Plant: (IIC): One 1,415 hp Rolls-Royce Merlin 45 or 46. (L.IIC): One 1,640 hp Rolls-Royce Merlin 32. (F.III): One 1,470 hp Rolls-Royce Merlin 55. (L.III and F.R.III): One 1,585 hp Rolls-Royce Merlin 55M.

Dimensions: Span, 36 ft 10 in. Length, 30 ft 2½ in. Height, 11 ft 2 in. Wing area, 242 sq ft.

Weights: (IIC): Empty, 6,103 lb. Loaded, 7,004 lb. (F.III): Empty, 6,204 lb. Loaded, 7,104 lb. (F.R.III): Empty, 6,286 lb. Loaded, 7,508 lb.

Performance: (IIC): Maximum speed, 332 mph at 14,000 ft; 285 mph at sea level. Service ceiling, 28,000 ft. Endurance, 1½ hr. (L.IIC): Maximum speed, 335 mph at 6,000 ft; 316 mph at sea level. Initial climb, 4,600 ft/min. Climb, 1.7 min to 5,000 ft. Range, 280 miles with 45-gallon drop tank. Service ceiling, 22,000 ft. (F.III): Maximum speed, 352 mph at 12,250 ft; 304 mph at sea level. Initial climb, 3,250 ft/min. Climb, 8.1 min to 20,000 ft. Range, 400 miles with 90-gallon drop tank. Service ceiling, 35,000 ft. (L.III): Maximum speed, 348 mph at 6,000 ft; 331 mph at sea level. Climb, 2,650 ft/min; 5½ min 15,000 ft. Range (with 45-gallon drop tank), 280 miles; (with 90-gallon drop tank), 400 miles. Service ceiling, 24,000 ft.

Armament: (F.IIC and subsequent variants): Two 20-mm guns and four 0.303 guns in wings and provision for one 500 lb bomb under fuselage or two 250 lb bombs under wings.

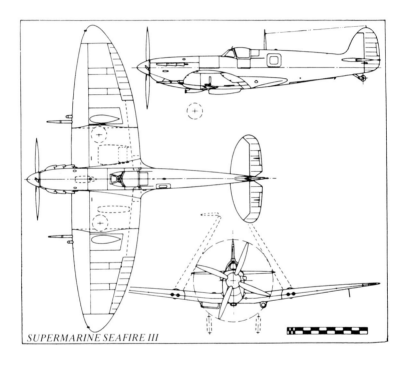

SUPERMARINE SEAFIRE III

Seafire XVII (SX194) of No.781 Squadron from Lee-on-Solent. *(Crown Copyright)*

Supermarine Seafire
(Griffon variants)

Griffon-engined Seafires were just entering service with the FAA when the Second World War came to an end. If the war had continued for a few months longer, the Seafire XV would have superseded the Seafire III in carriers of the British Pacific Fleet. As events turned out, however, the Seafire XV saw only a brief period of service with squadrons based in the United Kingdom before VJ-Day and subsequent Griffon-engined Seafires did not enter the FAA until the post-war years.

The Seafire XV, the first Griffon variant, was developed to Spec N.4/43 and the first three prototypes were NS487, NS490 and NS493. The first flew in February 1944, and production Seafire XVs were manufactured by Cunliffe-Owen Aircraft Ltd, which built 134, and by Westland Aircraft Ltd, which built 250. Apart from the installation of the Griffon VI engine, the Mark XV also differed from earlier Seafires in having increased fuel capacity, with tanks inside the wings, and from the 51st aircraft the sting-type arrester hook was standardised. This hook was mounted in the extreme tail, and the bottom of the rudder had to be cut away to accommodate it. It eventually replaced the old type V frame hook on most naval aircraft. All Seafire XVs (and subsequent marks except 45 and 46) had the folding wing incorporated as standard, and RATOG (rocket-assisted take-off gear) was added from the 75th aircraft. Cunliffe-Owen Seafire XVs were serialled between PR338 and 506, and Westland between SR446 and 645 and SW781 and 921.

The Seafire XV first entered service with No.802 Squadron at Arbroath in August 1945, subsequently embarking in the carriers *Premier*, *Berwick* and *Vengeance*. Other squadrons to receive the type were No.803, seconded to the Royal Canadian Navy for service in *Warrior*, and Nos.805 and 806, which saw service in the post-war light fleet-carriers *Ocean* and *Glory*.

The first type of Seafire to enter the FAA after the close of the Second World War was the Mk.XVII, which joined Nos.809 and 879 Squadrons at Nutts Corner, Northern Ireland, in November 1945. The Seafire XVII was a refinement of the Mk.XV, and the prototype (NS493) which flew in 1945 was in fact a conversion of the third prototype Seafire XV. It differed from all but the last 30 XVs in having a clear-view bubble hood and a cutaway rear fuselage and was built in two versions: the F.XVII and the F.R.XVII. The Seafire XVII also had more fuel capacity than the Mk.XV, as a 33-gal tank was mounted in the rear fuselage. It also had a much strengthened long-stroke undercarriage. Total production of the Seafire XVII was 232, of which Cunliffe-Owen Aircraft Ltd built 20 serialled between SP323 and 355, and Westland 212 from SW986 to SX389. The last aircraft was delivered in October 1946.

The Seafire XVII eventually proved to be the longest-lived of the post-war variants and, after retirement from first-line squadrons, continued to give good service with air squadrons of the RNVR and with training squadrons until November 1954.

Whilst the Seafire XV and XVII were in production, development work proceeded at the Cunliffe-Owen factory with a FAA version of the Spitfire Mk.21, designated Seafire 45. This Seafire was produced to the requirements of Spec N.7/44 and the prototype (TM379) was a converted Spitfire F.21. Alterations included the fitting of naval radio equipment, a stinger-type arrester hook and modified undercarriage leg fairings and tail wheel-guard to facilitate the use of arrester wires. The Seafire 45 also differed from the earlier Griffon variants in mounting the Series 61/85 engine and in having four 20-mm guns as standard. The new Griffon engine resulted in a change to a five-bladed airscrew. As the Seafire 45 emerged as the war ended, production was limited to 50 aircraft (LA428–457 and LA480–499) built at South Marston. The Seafire 45 never became operational, but it served with eight second-line squadrons until February 1948. One example (LA494) reached Mach 0.88 on trials to become the Fleet Air Arm's fastest piston-engined aircraft in history.

Just as the Spitfire 21 became the Seafire 45 when modified for naval service, so did the Spitfire 22 become the Seafire 46. This variant was generally similar to its predecessor, but introduced the bubble hood and cutaway rear fuselage. It appeared both with a five-blade airscrew and six-blade contra-rotating airscrews, the majority having the latter, and could also be seen with two types of tail assembly. Early Seafire 46s had the original tail, but later aircraft incorporated the revised fin and rudder of increased area as used on the Spiteful and Spitfire 24. The prototype Seafire 46 (TM383) was converted from the second prototype Seafire 45. It was followed by a small production batch of 24 aircraft (LA541 to LA564) from the South Marston factory, the original contract for 200 having been curtailed. A few Seafire 46s were fitted with a single oblique F.24 camera behind the pilot and designated F.R.46. The Seafire 46, like the Mk.45, did not enter first-line squadron service with the FAA, but it served with seven second-line squadrons between May 1945 and August 1950 and with No.1832 Squadron of the RNVR at Culham until January 1950.

The final version of the Seafire to enter service was the Mk.47, the naval version of the Spitfire 24. This differed from the Mks.45 and 46 in that it was fully navalised, with folding wings; those of the Seafire 45 and 46 were fixed. The Seafire 47's wing fold (power-operated from PS948) differed from all preceding Seafires in having a hinge at only one point in the mainplane panel. The entire wing folded upwards just outboard of the wheel wells: the wing tips did not fold back as on earlier Seafires. The six-bladed contra-rotating airscrew, bubble hood and Spiteful-type tail assembly was standard on all Seafire 47s:

Seafire XV (SW847) built by Westland. *(Charles E Brown)*

Seafire 45 (LA428) with five-blade airscrew *(Vickers)*

externally it was identical with the later production Seafire 46s except for the re-positioning of the carburettor air intake as a lip just behind the spinner and the use of the short-barrel Hispano guns. Internally, fuel capacity was increased by the installation of a 32-gal tank in the rear fuselage and, for maximum range, this could be augmented by a 90-gal flush-fitting drop tank below the fuselage and two 23-gal blister tanks under the mainplanes. This gave the Seafire 47 a grand total of 287 gal of fuel and bestowed a range of about 500 miles.

The prototype Seafire 47 (PS944) was followed by production aircraft from the South Marston, Swindon, factory of Supermarine, most of which were fitted out for fighter-reconnaissance and designated F.R.47. A contract was placed for 150 Seafire 47s but only 90 of these were built, serialled PS944–957, LA193 and 195, VP427–495 and VR961–972. The last was completed in January 1949.

The Seafire 47 entered first-line service in the FAA with No.804 Squadron at Ford in January 1948. It eventually joined No.800 Squadron, which received Seafire 47s at Donibristle in April 1949 and subsequently embarked in the light fleet-carrier *Triumph*. From October 1949 until February 1950 No.800 Squadron took part in rocket strikes against bandit hideouts in Malaya. With the outbreak of war in Korea in June 1950 *Triumph* sailed for Okinawa and No.800 Squadron's aircraft became the only Seafires to take part in the Korean War.

Seafire 46 (LA542) built by Vickers at South Marston. *(Charles E Brown)*

Seafire 47 (VP447), showing wing-folding arrangement. *(Vickers)*

Seafire 47 of No.800 Squadron leaves *Triumph* during the Korean War. *(MoD)*

They had a distinguished record, flying 360 sorties comprising 245 offensive fighter patrols and 115 ground-attack operations.

With the emergence of the Attacker, the FAA's first operational jet fighter, the Seafire 47 was superseded in first-line squadrons from 1950, but it continued to operate with air squadrons of the RNVR, alongside the older Seafire 17s. The last squadron to use Seafire 47s was No.1833 (Midland Air Division) at Bramcote: they were finally supplanted by Hawker Sea Furies in May 1954.

Credit for being the last Seafire in service must, however, be awarded to the Seafire XVII. The only remaining unit of Seafires in the FAA, No.764 Squadron, was finally retired at Yeovilton on 23 November 1954.

The sole surviving Seafire XVII in the United Kingdom (SX137) is preserved in the FAA Museum at Yeovilton, Somerset.

UNITS ALLOCATED

(*Seafire XV*): No.800 Squadron (Eglinton), No.801 Squadron (Australia, *Implacable*), No.802 Squadron (*Venerable*), No.803 Squadron (Arbroath and *Warrior*), No.804 Squadron (Eglinton and *Theseus*), No.805 Squadron (Machrihanish and *Ocean*), No.806 Squadron (Machrihanish and *Glory*), No.809 Squadron (Nutts Corner), No.883 Squadron (Nutts Corner, Arbroath and Machrihanish). RNVR: No.1831 Squadron (Stretton), No.1832 Squadron (Culham) and No.1833 Squadron (Bramcote). *Second-line squadrons:* Nos.700, 701, 706, 709, 715, 718, 721, 728, 733, 736, 737, 751, 759, 761, 766, 767, 768, 771, 773, 777, 778, 780, 781, 787, 790, 791 and 799. (*Seafire XVII*): No.800 Squadron (Eglinton and *Triumph*), No.805 Squadron (*Ocean*), No.807 Squadron (Nutts Corner and *Vengeance*), No.809 Squadron (Nutts Corner) and No.879 Squadron (Nutts Corner). RNVR: No.1830 Squadron (Abbotsinch), No.1831 Squadron (Stretton) and No.1833 Squadron (Bramcote). *Second-line squadrons:* Nos.701, 703, 727, 728, 736, 737, 738, 746, 759, 761, 764, 766, 778, 781, 782, 787 and 799. (*Seafire 45*): *Second-line squadrons:* Nos.700, 703, 709, 771, 777, 778, 780 and 787. (*Seafire 46*): RNVR: No.1832 Squadron (Culham). *Second-line squadrons:* Nos.736, 738, 767, 771, 777, 778 and 781. (*Seafire 47*): No.800 Squadron (Donibristle and *Triumph*), No.804 Squadron (Ford, Eglinton and *Ocean*). RNVR: No.1833 Squadron (Bramcote). *Second-line squadrons: Nos.759, 777, 778 and 787.*

Description: Single-seat carrier-borne fighter, figher-bomber or fighter-reconnaissance aircraft. All-metal stressed-skin construction.

Manufacturers: Supermarine Division of Vickers-Armstrongs Ltd, Castle Bromwich and South Marston, Swindon. Mks.XV and XVII sub-contracted by Cunliffe-Owen Aircraft Ltd, and Westland Aircraft Ltd.

Power Plant: (Mks.XV and XVII): One 1,815 hp Rolls-Royce Griffon VI. (Mk.45): One 2,035 hp Rolls-Royce Griffon 61. (Mk.46): One 2,375 hp Rolls-Royce Griffon 85. (Mk.47): One 2,350 hp Rolls-Royce Griffon 88.

Dimensions (Mks.XV and XVII): Span, 36 ft 10 in. Length, 32 ft 3 in. Height, 10 ft 8 in. Wing area, 242 sq ft. (Mks.45 and 46): Span, 36 ft 11 in. Length, 33 ft 7 in. Height, 12 ft 9 in. Wing area, 244 sq ft. (Mk.47): Span, 36 ft 11 in. Length, 34 ft 4 in. Height, 12 ft 9 in. Wing area, 244 sq ft.

Weights: (Mk.XV): Empty, 6,200 lb. Loaded, 8,000 lb. (Mk.VXII): Empty, 7,015 lb. Loaded, 8,010 lb. (Mk.45): Empty, 8,090lb. Loaded, 9,400 lb. (Mk.46): Empty, 8,530 lb. Loaded, 10,078 lb. (Mk.47): Empty, 8,680 lb. Loaded, (normal); 10,700 lb; (maximum), 12,530 lb.

Performance: (Mk.XV): Maximum speed, 384 mph at 13,500 ft; 369 mph at 5,000 ft. Climb, 3,450 ft/min. Range, 300 miles. Service ceiling, 32,000 ft. (Mk.XVII): Maximum speed, 387 mph at 13,500 ft. Climb, 3,300 ft/min; 6 min to 20,000 ft. Range, 440 miles (with auxiliary tanks). Service ceiling, 31,000 ft. (Mk.47): Maximum speed, 452 mph at 24,250 ft; 405 mph at 9,500 ft; 353 mph at sea level. Climb, 4,800 ft/min at sea level; 4.9 min to 20,000 ft. Range, 500 miles (with auxiliary tanks). Service ceiling, 43,100 ft.

Armament (Mk.XV): Two 20-mm guns and four 0.303 guns (Mk.XVII): Two 20-mm guns and four 0.303 guns plus four 60 lb rocket projectiles below the wings. (Mk.45 and 46): Four 20-mm guns. Provision for one 500 lb bomb below fuselage. (Mk.47): Four 20-mm guns plus four 60 lb rocket

Seafire 46 (LA561) of No.1832 Squadron from Culham (*'Flight'*)

projectiles below the wings. Provision for one 500 lb bomb below fuselage and two 250 lb bombs below wings.

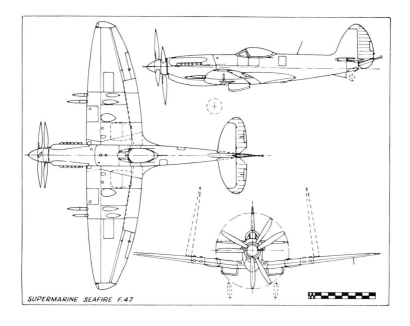

SUPERMARINE SEAFIRE F.47

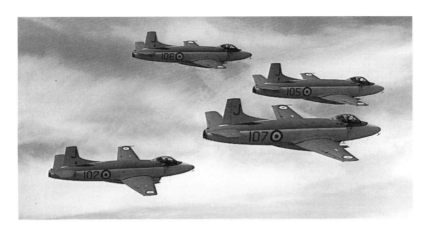

Attacker F.B.2s of No.800 Squadron from HMS *Eagle*. (*RAF Museum*)

Supermarine Attacker

The Attacker has a special place in FAA history as the first jet fighter to be standardised in first-line squadrons. It was originally conceived as a land-fighter for the RAF, and work began on its design in October 1944. Produced to Spec E.10/44, the first prototype (TS409) flew at Chilbolton on 27 July 1946. It incorporated the Spiteful's laminar flow wing and was the first aircraft to use the Rolls-Royce Nene turbojet. No RAF orders materialised, but the second and third prototypes (to Spec E.1/45) had long-stroke undercarriages, lift spoilers and deck-arrester hooks to meet naval requirements. The first naval prototype (TS413) flew on 17 June 1947 and carrier trials were concluded aboard HMS *Illustrious* in October 1947. Production contracts for the FAA were placed in November 1949 and the first F.1 (WA469) flew on 5 May 1950 and the first F.B.1 (WA527) on 7 January 1952. A total of 145 Attackers was built for the FAA, the last aircraft (WZ302) being delivered in 1953. The Attacker F.1 and F.B.1 with the Nene 3 was succeeded (from WK319) by the F.B.2 which had the Nene 102 engine, modified ailerons and cockpit hood and flew on 25 April 1952. Initial production aircraft did not have the dorsal fin extension, which first appeared early in 1951. Sixty-one Attacker F.1 and F.B.1s were built, and 84 F.B.2s. Serial blocks were WA469 to 498, WA505 to 534, WK319 to 342, WP275 to 304, WT851 and WZ273 to 302.

Attackers first entered service with No.800 Squadron at Ford on 17 August 1951: this was the pioneer operational jet squadron of the FAA. Standard equipment in service included Martin-Baker ejection seat, RATOG, accelerator hooks in the wheel bays and a somewhat cumbersome 250-gal drop tank below the fuselage. By the time of the Naval Review at Spithead in 1953, Attackers equipped Nos.800, 803 and 890 Squadrons as well as No.736 Squadron, all of which participated in the Fly-past. In 1954 Nos.800 and 803 Squadrons re-armed with Sea Hawks and No.890 Squadron with Sea Venoms and the Attacker passed from first-line service. However, it continued to serve with air squadrons of the RNVR from 1955 until their disbandment early in 1957. No.1831 Squadron received Attackers in exchange for Sea Furies at Stretton on 14 May 1955, becoming the first jet squadron of the RNVR.

UNITS ALLOCATED

(*F.1*): Nos.800, 803 and 890 Squadrons (Ford and *Eagle*). *Second-line squadrons:* Nos.702 (Culdrose), 703 (Ford), 736 (Culdrose and Lossiemouth), 767 (Stretton), 787 (West Raynham). (*F.B.1*): Nos.800 and 890 (Ford and *Eagle*). *Second-line squadrons:* Nos.703 (Ford), 767 (Stretton) and 787 (West Raynham). (*F.B.2*): Nos.800, 803 and 890 Squadrons (Ford and *Eagle*). *RNVR* Nos.1831 (Stretton), 1832 (Benson) and 1833 (Honiley). *Second-line squadrons:* Nos.703 (Ford), 767 (Stretton) and 787 (West Raynham).

TECHNICAL DATA (ATTACKER F.1)

Description: Single-seat carrier-borne fighter. All-metal stressed-skin.
Manufacturers: Supermarine Division of Vickers-Armstrongs Ltd, South Marston, Swindon, Wilts.
Power Plant: One 5,100 lb thrust Rolls-Royce Nene 3.
Dimensions: Span, 36 ft 11 in. Length, 37 ft 6 in. Height, 9 ft 11 in. Wing area, 226 sq ft.
Weights: Empty, 8,434 lb. Loaded, 12,211 lb.
Performance: Maximum speed, 590 mph at sea level; 583 mph at 10,000 ft; 561 mph at 20,000 ft; 538 mph at 30,000 ft. Cruising speed 355 mph. Climb, 6,350 ft/min at sea level; 6.6 min to 30,000 ft. Range, 590 miles (normal) or 1,190 miles (with auxiliary ventral tank). Service ceiling, 45,000 ft.
Armament: Four 20-mm guns in wings. F.B.1 and 2 also equipped for eight 60 lb rocket projectiles or two 1,000 bombs below wings.

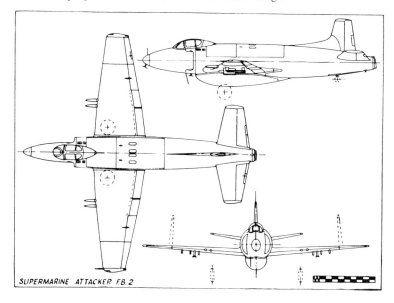

SUPERMARINE ATTACKER F.B.2

Scimitar (XD268) of No.800B Squadron from *Eagle*. *(FAA Museum)*

Supermarine Scimitar

The Scimitar was the first swept-wing single-seat fighter to be produced for the FAA and also the first to be capable of supersonic flight, attained in a shallow dive. It was also the first FAA aircraft equipped to carry an atomic bomb. Designed to meet the requirements of Naval Spec N.113D, the Scimitar first appeared as the Supermarine Type 544, a development of the Type 525 (VX138) which first flew on 27 April 1954. This had been preceded by two earlier straight-winged prototypes with a butterfly tail, the Type 508 (VX129), which first flew on 31 August 1951 and the Type 529 (VX136) which first flew on 29 August 1952. The first prototype Type 544 (WT854) flew on 19 January 1956. The second and third prototypes (WT859 and WW134) flew later in 1956.

The Scimitar prototype differed from the earlier Type 525 in a number of respects. Its fuselage was redesigned on the area rule principle; it had a longer nose and larger air intakes. Also new was the long dorsal spine, terminating in an intake. Blown flaps, tested experimentally in the Type 525, became standard in the Scimitar. This innovation reduced the safe approach speed, an obvious advantage for carrier operation, and also lowered the speed at which catapult launches of this very heavy aircraft were made. The system was operated by high-pressure air fed from each Avon compressor to the top surface of the wing-flaps; the effect was to delay the onset of turbulence over the wing at high angles of attack and low speeds. Another innovation in the Scimitar was the Fairey power-operated control system, the first of its kind in a British naval aircraft.

The initial contract was for over 100 Scimitars and the first production aircraft (XD212) flew on 11 January 1957. Later, 24 were cancelled.

Capable of low-level attacks at supersonic speeds with tactical nuclear weapons, high-level interception with air-to-air guided missiles, or fighter-reconnaissance at extreme ranges, the Scimitar represented a sensational advance on the Sea Hawk, which it superseded as the FAA's standard single-seat strike fighter. The first Scimitars reached No.700X Trials Flight for intensive flying trials in August 1957 at Ford, and the first operational squadron (No.803) was formed at Lossiemouth in June 1958.

Subsequently, three more operational squadrons equipped with the Scimitar

346

before it ceased production after 76 had been built in September 1960. Serials were XD212 to 250, XD264 to 282 and XD316 to 333. Two squadrons became famous for their aerobatic performances: No.807 (Lt-Cdr K A Leppard, RN), which appeared at the Farnborough Air Show in 1959, and No.800 (Lt-Cdr D P Norman, AFC, RN), which performed in 1961. No.800 Squadron, the premier fighter unit of the FAA, also appeared at the Paris Air Show in June 1961, as well as operating during the Kuwait crisis. The Scimitar's nuclear strike capability was taken over by the Buccaneer from 1966.

UNITS ALLOCATED

No.800 Squadron (Lossiemouth and *Ark Royal*). No.803 Squadron (Lossiemouth, *Victorious*, *Hermes* and *Ark Royal*). No.804 Squadron (Lossiemouth and *Hermes*). No.807 Squadron (Lossiemouth, *Ark Royal* and *Centaur*). *Second-line squadrons:* Nos.700 (Ford and Yeovilton), 700X (Ford), 736 (Lossiemouth), 764 (Lossiemouth) and 764B (Lossiemouth). *Flight Refuelling:* No.800B Squadron used Scimitar tankers to support Buccaneer S.1s in *Eagle*, 1964–1966.

TECHNICAL DATA (SCIMITAR F.1)

Description: Single-seat carrier-borne medium- or high-level interceptor fighter, fighter reconnaissance or low-level nuclear strike aircraft. All-metal stressed-skin construction.
Manufacturers: Supermarine Division of Vickers-Armstrongs Ltd, South Marston, Swindon, Wilts.
Power Plant: Two Rolls-Royce Avon 202 turbojets, each of 11,250 lb static thrust.
Dimensions: Span, 37 ft 2 in. Length, 55 ft 4 in. Height, 17 ft 4 in. Wing area, 485 sq ft.
Weights: Empty, 23,962 lb. Loaded, 34,200 lb.

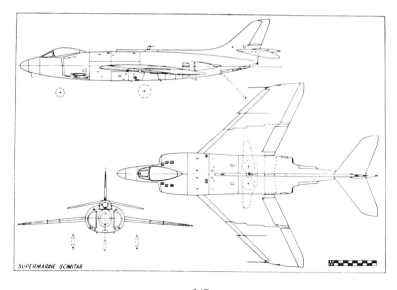

SUPERMARINE SCIMITAR

347

Performance: Maximum speed, 710 mph at sea level; Mach 0.97 at altitude. Rate of climb, 12,000 ft/min. Range, 1,422 miles. Service ceiling, 47,000 ft.

Armament: Four 30-mm Aden guns or four Bullpup air-to-ground missiles or four Sidewinder air-to-air missiles. Typical strike loads: four 500 lb or 1,000 lb bombs, or twenty-four 3-in rockets. Additionally, nuclear strike capability.

Scimitars of No.807 Squadron.

Chesapeake Is of No.811 Squadron. Lee-on-Solent

Vought-Sikorsky Chesapeake

The Chesapeake was the British version of the Vought V-156, which was first designed by R B Beisel in 1935 as a scout-bomber for the US Navy with the designation XSB2U-1. The prototype made its first flight on 5 January 1936 and the type was subsequently built for the US Navy under the designations SB2U-1, SB2U-2 and SB2U-3. It supplanted the SBU-1, a Vought biplane scout-bomber which had served for a number of years with the 1st, 2nd and 3rd Scouting Squadrons, and was in fact one of the first monoplane types with the US Navy, where the biplane lingered longer than in the US Army Air Corps.

In 1938 the Vought V-156 was offered for export sales and attracted the attention of the French Government, who ordered it for their Naval Air Service. Deliveries had begun when France was defeated in 1940, and a number of aircraft served with French Aeronavale squadrons AB-1, AB-2 and AB-3.

With the French capitulation, Britain ordered 50 V-156-B1s, the residue of the French contract, and allotted the airframe serial numbers AL908 to 957. These aircraft, named Chesapeake I, differed from the French V-156-F3 in having four forward-firing guns instead of one and in certain details such as the installation of the British-type arrester gear. Chesapeakes first arrived in Britain early in 1941, and were assembled at the Burtonwood Aircraft Repair Depot, near Liverpool. The only operational squadron to be equipped was No.811 at Lee-on-Solent, which received 14 Chesapeakes and two Sea Hurricanes on 14 July 1941. In the event, the Chesapeake proved unsuitable for escort-carrier work, for which it had been intended, and in November 1941 No.811 Squadron replaced it with Swordfish. It was thereafter relegated to training duties in the FAA, though with the US Marine Corps it saw active service in the Pacific until 1942 with VMSB-131 and VMSB-231 under the name Vindicator. Chesapeakes were retired from FAA service in June 1944.

UNITS ALLOCATED

No.811 Squadron (Lee-on-Solent). *Second-line squadrons:* Nos.770 (Crail and Dunino), 771 (Hatston and Twatt), 772 (Machrihanish), 776 (Lee-on-Solent and Speke), 778 (Arbroath), 781 (Lee-on-Solent), 784 (Lee-on-Solent and Drem), 786 (Crail) and 787 (Duxford).

Description: Two-seat carrier-borne or land-based dive-bomber. Metal structure, with metal and fabric covering.

Manufacturers: Vought-Sikorsky Aircraft Division of the United Aircraft
Corporation, Stratford, Connecticut.

Power Plant: One 825 hp Pratt & Whitney Twin Wasp Junior SB4-G.

Dimensions: Span, 42 ft. Length, 33 ft 11¾ in. Height, 9 ft 9½ in. Wing area,
305 sq ft.

Weights: Empty, 4,500 lb. Loaded, 6,953 lb.

Performance: Maximum speed, 200 mph at 11,000 ft. Initial climb, 600 ft/min.
Range, 700 miles. Service ceiling, 16,000 ft.

Armament: Four fixed machine-guns forward and one free-mounted gun aft.
Bomb-load of 1,500 lb comprising three 500 lb or 12 116 lb bombs.

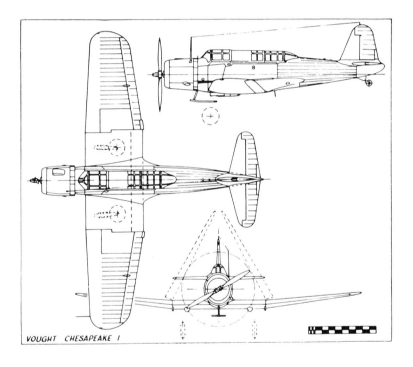

VOUGHT CHESAPEAKE I

Kingfisher seaplane (FN678) of No.765 Squadron. *(Charles E Brown)*

Vought-Sikorsky Kingfisher

The Kingfisher was designed by R B Beisel as an observation scout for the US Navy under the designation XOS2U-1, and made its first flight in 1939. Production aircraft were delivered to the US Navy from 1940 with the designations OS2U-1, OS2U-2 and OS2U-3, and over 1,800 were built. The parent company delivered 1,525 of the seaplane version and a further 300 landplanes emerged from the Naval Aircraft Factory under the designation OS2N-1. US Navy Kingfishers gave excellent service in the Pacific and figured in a number of spectacular rescue operations, including a successful search for Capt Eddie Rickenbacker at the end of 1942. Rickenbacker and his companions, lost in the South Pacific, were rescued by a Kingfisher pilot, who taxied across 40 miles of rough sea to bring them to safety. On another occasion, during the first American attack on the Japanese in the Aleutians, Kingfishers went into action as dive-bombers, each carrying a bomb-load 50 per cent in excess of normal.

With the FAA the Kingfisher was the second Vought-Sikorsky type to enter service. It first appeared in Great Britain in the summer of 1942; the previous year the FAA had received a batch of Vought-Sikorsky Chesapeake dive-bombers. Like the Curtiss Seamew, the Kingfisher was supplied under Lend-Lease arrangements. A total of 100 (FN650 to 749) reached the FAA as landplanes and seaplanes.

The first unit to be equipped with Kingfishers in the FAA was No.703 Squadron, which had 11 seaplanes on its strength. From July 1942 Kingfishers saw service as catapult-launched reconnaissance aircraft at sea with armed merchant cruisers such as HMS *Cilicia*, and *Corfu* in the South Atlantic and HMS

Canton with the Eastern Fleet, the Royal Navy cruisers *Emerald* and *Enterprise*, and as trainers with FAA seaplane flying schools at Lawrenny Ferry in Pembrokeshire and Sandbanks near Poole.

UNITS ALLOCATED

No.703 Squadron with seaplanes embarked in *Canton, Cicilia, Corfu, Emerald, Enterprise, Fidelity, Ranpura. Second-line squadrons:* Nos.726 (South Africa), 740 (Arbroath), 764 (Lawrenny Ferry and *Pegasus*) and 765 (Sandbanks).

TECHNICAL DATA (KINGFISHER I)

Description: Two-seat reconnaissance aircraft, with interchangeable land or float undercarriage, suitable for catapult launch from warships. All-metal structure, with metal and fabric covering.

Manufacturers: Vought-Sikorsky Aircraft Division of the United Aircraft Corporation, Stratford, Connecticut.

Power Plant: One 450 hp Pratt & Whitney Wasp Junior R-985-SB3.

Dimensions: Span, 35 ft 11 in. Length (seaplane), 33 ft 7¾ in; (landplane), 30 ft 1 in. Height (seaplane), 14 ft 8 in; (landplane), 13 ft.

Weights (Seaplane): Empty, 3,335 lb. Loaded, 4,980 lb. (Landplane): Empty, 2,915 lb. Loaded, 4,619 lb.

Performance: (Seaplane): Maximum speed, 161 mph. Cruising speed, 120 mph. Climb, 960 ft/min. Range, 582 miles. Service ceiling, 15,300 ft. (Landplane): Maximum speed, 171 mph. Cruising speed, 130 mph. Range, 710 miles. Service ceiling, 16,700 ft.

Armament: One fixed 0.30 gun forward and one free-mounted machine-gun aft. Provision for 500 lb of bombs carried externally below the wings.

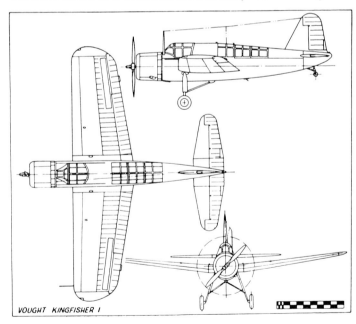

VOUGHT KINGFISHER I

Walrus (N9500). *(Westland)*

Westland Walrus

The Westland Walrus was one of the curious collection of ugly ducklings used on Fleet spotting duties in the years immediately following the First World War. It was the first British aeroplane designed for naval duties after the Armistice and the prototype first flew in 1920. It first entered squadron service in 1922 and was still employed on first-line duties until May 1925 as a contemporary of the Parnall Panther, the Avro Bison and the Blackburn Blackburn.

The Walrus was the outcome of an Air Ministry plan to effect financial economies in the lean 'twenties by adapting the RAF's D.H.9A day bomber into a three-seat deck-landing aircraft. The first stage in this transformation was the alteration of the fuselage to accommodate an observer in a third cockpit, behind the gunner, and a large ventral bulge was added to provide the observer with a prone position. This prototype (J6585) was produced by Armstrong Whitworth and was known as the Tadpole: it differed from the production Walrus in retaining the original Liberty engine with frontal radiator. In the Walrus proper (all built by Westland) the Napier Lion engine was substituted and additional modifications included detachable wings, emergency flotation bags, a jettisonable undercarriage fitted with a hydrovane, jaws on the spreader bars to engage fore-and-aft arrester wires and an arrangement to convert the fuel-tank, if required, into an additional flotation chamber. In both the Tadpole and the Walrus the original stagger of the D.H.9A's wings was heavily reduced, and the final result was to produce one of the ugliest imaginable aeroplanes, which, according to all accounts, handled extremely badly.

All production aircraft were fitted with horn-balanced ailerons and an oleo undercarriage and N9500 (illustrated) was later brought up to this standard. Total output of the Walrus amounted to 36, N9500 to N9535.

The Walrus first entered service at Leuchars in January 1922 where it equipped No.3 Squadron of the Royal Air Force until that unit split up to form Nos.420, 421 and 422 Fleet Spotter Flights on 1 April 1923. For the last five months of their stay with No.3 Squadron, the Walruses were based at Gosport. Subsequently, they served in three aircraft carriers until superseded by Bisons and Blackburns.

UNITS ALLOCATED

No.420 Flight (embarked *Furious*), No.421 Flight (embarked *Furious*), No.422 Flight (embarked *Eagle*) and No.423 Flight (embarked *Argus*). No.3 Squadron, RAF (Leuchars and Gosport).

TECHNICAL DATA (WALRUS)

Description: Three-seat carrier-borne spotter-reconnaissance aircraft. Wooden structure, with wood and fabric covering.
Manufacturers: Westland Aircraft Ltd, Yeovil, Somerset.
Power Plant: One 450 hp Napier Lion II.
Dimensions: Span, 45 ft 10 in. Length, 30 ft. Height, 11 ft 7 in. Wing area, 496 sq ft.
Weight: Loaded, 4,994 lb.
Performance: Maximum speed, 124 mph. Climb, 10 min to 9,840 ft.
Armament: One Vickers gun forward and one Lewis aft on a Scarff ring.

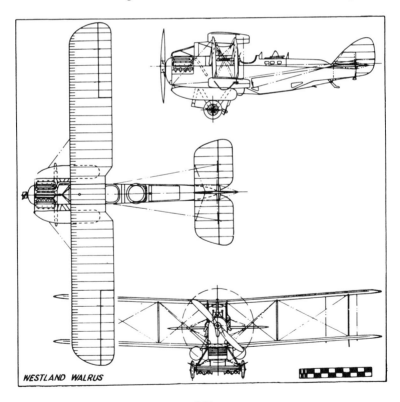

WESTLAND WALRUS

354

Westland Wyvern T.F.1

The original Wyvern torpedo-strike fighter was designed to Spec N.11/44 and the prototype (TS371) flew on 12 December 1946. Illustrated is the second prototype (TS375): there were seven production aircraft (VR131–137). All these early Wyverns had the 2,690 hp Rolls-Royce Eagle 22 piston engine. Loaded weight, 21,879 lb. Maximum speed, 456 mph at 23,000 ft. Range (maximum), 1,180 miles. Service ceiling, 32,100 ft. Span, 44 ft. Length, 39 ft 3 in. A production Wyvern T.F.1 (VR133) was used for trials aboard HMS *Eagle* in 1952.

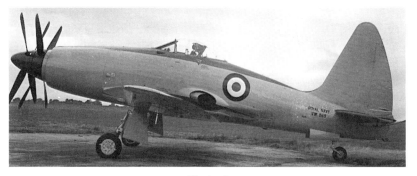

Westland Wyvern T.F.2

The Wyvern T.F.2, the first variant with a propeller-turbine, was produced to Spec N.12/45. First flight was by VP120 on 18 January 1949, powered by a Rolls-Royce Clyde of 4,030 ehp. On 22 March 1949 the first Armstrong Siddeley Python version (VP109) made its first flight. A production batch of 20 T.F.2s (VW867–886) was ordered: 13 were delivered as such and the remaining seven converted to S.4 standard (see pages 356–8). The third production T.F.2 (VW869) is illustrated.

Wyvern S.4 (WN334) of No.831 Squadron from Ford. *(Flight)*

Westland Wyvern S.4

The Wyvern, which was the first Westland-designed aircraft used in the FAA since the Walrus of the 'twenties, had more than the average share of teething troubles: nearly seven years elapsed between the maiden flight and the equipping of the first operational squadron. This is not surprising when it is realised that its three successive power plants (Eagle, Clyde and Python) were all new and untried engines. The final hurdle was the problem of adapting the Python and the huge eight-bladed contra-rotating airscrew for the special techniques demanded by deck-flying: this was eventually solved in 1953 by the installation of the Rotol inertia controller.

Originally designed to Spec N.11/44, the Wyvern was from the outset intended for propeller-turbine power, but as such engines did not become available until 1948 the five prototype and seven pre-production T.F.1s were fitted with the Rolls-Royce Eagle piston engine. The first turbine Wyverns, designated T.F.2, were produced to Spec N.12/45 and flew in 1949.

The first Wyvern to reach operational status was the S.4, originally T.F.4 until this designation was abolished in 1953. The S.4 (which first flew in May 1951) featured a cut-back engine cowling to permit cartridge starting, stiffened cockpit canopy, modified aileron tabs and auxiliary tail fins on a dihedral tailplane. The last seven T.F.2s (VW880 to 886) were completed to S.4 standards and followed by 87 production S.4s, serialled VZ745 to 766, VZ772 to 799, WL876 to 888, WN324 to 336 and WP336 to 346.

The Wyvern S.4 first entered service with No.813 Squadron (formerly Firebrands) in May 1953 and was shore-based until 1954, when it embarked first in *Albion* and later in *Eagle*. The second Wyvern squadron was No.827, which embarked in *Eagle* in May 1955. Finally, in November 1955, Nos.830 and 831 Squadrons re-formed with Wyverns at Ford, Sussex, joining *Eagle* in April 1956. Only No.830 Squadron flew their Wyverns operationally, on ground-attack sorties during the Anglo-French intervention in Egypt in November 1956. Nine Wyverns were deployed on 82 sorties between 1 and 6 November, mainly in bombing and strafing attacks on Dekheila and Port Said.

Wyvern S.4 (VZ782) from No.703 Squadron during trials on board *Ark Royal*. *(Royal Navy)*

Wyvern S.4s of No.813 Squadron from RNAS Ford. (*RAF Museum*)

The Wyvern remained in service until No.813 Squadron disbanded at RNAS Ford in March 1958. One surviving Wyvern, VR137, is retained by the FAA Museum at Yeovilton.

UNITS ALLOCATED

No.813 Squadron (Ford, *Albion* and *Eagle*), No.827 Squadron (Ford and *Eagle*), No.830 Squadron (Ford and *Eagle*) and No.831 Squadron (Ford, *Ark Royal* and *Saratoga*). *Second-line squadrons:* Nos.700 (Ford), 703 (Ford), 764 (Ford) and 787 (West Raynham—Naval Air Fighting Development Unit).

TECHNICAL DATA (WYVERN S.4)

Description: Single-seat carrier-borne strike aircraft. All-metal stressed-skin construction.
Manufacturers: Westland Aircraft Ltd, Yeovil, Somerset.
Power Plant: One 4,110 ehp Armstrong Siddeley Python A.S.P.3.
Dimensions: Span, 44 ft (20 ft folded). Length, 42 ft 3 in. Height, 15 ft 9 in. Wing area, 355 sq ft.
Weights: Empty, 15,608 lb. Loaded, 21,200 lb (normal) or 24,500 lb (maximum).
Performance: Maximum speed, 383 mph at sea level. Cruising speed, 343 mph at 20,000 ft. Climb, 2,350 ft min at sea level. Range, 904 miles. Service ceiling, 28,000 ft.
Armament: Four 20-mm guns in wings and provision for 16 rocket projectiles or a single torpedo or three 1,000 lb bombs.

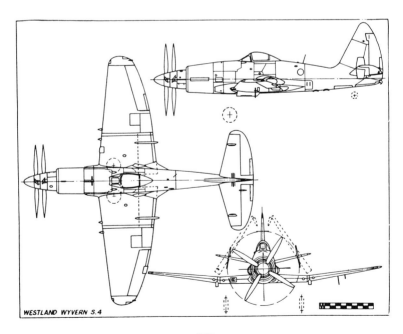

WESTLAND WYVERN S.4

Dragonfly H.R.3 (WG668) aboard *Bulwark*. *(MoD)*

Westland Dragonfly

The Royal Navy was quick to appreciate the value of the helicopter, and its No.705 Helicopter Squadron, formed at Gosport, was probably the first all-helicopter squadron to be formed outside the USA. Initial experiments had taken place with American-built Hoverflies (see Appendix) some five years previously, but the Westland-Sikorsky Dragonfly was the first British-built helicopter to serve with the Royal Navy, and this type was chosen as the initial equipment of the pioneer No.705 Squadron from January 1950. In 1949 it was used for trials on board the carrier *Vengeance*.

The Dragonfly, also supplied to the RAF, was the British-built version of the American Sikorsky S-51, for which the Westland concern acquired the manufacturing rights in 1947. The total production of Dragonflies built for the Royal Navy was 72. The initial production version for the Royal Navy was the Dragonfly H.R. Mark.1, which had a three-blade rotor of composite construction and was equipped for a general utility and rescue rôle. The maiden flight was on 22 June 1949. Thirteen of these were built, serialled VX595 to 600 and VZ960 to 966. This was followed by the principal production variant for the Royal Navy, the Dragonfly H.R. Mk.3, which differed in having a three-blade metal rotor and a hydraulic servo-controlled mechanism. The last Dragonfly H.R.3 for the Royal Navy was delivered on 28 September 1953. Fifty were built, serialled between WG661 and WP504. The final variant was the H.R.5, of which nine were built, serialled WN492 to 500. Additionally, about 25 Mk.1 and Mk.3 were modified to Mk.5 at Donibristle.

Dragonflies were used extensively aboard aircraft-carriers, both for ship-to-shore communications flying and for 'plane-guard' duties, hovering in attendance during deck-flying operations to provide rapid air-sea rescue facilities if needed. In this latter rôle they superseded the destroyer's traditional duties, proving at once more efficient and more economical. Two Dragonflies were also issued to every coastal air station of the Royal Navy, where they supplanted the well-tried Sea Otter amphibian in the air-sea rescue rôle. Naval Dragonflies took part in many civilian rescue operations and did valiant work in Holland during the floods of 1953. In June 1953 12 Dragonflies were accorded the honour of leading the massed fly-past of aircraft in the Royal Naval Coronation Review at Spithead.

In 1960 the Dragonfly was issued to a special air experience flight for the training of officer cadets at the Royal Naval College, Dartmouth. These flew from Roborough and were the last in RN service when withdrawn in June 1967.

UNITS ALLOCATED

(*H.R.1*): No.700, No.705 (Portland and Lee-on-Solent). (*H.R.3*): No.705 (Portland, Lee-on-Solent and Culdrose), No.728 (Malta) and No.744 (Malta). (*H.R.5*): No.701 (Lee-on-Solent and *Victorious*), No.705 (Lee-on-Solent and Culdrose), No.727 (Brawdy) and No.771 (Portland).

TECHNICAL DATA (DRAGONFLY H.R.3)

Description: Carrier-borne or shore-based air-sea rescue and communications helicopter. Crew of two.
Manufacturers: Westland Aircraft Ltd, Yeovil, Somerset.
Power Plant: One 550 hp Alvis Leonides 50.
Dimensions: Rotor diameter, 49 ft. Length, 57 ft 6½ in. Height, 12 ft 11 in.
Weights: Empty, 4,397 lb. Loaded, 5,870 lb.
Performance: Maximum speed, 95 mph. Cruising speed, 81 mph. Climb, 970 ft/min. Service ceiling, 13,200 ft. Range, 300 miles.

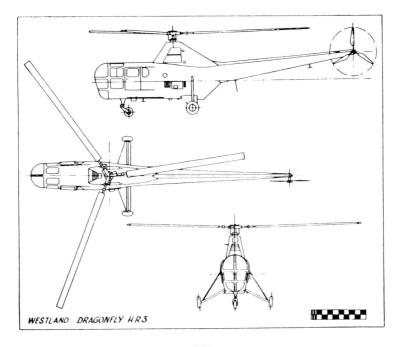

WESTLAND DRAGONFLY H.R.3

Whirlwind H.A.S.7 (XK934) of No.820 Squadron from *Albion*. *(Flight)*

Westland Whirlwind (Mks.1 to 7)

The Whirlwind, British-built version of the American Sikorsky S-55 helicopter, first entered service with the Royal Navy, but was eventually adopted by the RAF as well. The prototype Whirlwind H.A.R.1 (XA862) first flew on 15 August 1953 and the 10 production aircraft replaced Whirlwind H.A.R.21s in No.848 Squadron in October 1954. The latter were American-built aircraft (see Appendix) delivered in 1952 under MDAP.

The small production batch of Whirlwind H.A.R.1 (XA862 to 871) was followed by the second naval version, the H.A.R.3, which differed from the earlier model in having the 700 hp Wright Cyclone R-1300-3 engine instead of the 600 hp Pratt & Whitney Wasp R-1340-40. The 27 production H.A.R.3s were serialled XG572 to 585, XG587 and 588 and XJ393 to 402. The first in service went to No.845 Squadron in October 1955.

Final version of the Whirlwind in FAA service was the H.A.S.7 powered by a British engine, the Alvis Leonides Mk.5. It incorporated a torpedo bay and first served with No.700H Squadron at Lee-on-Solent from March 1957.

The H.A.S.7 prototype (XG586) flew for the first time on 17 October 1956. Whereas the H.A.R.1 and 3 had been equipped only for non-combat rôles such as search and rescue and communications, the H.A.S.7 was designed for first-line duties in the anti-submarine rôle and was in fact the first British helicopter for this kind of work. Equipment included radar and dipping Asdic, for submarine detection. The first operational squadron was No.845, equipped in June 1957. From April to November 1959, H.A.S.7s were withdrawn from service for modifications to the engine and transmission system. First operational squadron to resume service with the modified Whirlwinds was No.815. Thereafter the Whirlwind gradually superseded the Gannet in FAA anti-submarine squadrons. H.A.S.7s also served on Commando duties in Brunei and Borneo in 1959–1964. The last first-line unit (No.829 Squadron) used H.A.S.7s until June 1967.

Total production of the H.A.S.7 was 130, with serials ranging from XG587 to XN387. It finally left RN service in December 1974.

UNITS ALLOCATED

(H.A.R.1): No.829 (Culdrose) and No.848 (Kuala Lumpur). *Second-line squadrons:*

Nos.700, 701, 705, 771, 781. (*H.A.R.3*): No.815 (Portland) and No.845 (Lee-on-Solent and Lossiemouth). *Second-line squadrons:* Nos.700, 701, 705, 728, 737, 771 and 781. (*H.A.S.7*): No.814 (Culdrose, Portland and *Hermes*), No.815 (Eglinton, Culdrose, Portland and *Albion*), No.819 (Eglinton and Brawdy), No.820 (Eglinton, *Eagle, Ark Royal* and *Albion*), No.824 (Eglinton, *Victorious, Eagle* and *Ark Royal*), No.825 (Culdrose, Portland and *Victorious*), No.829 (Culdrose), No.845 (*Bulwark*), No.846 (Culdrose, *Albion* and Brunei), No.847 (Culdrose and *Bulwark*) and No.848 (Culdrose, *Albion* and Aden).

TECHNICAL DATA (WHIRLWIND H.A.S.7)

Description: Carrier-borne or shore-based anti-submarine helicopter with a
    crew of three. All-metal construction. Eight troops in commando rôle.
Manufacturers: Westland Aircraft Ltd, Yeovil, Somerset.
Power Plant: One 750 hp Alvis Leonides Major 755/1.
Dimensions: Rotor diameter, 53 ft. Length, 41 ft 8½ in. Height, 13 ft 2½ in.
Weights: Empty, 5,170 lb. Loaded, 7,800 lb.
Performance: Maximum speed, 106 mph at sea level. Maximum inclined climb
    at sea level, 910 ft/min. Range, 290 nautical miles. Service ceiling,
    9,400 ft.
Armament: Provision for Mk.30 or Mk.44 homing torpedo in recess in fuselage
    bottom.

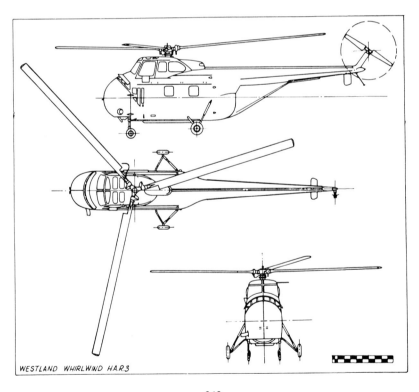

WESTLAND WHIRLWIND H.A.R.3

H.A.R.9 (XL889) from SAR Flight, Culdrose.

Westland Whirlwind H.A.R.9

The Whirlwind H.A.R.9 was first introduced to FAA service in January 1966 as a turbine-engined conversion of the piston engined Whirlwind Mk.7 It was the Fleet Air Arm equivalent of the RAF's Whirlwind H.A.R.10 which was also a turbine conversion of the Leonides-engined Mk.7.

The first H.A.R.9 conversion for the Royal Navy was XN387. Altogether, seventeen Whirlwinds were converted to Mk.9 standard.

The H.A.R.9 was used for search-and-rescue operations, based mainly at RNAS Brawdy, RNAS Lee-on-Solent and RNAS Culdrose. It also served in HMS *Protector* and *Endurance* on ice patrol duties in the Antarctic. No.829 Squadron at Culdrose was the main user of the H.A.R.9, from July 1967 to August 1976.

Accommodation was provided for six to eight, including pilot, aircrewman and aircrew diver.

The Whirlwind H.A.R.9 was finally superseded on search and rescue duties by the Wessex Mk.5, the last example being retired in March 1977.

One 1,050 shp Rolls-Royce Gnome H 1000 engine. Rotor diameter, 53 ft. Length (fuselage), 44 ft 2 in; (overall): 62 ft 4 in. Height, 13 ft 2½ in. Maximum speed, 106 mph. Maximum weight, 8,000 lb. Range, 300 miles. Service ceiling, 10,000 ft.

Whirlwind H.A.R.9 (XL839) from HMS *Protector*. (*Royal Navy*)

363

Wessex H.A.S.1 (XS882) of No.814 Squadron. *(MoD (Royal Navy))*

Westland Wessex H.A.S.1

Produced as a replacement in the FAA for the Westland Whirlwind, the Wessex was the first helicopter in the world to be manufactured in quantity with a free gas turbine as its power plant. It was developed from the American Sikorsky S-58, used as a 16-seat transport by the US Army and as an anti-submarine helicopter by the US Navy under the designations H-34A, HSS-1 and HUS-1. The original S-58 was powered by an orthodox piston engine, a 1,525 hp Wright R-1820-84.

The prototype Wessex (XL722) was an imported S-58 airframe modified to take the Napier Gazelle gas-turbine engine. It made its first flight at Yeovil on 17 May 1957, after a series of ground running tests of the Gazelle engine with the helicopter tethered.

The Wessex was the first helicopter ordered for the FAA to have been designed from the outset as an anti-submarine aircraft. Fitted with an automatic pilot, it could operate by day or night in all weathers. It could also be used, like its predecessors, for search and rescue and communications duties. Compared with its piston-engined counterpart, the Wessex carried a higher disposable load as well as being smoother and quieter. All these benefits derived from the Gazelle engine which also enabled the Wessex to be airborne from a cold start within 45 sec, and finally eliminated the necessity to carry petrol as well as kerosene in aircraft-carriers. This latter point was important to the Royal Navy, as jet engine fuel can be stowed in ships' tanks in the same way as ship's boiler fuel, leading to economies in storage space.

The first Wessex built entirely at Yeovil (XL727) made its maiden flight on 20 June 1958, and evaluation of the pre-production batch was undertaken by No.700H Flight of the FAA at Culdrose, Cornwall from April 1960. Total production of the H.A.S.1 was 137, serials ranging from XM299 to XS889. Forty were later converted to H.A.S.3 configuration.

The first front-line unit of the FAA to be equipped with the Wessex was No.815, commanded by Lt-Cdr A L L Skinner, RN, which commissioned at Culdrose on 4 July 1961. No.815 Squadron's aircraft embarked in *Ark Royal* in

September 1961, this being the first carrier to accommodate Wessex helicopters in an operational rôle.

From April 1962, some Wessex H.A.R.1s were converted from anti-submarine to commando duties and operated with No.845 Squadron in North Borneo. In 1969, H.A.S.1s were assigned to the new helicopter cruisers *Tiger*

Wessex H.A.S.1s of No.700 H Flight from Culdrose (*Flight*)

Wessex H.A.S.1 (XM920) of No.814 Squadron from *HMS Hermes*.

and *Blake*. The Wessex Mk.1 was finally retired from FAA service in August 1979.

UNITS ALLOCATED

No.814 Squadron (Culdrose, *Hermes* and *Victorious*, No.815 (Culdrose, *Ark Royal* and *Centaur*), No.819 (Eglinton, *Centaur*, *Hermes* and *Ark Royal*), No.820 (Culdrose and *Eagle*), No.826 (Culdrose and *Hermes*), No.829 (County Class Destroyers) and No.845 (Culdrose, Yeovilton, *Albion* and *Bulwark*). *Second-line squadrons:* Nos.700H, 706, 706B, 737, 771, 772.

TECHNICAL DATA (WESSEX H.A.S.1)

Description: All-weather anti-submarine search and strike or commando transport helicopter. Crew of four (two pilots, one observer and one underwater control crewman). As transport carried 16 fully-equipped marines.

Manufacturers: Westland Aircraft Ltd, Yeovil, Somerset.

Power Plant: One 1,450 shp Napier Gazelle 161 free turbine engine.

Dimensions: Rotor diameter, 56 ft. Length, 65 ft 10 in (38 ft 2 in with tail folded). Height (to top of tail rotor), 15 ft 10 in.

Weights: Empty, 7,600 lb. Loaded, 12,600 lb.

Performance: Maximum speed, 135 mph. Rate of climb at sea level, 1,750 ft/min. Range (with standard tankage): 390 miles. Duration, 2½ hr. Service ceiling, 7,000 ft.

Armament: Anti-submarine weapons (usually two Mk.44 homing torpedoes) carried externally or two Mk.11 depth charges.

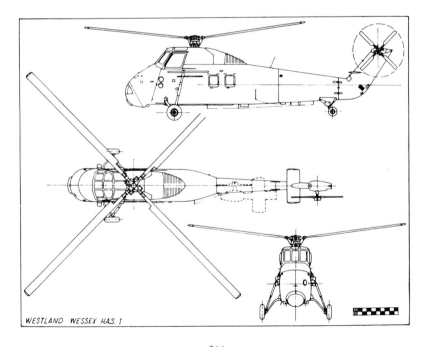

WESTLAND WESSEX HAS. 1

Wessex H.A.S.3 (XM328) of No.737 Squadron. RNAS Portland. *(FAA Museum)*

Westland Wessex H.A.S.3

Following trials with No.700H Squadron from January 1967, the Wessex H.A.S.3 first entered first-line service with the Fleet Air Arm when it joined No.814 Squadron in August 1967. The H.A.S.3 was a more powerful version of the H.A.S.1 which first entered first-line service with the FAA in July 1961. In place of the earlier aircraft's 1,450 shp Gazelle 161 engine a Gazelle 165 of 1,600 shp was installed.

An easily recognisable external feature identifying the Wessex H.A.S.3 was the 'hump' behind the rotor head which was part of the advanced radar system and earned it the nickname 'the Camel'. It carried an altogether more sophisticated weapons system than the H.A.S.1 and had an automatic flight control system enabling it to operate with greater facility in varying climatic conditions, and with improved Doppler navigation.

The vast majority of the 43 Wessex H.A.S.3s were conversions from H.A.S.1s, but three aircraft (XT255 to 257) were in fact built as H.A.S.3s from the outset. The converted aircraft were serialled XM327, 328, 331, 832, 833, 834, 836, 837, 838, 844, 870, 871, 872, 916, 918, 919, 920, 923 and 927, XP103, 104, 105, 110, 116, 118, 137, 138, 139, 140, 142, 143, 147, 150, 153 and 156, XS119, 121, 122, 126, 127, 149, 153 and 862.

The Wessex H.A.S.3 was the first Fleet Air Arm helicopter to utilise in-flight refuelling (HIFR), taking on fuel from a ship whilst airborne. It remained the Royal Navy's standard anti-submarine helicopter until superseded by the Sea King from 1970. The last first-line squadron with Wessex H.A.S.3s (No.819) disbanded on 29 January 1971 but single aircraft remained on board destroyers of the 'County' Class such as HMS *Antrim* until December 1982.

Two Wessex H.A.S.3 helicopters of No.737 Squadron played an important rôle in the Falklands War in 1982. They were embarked in the guided missile

destroyers *Antrim* and *Glamorgan* and one of them (XP142, known affection-
ately by its crew as 'Humphrey') survives in the Fleet Air Arm Museum at
Yeovilton.

UNITS ALLOCATED

No.814 Squadron (Culdrose and *Hermes*), No.819 (Ballykelly, *Engadine, Tidepool, Olma*
and *Olmeda*), No.820 (Culdrose, *Blake, Olmeda, Tidepool* and *Engadine*), No.826
(Culdrose and *Eagle*) and No.829 (County Class Destroyers). *Second-line squadrons:*
Nos.700H, 706 and 737.

TECHNICAL DATA (WESSEX H.A.S.3)

Description: Carrier-borne, ship-borne or shore-based anti-submarine strike
helicopter with a crew of four (two pilots, observer and sonar operator).
Manufacturers: Westland Aircraft Ltd, Yeovil, Somerset.
Power Plant: One 1,600 shp Napier Gazelle 165 gas turbine engine.
Dimensions: Rotor diameter, 56 ft. Overall length (including rotors), 65 ft
10½ in. Height, 14 ft 5 in. Overall length (with tail folded), 38 ft 6 in.
Weights: Empty, 9,350 lb. Loaded, 13,500 lb.
Performance: Maximum speed, 135 mph at sea level. Endurance, 1 hr 33 min.
Range, 390 miles. Climb, 1,640 ft/min. Service ceiling, 12,000 ft.
Armament: Two Mk.44 or Mk.46 homing torpedoes, carried externally on
either side of the fuselage.

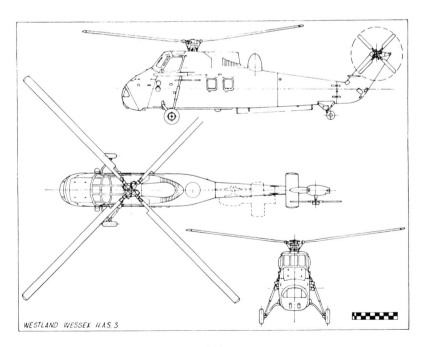

WESTLAND WESSEX H.A.S.3

Wessex H.U.5s of No.845 Squadron from *Bulwark*.

Westland Wessex H.U.5

The Wessex H.U.5 was produced to meet the operational requirement of the Royal Marine Commandos for a helicopter capable of taking a dozen or more fully-armed combat troops into action from the deck of an aircraft carrier or commando carrier to make an assault on an enemy beach-head. Artillery, Land-Rovers, or bulky loads of fuel and ammunition could also be slung underneath the aircraft and released from the hover. The Wessex H.U.5 could also go into action against ground targets with wire-guided air-to-surface missiles or as a 'gun-ship'.

Design work began in April 1962 and construction of the prototype was started in May 1962. The prototype H.U.5 (XS241) flew for the first time on 31 May 1963 and the first production aircraft (XS479) followed on 17 November 1963. The FAA took delivery of 100 Wessex H.U.5s, the serial numbers allocated being XS479 to 500, XS506 to 523, XT448 to 487 and XT755 to 774.

First delivery to the Royal Navy was in October 1963 when six aircraft for No.700V Intensive Flying Trials Unit arrived at RNAS Culdrose, Cornwall. Wessex H.U.5s then equipped No.707 Squadron at Culdrose from December 1964 and it was with this unit that the Prince of Wales trained in 1974.

The Wessex H.U.5 entered first-line duties with No.848 Squadron in May 1964 and eventually equipped four commando assault helicopter squadrons. Its exploits on anti-terrorist operations in Aden, Borneo, Cyprus and Northern Ireland have become legendary, operating both from commando carriers and shore bases. It made a massive contribution in the Falklands in 1982 when more than 50 were deployed by Nos.845, 847 and 848 Squadrons. They took part in the landing of troops and supplies on the beaches of San Carlos and attacked targets at Port Stanley with A.S.12 missiles. The H.U.5 was not finally withdrawn from service until March 1988.

UNITS ALLOCATED

No.829 Squadron (*Regent* and *Resource*), No.845 (Culdrose, *Bulwark*, *Albion*, *Fearless*, *Intrepid*, *Invincible*, *Hermes* and *Atlantic Conveyor*), No.846 (Culdrose, *Fearless*, *Engadine* and *Bulwark*), No.847 (*Albion*, *Bulwark* and *Intrepid*) and No.848 (Culdrose, *Albion*, *Intrepid*, *Bulwark*, *Fearless* and *Atlantic Conveyor*). Second-line squadrons: Nos.700V, 707, 771, 772 and 781.

TECHNICAL DATA (WESSEX H.U.5)

Description: Carrier-borne, ship-borne or shore-based troop-carrying assault helicopter. Crew of one to three, plus 16 troops.

Manufacturers: Westland Aircraft Ltd, Yeovil, Somerset.

Power Plant: Two coupled Rolls-Royce Gnome H1200 turboshafts, each of 1,350 shp.

Dimensions: Rotor diameter, 56 ft. Fuselage length, 48 ft 4½ in. Height, 14 ft 5 in.

Weights: Empty, 8,657 lb. Loaded, 13,500 lb.

Performance: Maximum speed, 132 mph at sea level. Range, 478 miles. Climb, 1,650 ft/min. Service ceiling, 5,500 ft.

Armament: Provision for carrying one fixed forward-firing machine-gun, rocket launchers and Nord S.S.11 or A.S.12 air-to-surface missiles.

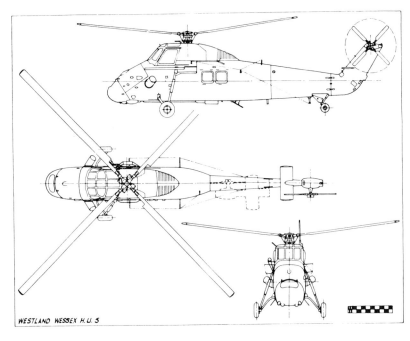

WESTLAND WESSEX H.U. 5

370

Wasp H.A.S.1 (XT434) of No.829 Squadron. *(MoD (Royal Navy))*

Westland Wasp

The Wasp was the first Fleet Air Arm helicopter to operate extensively from platforms on frigates and other smaller vessels, and by August 1968 no fewer than 15 *Leander* Class frigates, four Tribal Class frigates and three *Rothesay* Class frigates were operating Small Ship Wasp Flights. The first Small Ship Flight (for *Leander*) formed on 11 November 1963.

Developed from the early Saunders-Roe P.531 which first flew in July 1958, the Wasp (originally known as the Sea Scout) was manufactured by the Fairey Division of Westland at Hayes, and the first pre-production aircraft (XS463) made its first flight, piloted by Ron Gellatly, from White Waltham on 28 October 1962. A second pre-production Wasp (XS476) was followed by the first full production H.A.S.1 (XS527) in January 1963. Eventually, a total of 96 Wasps was supplied to the RN, serialled XS527 to 545, XS562 to 572, XT414 to 443, XT778 to 795 and XV622 to 639.

Production Wasps differed from the earlier prototypes in having four individual undercarriage legs with castoring wheels and a folding tail boom. The Initial Flying Trials Unit (No.700W Squadron) formed at Culdrose on 4 June 1963 and was finally disbanded on 4 March 1964. The following day No.829 Squadron commissioned as the Headquarters Squadron for all Small Ships Flights, moving to RNAS Portland, Dorset, in December 1964.

Wasps operated up to 10 nautical miles from the parent ship, fired their torpedoes (or depth charges in shallow water attacks) and stayed on patrol for about one hour. From 1969, the Wasp also became operational carrying Nord

A.S.12M air-to-surface missiles with an automatic guidance system.

Flying from *Plymouth* and *Endurance*, Wasps of No.829 Squadron used A.S.12 missiles effectively during the Falklands conflict in attacks on the Argentine submarine *Santa Fé*. Wasps finally left RN service in March 1988.

UNITS ALLOCATED

No.829 Squadron (Portland), No.845 (*Bulwark, Fearless, Eagle, Hermes* and *Albion*) and No.848 (*Albion, Intrepid* and *Bulwark*). *Second-line squadrons:* Nos.700W, 703, 705, 706 and 771.

TECHNICAL DATA (WASP H.A.S.1)

Description: Light anti-submarine strike helicopter for operation from platforms on small ships. Crew of two.

Manufacturers: Westland Aircraft Ltd, Hayes, Middlesex.

Power Plant: One 710 shp Rolls-Royce Nimbus 503 shaft-turbine.

Dimensions: Rotor diameter, 32 ft 3 in. Overall length, 40 ft 4 in. Length (folded), 25 ft 9 in. Height, 8 ft 10 in.

Weights: Empty, 3,425 lb. Loaded, 5,500 lb.

Performance: Maximum speed 120 mph at sea level. Climb, 1,440 ft/min. Range, 303 miles. Service ceiling, 12,200 ft.

Armament: Two Mk.44 homing torpedoes carried externally. Alternatively, depth charges or Nord A.S.12 air-to-surface missiles.

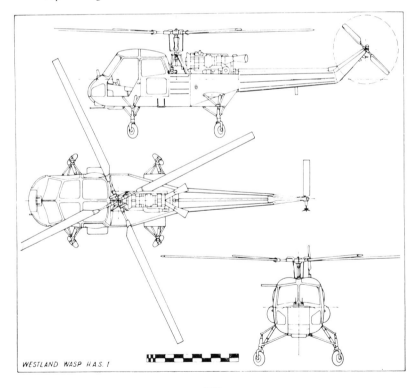

WESTLAND WASP H.A.S. 1

Sea King H.A.S.1 (XV647) of No.700S Squadron from Culdrose. *(Westland)*

Westland Sea King H.A.S.1

With the entry into front-line service of the Sea King, the Fleet Air Arm acquired one of the world's leading hunter-killer helicopter weapons systems. Capable of flying sorties of four hours (twice that of the Wessex), it also covered a search area four times greater. Using the basic airframe of the American Sikorsky S-61B of 1959, the Sea King featured a power-folding, five-bladed main rotor, retractable undercarriage and a boat-type hull, with sponsons. The prototype (XV370) flew on 8 September 1967. It was the first of four (XV370–373) assembled from imported parts.

The Sea King Intensive Flying Trials Unit, No.700S Squadron, was commissioned on 19 August 1969 at RNAS Culdrose. The first deck-landing by a Sea King had taken place on the Royal Fleet Auxiliary *Engadine* in the Portland area on 2 July 1969.

The first operational unit to be equipped with Sea Kings was No.824 Squadron which formed on 24 February 1970 at Culdrose and subsequently embarked in HMS *Ark Royal*. The second Sea King squadron, No.826, formed at Culdrose on 2 June 1970 and later embarked in HMS *Eagle*. Sea Kings act as tactical co-ordinators during submarine detection, directing either another anti-submarine helicopter, a surface vessel or a maritime patrol aircraft to the actual attack.

The Royal Navy's first production contract for Sea Kings totalled 56 aircraft, serialled between XV642 and XV714. Some of these aircraft were retrospectively modified to Mk.2A standard.

From February 1978, Sea King Mk.1s were allocated to Royal Fleet Auxiliary ships, starting with *Fort Grange*.

During the Turkish invasion of Cyprus in 1974, Sea Kings of No.814 Squadron (HMS *Hermes*) helped to rescue about 1,500 civilians from a beach near Kyrenia.

UNITS ALLOCATED

No.814 Squadron (Prestwick, *Bulwark* and *Hermes*), No.819 Squadron (Culdrose and *Engadine*), No.820 Squadron (Culdrose and *Blake*), No.824 Squadron (Culdrose and *Ark*

Royal) and No.826 Squadron (Culdrose, *Eagle, Engadine* and *Tiger*). *Second-line squadrons:* Nos.700S, 706 and 737.

TECHNICAL DATA (SEA KING H.A.S.1)

Description: All-weather anti-submarine search and strike helicopter. Crew of four (pilot, co-pilot, observer and underwater control rating).

Manufacturers: Westland Aircraft Ltd, Yeovil, Somerset.

Power Plant: Two 1,500 shp Rolls-Royce Gnome H.1400 shaft-turbine engines.

Dimensions: Rotor diameter, 62 ft. Overall length, 55 ft 9¾ in. Overall height, 15 ft 6 in.

Weights: Empty, 12,170 lb. Loaded, 20,500 lb.

Performance: Maximum speed, 161 mph. Climb, 3,000 ft/min. Service ceiling, 10,500 ft. Range, 598 miles. Endurance 4 hr.

Armament: Four Mk.44 homing torpedoes carried externally, or similar numbers of Mk.11 depth charges or one nuclear depth bomb.

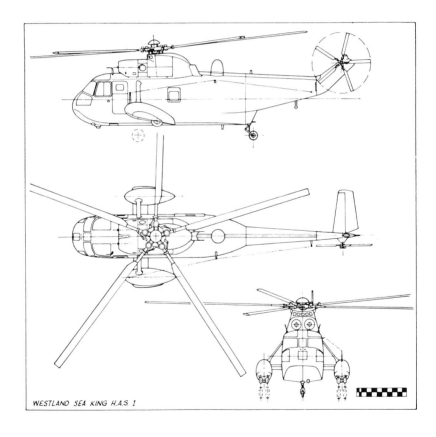

WESTLAND SEA KING H.A.S. 1

374

Sea King H.A.S.1s of No.706 Squadron from RNAS Culdrose in echelon over the Lizard Peninsula, Cornwall. *(RNAS Culdrose)*

Sea King A.E.W.2 (XV704) converted airframe.

Westland Sea King H.A.S.2 and A.E.W.2A

Following the success of the Sea King as the Fleet Air Arm's primary anti-submarine strike helicopter from 1970, it was decided to further improve the operational qualities of the aircraft and as a result the Sea King H.A.S.2 was evolved. This improved variant could be distinguished externally from the earlier version by its six-bladed tail rotor. Its power plant was uprated to a 1,660 shp Gnome.

In 1975, a total of 21 Sea King H.A.S.2s (XZ570–582 and XZ915–922) were ordered for Fleet Air Arm service and the first made its maiden flight at the Westland airfield at Yeovil on 18 June 1976. In addition to the newly-built aircraft, it was arranged to retrofit existing H.A.S.1 helicopters to the new standard and eventually the FAA had 52 Sea King H.A.S.2s in service, including all the updated Mk.1 airframes. From 1981 these were converted yet again to Mk.5 standard.

The first operational Fleet Air Arm unit to re-equip with the Sea King H.A.S.2 was No.826 Squadron at RNAS Culdrose, Cornwall, in December 1976.

A late development of the Sea King Mk.2 was the A.E.W.2A equipped for the Airborne Early Warning rôle. The Falklands conflict in 1982 had signalled the urgent need for such an aircraft (the FAA had not had its A.E.W. Gannets since 1978) and two Sea King Mk.2s (XV650 and XV704) were converted to carry Thorn-EMI Searchwater radar on a rotatable mounting on the starboard side of the fuselage. These aircraft joined *Illustrious* on 2 August 1982 and by early 1990 a further ten Sea Kings had been converted to A.E.W.2A standard.

Sea King A.E.W.2s entered service with No.849 Squadron on 31 May 1985.

UNITS ALLOCATED

(*H.A.S.2/2A*): No.814 Squadron (Culdrose, *Hermes* and *Bulwark*), No.819 Squadron (Prestwick and *Hermes*), No.820 Squadron (Prestwick, *Blake*, Culdrose and *Invincible*), No.824 Squadron (Culdrose, *Ark Royal*, *Olmeda* and *Fort Grange*), No.825 Squadron

(Culdrose, *Queen Elizabeth, Atlantic Causeway* and *Canberra*) and No.826 Squadron (Lossiemouth, *Engadine*, Culdrose, *Tiger, Hermes* and *Bulwark*). *Second-line squadrons:* No.706. (*A.E.W.2A*): No.824D (Culdrose, Yeovilton and *Illustrious*) and No.849 (Culdrose, *Illustrious, Invincible* and *Ark Royal*).

TECHNICAL DATA (SEA KING H.A.S.2)

Description: All-weather anti-submarine search and strike helicopter. Crew of four (pilot, co-pilot, observer and rating sonar operator).
Manufacturers: Westland Helicopters Ltd, Yeovil, Somerset.
Power Plant: Two 1,660 shp Rolls-Royce Gnome H 1400-1 shaft-turbines.
Dimensions: Rotor diameter, 62 ft. Overall length (fuselage), 55 ft 9¾ in. Overall height, 15 ft 6 in.
Weights: Empty, 13,000 lb. Loaded, 21,000 lb.
Performance: Maximum speed, 161 mph. Climb, 3,000 ft/min. Service ceiling, 10,500 ft. Endurance, 4 hr. Range, 764 miles.
Armament: Four Mk.46 torpedoes or four Mk.11 depth charges or one nuclear depth bomb.

TECHNICAL DATA (SEA KING A.E.W.2)

Description: All-weather airborne early warning helicopter. Crew of three (pilot and two observers).
Manufacturers: Westland Helicopters Ltd, Yeovil, Somerset.
Power Plant: Two 1,660 shp Rolls-Royce Gnome H 1400-1 shaft-turbines.
Dimensions: Rotor diameter, 62 ft. Overall length (fuselage), 55 ft 9¾ in, (including rotors), 72 ft 8 in. Overall height, 15 ft 6 in.
Weight: Loaded, 21,500 lb.
Performance: Maximum speed, 151 mph. Cruising speed, 144 mph. Service ceiling, 10,000 ft. Range, 420 nautical miles. Endurance, 4 hr.

Sea King H.C.4 of No.846 Squadron from HMS *Bulwark*. *(Westland)*

Westland Sea King H.C.4

From November 1979 a new version of the Sea King, the H.C.4, entered service with the Fleet Air Arm. Equipped as a troop transport and logistic support aircraft, the Sea King H.C.4 made its first flight at Yeovil on 26 September 1979. Designed primarily to supersede the Wessex H.U.5 as the main lift helicopter for the Royal Marines' commando forces, the Sea King H.C.4 lifted 8,000 lb compared with the 2,700 lb of its predecessor. A fixed undercarriage was substituted for the retractable version (and sponsons) in other Sea Kings.

The Sea King H.C.4 was equipped to carry 27 fully equipped Royal Marine commando or other troops and could operate in arctic or tropical conditions. A total of fifteen was ordered initially for the Royal Navy, the serial numbers allotted to the aircraft being ZA290–299 and ZA310–314. Later, 19 more were delivered serialled ZD476–480, ZD625–627, ZE425–428 and ZF116–124. Total production was 34.

No.846 Squadron took the Sea King H.C.4s into service from November 1979. Home-based at RNAS Yeovilton, its main assignment was to provide helicopter lift amenities for the Anglo-Dutch amphibious forces committed to the defence of NATO's northern flank. Operating from the carrier HMS *Bulwark*, exercises took place under the code-name *Clockwork* in the north of Norway. H.C.4s also operated in the Lebanon and in Cyprus.

During the Falklands conflict in 1982, thirteen Sea King H.C.4s of No.846 Squadron were operational during the landings at San Carlos and they also operated at night with the SBS and the SAS.

In 1984, No.846 Squadron's H.C.4s formed part of the Peacekeeping Force in Cyprus during the troubles in the Lebanon.

UNITS ALLOCATED

No.845 Squadron (Yeovilton, *Hermes, Fearless* and *Invincible*) and No.846 Squadron (Yeovilton, *Bulwark, Hermes, Fearless, Intrepid* and *Canberra*). *Second-line squadron:* No.707.

TECHNICAL DATA (SEA KING H.C.4)

Description: All-weather tactical support and heavy-lift helicopter. Crew of three in commando rôle, with two pilots, one aircrewman and 27 fully-equipped troops.
Manufacturers: Westland Helicopters Ltd, Yeovil, Somerset.
Power Plant: Two 1,660 shp Rolls-Royce Gnome H-1400-1 shaft-turbine engines.
Dimensions: Rotor diameter, 62 ft. Length, 55 ft 9¾ in. Height, 16 ft 6 in.
Weights: Empty, 12,566 lb. Loaded, 21,000 lb.
Performance: Maximum speed, 161 mph. Service ceiling, 10,000 ft. Range, 598 miles.
Armament: One general purpose machine-gun and 2-inch rockets.

Sea King H.C.4 of No.846 Squadron exercising with Royal Marines in Norway. *(Westland)*

Sea King H.A.S.5 (ZA127) from No.820 Squadron, *Invincible*

Westland Sea King H.A.S.5

With its emergence as the major anti-submarine warfare aircraft of the Fleet Air Arm, the Sea King helicopter was developed still further with the arrival of the H.A.S.5 which first entered service with the Royal Navy from 2 October 1980. The prototype Sea King H.A.S.5 was a converted H.A.S.2 (XZ916) and a total of 30 new-build aircraft (ZA126–137, ZA166–170, ZD630–637 and ZE418–422) were ordered for the Royal Navy. Ultimately, the existing force of around 50 Sea King H.A.S.2 helicopters was converted to H.A.S. Mk.5 standard.

No.820 Squadron was the first FAA unit to be equipped with the Sea King H.A.S.5, embarked in HMS *Invincible*, which became operational in June 1981.

With more sophisticated equipment than its predecessor, the H.A.S.2, the H.A.S.5 was identifiable externally by a larger radome above the fuselage. The Sea King Mk.5 incorporated a Decca 71 radar, Sea Searcher radar, improved tactical air navigation system and LAPADS (lightweight acoustic processing and display system) working in conjunction with signals from Jezebel passive sonobuoys. To accommodate the extra equipment, the cabin was enlarged by moving the rear bulkhead about six feet further aft.

The Sea King H.A.S.5's enhanced submarine-hunting rôle enabled it to operate at far greater ranges than before to monitor signals from its own sonobuoys as well as those dropped by RAF Nimrods and to strike with Mk.44 or 46 homing torpedos or the Sting Ray. In the search and rescue rôle, Sea Kings were designated H.A.R.5.

During the Falklands conflict in 1982, five Sea King squadrons of the FAA made a major contribution to victory. Of these, Nos.820 and 826 Squadrons were equipped with H.A.S.5s, flying from the carriers *Invincible* and *Hermes* respectively. One H.A.S.5 of No.826 Squadron (XZ577) made a record operational sortie lasting no less than 10 hr 20 min, refuelling in the air from *Brilliant* and *Yarmouth*.

No.810 Squadron (Portland and *Engadine*), No.819 (Prestwick, in SAR rôle), No.820 (Culdrose and *Invincible*), No.824 (Culdrose and *Illustrious*) and No.826 (Culdrose, *Hermes*, Prestwick, *Tidespring* and *Fort Grange*). *Second-line squadron:* No.706 (Culdrose) and 771 (Culdrose).

TECHNICAL DATA (SEA KING H.A.S.5)

Description: All-weather anti-submarine warfare helicopter. Crew of four, including two pilots.
Manufacturers: Westland Helicopters Ltd, Yeovil, Somerset.
Power Plant: Two 1,660 shp Rolls-Royce Gnome H-1400-1 shaft-turbine engines.
Dimensions: Rotor diameter, 62 ft. Length (fuselage), 55 ft 9¾ in, (including rotors turning), 72 ft 8 in. Height, 16 ft 6 in.
Weights: Empty, 14,051 lb. Loaded, 21,000 lb.
Performance: Maximum speed, 161 mph. Cruising speed, 129 mph. Climb, 3,000 ft/min. Range, 764 miles. Endurance (normal), 4 hr.
Armament: Four Mk.44 torpedoes or four Mk.11 depth charges, a nuclear depth bomb or Sting Ray homing torpedo.

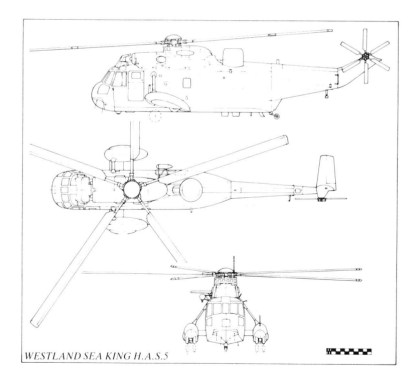

WESTLAND SEA KING H.A.S.5

Sea King H.A.S.6 (ZA135) of No.819 Squadron from RNAS Prestwick. (*HMS Gannet*)

Westland Sea King H.A.S.6

In 1987 the Sea King had been in service with the Royal Navy as its primary anti-submarine warfare aircraft for eighteen years and during this time had been progressively improved through four different variants. Over 150 had entered service but there was still room for further development.

The Sea King H.A.S.6 offered improvements both to the basic airframe and the main transmission system as well as still more sophisticated ASW sonics, sonar and MAD systems and the capacity to launch Sea Eagle anti-ship missiles. Initial plans in 1987 called for 29 Sea King H.A.S.6s to be supplied to the Fleet Air Arm, comprising four new build aircraft and 25 converted H.A.S.5s.

In 1988, No.824 Squadron at RNAS Prestwick was assigned its first Sea King H.A.S.6, thereafter forming an Intensive Flying Trials Unit. The first H.A.S.6 in service with No.824 Squadron was ZA136 (a converted Mk.5) and later No.819 Squadron received its first H.A.S.6, serialled ZA135.

No.824 Squadron disbanded in 1989, but the H.A.S.6 continued in service with Nos.819 and 820 Squadrons.

Gazelles of No.705 Squadron at RNAS Culdrose.

Westland/Aérospatiale Gazelle

The SA-341 light utility helicopter, later named Gazelle, was first conceived as part of the 1967 Anglo-French collaborative helicopter programme. In the Royal Navy it was adopted as a replacement for the Hiller H.T.2 and the Whirlwind H.A.S.7 in the training rôle. With the Fleet Air Arm it was designated Gazelle H.T.2.

The first of 35 Gazelles for the Royal Navy, (XW845) made its first flight in July 1972 and production aircraft joined service with the Fleet Air Arm at Royal Naval Air Station Culdrose, Cornwall, in March 1974, later forming the entire equipment of No.705 Squadron from March 1975 when the last Hiller departed.

This versatile helicopter, fundamentally a military development of the famous Alouette, had by the autumn of 1977 been built jointly by British and French factories to a total exceeding 700, including 203 for the British Army, 34 for the Royal Air Force, and 35 for the Fleet Air Arm. About 30 per cent of each Gazelle airframe was built at the Weston-super-Mare (Old Mixon) factory of Westland Helicopters Ltd, the remainder being fabricated by Aérospatiale at Marignane in France.

Nine Gazelles participated in the all-helicopter flypast during HM the Queen's Review of the Fleet at Spithead on 28 June 1977. Six were drawn from No.705 Squadron and three from the Royal Marines.

Serial numbers allocated to Gazelle H.T.2s for the Fleet Air Arm ranged between XW845 and 907, XX391 and 451, XZ 938 and 942 and ZB647 to 649.

The Fleet Air Arm's Gazelle is probably best known to the British public for its spectacular displays with the renowned *Sharks* formation display team. This

383

consists of six Gazelle H.T.2s operating from their base at Culdrose and performing regularly at air shows all over the United Kingdom every summer.

UNITS ALLOCATED

Second-line squadron: No.705 (Culdrose).

TECHNICAL DATA (GAZELLE H.T.2)

Description: Multi-rôle utility and training helicopter with a normal crew of two.
Manufacturers: Westland/Aérospatiale in England and France.
Power Plant: One 592 shp Turboméa Astazou XIV turboshaft engine.
Dimensions: Rotor diameter, 34 ft 5½ in. Overall length, 31 ft 2¾ in. Height, 9 ft 0¼ in.
Weights: Empty, 2,002 lb. Loaded, 3,970 lb.
Performance: Maximum speed, 164 mph. Maximum range, 403 miles. Climb, 1,675 ft/min. Service ceiling, 14,105 ft.
Armament: Various options including AS.11 or AS.12 air-to-surface missiles or 36-mm rocket pods.

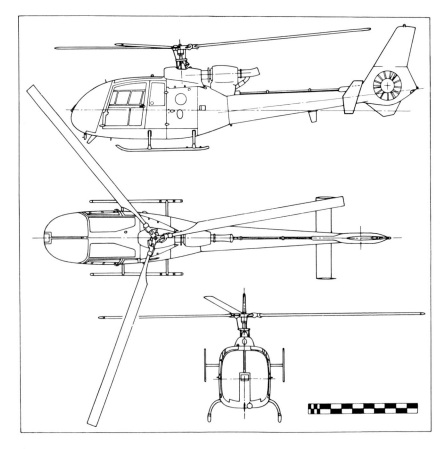

Lynx H.A.S.2 (XZ232) of No.702 Squadron from Yeovilton. *(Royal Navy)*

Westland/Aérospatiale Lynx H.A.S.2

Under the design leadership of Westland, the Lynx was evolved in collaboration with Aérospatiale under an Anglo–French agreement of February 1967. The Lynx superseded the Wasp as the Fleet Air Arm's standard anti-submarine hunter-killer for service from frigate-sized warships and guided-missile destroyers.

The first of five development prototype aircraft (XW835) flew on 21 March 1971 but the original Royal Navy prototype (XX469) did not fly until 25 May 1972. The second RN prototype (XX510) followed on 5 March 1973 and became the first Lynx to alight on a ship at sea, this being the Royal Fleet Auxiliary *Engadine* during trials off the Dorset coast.

Contracts were placed for 60 Lynx H.A.S.2s for the Royal Navy in May 1974. They were serialled XZ227–252, XZ254–257, XZ689–700 and XZ719–736 and the first of them flew on 10 February 1976. First deliveries were made in September 1976 to No.700L Squadron at Yeovilton and trials took place in HMS *Birmingham* and *Sheffield*. Finally, in January 1978, the Lynx was issued to No.702 Squadron which served as the Headquarters for 15 Lynx Ship's Flights deployed in frigates and destroyers other than *Rothesay* Class frigates, which retained their Wasps due to hangar limitations.

From January 1981, No.815 Squadron became the Headquarters Squadron for Ship's Flights, the shore base becoming Portland in July 1982. By this time, No.815 Squadron was supplying Lynx helicopters for the British Naval Task Force in the Falklands conflict where they flew over 1,800 sorties. The newly introduced Sea Skua missile was used by Lynx to sink the Argentine ships *Somellera* and *Río Carcarana*. Another notable engagement was the torpedo attack by a Lynx H.A.S.2 from HMS *Brilliant* on the submarine *Santa Fé*.

No.815 Squadron (Yeovilton and Portland, HQ for aircraft in 15 Ships' Flights). *Second-line squadrons:* Nos.700L (Yeovilton) and 702 (Yeovilton and Portland).

TECHNICAL DATA (LYNX H.A.S.2)

Description: All-weather anti-submarine search and strike helicopter with a basic crew of two.

Manufacturers: Westland/Aérospatiale of England and France.

Power Plant: Two 900 shp Rolls-Royce Gem 2 Mk.100 shaft-turbines.

Dimensions: Rotor diameter, 42 ft 0 in. Length overall, 49 ft 9 in. Fuselage length, 39 ft 1 in. Height, 11 ft 5 in.

Weights: Empty, 6,040 lb. Loaded, 10,500 lb.

Performance: Maximum speed, 144 mph. Range, 418 miles. Ceiling, 8,450 ft.

Armament: Two Sea Skua or A.S.12 air-to-surface missiles or two Mk.44 or 46 torpedoes or nuclear depth bomb.

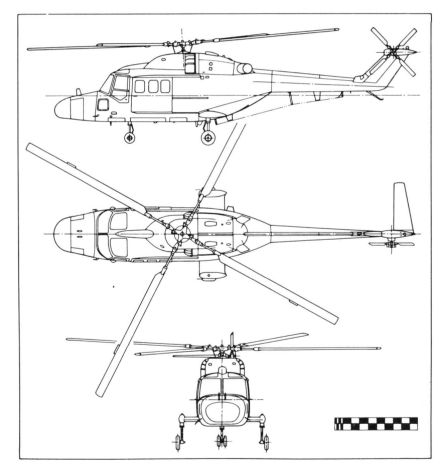

Lynx H.A.S.2 (XZ229) arriving at RNAS Yeovilton. *(Westland)*

Lynx H.A.S.3 (ZD264) of No.815 Squadron from RNAS Portland. (*HMS Osprey*)

Westland Lynx H.A.S.3 and 8

Just too late to see service in the Falklands conflict where its predecessor the Lynx H.A.S.2 played a prominent rôle, the Lynx H.A.S.3 was first delivered to the Fleet Air Arm in March 1982. The first Lynx H.A.S.3s went to No.702 Squadron at Portland and later to No.815 Squadron at the same base. The prototype (ZD249) had first flown on 26 August 1980.

Compared with the earlier variants, the Lynx H.A.S.3 had the new Gem 41 engine developing 1,120 shp with a strengthened transmission and an improved electronic surveillance system known as Orange Crop. The Royal Navy placed an order for 20 H.A.S.3s (ZD249–268), later increased to 30 including three (ZD565–567) ordered immediately after the Falklands conflict to replace battle losses. Lynx H.A.S.3s served with ships of the Armilla Patrol in the Gulf, carrying Yellow Veil jamming pods.

A still later development of the Lynx currently under test for the Royal Navy is the H.A.S.8 notable for its Sea Spray 360 degree radar scanner in a cylindrical radome under the nose. This variant introduced carbonfibre composite rotor blades, an increased loaded weight of 11,300 lb and for the first time in a Lynx a CTS (central tactical system). It is expected that the H.A.S.8 will eventually be standardised for Fleet Air Arm use by up-dating earlier Marks.

TECHNICAL DATA (LYNX H.A.S.3)

Description: All-weather anti-submarine search and strike helicopter. Crew of two.

Manufacturers: Westland/Aérospatiale of United Kingdom and France.
Power Plant: Two 1,120 shp Rolls-Royce Gem 42–1 shaft-turbines.
Dimensions: Rotor diameter, 42 ft. Length (fuselage), 39 ft 1¼ in. Length (overall, including rotors), 49 ft 9 in. Height, 11 ft 3 in.
Weights: Empty, 6,836 lb. Loaded, 10,500 lb.
Performance: Maximum speed: 184 mph. Range: 418 miles. Service ceiling, 9,678 ft. Endurance: 2½ hr.
Armament: Four Sea Skua air-to-surface missiles or Mk.11 depth charges or two Sting Ray homing torpedoes.

UNITS ALLOCATED

No.815 Squadron (Portland) providing aircraft for embarkation in nearly 50 frigates, destroyers and survey ships. *Second-line squadron:* No.702 (Portland).

Lynx H.A.S.8 (ZD267) on test at Yeovil. (*Westland*)

Merlin (ZF649) on test at Yeovil. (*Westland*)

Westland EH 101 Merlin

The Merlin was designed to replace the long-serving Sea King as the Royal Navy's standard anti-submarine warfare helicopter. The first fully navalised prototype EH 101 (ZF649) flew for the first time at Yeovil on 24 October 1989. The envisaged rôle was to operate from Type 22/23 frigates as well as ASW carriers and the EH 101 was planned to enter Fleet Air Arm service around the middle of the 1990s.

As a joint project between Westland and Agusta of Italy, the EH 101 was first launched in 1979 and the original prototype (ZF641), which was not navalised, flew for the first time on 9 October 1987. Initial plans were to produce 50 of the Royal Navy's Merlin variant, to be equipped with Blue Kestrel search radar in a chin radome. A formidable array of 'state of the art' avionics was incorporated, including an aircraft management computer and integrated mission sensors. General Electric T 700–401 turbine engines in the early aircraft were scheduled to be superseded by Rolls-Royce Turboméca RTM 322s in later production examples.

First deck landings by a pre-production Merlin were first conducted by Colin Hague, Westland's chief test pilot, on board HMS *Norfolk*, the first Type 23 frigate during sea trials in November 1990.

TECHNICAL DATA (EH 101 MERLIN)

Description: All-weather anti-submarine warfare helicopter. Crew of three (one pilot).

Manufacturers: Westland Helicopters, Yeovil, Somerset, and Agusta, Italy.

Power Plant: Three 1,680 shp General Electric T 700-401C turbine engines driving a five-bladed rotor. Alternatively, three 2,100 shp Rolls-Royce Turboméca RTM 322 engines.

Dimensions: Rotor diameter, 61 ft 0 in. Length (rotors turning), 74 ft 10 in. Height, 21 ft 10 in.

Weight: Loaded, 28,500 lb approx.

Performance: Maximum speed, 190 mph. Endurance, 5 hr. Service ceiling, 15,000 ft.

Armament: Up to four Mk.46 or Sting Ray homing torpedoes, four Mk.11 depth bombs, nuclear depth charges.

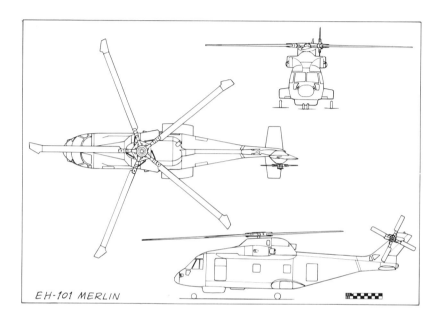

EH-101 MERLIN

Pre-production Merlin (PP5) on trials with HMS *Norfolk*.

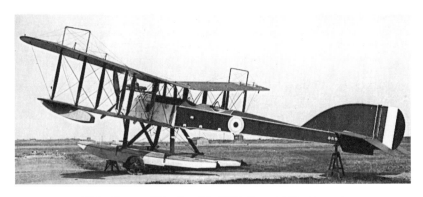

Wight 'Converted' Seaplane (No.9853). *(Imperial War Museum)*

Wight 'Converted' Seaplane

The Wight 'Converted' Seaplane was descended from a single-engined landplane bomber (N501) of 1916 which did not enter production. It was the third type of Wight seaplane to be used in numbers by the RNAS, the others being the Pusher Seaplane of 1913 and the Admiralty Type 840 of 1915, both of which are described and illustrated in the Appendix.

As its name indicated, the Seaplane was a straightforward adaptation of the Bomber, and apart from the undercarriage differed only in minor details such as the installation of double-acting ailerons and modified kingposts on the top wing. The same Rolls-Royce Eagle engine was retained in the first production 'Converted' Seaplanes, but the later batches had a Sunbeam Maori.

Although it was not used in such large numbers as some other types of RNAS seaplanes, the Wight 'Converted' put in a great deal of work on maritime patrols, and one of them is alleged to have destroyed a U-boat, the first to be sunk in the English Channel by direct air attack from a British aircraft. The date was 22 September 1917. The Wight hit its quarry with its first 100 lb bomb. It was operating from the RNAS Station at Cherbourg and was flown by F/Sub-Lt C S Mossop and Air Mechanic A E Ingledew.

A total of 50 Wight 'Converted' Seaplanes was ordered for the RNAS, but only 37 were built, as it was decided to standardise on the Short 184. The serial numbers allocated were 9841 to 9860, N1280 to 1289 and N2180 to 2199.

Only a handful of 'Converted' Seaplanes remained at RNAS Stations by the Armistice. Official records listed seven on 31 October 1918. The type was withdrawn in June 1919.

UNITS ALLOCATED

No.241 Squadron (Portland) and No.243 Squadron (Cherbourg).

TECHNICAL DATA (WIGHT 'CONVERTED')

Description: Two-seat anti-submarine patrol seaplane. Wooden structure with fabric covering.

392

Manufacturers: J Samuel White & Co, East Cowes, Isle of Wight.

Power Plant: One 322 hp Rolls-Royce Eagle VI or 265 hp Sunbeam Maori.

Dimensions: Span, 65 ft 6 in. Length, 44 ft 8½ in. Height, 16 ft. Wing area, 715 sq ft.

Weights: Empty, 3,758 lb with Eagle engine and 3,957 lb with Maori engine. Loaded, 5,556 lb with Eagle engine and 5,394 lb with Maori engine.

Performance (Eagle engine): Maximum speed, 84½ mph at 2,000 ft; 82½ mph at 6,500 ft. Climb, 4 min 20 sec to 2,000 ft; 42½ min to 10,000 ft. Endurance, 3½ hr. Service ceiling, 9,600 ft.

Armament: One Lewis machine-gun on Scarff mounting aft and provision for four 100 lb or 112 lb bombs below the wings.

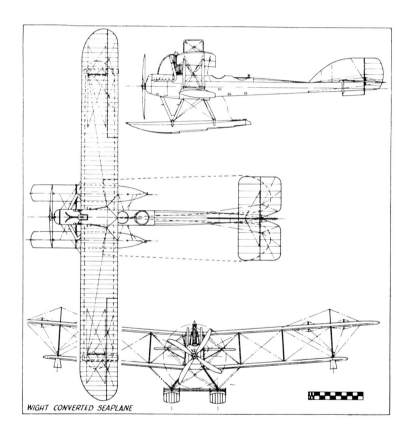

WIGHT CONVERTED SEAPLANE

Other types of aircraft in service with the Royal Flying Corps (Naval Wing), the Royal Naval Air Service and the Fleet Air Arm since 1912

This section deals with all British naval aircraft (including those of foreign origin) not otherwise described and illustrated in the main text. It includes:

(i) Early naval types used only in small quantities. This category embraces the less important aircraft of the 1914–18 period and also the miscellaneous types which were included in the standard numbering system for British Service aircraft introduced during 1912. The Admiralty was allotted the numbers 1 to 200, 801 to 1600, 3001 to 4000 and 8001 to 10000.

(ii) Aircraft of all periods used for training duties, or other second-line rôles such as transport or target-towing, but not designed primarily for naval purposes.

(iii) Variants of first-line types.

(iv) First-line aircraft supplied in limited numbers but with no actual operational service to their credit.

Note on RAF aircraft used by the Royal Navy 1939–45

This appendix does *not* include a number of aircraft types produced primarily for the Royal Air Force, but which were seconded for various duties to units of the Fleet Air Arm, mainly in training or transport rôles.

Types falling into this category include various Austers, the Canadian-built Avro Anson II, the Avro Lancaster, the Armstrong Whitworth Whitley, the Blackburn Botha, the Bristol Blenheim, the Bristol Beaufighter X, the de Havilland Mosquito P.R.XVI, the D.H.86, the Hawker Hart Trainer, the Handley Page Harrow, the Percival Petrel and Spitfires Mks.I, II, V, IX, XII, XIII and XVI. Full details of these aircraft can be found in the companion volume *Aircraft of the Royal Air Force since 1918*. The appendix *does* include RAF aircraft used in considerable numbers such as the Beaufort, Beaufighter II, Mosquito B.25, Master I and II, Martinet, Wellington and Lysander.

A.D. FLYING-BOAT

Two-seat patrol flying-boat designed by the Air Department of the Admiralty and constructed by Pemberton-Billing, Ltd (later Supermarine), at Woolston, Southampton. First flown 1917. Prototypes (1412 and 1413) followed by 27 production aircraft (N1290, N1520 to 1529, N1710 to 1719 and N2450 to 2455). One 150 hp or 200 hp Hispano-Suiza engine, loaded weight 3,327 lb and 3,567 lb respectively. Span, 50 ft 4 in. Length, 30 ft 7 in. Maximum speed, 100 mph at 2,000 ft. Climb, 30 min to 10,000 ft. Endurance, 4½ hr.

AIRSPEED ENVOY

Twin-engined development of Courier first flown in 1934. Envoy (P5629) illustrated was used during 1939–43 for communications duties by the Royal Navy. Two 350 hp Armstrong Siddeley Cheetah IX engines and loaded weight of 6,600 lb. Maximum speed, 203 mph. Climb, 1,250 ft/min. Range, 620 miles. Service ceiling, 22,000 ft.

AIRSPEED OXFORD

Military training development of the Envoy, first flown 1937. Used predominantly by the RAF but also entered service with the FAA during 1939–45. Naval example illustrated is R6180. Served with Nos.700, 701, 702, 703, 720, 727, 728, 729, 730, 739, 740, 744, 750, 751, 758, 759, 760, 761, 762, 765, 766, 771, 775, 776, 780, 781, 782, 787, 789, 790, 792, 798, 799 and 1701 Squadrons. Two 370 hp Armstrong Siddeley Cheetah X engines and loaded weight of 8,000 lb. Maximum speed, 188 mph. Climb, 960 ft/min. Service ceiling, 19,500 ft. Span, 53 ft 4 in. Length, 34 ft 6 in.

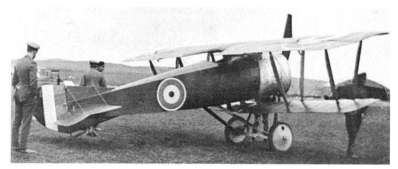

ALCOCK SCOUT

Devised but not flown by F/Lt J W Alcock (later to achieve fame in the Vimy Atlantic crossing of 1919), this single-seat scout was operated by No.2 Wing of the RNAS at Mudros in 1917–18. It was comprised of components from the Sopwith Triplane and Pup and had a 100hp Monosoupape or 110 hp Clerget engine. Armament was twin Vickers machine-guns. No other details available.

ARMSTRONG WHITWORTH F.K.10

Four of these unconventional two-seat quadruplanes were built for the RNAS in 1917, serialled N511–514. They were built under licence by the Phoenix Dynamo Manufacturing Company of Bradford. The first naval F.K.10 was equipped as a two-seat fighter and the second as a bomber. One 130 hp Clerget engine. Loaded weight, 2,019 lb. Maximum speed, 84 mph at 6,500 ft. Service ceiling, 10,000 ft. Span, 27 ft 10 in. Length, 22 ft 3 in.

ARMSTRONG WHITWORTH A.W.XVI

First flew in 1930, having been designed to Specification N.21/26 as a deck-landing fighter. It was in competition with the Parnall Pipit (N232), Fairey

Firefly IIIM (S1592), Hawker Hoopoe (N237), Gloster Gnatsnapper (N227) and Vickers 141 Scout. Serialled S1591, the A.W.XVI was attached for trials to No.402 Flight of the Fleet Air Arm whose crest it bore on its fin. It never entered production as the FAA's next standard fighter was to be the Hawker Nimrod. One 500 hp Armstrong Siddeley Panther IIIA engine. Span, 33 ft 0 in. Length, 25 ft 6 in. Height, 11 ft 0 in. Loaded weight, 4,067 lb. Maximum speed, 203 mph at 10,000 ft. Climb, 18 min to 20,000 ft. Service ceiling, 28,650 ft.

ARMSTRONG WHITWORTH METEOR T.T.20

The Meteor T.T.20 was a special target-tug conversion from the Meteor N.F.11 for the use of Fleet Requirements Units. Modification began at the Armstrong Whitworth factory at the end of 1957, and the first of 29 Meteor T.T.20s entered service with the FAA in March 1958. Mainly used by No.728 Fleet Requirements Unit at Hal Far, Malta, where it replaced Sturgeons. Finally left RN service in March 1971. The T.T.20 carried four 3 ft by 15 ft (or 4 ft by 20 ft) high-speed radar-responsive sleeve targets and a 6,100 ft towing cable operated by a windmill winch on the starboard wing. Two Rolls-Royce Derwent turbojets. Span, 43 ft. Length, 48 ft 6 in. Maximum speed, 554 mph. Service ceiling, 40,000 ft.

AVRO 500 (TYPE E)

Two-seater used for training by both the Naval and Military Wings of the RFC from 1912. Used by RNAS flying school at Chingford after outbreak of war in 1914. Naval Wing allotted Nos.41, 51 to 53, 94, and 150. One 50 hp Gnome engine and loaded weight of 1,300 lb. Maximum speed, 62 mph. Span, 36 ft. Length, 29 ft.

AVRO 501

Avro's first seaplane, produced in January 1913. One only supplied to RNAS as No.16, was converted from amphibian to a landplane and flown at Eastchurch Naval air station, where it was used for training. One 100 hp Gnome engine and a loaded weight of about 2,200 lb. Span, 50 ft. Length, 33 ft 6 in.

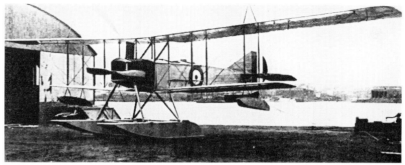

AVRO 510

Two-seat patrol seaplane used by RNAS coastal air stations from 1914 at Dundee, Isle of Grain and Killingholme. Allotted Nos.130 to 134. One 150 hp Sunbeam Crusader engine and loaded weight of 2,800 lb. Maximum speed, 70 mph. Climb, 15 min to 3,000 ft. Endurance, 4½ hr. Span, 63 ft. Length, 38 ft.

AVRO 519

Two only (Nos.8440 and 8441) supplied to the RNAS in 1916. So far as is known, the type saw no operational service. Originally built as a two-seater, a single-seat version (No.8441) is illustrated: it had folding wings. One 150 hp Sunbeam Nubian engine.

(Charles E Brown)

AVRO ANSON

No Ansons were supplied to the Royal Navy directly by the manufacturers but some (like the Mk.I, DJ331, illustrated) were handed over by the RAF and used post-war for the training of air observers. Served with Nos.700, 701, 703, 707, 710, 711, 719, 720, 724, 725, 728, 732, 735, 737, 739, 740, 742, 743, 744, 745, 747, 749, 750, 751, 758, 762, 763, 766, 771, 772, 773, 778, 781, 782, 783, 784, 785, 786, 787, 789, 790, 792, 798, 799, 809, 1830 ,1832, 1833, 1840 and 1841 Squadrons. Two 350 hp Armstrong Siddeley Cheetah IX engines and a loaded weight of 8,000 lb. Maximum speed, 188 mph at 7,000 ft. Climb, 720 ft/min. Range, 790 miles. Service ceiling, 19,000 ft. Span, 56 ft 6 in. Length 42 ft 3 in.

(Imperial War Museum)

B.E.2A

The B.E.2a served with both the Military and Naval Wings of the RFC from 1912. Naval Wing was allotted Nos.46, 47, 49 and 50, the last of these becoming the favourite mount of the famed Cdr Samson. It accompanied the Eastchurch Squadron to Belgium in August 1914 and served again with Samson in the Dardanelles region. One 70 hp Renault engine and a loaded weight of 1,600 lb. Maximum speed, 70 mph at sea level. Climb, 5 min to 7,000 ft. Endurance, 3 hr. Service ceiling, 10,000 ft. Span, 38 ft 7½ in. Length, 29 ft 6½ in.

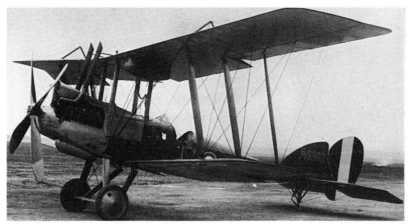

(Imperial War Museum)

B.E.2E

Two-seat Corps reconnaissance aircraft, a development of the B.E.2c and B.E.2d, used mainly by the RFC but some 95 were transferred to the RNAS for service at training schools such as Cranwell. Some of the RNAS trainers had the 75 hp Rolls-Royce Hawk engine instead of the standard 90 hp RAF 1A. Loaded weight, 2,100 lb. Maximum speed 90 mph at sea level. Climb, 53 min to 10,000 ft. Endurance, 4 hr. Service ceiling, 9,000 ft. Span, 40 ft 9 in. Length, 30 ft 6 in.

(Imperial War Museum)

B.E.8

Commonly known as 'The Bloater', the B.E.8 was used from 1912 as a trainer at the Central Flying School and one example was still serving with No.3 Flight, RNAS Westgate, in July 1915. One 80 hp Gnome engine. Maximum speed, 70 mph at sea level. Climb, 10½ min to 3,000 ft. Span, 39 ft 6 in. length, 27 ft 3 in.

BEECH TRAVELLER

Five-seat communications aircraft. Lend–Lease deliveries totalled 93 to the Royal Navy. Serial numbers were FL653 to 670, FZ428 to 439 and FT461 to 535. Served with Nos.701, 712, 730, 740, 776, 778, 781, 782, 787 and 799 Squadrons. One 450 hp Pratt & Whitney Wasp Junior and loaded weight of 4,250 lb. Maximum speed, 198 mph. Climb, 1,400 ft/min. Range, 700 miles. Service ceiling, 25,000 ft. Span, 32 ft. Length, 26 ft.

BEECH EXPEDITER

Six–eight-seat communications aircraft used by the US Army as UC-54A and US Navy as the JRB-1. Lend–Lease supplied 76 to the Royal Navy. Photograph shows Expediter II KP110. Expediters were serialled FT975 to 996, HD752 to 762, HD772 to 776 and KP100 to 124. Served with Nos.701, 712, 723, 724, 728, 730, 739, 742, 755, 781, 782 and 791 Squadrons. Two 450 hp Pratt & Whitney Wasp Junior engines and loaded weight of 7,850 lb. Maximum speed, 230 mph at sea level. Climb, 1,850 ft/min. Range, 900 miles. Service ceiling, 27,000 ft. Span, 47 ft 8 in. Length, 34 ft 3 in.

BLACKBURN NAUTILUS

Designed to Spec O.22/26 for a carrier-borne Fleet spotter with fighter capability, the Nautilus was in competition with the Fairey Fleetwing, the Short Gurnard and the naval version of the Hawker Hart which (as the Osprey) was eventually chosen. First flown in May 1929, the Nautilus (N234) saw brief service in 1930–31 with No.405 Flight of the Fleet Air Arm on board the carrier *Furious*. It was ultimately converted for ship-to-shore communications duties. One 525 hp Rolls-Royce F.XIIMS engine. Span, 37 ft 0 in. Length, 31 ft 8 in. Maximum speed, 154 mph at 5,000 ft. Initial climb, 1,260 ft/min. Range, 375 miles. Service ceiling, 18,800 ft.

BLÉRIOT TYPE XI

Fundamentally similar to the aircraft used by Louis Blériot for his historic crossing of the English Channel in 1909, this type was used by both the Naval and Military Wings of the RFC and subsequently by the RNAS from 1912 to early 1915. One 80 hp Gnome engine and a loaded weight of 1,388 lb. Maximum speed, 66 mph at sea level. Climb, 230 ft/min. Span, 34 ft 3 in. Length, 27 ft 6 in.

(Imperial War Museum)

BLÉRIOT PARASOL

This was a development of the earlier Blériot XI. Served with the RFC and RNAS (Nos.1538–1549) during 1914–15.

(Peter Moss)

BOREL SEAPLANE

One of the first seaplanes used for British naval flying, the Borel was of French manufacture and was first purchased by the British Government in 1912. At least eight were in service with the Naval Wing before 1914, including Nos.37, 48, 83, 84, 85, 86, 87 and 88. No.48 was embarked in HMS *Hermes* for the Fleet manoeuvres of July 1913 and at about the same period Lt A M Longmore (later Air Chief Marshal Sir Arthur Longmore) piloted Admiral Jellicoe in a Borel at Cromarty naval air station. The Borel was powered by an 80 hp Gnome engine.

BOULTON PAUL DEFIANT TARGET-TUG

These aircraft, shore-based, were used by Fleet Requirements Units between 1942 and 1945. The aircraft illustrated belonged to No.777 Squadron. Also equipped were the second-line squadrons Nos.721, 726, 727, 728, 770, 771, 772, 774, 775, 776, 779, 788, 789, 791, 792, 794 and 797. One 1,260 hp Rolls-Royce Merlin XX engine. Maximum speed, 260 mph at 20,000 ft. Span, 39 ft 4in. Length, 35 ft 4 in.

BOULTON PAUL SEA BALLIOL T.21

Deck-landing version of the RAF's Balliol trainer. The first prototype (VR599) flew in October 1952 and 30 Sea Balliols were delivered to the FAA with the serial numbers WL715 to 734 and WP324 to 333. The last was delivered on 7 December 1954. Units equipped were Nos.702, 703, 727, 765, 781 and 796 Squadrons and Nos.1831, 1832, 1834, 1840, and 1844 Squadrons of the RNVR. One 1,280 hp Rolls-Royce Merlin 35 engine and a loaded weight of 8,410 lb. Maximum speed, 288 mph. Climb, 1,790 ft/min. Service ceiling, 32,500 ft. Span, 39 ft 4 in. Length, 35 ft 1½ in.

(*Imperial War Museum*)

BREGUET C2/U2

The early type of Breguet biplane was used by the Naval Wing of the RFC from 1912. The first to be purchased from France (No.6) was delivered to Eastchurch in August 1912 and early in 1914 was stationed at Felixstowe. Originally fitted with the 80 hp Chenu engine, it later had the 110 hp Canton Unné installed.

(*J M Bruce*)

BREGUET BUC/BLC *DE CHASSE*

Seventeen of these Breguet BUC/BLC pusher biplanes were supplied to the RNAS, where they served with 'A' and 'B' Squadrons of No.5 Wing in Belgium from April to June 1916. Named *de Chasse* by the Royal Navy, they were serialled 1390–1394, 3209–3213, 3883–3887 and 3946. One 225 hp Sunbeam Mohawk engine. Span, 53 ft 9½ in. Length, 31 ft 2 in. Maximum speed, 86 mph at sea level. Service ceiling, 12,140 ft.

BREGUET TYPE 5 *CONCOURS*

The RNAS took this large pusher aircraft into service for use as a bomber, primarily with No.3 Wing during 1916. Twenty-seven examples were supplied by the French manufacturers (3946, 1398–1399 and 9175–9200) and an additional 10 were built in Britain by Grahame-White (9426–9435) and designated Type XIX. They did not prove very successful and were soon withdrawn. One 225 hp Renault or 250 hp Rolls-Royce engine. Maximum speed, 88 mph at sea level. Climb, 15½ min to 6,500 ft. Range, 435 miles. Service ceiling, 14,000 ft. Span, 57 ft 9 in. Length, 32 ft 6 in.

BREWSTER BUFFALO

During 1941 about 15 went to the Royal Navy and served with No.805 Squadron at Aboukir and No.885 Squadron at Dekheila. Also with Nos.759 and No.760 Squadrons at Fighter Pool at Yeovilton and a few examples to Nos.804 and 813 Squadrons. One 1,200 hp Wright Cyclone engine and a loaded weight of 6,840 lb. Maximum speed, 313 mph at 13,500 ft. Climb, 2,070 ft/min. Range, 650 miles. Service ceiling, 30,500 ft. Span, 35 ft. Length, 26 ft.

(Bristol)

BRISTOL BOXKITE

First appeared in June 1910 and used by the RFC from its formation in May 1912. Six (Nos.942 to 947 inclusive) ordered by the Admiralty remained in service at RNAS training schools at Eastbourne, Eastchurch and Hendon until about the middle of 1915. One 50 hp Gnome engine and a loaded weight of 900 lb. Maximum speed, 40 mph Span, 46 ft 6 in. Length, 38 ft 6 in. At least one Boxkite was fitted with flotation bags.

BRISTOL T.B.8

First flown in 1913. The first T.B.8 for the Admiralty, delivered in January 1914, had twin floats: subsequent aircraft were landplanes. Forty-five T.B.8 landplanes went to the RNAS (including 14 diverted from the RFC) and served until 1916. The aircraft illustrated (No.1216) was the first of a batch of twelve (Nos.1216 to 1227) diverted from the RFC to the RNAS at the end of 1914. Two T.B.8s served with Eastchurch Squadron at Ostend and Dunkirk and four with No.1 Squadron at Gosport and Newcastle-on-Tyne. Others were used at Barrow-in-Furness, Chingford, Hendon, Killingholme, Kingsnorth and Redcar. One 80 hp Gnome, Le Rhône or Clerget engine. Loaded weight, 1,665 lb. Maximum speed, 75 mph. Climb, 11 min to 3,000 ft. Span, 37 ft 8 in. Length, 29 ft 3 in.

BRISTOL BEAUFIGHTER II

This version of the Beaufighter, with two 1,280 hp Rolls-Royce Merlin XX engines, was used by various Fleet Requirements Units of the FAA between 1941 and 1945. FAA units with Beaufighters were Nos.721, 726, 728, 733, 762, 775, 779, 781, 788, 789, 797 and 798 Squadrons. Aircraft illustrated is from No.798 Squadron at Lee-on-Solent. Maximum speed, 330 mph. Range, 1,500 miles. Span, 57 ft 10 in. Length, 41 ft 8 in.

(*FAA Museum*)

BRISTOL BEAUFORT

Small numbers of Beauforts (both Mk.I and II) were supplied to the Royal Navy from October 1943 and a few examples remained as late as August 1946. They were chiefly used by No.762 Squadron, a twin-engine conversion unit, at Yeovilton and Dale but some were also to be found with No.728 Squadron in Malta (see photo), No.733 Squadron in Ceylon, No.788 Squadron at Mombasa and No.798 Squadron at Lee-on-Solent. Two 1,130 hp Bristol Taurus VI engines. Span, 57 ft 10 in. Length, 44 ft 7 in. Maximum speed, 265 mph at 6,000 ft. Range, 1,035 miles. Service ceiling, 16,500 ft.

BRITISH AEROSPACE BAe 125

This modified BAe 125–600B executive jet (ZF130) played a key rôle in the development of the Royal Navy's Sea Harrier F.R.S.2 fighter by serving as a test bed. It was fitted with Sea Harrier F.R.S.2 controls and avionics including the Ferranti Blue Vixen radar in an extended nose. A pylon below the starboard wing carried a Sidewinder missile and a simulated AMRAAM system was installed.

A second B.Ae 125 in service with the Royal Navy operated as a communications aircraft, based at Northolt.

Two Garrett turbofans. Span, 47 ft. Length, 50 ft 6 in. Maximum speed, 570 mph. Service ceiling, 41,000 ft.

BURGESS GUNBUS

Thirty-six of these pusher biplanes (Nos.3657 to 3681 and 8258 to 8268) were purchased from the USA by the Admiralty in 1915. Some of them were test-flown at Hendon, but they were not a success and never entered squadron service. They went into storage at the White City and were finally condemned in May 1916. The power plant was a single 140 hp Sturtevant engine.

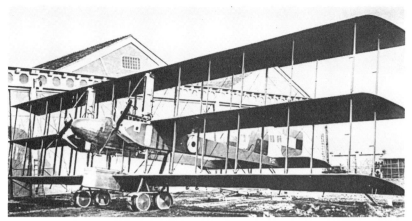

(Imperial War Museum)

CAPRONI CA.42 TRIPLANE

Six examples of this three-engined triplane bomber were purchased from Italy for the RNAS, but were not, so far as is known, used operationally although originally intended for No.227 Squadron at Pizzone, in April 1918. They had the serial numbers N526 to 531 inclusive: N527 is illustrated.

(Imperial War Museum)

CAUDRON G.3

The RNAS used 140 of these aeroplanes, mostly for training purposes at Vendome in France. The G.3 was the single-engined forerunner of the G.4 (see main text) and earlier G.2s (Nos.40, 55, 56 and 57) were in service as seaplanes with coastal air stations prior to 1914. No.55, an amphibian, was embarked in HMS *Hermes* at Great Yarmouth in July 1913 and operated from the forward flying-off deck. The pre-war Caudrons had an 80 hp or 100 hp Gnome engine. Some G.3s, like No.3066 illustrated, mounted the 100hp Anzani engine. Loaded weight, 1,619 lb. Maximum speed, 70 mph. Climb, 20 min to 6,500 ft. Service ceiling, 10,000 ft. Span, 43 ft 5 in. Length, 22 ft 6 in.

CURTISS TWIN CANADA

One hundred of these bombers were ordered for the RNAS in 1915 (Nos.9500 to 9599), but the contract was subsequently cancelled. One example (No.3700) was eventually delivered to Hendon in November 1916. Designed by Curtiss and built in Canada, the Twin Canada had two 160 hp Curtiss XV engines.

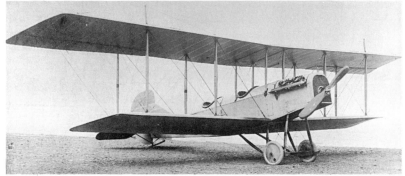

CURTISS R-2 and R-4

Eighty-four delivered to the RNAS in 1915 (Nos.3445 to 3529) for reconnaissance duties. The type proved unsuccessful because its 160 hp Curtiss XV engine was unreliable and in British service was replaced by a 200 hp Sunbeam but a few are believed to have served for armament training duties until as late as 1918. Nos.3455 and 3459 went to the RNAS at Luxeuil and Nos.3462, 3463 and 3464 to Mudros.

CURTISS JN-3

The JN-3 was the forerunner of the more famous JN-4 Jenny trainer, and six (Nos.1362 to 1367) were ordered for the RNAS in 1914; deliveries followed in March 1915. A further 79 (Nos.3345 to 3423) were produced to Admiralty orders by the parent firm and 12 (Nos.8392 to 8403) by Curtiss (Canada) at Toronto. All were fitted with the 90 hp Curtiss OX-5 engine.

CURTISS JN-4

The celebrated 'Jenny' trainer, used both by the RFC and RNAS. The Admiralty ordered 250, but only 80 entered service with the RNAS. One hundred were transferred to the RFC and 70 were not delivered. The RNAS trainers were allotted the serial numbers 3424–3444, 8802–8880, 8901 and N5670–5673. One 90 hp Curtiss OX-2 engine. Loaded weight, 2,130 lb. Maximum speed, 70 mph at 6,500 ft. Climb, 10 min to 3,000 ft. Span, 43 ft 9 in. Length, 27 ft 4 in. The JN-4A illustrated had increased dihedral (4 deg) over the original JN-4.

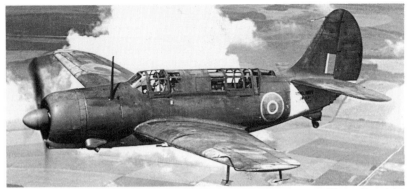

CURTISS HELLDIVER

Twenty-six of these dive-bombers, serialled JW100 to 125, were delivered to the FAA under Lend-Lease arrangements. Nine Helldivers were used to form No.1820 Squadron at Squantum, USA, on 1 April 1944. They were shipped to the United Kingdom in HMS *Arbiter*, but saw no operational service. Shore-based at Burscough and disbanded December 1944. The FAA's Helldivers were built by the Canadian Car and Foundry Factory with the designation SBW-1B. Illustrated is JW117. One 1,650 hp Wright Double-Row Cyclone engine. Loaded weight, 13,880 lb. Maximum speed, 284 mph. Climb, 2,500 ft/min. Range, 695 miles. Service ceiling, 24,000 ft. Span, 47 ft. Length, 39 ft 2 in. Armament: Four 0.50 calibre guns forward and one 0.50 gun aft. Bomb-load, 1,000 lb.

CURTISS-WANAMAKER TRIPLANE

Twenty of these enormous triplane flying-boats were ordered from the USA for the equipment of the RNAS in 1915. They were intended to carry a crew of six and to be heavily armed for anti-Zeppelin patrols over the North Sea. They were allotted the serial numbers 3073 to 3092, but in the event only one (No.3073) reached the RNAS in 1916. Power was provided by four 250 hp Rolls-Royce Mk.I engines. Loaded weight, 22,000 lb. Maximum speed, 100 mph. Span, 134 ft. Length, 58 ft 10 in.

(*Flight Refuelling*)

DASSAULT FALCON 20

The Falcon 20 was selected in 1983 as the replacement for the Canberra T.22 in service with the Fleet Requirement and Aircraft Direction Unit (FRADU) at Yeovilton. Flight Refuelling Aviation Ltd, which managed FRADU, acquired 16 Falcon 20s and modified them to perform all the Canberra's previous duties, including radar calibration, anti-ship simulated missile attacks and target-towing, where they replaced Canberra T.T.18s. They also operate in the electronic warfare rôle. Although on Royal Navy duties, the Falcon 20s retained their civil markings. Two 4,315 lb thrust CF 700 turbojets. Span, 53 ft 6 in. Length, 56 ft 3 in. Maximum speed, 651 mph. Range, 1,530 miles. Service ceiling, 42,000 ft.

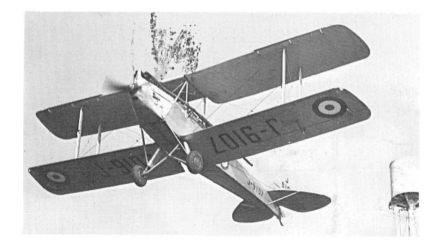

DE HAVILLAND 60M MOTH

Illustrated is J9107, a D.H.60M Moth supplied to the FAA at Gosport for deck-landing training in June 1938. Also served with No.769 Squadron (K1898) at Donibristle from July 1939 to April 1940.

419

DE HAVILLAND QUEEN BEE

The Queen Bee, a special radio-controlled version of the Tiger Moth for anti-aircraft gunnery practice, first flew in January 1935 and subsequently entered service both with the RAF and the FAA. The seaplane version was catapulted from warships and employed on Fleet gunnery exercises. The Queen Bee remained in production until July 1944 and a total of 380 was built. The aircraft illustrated, K5114, is a Mk.II serving in Malta.

DE HAVILLAND TIGER MOTH

Tiger Moths served with the Royal Navy for a variety of duties in 27 second-line squadrons and provided air experience for naval cadets at Roborough until replaced by Chipmunks in 1966. One 130 hp D.H. Gipsy Major engine. Loaded weight, 1,770 lb. Maximum speed, 109 mph at 1,000 ft. Climb, 673 ft/min. Range, 302 miles. Service ceiling, 13,600 ft. Span, 29 ft 4 in. Length, 23 ft 11 in.

DE HAVILLAND FLAMINGO

The D.H.95 Flamingo, which was just entering service as a civil airliner in 1939, was taken over by the RAF and two also served with the Royal Navy. Naval Flamingos were operated by No.782 Squadron at Donibristle on services to the Orkneys, the Shetlands and Northern Ireland. Illustrated is BT312 (*Merlin VI*) which joined RN service in November 1940. Two 930 hp Bristol Perseus XVI engines. Loaded weight, 17,600 lb. Maximum speed, 239 mph. Range, 1,210 miles. Span, 70 ft. Length, 51 ft 7 in.

(Crown Copyright)

DE HAVILLAND DOMINIE

FAA Dominies were, like their counterparts in the RAF, used for training and communications duties from 1940 and some remained in service post-war until as late as 1958. A total of 65 entered the Royal Navy and served with Nos.701, 703, 712, 736, 739, 740, 744, 767, 776, 778, 781, 782, 787, 790 and 799 Squadrons. The Dominie illustrated, HG708, entered service in April 1945 and has the markings of the Royal Naval Air Station, Culham. Two 200 hp D.H. Gipsy Six engines. Loaded weight, 5,500 lb. Maximum speed, 157 mph at 1,000 ft. Range, 570 miles. Capacity for ten as a communications aircraft.

(*FAA Museum*)

DE HAVILLAND MOSQUITO B.25

Eleven second-line squadrons of the Fleet Air Arm had examples of the Mosquito B.25 on their strength between 1945 and 1948. Seventy B.25s were allocated to the Royal Navy and they served on Fleet Requirements duties or for training. Nos.704, 762, 770, 771, 772, 777, 778 and 790 Squadrons were in the United Kingdom, No.728 in Malta (see photo) and Nos.733 and 797 in Ceylon. The Mosquito B.25 was Canadian-built and had two 1,620 hp Packard Merlin 225 engines. Span, 54 ft 2 in. Length, 41 ft 6 in. Maximum speed, 410 mph.

(*MoD*)

DE HAVILLAND SEA DEVON C.20

The Sea Devon C.20 eight-seat light transport was first acquired for the Royal Navy in 1955 and served with No.781 Squadron at Lee-on-Solent and Culdrose. Also issued to Nos.728, 750, 765 and 771 Squadrons. Finally retired from RN service in December 1989. Initially, 10 Sea Devons were delivered, the serial numbers being XJ319 to 324 and XJ347 to 350. Three more (XK895–897) were added later. Two 340 hp D.H. Gipsy Queen 70 engines. Loaded weight, 8,500 lb. Maximum speed, 210 mph at 8,000 ft. Span, 57 ft. Length, 39 ft 3 in.

(Flight)

DE HAVILLAND SEA HERON

Five Sea Heron C.1s supplemented Sea Devons with No.781 Squadron at RNAS Lee-on-Solent from May 1961 to March 1981. The first two, XR441 and XR442, were formerly of Jersey Airlines. Sea Herons XR443 to 445 were previously of West African Airways. A sixth aircraft (XM296) was added in July 1972, equipped as an Admiral's Barge and designated C.4. Finally retired from RN service in December 1989. Four 250 hp D.H. Gipsy Queen 30 engines. Maximum cruising speed, 183 mph at 8,000 ft. Span, 71 ft 6 in. Length, 48 ft 6 in.

(Aviation Photo News)

DE HAVILLAND CHIPMUNK T.10

Sixteen ex-RAF Chipmunks entered service with the Fleet Air Arm from June 1966 to provide air experience for cadets of the Royal Naval College, Dartmouth, based with the Britannia Flight at Plymouth. The Chipmunks were serialled WB575, WB657, WB671, WD374, WK511, WK574, WK608, WK634, WK635, WK776, WP795, WP801, WP809, WP856, WP904 and WP906. Chipmunks also serve as partial equipment of No.771 Squadron.

One 145 hp de Havilland Gipsy Major 8 engine. Loaded weight, 2,000 lb. Maximum speed, 138 mph at sea level. Span, 34 ft 4 in. Length, 25 ft 8 in.

DEPERDUSSIN MONOPLANE

This type, one of the earliest products of the French aircraft industry, was to be seen at most of the pre-1914 flying meetings. A number entered service with the Naval Wing of the RFC from 1912 and were used both as landplanes and seaplanes. No.7 was acquired in July 1912 and flown from Lake Windermere: its engine was a 70 hp Gnome. Others were Nos.22, 30, 36 and 44, all with the 80 hp Anzani engine. The example illustrated has the early Naval Wing serial number M.1 on its rudder.

DOUGLAS BOSTON

A few served with FAA second-line squadrons, notably Nos.771, 772 and 778 in 1941/42. They were similar in all respects to the RAF Bostons. Two 1,200 hp Pratt & Whitney Twin Wasp engines. Maximum speed, 295 mph. Span, 61 ft 4 in. Length, 46 ft 11¾ in.

424

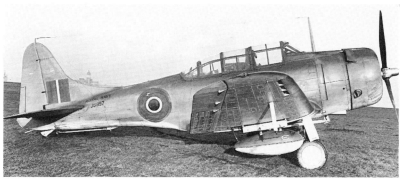

(Crown Copyright)

DOUGLAS DAUNTLESS

Nine of these dive-bombers, equivalent to the US Navy's SBD-5, were delivered to the UK and received the designation Dauntless D.B. Mk.I in January 1945. Their serial numbers were JS997 to 999 and JT923 to 928. The aircraft illustrated is JS997. They served in Nos.700 and 787 Squadrons but were rejected for FAA first-line use. One 950 hp Wright Cyclone engine. Loaded weight, 9,519 lb. Maximum speed, 255 mph at 14,000 ft. Climb, 1,428 ft/min. Range, 773 miles. Service ceiling, 25,200 ft. Span, 41 ft 6 in. Length, 33 ft. Nearly 6,000 of these famous dive-bombers had been built for the US Navy, US Marine Corps and USAAF when production ceased in July 1944.

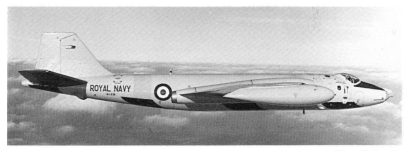

(Peter R March)

ENGLISH ELECTRIC CANBERRA T.T.18

Twelve Canberra T.T.18 target facilities aircraft were supplied to the Royal Navy from September 1969 for service mainly with the Fleet Requirements Unit at Hurn, Hampshire and subsequently at RNAS Yeovilton. They were all converted from Canberra B.2s, including WJ636 illustrated, and superseded Meteor T.T.20 target-tugs. Other T.T.18s were WE122. WH887, WJ574, WJ614, WJ636, WK123, WK124, WK126 and WK142.

ENGLISH ELECTRIC CANBERRA T.22

Seven of these aircraft were specially converted from P.R.7s in 1973 initially to train Buccaneer navigators but later for radar calibration duties. They could be distinguished externally by the light grey overall finish, with dayglow bands in orange round the outer wings and rear fuselage, and a long pointed nose housing Blue Parrot radar. Serials were WH780, WH797, WH801, WH803, WT510, WT525 and WT535.

The first Royal Navy Canberra T.22 made its maiden flight at Samlesbury on 28 June 1973.

(MoD (Royal Navy))

ENGLISH ELECTRIC CANBERRA U.14

Six Canberra B.2s were converted by Shorts to Canberra U.14 pilotless aircraft for use by No.728B Squadron at Hal Far, Malta. These Canberras were used for trials with Seacat missiles fired from HMS *Girdleness* in 1961.

Two Rolls-Royce Avon turbojets. Span, 63 ft 11½ in. Length, 65 ft 6 in.

FAIREY IIIA

The Fairey IIIA was a landplane conversion of the earlier N.10 twin-float seaplane and fifty were built for the RNAS with the serial numbers N2850 to 2899. Only one (N2850) had been delivered (to Luce Bay) by the Armistice. Served post-war with No.258 Squadron (Luce Bay) and No.272 Squadron (Machrihanish) until March 1919. One 260 hp Sunbeam Maori II engine. Loaded weight, 3,694 lb. Maximum speed, 109½ mph at sea level. Climb, 10 min to 6,500 ft. Endurance, 4½ hr. Service ceiling, 15,000 ft. Span, 46 ft 2 in. Length, 31 ft.

FAIREY IIIB

The Fairey IIIB was designed for bombing duties to the requirements of the Admiralty's N.2B specification. Twenty-five IIIBs were built (N2230–2254) and served with No.219 Squadron (Westgate), No.230 Squadron (Felixstowe) and No.229 Squadron (Great Yarmouth). Withdrawn in February 1920. One 260 hp Sunbeam Maori II engine. Loaded weight, 4,892 lb. Maximum speed, 95 mph at 2,000 ft. Climb, 17 min 50 sec to 6,500 ft. Endurance, 4½ hr. Service ceiling, 10,300 ft. Span, 62 ft 9 in. Length, 37 ft 1 in.

(*Quadrant Picture Library*)

FAIREY FIREFLY IIIM

The Firefly IIIM (S1592) was built to meet the requirements of Specification N.21/26 for a deck-landing fighter. It first flew on 17 May 1929 and in June 1930 underwent carrier trials on board HMS *Furious*. It was not adopted by the Fleet Air Arm and the Hawker Norn (later named Nimrod) was selected instead. One 480 hp Rolls-Royce F.XIS engine. Span, 33 ft 6 in. Length, 25 ft 4 in. Height, 9 ft 10 in. Loaded weight, 3,479 lb. Maximum speed, 188 mph at sea level. Climb, 2 min 48 sec to 5,000 ft.

FAIREY FLEETWING

The Fleetwing (N235) was designed to meet Specification O.22/26 for a two-seat spotter-reconnaissance deck-landing aircraft with a fighter capability. It first flew on 16 May 1929 and between January and March 1930 was attached to No.405 Flight of the Fleet Air Arm for trials on board HMS *Furious*, whose red carrier band it displayed. In April 1932, operating as a seaplane, it did catapult trials from HMS *Norfolk*. The Fleetwing was in competition with the Blackburn Nautilus (N234) and Short Gurnard (N228) but in the event none of these types was chosen and the contract went to the Hawker Osprey. One 480 hp Rolls-Royce F.XI engine. Span, 37 ft. Length (landplane), 29 ft 4 in (seaplane), 32 ft. Loaded weight (landplane), 4,737 lb. Maximum speed, 169 mph (landplane) and 156 mph (seaplane).

(Crown Copyright)

FAIREY SPEARFISH

Designed as a replacement for the Barracuda, the Spearfish was too late to see war service. It was built to Spec O.5/43 and the prototype (RA356) first flew on 5 July 1945. A production order for 40 Spearfish T.B.D.Mk.I, in hand at Stockport in 1946, was subsequently cancelled, but one production aircraft (RN241, illustrated) was flown as well as the second and third prototypes, RA360 and RA363. One Spearfish was still flying with the Carrier Trials Unit at Ford (earlier at Lee-on-Solent) until the summer of 1952. One 2,585 hp Bristol Centaurus 58, 59 or 60 engine. Loaded weight, 22,083 lb. Maximum speed, 292 mph at 14,000 ft. Initial climb, 1,720 ft/min, 12 min 40 sec to 15,000 ft. Range, 1,036 miles. Service ceiling, 25,000 ft. Span, 60 ft 3 in. Length, 44 ft 7 in.

(Imperial War Museum)

FARMAN F.40

Fifty of these aeroplanes (usually known as Horace Farmans) entered service with the RNAS. They were frequently fitted with Le Prieur rockets on the interplane struts (as on the example illustrated). The Farman F.40 was used by No.5 Wing of the RNAS. One 160 hp Renault engine. Maximum speed, 84 mph at 6,560 ft. Span, 57 ft 8 in.

(Imperial War Museum)

FRANCO-BRITISH AVIATION TYPE 'C'

Some 128 of these small two-seat flying-boats served with the RNAS for training purposes in the 1914–18 war. Forty-four were provided by the original French manufacturers and 80 were built in Britain by the Norman Thompson and Gosport Aviation concerns. Another four (N1075 to 1078) were handed over by Italy and used by the RNAS at Otranto. The Norman Thompson aircraft were serialled N1040–1059 and the Gosport-built boats N2680–2739. One 100 hp Gnome engine. Maximum speed, 60 mph. Span, 45 ft. Length, 30 ft.

(MoD)

GLOSTER METEOR III

The aircraft illustrated (EE387) was one of two Meteor IIIs fitted with Derwent V engines in short nacelles and arrester hooks. They were used in 1948 for special investigations into the problems of jet flying aboard carriers. EE387 flew from *Illustrious* and EE337 from *Implacable*.

(MoD)

GLOSTER METEOR T.7

The Meteor T.7 dual-control jet trainer was adopted by the FAA as well as the RAF. Thirty-one supplied to RN. The aircraft illustrated display the markings of the Royal Naval Air Station, Hal Far, Malta. The FAA Meteor T.7s were shore-based only and not fitted for deck-flying. They served with Nos.700, 702, 703, 728, 736, 759, 767, 771 and 781 Squadrons and finally retired in March 1971. Two 3,600 lb thrust Rolls-Royce Derwent V or 8 engines. Maximum speed, 585 mph. Climb, 7,600 ft/min. Service ceiling, 35,000 ft. Span, 37 ft 2 in. Length, 43 ft 6 in.

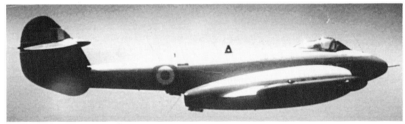

(FAA Museum)

GLOSTER METEOR U.15 AND U.16

The Meteor U.15 and U.16 were in service as target-drones (radio-controlled and pilotless) with No.728B Squadron of the Fleet Air Arm at Hal Far in Malta between 1959 and 1961. They had replaced the Firefly U.8 and U.9 and were used for co-operation with HMS *Girdleness* when it was running trials of the Seaslug missile. The U.15 was converted from the Meteor F.4 fighter and the U.16 was a conversion of the F.8. Seventeen U.15s and four U.16s went to the Royal Navy.

The photograph is of a U.15 (VT310) of No.728B Squadron in Malta early in 1960.

(J M Bruce)

GRAHAME-WHITE TYPE XV

Known as the Type 1600 in RNAS service (the prototype, No.1600, is illustrated), this pusher biplane was extensively used as a trainer in the first part of the First World War, operating at the Royal Naval Air Station at Chingford as well as other schools. The RNAS received about 80, serial numbers 3151 to 3162, 3607 to 3616, 8305 to 8316 and 8752 to 8801. It was fitted with an 80 hp Gnome or Le Rhône rotary engine.

(Imperial War Museum)

GRAIN GRIFFIN

Produced by the Port Victoria design staff at the Isle of Grain, the Griffin reconnaissance aircraft was based closely on the concept represented by the Sopwith B.1 single-seat bomber prototype of 1917. The Griffin introduced a second cockpit for an observer and folding wings for carrier operations. Prototype (N50) was followed by seven production aircraft (N100–106). The type saw very little service but one (N100) was reportedly embarked in HMS *Vindictive* during 1919. One 200 hp Sunbeam Arab or 230 hp Bentley B.R.2 engine. Span, 42 ft 6 in. Length, 27 ft 3 in. Maximum speed, 115 mph at 5,000 ft. Climb, 12 min to 10,000 ft. Endurance, 3 hr. Service ceiling, 19,000 ft.

GRUMMAN GOOSE

Fifty-five Goose amphibians were supplied to both the RAF and the Fleet Air Arm. With the Royal Navy, it entered service with the Royal Naval Air Station at Piarco, Trinidad, in 1942 and was used (alongside Proctors and Reliants) for the training of air observers with No.749 Squadron. Serial numbers were FP470–524.

Two 450 hp Pratt and Whitney Wasp Junior engines and a loaded weight of 8,000 lb. Maximum speed, 200 mph. Range, 800 to 1,050 miles. Service ceiling, 22,000 ft. Span, 49 ft. Length, 38 ft 4 in.

(A J Jackson)

GRUMMAN WIDGEON

Fifteen of these small amphibians, supplied from the USA under Lend-Lease, were used by the Royal Navy for communications duties mainly in the West Indies between 1943 and 1945. In British service the type was originally known as the Gosling. The serial numbers allocated were FP455 to 469, and FP456 is illustrated. Two 200 hp Ranger engines. Loaded weight, 4,500 lb. Maximum speed, 164 mph. Climb, 1,000 ft/min. Range, 775 miles. Service ceiling, 15,500 ft. Span, 40 ft. Length, 31 ft.

(J M Bruce)

HANDLEY PAGE TYPE 'G'

First flown in 1913, this biplane was unusual in having wings with curved swept-back leading edges. It was acquired by the Admiralty soon after the outbreak of war in 1914 and served with the RNAS for training and Home Defence duties at Hendon and Chingford until August 1915. It had the serial number 892. One 100 hp Anzani engine. Maximum speed, 73 mph at sea level. Span, 44 ft. Length, 25 ft 1 in.

(Fleet Air Arm Museum)

HAWKER HENLEY T.T.III

Although used primarily by RAF gunnery schools and anti-aircraft co-operation units, a few examples of the Henley target-tug entered Fleet Air Arm service between 1939 and 1943. As in the example illustrated, they appeared on the strength of No.771 Squadron. One 1,030 hp Rolls-Royce Merlin II or III engine. Span, 47 ft 10½ in. Length, 36 ft 5 in. Maximum speed, 272 mph (with drogue). Range, 950 miles. Service ceiling, 27,000 ft.

(The Aeroplane)

HILLER H.T.1

Twenty of these American two-seat training helicopters were supplied to the Royal Navy in 1953 under MDAP arrangements. Serial numbers allocated were XB474 to 481 and XB513 to 524. The Hillers were used by Nos.705 and 706 Squadrons and one from 705 led the Coronation Review Flypast on 15 June 1953. One 210 hp Franklin engine. Loaded weight, 2,500 lb. Maximum speed, 84 mph. Service ceiling, 9,400 ft. Range, 135 miles. Rotor diameter, 35 ft. Length, 38 ft 8 in. Height, 9 ft 6 in.

HILLER H.T.2

Fourteen of these helicopters entered service with No.705 Training Squadron at RNAS Culdrose in September 1962. The first batch of Hiller H.T.2s were serialled XS159 to 172. Later, deliveries were increased to 21 with the addition of XS700 to 706. Served operationally in Borneo in 1964/65 with No.845 Squadron. Hiller H.T.2s were finally retired from FAA service after a farewell formation flypast at Culdrose on 25 March 1975. They were superseded by Gazelles.

One 305 hp Lycoming VO-540 piston engine. Maximum speed, 96 mph. Service ceiling, 13,200 ft. Range, 205 miles. Loaded weight, 2,800 lb. Rotor diameter, 35 ft 5 in. Length, 28 ft. Height, 10 ft 1½ in.

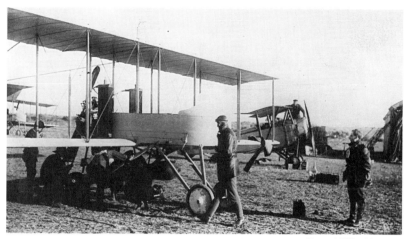

HENRY FARMAN F.27

Extensively employed by the RNAS in the Aegean war theatre in 1915–16, the Henry Farman F.27 had first appeared in 1914. It was notable for its all-steel tubular airframe construction which was very rugged and suitable for the hot climates where it mainly operated. Unlike other Henry Farman variants, it had equal-span wings and a four-wheeled undercarriage. It could carry eight 16 lb bombs and served at the Dardanelles with No.2 Wing, RNAS. Commander C.R. Samson describes his experiences in his Henry Farman F.27 (No.1241) in his entertaining book *Fights and Flights*. On 14 December 1914 he bombed enemy batteries near Ostend during the first night flight of the War by either side. Later, in 1915, he flew No.1241 during the Dardanelles campaign. About eighty were supplied to the RNAS including 3617–3636, 3900–3919, 8243–8249 and N3000–3024. One 140 hp or 160 hp Canton-Unné (Salmson) engine. Span, 53 ft. Length, 30 ft 3 in. Maximum speed, 90 mph at 6,500 ft. Climb, 14 min to 6,500 ft. Endurance, 4 hr.

(Imperial War Museum)

H.R.E.2 SEAPLANE

Designed as a two-seat seaplane for the Naval Wing of the RFC by the Royal Aircraft Factory in 1913. Despite its intended purpose (the designation signified 'Hydro Reconnaissance Experimental') it was first flown as a landplane, was unsuccessful as a seaplane, and reverted finally to landplane form. With the serial number 17, the H.R.E.2 was still in service with the RNAS when war began in 1914. One 70 hp or 100 hp Renault engine. Span, 45 ft 3½ in. Length, 32 ft 3 in.

(Sir Murray Sueter)

MANN EGERTON TYPE B

This seaplane was a modified version of the Short 184, previously built by Mann, Egerton of Norwich to Admiralty contracts. Mann, Egerton built 10 of their own Type B (Nos.9085 to 9094 inclusive) and they were delivered to the RNAS in 1916, seeing service at Calshot. The Type B No.9085 is illustrated. The engine was a 225 hp Sunbeam.

MARTIN MARYLAND

The Maryland light bomber, supplied to Britain from the USA in 1940, was used mainly by the RAF, but a few examples (including AR720, AR736 and AR740) found their way to the FAA, where they were used for photographic reconnaissance and target-towing duties from shore bases. It was a Maryland of No.771 Squadron which on 22 May 1941 took off from Hatston (HMS *Sparrowhawk*) in the Orkneys in appalling weather conditions to report that *Bismark* and *Prinz Eugen* had put to sea from their Norwegian fiord. On this information the Home Fleet put to sea in pursuit. The crew of the Maryland on this historic flight consisted of Lt N E Goddard, RNVR, and Cdr G A Rotheram, OBE, RN. The Maryland had two 1,200 hp Pratt & Whitney Twin Wasp engines and a maximum speed of 278 mph at 11,800 ft. Service ceiling 26,000 ft. Span, 61 ft 4 in. Length, 46 ft 8 in.

MARTIN BALTIMORE

Between September 1944 and October 1946, Baltimores were employed in small numbers for Fleet Requirements duties by No.728 Squadron. They were based in Malta and operated alongside Beauforts and Mosquitoes on similar duties. Examples of both the Mk.IV and Mk.V were to be seen in Royal Navy markings. Two 1,660 hp Wright Double-Row Cyclone engines. Span, 61 ft 4 in. Length, 48 ft 5¾ in. Maximum speed, 302 mph at 11,000 ft. Climb, 12 min to 15,000 ft. Range, 950 miles. Service ceiling, 24,000 ft.

(G S Leslie)

MAURICE FARMAN LONGHORN

The Maurice Farman S.7 Longhorn preceded the S.11 Shorthorn (described in the main text) and could be readily distinguished by the presence of the forward elevator mounted on outriggers ahead of the nacelle. About 16 Longhorns were in service with the Naval Wing of the RFC before 1914. From 1915 the Longhorn served mainly for training purposes. The pre-1914 Longhorns were built by the Aircraft Manufacturing Company Ltd; the later trainers by the Brush, Robey and Phoenix Dynamo concerns. Brush built Nos.8921 to 8940 with 70 hp Renault engines and N5030 to 5059 with the 80 hp Renault. Robey built N5000 to 5016 with the 75 hp Rolls-Royce Hawk engine and the same power plant was used in the batches N5330 to 5349 and N5750 to 5759 (one of which is illustrated) built by the Phoenix Dynamo Manufacturing Company of Bradford. The Longhorn had a maximum speed of 59 mph at sea level. Span, 51 ft. Length, 37 ft 3 in. Loaded weight, 1,887 lb.

(Imperial War Museum)

MILES MAGISTER

Many FAA pilots took their *ab initio* flying instruction on this type during the Second World War, mainly at Luton or Elmdon. Some Magisters flew on communications work with No.780 Squadron at Lee-on-Solent. One 130 hp de Havilland Gipsy Major engine. Loaded weight, 1,900 lb. Maximum speed, 132 mph at 1,000 ft. Span, 33 ft 10 in. Length, 24 ft 7½ in.

MILES MASTER

The Master II (illustrated) was the variant predominantly used by the FAA second-line squadrons from April 1943 but the earlier Mk.I with a Kestrel engine was also in service, being first introduced in No.760 Squadron at Eastleigh in June 1940. Master Is were used by Nos.748, 759, 760, 761, 762, 780, 785, 792, 794 and 798 Squadrons and Master IIs by Nos.700, 715, 718, 719, 736, 748, 759, 761, 766, 772, 780, 794 and 798 Squadrons. All FAA Masters had been displaced by Harvards by 1946. Mk.II: One 870 hp Bristol Mercury XX engine. Maximum speed, 242 mph at 6,000 ft. Initial climb, 2,120 ft/min. Range, 393 miles. Service ceiling, 25,100 ft. Span, 39 ft. Length, 29 ft 6 in.

The aircraft illustrated is W9026 of No.794 Squadron at RNAS Dale.

MILES MARTINET

This target-tug was widely used by the FAA at its Fleet Requirements Units at home and abroad from 1943. FAA units with Martinets on strength were Nos.722, 723, 725, 726, 728, 733, 736, 766, 770, 771, 772, 773, 775, 776, 779, 789, 792, 793 and 794 Squadrons. One 870 hp Bristol Mercury XX or XXX engine. Loaded weight, 6,600 lb. Maximum speed, 237 mph at 15,000 ft. Span, 39 ft. Length, 30 ft 11 in. Illustrated is Martinet RG958 of No.723 Squadron.

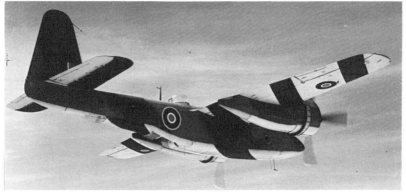

(*Crown Copyright*)

MILES MONITOR

The Monitor high-speed target tug originally produced to Spec Q.9/42 first flew on 5 April 1944 and in its Mk.II form entered production for the Royal Navy in the autumn of 1945. Twenty were built (NP406 to 425) but not all were delivered and in the event the Fleet Requirements Units for which the Monitors had been intended were equipped instead with Mosquito T.T.39s. Two 1,750 hp Wright Double-Row Cyclone engines. Span, 55 ft 3 in. Length, 46 ft 8 in. Maximum speed, 360 mph at 20,000 ft. Climb, 5 min to 10,000 ft. Range, 1,000 miles.

(*J M Bruce*)

MORANE-SAULNIER TYPE BB BIPLANE

A few examples of this French two-seat biplane entered service with the RNAS in 1915–16 and a naval aircraft (No.3683) is illustrated. No.4 Squadron, RNAS, is recorded as having used the Morane Biplane. The engine was an 80 hp Le Rhône rotary.

NIEUPORT TYPE VI.H SEAPLANE

Twelve of these early seaplanes were used by the RNAS, the serial numbers being 3187 to 3198. Two of them, Nos.3194 and 3197, were employed for the training of seaplane pilots on Lake Windermere and others served at RNAS Bembridge, Calshot, Walney and Westgate.

NIEUPORT 10

This was the first of all the historic Nieuport biplanes to enter service with the RNAS early in 1915. Although a two-seater, it was often flown as a single-seater (with the front seat removed) and a machine-gun on the top wing. Fifty were supplied to the RNAS (3163–3186, 3920–3921, 3962–3973 and 8516–8517) and they served with No.1 Wing RNAS at Dunkirk and No.2 Wing in the Agean including the Dardanelles campaign. One 80 hp Gnome engine. Maximum speed, 87½ mph. Climb, 16 min to 6,500 ft. Span, 25 ft 11 in. Length, 22 ft 11 in.

(H H Russell)

NIEUPORT 11 SCOUT

The Nieuport 17bis Scouts described in the main text were preceded in RNAS service by the Nieuport 11 (sometimes known as the *Bebe*), a slightly smaller machine with a lower-powered (80 hp Le Rhône) engine. Nieuport 11s entered service early in 1916 and took part in some historic operations with the RNAS No.1 Wing at Dunkirk and No.2 Wing in the Aegean theatre. They also equipped one flight of the famous 'Naval Eight' Squadron for a few months in 1916, flying alongside Sopwith Pups. RNAS serial numbers were 3974–3994. Maximum speed, 97 mph at sea level. Climb, 5 min to 3,280 ft, 18 min to 9,800 ft. Service ceiling, 18,000 ft. Span, 24 ft 9 in. Length, 18 ft 8 in.

(Aeroplane Photo Supply)

NIEUPORT 21

Known in the RNAS as the '17B', the Nieuport 21 was similar to the Nieuport 17 and of the same dimensions but reverted to the 80 hp Le Rhône engine. At least 10 entered RNAS service with the serial numbers 3956–3958 and 8745–8751. Units with them on strength included Nos.8, 9 and 11 RNAS Squadrons. Maximum speed, 93 mph. Climb, 8¾ min to 6,500 ft.

NORMAN THOMPSON N.T.2B

Two-seat dual-control training flying-boat used by the RNAS in 1917–18. It entered service at Calshot, Felixstowe and Lee-on-Solent, and 79 were still on charge at the time of the Armistice. It was built under licence by S E Saunders Ltd of Cowes and the Supermarine Aviation Works as well as by the parent company. The example illustrated (N2569) is one of the later production versions built by Norman Thompson and is fitted with a 200 hp Hispano-Suiza engine. Earlier versions had the 160 hp Beardmore or the 200 hp Sunbeam Arab engines. Total production was 134, serialled N1180–1189, N2260–2294, N2400–2429, N2500–2516, N2555–2579 and N2760–2778. Maximum speed with the Arab engine was 85 mph at 2,000 ft and the service ceiling 11,400 ft. Loaded weight, 3,169 lb. Span, 48 ft 4¾ in. Length, 27 ft 4½ in.

(Air-Britain)

NORTH AMERICAN HARVARD

The Harvard III was the version of this widely-used trainer mainly used by the FAA, but some Mk.IIBs (such as KF558 of No.780 Squadron illustrated) also entered naval service. One hundred and eighty-seven entered service (54 Mk.IIB and 133 Mk.III) with 36 second-line and six RNVR Squadrons. One 550 hp Pratt & Whitney Wasp engine. Loaded weight, 5,250 lb. Maximum speed, 205 mph at 5,000 ft. Service ceiling, 21,500 ft. Span, 42 ft. Length, 29 ft.

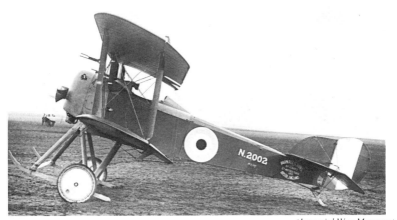

(Imperial War Museum)

PARNALL HAMBLE BABY CONVERT

Seventy-four of these landplane converts of the Hamble Baby seaplane (see main text) were built by Parnall at their Bristol works, the serial numbers being N1986 to 2059. They were employed mainly for training at various RNAS flying schools, including Cranwell.

(Flight)

PARNALL PETO

This small two-seat reconnaissance seaplane of the late 'twenties was unusual in that it was designed to operate from the Royal Navy's submarine *M.2*, in which a special hangar was provided. The Peto was built of stainless steel and could be catapulted from the submarine's deck. Two prototypes were built: N181 and N182 with a 135 hp Bristol Lucifer IV engine initially and later with a 135 hp Armstrong Siddeley Mongoose engine. The Peto illustrated, N255, was a re-build of N181. The first two pilots to fly the Peto aboard a submarine were Lt C W Byas and Lt C Keighley-Peach, and they were fortunate in that they received both flying pay and submarine pay. The Peto was not an unqualified success and lacked an adequate ceiling. It is believed that the loss of the *M.2* off Weymouth on 26 January 1932 was due to the misinterpretation of an order concerning the opening of the Peto's hangar doors. The Peto had a maximum speed of 113 mph at sea-level and could climb to 5,000 ft in 11 min. Its endurance was 2 hr and its loaded weight 1,950 lb. Span, 28 ft 5 in (8ft folded). Length, 22 ft 6¼ in.

(J M Bruce)

PEMBERTON-BILLING P.B.9

This little single-seat scout was designed and built in the surprisingly short time of eight days, and it made its first flight in August 1914. It was not produced in quantity, but the prototype was purchased by the Admiralty and served for a time as a trainer at the RNAS flying school at Hendon. One 50 hp Gnome rotary engine. Maximum speed, 78 mph. Climb, 500 ft/min. Endurance, 3 hr. Span, 26 ft. Length, 20 ft.

(J M Bruce)

PEMBERTON-BILLING P.B.25

Twenty P.B.25 single-seat scouts entered service with the RNAS at Eastchurch and Hendon during 1916. They had the serial numbers 9001 to 9020 and 9002 is illustrated. The P.B.25 was developed from the P.B.23 'Push-Proj' of 1915 and was armed with a single Lewis gun firing forward. One 100 hp Gnome or 110 hp Clerget engine. Maximum speed, 99 mph. Endurance, 3 hr. Span, 33 ft. Length, 24 ft 1 in.

PERCIVAL PROCTOR

Over 1,000 Proctors were built for the RAF and Royal Navy during the Second World War for use as trainers and communications aircraft. Of this total, the FAA received 100 Mk.IA and 50 Mk.IIA from the parent company at Luton and 100 Mk.IIA from Hills of Manchester. The Royal Navy's Proctors were mostly employed for the training of wireless telegraphists at Piarco (No.752), Arbroath (Nos.754 and 758) and Worthy Down (Nos.755 and 756). The Proctor IIA BV559 is illustrated. One 210 hp D.H. Gipsy Queen engine. Maximum speed, 160 mph. Climb, 1,020 ft/min. Range, 660 miles. Service ceiling, 17,000 ft. Span, 39 ft 6 in. Length, 25 ft 10 in.

PORTE BABY

This three-engined (two tractor and one pusher) flying-boat was built by May, Harden and May of Southampton to the designs of Sqn Cdr Porte. Eleven Porte Babies (Nos.9800 to 9810) were built and saw service on North Sea patrols from Felixstowe and Killingholme. The Baby first entered service in November 1916. Two 250 hp Rolls-Royce and one 260 hp Green engine in early versions: later Babies had three 325 hp Rolls-Royce Eagle VII or 360 hp Eagle VIII engines. Crew of five. Loaded weight, 18,600 lb. Maximum speed, 92 mph at sea level. Service ceiling, 8,000 ft. Span, 124 ft. Length, 63 ft.

R.E.5

The R.E.5, the first aeroplane to be produced in quantity at the Royal Aircraft Factory, Farnborough, made its appearance in 1914. It was used mainly by the RFC, but one example (No.26) reached the RNAS and was flown to Dunkirk on 27 September 1914 by Sqn Cdr A M Longmore (later Air Chief Marshal Sir Arthur Longmore). It was used for a bombing raid on Courtrai on 30 September 1914. One 120 hp Austro-Daimler engine. Maximum speed, 78 mph.

R.E.7

The R.E.7 was a development of the R.E.5, and it first appeared in 1915. It was used mainly by the RFC, but six examples were handed over for the use of the RNAS. It was fitted at various times with a great variety of engines, ranging from the 120 hp Beardmore to the 280 hp Rolls-Royce Eagle. Maximum speed with the 120 hp Beardmore was 82 mph. Span, 57 ft. Length, 31 ft 10½ in.

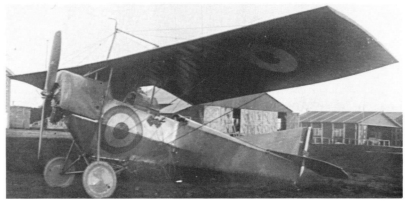

(G Haddow)

ROBERT ESNAULT-PELTERIE PARASOL

Twelve of these early monoplanes served with the RNAS before the First World War. Serialled 8454–8465. 110 hp Le Rhône engine. Speed, 68 mph. Span, 36 ft.

(Short Brothers)

SHORT TANDEM TWIN

This aeroplane, with the Triple Twin the first multi-engined aircraft ever built in Great Britain, was purchased by the Admiralty in 1911 and used at the Naval Flying School at Eastchurch. It was converted from a Short S.27 airframe. It had two 50 hp Gnome rotary engines, one driving a tractor and one a pusher airscrew, the pilot being seated between. Maximum speed, 55 mph. Span, 34 ft 2 in. Length, 40 ft 6 in.

SHORT S.39 TRIPLE TWIN

This early Short biplane, also used by the Naval Flying School at Eastchurch from 1911 (RNAS No.3) was powered by two 50 hp Gnome engines. The front engine drove twin airscrews and the rear engine a single pusher. Maximum speed, 55 mph. Span, 50 ft. Length, 45 ft.

In July 1913 it was re-built as a two-seater with no forward stabiliser and a single Gnome pusher and went to Belgium in 1914 with Cdr Samson's Eastchurch Squadron.

SHORT S.27

This box-kite biplane, fitted with an eight-cylinder E.N.V. engine, first appeared in 1910, and provided the basis for a series of Short biplanes, all of which were used in the earliest days of naval flying in Great Britain when Royal Navy officers were trained at the Royal Aero Club aerodrome at Eastchurch, at first on aeroplanes privately owned by Mr Frank McClean and loaned to the Admiralty. Maximum speed, 40 mph. Span, 34 ft 2 in. Length, 42 ft 1 in.

SHORT IMPROVED S.27 SERIES

These aeroplanes were a development of the S.27 from which they differed in having strut-braced extensions to the top wings. Later models were also to be seen with a small nacelle for the pilot and passenger. The most famous of the modified S.27s was S.38 (RNAS No.2), which was fitted with three air-bags (attached to the undercarriage struts and beneath the tail) enabling it to alight on water. On 1 December 1911 this feat was achieved by Lt A M Longmore (later Air Chief Marshal Sir Arthur Longmore), who flew the S.38 on to the River Medway. On 10 January 1912 Lt Samson used the same aeroplane to make the first take-off from the deck of a British warship (HMS *Africa*) whilst it was at anchor off Sheerness. On 9 May 1912 this performance was repeated from the deck of HMS *Hibernia* as it was steaming in Weymouth Bay at 10½ knots, and again from HMS *London* on 4 July 1912. The improved S.27 was fitted with a single 50 hp or 70 hp Gnome rotary engine. Maximum speed, 48 mph. Span, 46 ft 5 in.

SHORT S.36

Also known as the T.5 (Tractor Five), this was the first tractor biplane built by Short Brothers, and appeared early in 1912. The original model, with uncovered rear fuselage, was owned by Mr Frank McClean. The type was quickly adopted by the Admiralty, and served with the Naval Wing of the RFC both as a landplane and as a seaplane, the latter with a single centre float and two smaller floats below the wings. 70 hp Gnome rotary engine.

SHORT S.38 TRAINER

Developed from earlier Short pushers but introducing a crew nacelle and dual control, the S.38 trainer was widely employed by RNAS flying schools at Chingford and Eastchurch during 1915–16. Thirty-six were built by Supermarine (1580–1591), White and Thompson (3143–3148 and 8530–8541) and Norman Thompson (8434–8439). One 80 hp Gnome engine. Maximum speed, 58 mph. Span, 52 ft. Length, 35 ft 6 in.

SHORT S.57

Developed from Short S.41 (No.10) which first appeared early in 1912 as a landplane: later it was fitted with floats and was flown in the Review of the Fleet at Weymouth on 8 May 1912. An improved version (No.20, illustrated) entered service at Great Yarmouth in July 1913 and took part in the Naval Review of that year. No.20 remained in service on North Sea patrols until June 1915. It was used in early wireless experiments. One 100 hp twin-row Gnome engine. Maximum speed, 60 mph. Span, 50 ft. Length, 39 ft.

SHORT S.60

This type first appeared at the 1913 Olympia Exhibition as a seaplane. It bore a considerable resemblance to the S.41 from which it was developed. Purchased for the Naval Wing, it was allotted the official number 42 and participated in the 1913 Fleet manoeuvres. Afterwards it was given a land undercarriage and was one of the aeroplanes taken to Ostend with Cdr Samson's Eastchurch Squadron of the RNAS on 27 August 1914. One 80 hp Gnome engine. Maximum speed, 65 mph. Span, 48 ft. Length, 35 ft.

SHORT ADMIRALTY TYPE 74 SEAPLANE

Also known as the Improved S.41, this seaplane entered service with the RNAS in 1914 and took part in the Naval Review of July. Serial numbers allotted were Nos.74 to 80, 183 and 811 to 818. Three Type 74 seaplanes (Nos.811, 814 and 815) joined four other seaplanes in the historic raid on Cuxhaven from the carriers *Empress, Engadine* and *Riviera* on Christmas Day, 1914. The Type 74 had a 100 hp Gnome engine but two later examples (Nos.78 and 79) were powered by 160 hp twin-row Gnome engines.

SHORT S.64 FOLDER SEAPLANE

This was one of the earliest aeroplanes to incorporate folding wings. The first two Folders (Nos.81 and 82) had two-bay wings and were closely related to the S.41. Later Folders (including No.119 shown in the photograph) had three-bay wings. The original Folder, No.81, took part in the Naval manoeuvres of July 1913 and carried an early type of wireless transmitter. On 28 July 1914 a Short three-bay Folder (No.121) from Calshot flown by Sqn Ldr A M Longmore made the first successful air-torpedo drop in Great Britain. The weapon used on this historic occasion was a 14 in torpedo which weighed 810 lb. Two Short Folders (Nos.119 and 120) were among the seven RNAS seaplanes which raided Cuxhaven on Christmas Day, 1914. One 160 hp Gnome engine. Maximum speed, 78 mph. Span (three-bay version), 67 ft. Length, 39 ft.

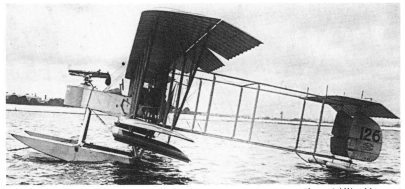

(Imperial War Museum)

SHORT S.81 SEAPLANE

This special seaplane, No.126, was supplied to the Naval Wing in 1913 for a series of experiments with 1½-pounder Vickers semi-automatic guns, one of which is seen in the photograph. The S.81 was known as the Gun-carrier; it served at Great Yarmouth, and in 1915 was carrying an even heavier gun, the 6-pounder Davis. The employment of such guns in aircraft did not prove a practical proposition and there were no operational applications of the weapon. The S.81 was fitted with a 160 hp Gnome engine.

(C H Barnes)

SHORT S.87 ADMIRALTY TYPE 135 SEAPLANE

The Type 135 was a development of the Short Folder, and it also had folding wings. Only two were built: No.135, with a 135 hp Salmson, and No.136 (illustrated), with a 200 hp Salmson engine.

The Short 135 seaplanes were both used in the celebrated RNAS raid on Cuxhaven on Christmas Day, 1914, and No.136 later served in the Dardanelles with the seaplane-carrier *Ark Royal*. Maximum speed, 65 mph. Span, 54 ft 6 in. Length, 39 ft.

SHORT S.90 ADMIRALTY TYPE 166 SEAPLANE

Originally the Short Type C, the Type 166 was designed to carry an 810 lb 14 in torpedo, though there is no record of this weapon having been used operationally by the aircraft in service. The parent firm built six (Nos.161 to 166) and the Westland Aircraft Works 20 (Nos.9751 to 9770); the photograph shows the first of the Westland-built Type 166 seaplanes on the Hamble River in 1916. The Type 166 was used by the RNAS at Calshot and Thasos and in the seaplane-carrier *Ark Royal*. One 200 hp Salmson engine. Loaded weight, 4,580 lb. Maximum speed, 65 mph. Span, 57 ft 3 in. Length, 40 ft 7 in.

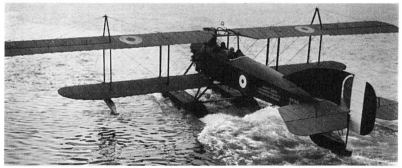

(Short Brothers)

SHORT (140 hp SALMSON) SEAPLANE

Ten seaplanes of this type were built, Nos.9781 to 9790, and No.9790 is illustrated. They served with the RNAS seaplane station at Calshot from 1916. The engine was a 140 hp Salmson radial.

SHORT SEAMEW A.S.1

In February 1955, the Royal Navy ordered 30 Seamew A.S.1s for service aboard carriers in a light-weight anti-submarine rôle. Carrier trials with prototype XA213 took place on board HMS *Bulwark* between July and December 1955. Although planned to replace Avengers in RNVR squadrons, the Seamew fell victim to defence cuts in 1957 and only seven were ever delivered. One 1,650 shp Armstrong Siddeley Mamba propeller-turbine. Span, 55 ft. Length, 41 ft. Maximum speed, 235 mph. Range, 750 miles. Endurance, 4.8 hr.

SIKORSKY HOVERFLY I

The Hoverfly I was the British version of the Sikorsky VS-316, designated R-4 in the USAAF. Forty-five were supplied to Britain under Lend-Lease and the photograph shows KK984 from the batch KK969 to KL113: initial trials aircraft for the FAA were FT833 to 839. Hoverfly I was the first type of helicopter to be used by the RAF and FAA and provided invaluable experience in service flying of this type of aircraft. Entered service with No.771 Fleet Requirements Unit at Portland in February 1945 and No.705 Squadron at Gosport in May 1947. One 180 hp Warner engine. Loaded weight, 2,530 lb. Maximum speed, 75 mph. Service ceiling, 8,000 ft. Range, 220 miles. Main rotor diameter, 38 ft. Length, 35 ft 3 in. Height, 12 ft 5 in.

SIKORSKY HOVERFLY II

This helicopter, the R-6A of the USAAF, was also supplied to Great Britain under Lend-Lease and served both with the RAF and the Royal Navy. Four equipped No.705 Squadron of the FAA for training and communications duties from 1947 until 1950. One 245 hp Franklin engine. Loaded weight, 2,600 lb. Maximum speed, 100 mph. Service ceiling, 10,000 ft. Main rotor diameter, 38 ft. Length, 47 ft 11 in.

(Flight)

SIKORSKY WHIRLWIND H.A.R.21 and H.A.S.22

These Whirlwinds, built by the parent company in the USA and supplied to Britain under MDAP arrangements, preceded the Westland-built Whirlwinds (see main text) in service with the FAA. Twenty-five were delivered, the H.A.R.21 being the equivalent of the US Marines' HRS-2 and the H.A.S.22 of the US Navy's HO4S-3. H.A.R.21s equipped the Royal Navy's first operational helicopter squadron (No.848) from 29 October 1952 and in January 1953 went into action for the first time in Malaya. No.848 Squadron performed general utility and transport duties. A second naval squadron (No.845) equipped with the H.A.S.22 became the Royal Navy's first helicopter anti-submarine unit. It was formed at RNAS Eglinton in Northern Ireland from No.706 Squadron. No.845's H.A.S.22s were equipped with dipping sonar gear and began operational duties on 15 March 1954. With sonar removed, they operated at Suez in the commando rôle in 1956. One of the Whirlwind Mk.22s (WV222) was used extensively by HRH the Duke of Edinburgh (including flights from the grounds of Buckingham Palace) for personal transport and designated V.V.I.P.22. The H.A.R.21 (illustrated) was powered by a single 550 hp Pratt & Whitney Wasp R-1340-57 and the H.A.S.22 by a 700 hp Wright Cyclone R-1300-3. The ten H.A.R.21s were serialled WV189 to 198 and the fifteen H.A.S.22s were numbered WV199 to 205 and WV218 to 225.

H.A.R.21: Loaded weight, 6,835 lb. Maximum speed, 105 mph. Service ceiling, 12,900 ft. Range, 440 miles. Main rotor diameter, 53 ft. Length, 42 ft 2 in. Height, 13 ft 4 in.

H.A.S.22: Loaded weight, 7,500 lb. Maximum speed, 101 mph. Service ceiling, 10,500 ft. Range, 400 miles. Main rotor diameter, 53 ft. Length, 42 ft 2 in. Height, 13 ft 4 in.

SOPWITH BAT BOAT

The Bat Boat, which first appeared in 1913, was the first flying-boat to be built in Great Britain. It entered service with the Naval Wing (No.38) and a second (No.118) took part in the Royal Naval Review of July 1914. On the outbreak of war it was used on sea patrols from Scapa Flow until November 1914. One 100 hp Green engine as illustrated. Later fitted with a 90 hp Austro-Daimler engine. Loaded weight, 1,700 lb. Maximum speed, 65 mph. Span, 41 ft. Length, 32 ft.

SOPWITH D.1

This biplane, which seated two passengers side-by-side in the front cockpit and the pilot in the rear cockpit, appeared at the same time as the Bat Boat in 1913. It was adopted by both the Naval and Military Wings of the RFC, and on the outbreak of war in 1914 the RNAS had two, Nos.103 and 104. They flew from Eastchurch and Calshot and on patrols from Scapa Flow. One 80 hp Gnome engine. Loaded weight, 1,550 lb. Span, 40 ft. Length, 29 ft.

SOPWITH SOCIABLE

Also known as the Tweenie and the Churchill, this two-seat side-by-side biplane was fitted with dual control and used for training by the Naval Wing of the RFC in 1913–14 at Hendon and Eastchurch. It was fitted first with an 80 hp and later a 100 hp Gnome engine and had the official serial number 149. The photograph shows the Tweenie at Hendon, where it was flown extensively by Lt Spenser Grey, RN.

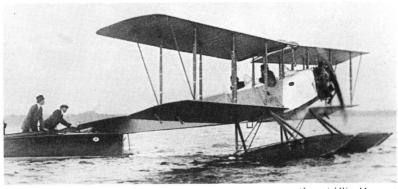

(Imperial War Museum)

SOPWITH H.T. SEAPLANE

Three seaplanes of this type were delivered to the Naval Wing of the RFC, beginning with No.58 in July 1913. The others were numbered 59 and 60. They were used at Cromarty and Great Yarmouth seaplane stations and one participated in the Naval Manoeuvres of 1913. The engine was a 100 hp Anzani radial.

(Imperial War Museum)

SOPWITH GUN BUS

This two-seat pusher biplane first appeared in 1913 as a seaplane trainer for the Greek Naval Air Service. Six further Gun Buses ordered by Greece were taken over by the Admiralty in 1914 and fitted with landplane undercarriages. Serial numbers allotted were No.801 to 806. These aircraft carried a machine-gun in the front cockpit and were fitted with a 100 hp Gnome Monosoupape engine. They were used mainly for training at Hendon. Later examples were also built, as illustrated, with a 150 hp Sunbeam engine and a modified nacelle. Maximum speed, 80 mph. Span, 50 ft. Length, 32 ft 6 in.

(Imperial War Museum)

SOPWITH ADMIRALTY TYPE 807 SEAPLANE

The Type 807, based on the earlier 'Round Britain' Contest seaplane, was first supplied to the RNAS in July 1914 and it incorporated the folding wings first patented in the Short Folders. At least 15 Sopwith 807s entered service and operated both at home (at Calshot and Great Yarmouth) and overseas (in the Dardanelles and East Africa). Some were carried in the seaplane-carrier *Ark Royal*. One 100 hp Gnome Monosoupape engine. Maximum speed, 80 mph.

SOPWITH ADMIRALTY TYPE 860 SEAPLANE

Used by the RNAS on patrols in home waters during 1915 and 1916, the Type 860 was designed to carry an 810 lb 14 in torpedo. Twenty-four were delivered to the RNAS, numbered 851 to 860, 880, 897 to 899 and 927 to 938. The engine was a 225 hp Sunbeam or 220 hp Canton-Unné.

SOPWITH SPINNING JENNY

Officially known as the Two-seater Scout, this aeroplane was more or less a landplane version of the Type 807 and at least 24 were delivered to the RNAS, being employed on anti-Zeppelin patrols from Hendon, Great Yarmouth and Killingholme. Armament was rudimentary and usually consisted of grenades, pistols or rifles. They enjoyed little success and were mostly withdrawn by the end of 1915. Serial numbers allocated were Nos.1051 to 1074 and No.1064 is illustrated. One 100 hp Gnome Monosoupape engine. Maximum speed, 69 mph. Service ceiling, 3,000 ft. Span, 36 ft.

(H H Russell)

SOPWITH B.1

The B.1, which bore a close relationship to the Cuckoo, was a single-seat bomber which first appeared early in 1917. Only one example was built, serialled B1496, but it saw service with the Fifth Wing of the RNAS at Dunkirk, where it was used on bombing raids alongside D.H.4s. One 200 hp Hispano-Suiza engine. Loaded weight, 2,945 lb. Maximum speed, 118½ mph at 10,000 ft. Climb, 15½ min to 10,000 ft. Service ceiling, 19,000 ft. Span, 38 ft 6 in. Length, 27 ft. The bomb load was 560 lb.

(J M Bruce)

SPAD S.7

This famous French fighting scout, which first flew in May 1916, was ordered for the RNAS by the Admiralty, and contracts for 120 placed with the firm of Mann, Egerton of Norwich. In December 1916 the Admiralty agreed to hand over 60 of its Spads to the RFC in exchange for Sopwith Triplanes. The following February it was agreed to divert all RNAS Spads to the RFC. The photograph shows a Spad S.7 with a RNAS serial number (N3399). One 140 hp Hispano-Suiza engine. Loaded weight, 1,632 lb. Maximum speed, 119 mph at 6,500 ft. Span, 25 ft 8 in. Length, 20 ft 3½ in.

STINSON RELIANT

This American civil aircraft first appeared in 1933. Over 500 military versions were transferred to the Royal Navy under Lend-Lease arrangements, and employed for navigation training and communications. Twenty-four second-line squadrons had Reliants on strength. The serial numbers allocated were FB523 to 845 and FK814 to FL163. The Reliant illustrated is FK815. One 290 hp Lycoming R-680 engine. Loaded weight, 4,000 lb. Maximum speed, 135 mph. Span, 41 ft 11 in. Length, 29 ft 6 in.

(The Aeroplane)

SUPERMARINE SEAFANG

The Seafang (to Spec N.5/45) was the naval counterpart of the Spiteful and 150 were ordered for the FAA in May 1945. Only 16 production aircraft were delivered, serialled VG471 to 480 (F.31) and VG481 to 490 (F.32). The Seafang 31 had a Rolls-Royce Griffon 61 engine and fixed wings: the Seafang 32, a Griffon 89 engine, contra-rotating airscrews and folding wings. Maximum speed, 475 mph at 21,000 ft. Climb, 4,630 ft/min. Range (maximum), 1,120 miles. Service ceiling, 42,000 ft. Span, 35 ft (27 ft folded). Length, 34 ft 1 in.

(J M Bruce)

TELLIER FLYING-BOAT

Two of these French-designed flying-boats were acquired for the RNAS. They were allocated the serial numbers N84 and N85. The Tellier boat N85 is illustrated in special camouflage whilst undergoing trials at the Isle of Grain. The RNAS flying-boats were delivered to the Isle of Grain in April 1918, having been purchased by the Royal Navy in November 1917. One 200 hp Hispano engine. Maximum speed, 90 mph. Span, 51 ft 2 in. Length, 38 ft 10 in.

(Peter M Bowers)

THOMAS T.2

This two-seat biplane was produced by the Thomas Bros. Aeroplane Company of the USA and designed by an Englishman, B D Thomas, who bore no relationship to the American proprietors. Twenty-four were ordered by the Admiralty for the RNAS in 1915: they were in two batches of 12 numbered 3809 to 3820 and 8269 to 8280. One 90 hp Curtiss OX-5 engine. Maximum speed, 83 mph. Climb, 10 min to 3,800 ft.

VICKERS ADMIRALTY TYPE 32 GUNBUS

The F.B.5 Gunbus, the first British two-seat fighter aeroplane, made its appearance in 1914. It was used mainly by the RFC but over 20 were delivered to the RNAS beginning with No.32. This resulted in the aeroplane being known as the Type 32 in the RNAS. Subsequent serials were 861 to 872, 1534 to 1535 and 3595 to 3606. Nos.1 and 4 Squadrons of the RNAS used at least one Gunbus each in France in 1915, but there is no operational record of other naval Gunbuses. One 100 hp Gnome Monosoupape engine. Loaded weight, 2,050 lb. Maximum speed, 70 mph at 5,000 ft. Service ceiling, 9,000 ft. Span, 36 ft 6 in. Length, 27 ft 2 in.

VICKERS WELLINGTON

Seven second-line squadrons of the Fleet Air Arm had some Wellingtons between 1944 and 1946. Mostly they were Wellington Mk.XIs, but there were also some Mk.Is, Mk.IIs, Mk.Xs and Mk.XIVs. They were used for a variety of training tasks in the ASV and ASR rôles as well as for twin-engine conversion and instrument training. FAA units equipped were Nos.716, 728, 736, 758, 762, 765 and 783. The Mk.XI had two 1,675 hp Bristol Hercules VI engines. Span, 86 ft 2 in. Length, 64 ft 7 in. Maximum speed, 255 mph. Range, 1,885 miles. Service ceiling, 22,000 ft.

The Wellington illustrated was serving with No.765 Squadron.

VOISIN III LA.S

About 30 Voisin III LA.Ss were in service with the RNAS between 1915 and 1917. They operated as bombers with No.1 Squadron (later No.1 Wing) and with No.2 Wing at Mudros. Four Voisins were also used by No.8 (Naval) Squadron in East Africa from March 1916. One 140 hp Canton Unné engine. Loaded weight, 2,959 lb. Maximum speed, 62 mph at 6,500 ft. Service ceiling, 10,000 ft. Span, 48 ft 5 in. Length, 31 ft 3 in.

(Crown Copyright)

VULTEE VENGEANCE

The Vengeance two-seat dive-bomber was supplied to Great Britain from the USA under Lend-Lease and used mainly by the RAF in Burma. Some of the later deliveries were converted for target-towing duties and saw service in this rôle both with the RAF and the Royal Navy. Fleet Requirements Units with the Vengeance T.T.IV were Nos.721, 723, 733 and 791 Squadrons. One 1,700 hp Wright Double-Row Cyclone engine. Loaded weight, 12,480 lb. Maximum speed, 279 mph. Service ceiling, 24,300 ft. Span, 48 ft. Length, 40 ft.

WESTLAND LYSANDER T.T.III

The Lysander first entered Royal Navy service in June 1941 when No.754 Squadron at Arbroath replaced its Percival Proctors. Subsequently they served at Worthy Down with Nos.755 (see photo) and 757 Squadrons on telegraphist air gunner and observer training duties, superseding Sharks and Skuas respectively. They were all equipped for drogue-towing. One 870 hp Bristol Mercury XX or XXX engine. Span, 50 ft. Length, 30 ft 6 in. Maximum speed, 219 mph. Range, 600 miles. Service ceiling, 26,000 ft.

WHITE AND THOMPSON FLYING-BOAT

Designed originally at the same time as a twin-engined flying-boat for the 'Round Britain' contest for seaplanes, cancelled on the outbreak of war, the type was adopted by the RNAS for anti-submarine patrol duties, and eight production aircraft (designated White and Thompson No.3) were delivered with the serial numbers 1195 to 1200, 3807 and 3808. One 120 hp Beardmore engine. Loaded weight, 2,400 lb. Maximum speed, 85 mph. Crew of two, side-by-side. Span, 45 ft. Length, 27 ft 6 in.

WHITE AND THOMPSON 'BOGNOR BLOATER'

This biplane, remarkable for its wooden monocoque fuselage, was first flown in March 1915. Nine were delivered to the RNAS with the serial numbers 1171 to 1179 and entered service at coastal air stations at Eastbourne, Great Yarmouth and Killingholme. One 70 hp Renault engine.

WIGHT A.I. IMPROVED NAVYPLANE

This larger pusher seaplane was developed from a type first shown at Olympia in February 1913. The five-bay wings, unusual in themselves, were made to fold in production aircraft. Eleven examples were built for the Admiralty with the serial numbers 155, 171 to 177 and 893 to 895. No.176, which appears in the photograph, was one of two Wight Pusher Seaplanes sent to the Dardanelles aboard the seaplane-carrier *Ark Royal* in February 1915. They were used for reconnaissance flights over the Turkish lines. One 200 hp Salmson radial engine. Loaded weight 3,500 lb. Maximum speed, 72 mph. Span, 63 ft.

WIGHT ADMIRALTY TYPE 840 SEAPLANE

The Wight Type 840 was designed as a torpedo-carrying seaplane to the same requirements as the more famous Short Type 184. It could carry a single 810 lb 14 in torpedo, but there are no records of this weapon having been used in action. It served with the RNAS at Felixstowe, Scapa Flow and Gibraltar on anti-submarine patrol between 1915 and 1917. No.835 (illustrated) was one of the batch 831 to 840 built by the parent company, which also produced Nos.1300 to 1319 and 1351 to 1354. About 70 Wight 840 seaplanes were delivered to the RNAS, including sub-contracted aircraft by Beardmore of Dalmuir and Portholme of Huntingdon. A landplane version also existed. One 225 hp Sunbeam engine. Loaded weight, 4,453 lb. Maximum speed, 81 mph. Span, 61 ft. Length, 41 ft.

Non-rigid, semi-rigid and rigid Airships supplied to British naval requirements 1914–1919

The construction of rigid airships began in Great Britain in 1908 with the commissioning from Vickers Ltd at Barrow-in-Furness of R.1 (unofficially named *Mayfly*) by the Admiralty. Launched on 22 May 1911, *Mayfly* was wrecked beyond repair whilst being taken from its shed on 24 September 1911, and naval airship development received a setback until in July 1913 the building of two further rigid and six non-rigid airships was authorised.

Meanwhile, the use of airships by the British Army continued, but from November 1913 they were all handed over to the Naval Wing of the RFC, which became the RNAS in July 1914. Airships then remained under naval control until December 1919, when all air units were transferred to the RAF, Coastal Area.

By the outbreak of war, the former Army airships *Beta, Gamma, Delta* and *Eta* had been augmented by *Astra-Torres* (a non-rigid bought from France in 1913) and Naval Airship No.4, a semi-rigid based on the German Parseval design. The latter two airships were the only ones to be used operationally by the RNAS (though three more Parsevals were later added) until from March 1915 the construction of small non-rigid airships was begun. These non-rigids served throughout the war on anti-submarine patrol, convoy escort and coastal reconnaissance and were developed through the Sea Scout, Coastal, Coastal Star and North Sea series.

Rigid airships made their appearance again from 27 November 1916, when R.9 (built by Vickers) made its maiden flight. Rigid-airship sheds for the RNAS were completed at Howden in December 1916, at Pulham in February 1917, at Longside in March 1917, at East Fortune in April 1917 and at Cranwell in June 1917. Nine rigid naval airships were completed. The last of these, the celebrated R.34, was launched in March 1919.

ASTRA-TORRES (NAVAL AIRSHIP No.3)

This non-rigid airship was used by the RNAS for patrols (each of about 12 hr duration) over the English Channel from 10 August 1914. It was the only British airship of its period to be armed, carrying a single Hotchkiss machine-gun. Two 220 hp Chenu engines. Length 248 ft. Gas capacity 230,000 cu ft.

PARSEVAL (NAVAL AIRSHIP No.4)

A design of German origin, the Parseval No.4 was used on Channel patrols in company with Naval Airship No.3 from 10 August 1914. It was based at Kingsnorth, the first RNAS airship station. It was later joined by other Parsevals (built by Vickers under licence), which were numbered 5, 6 and 7: all were used for training. Two 180 hp Maybach engines. Length 276 ft. Gas capacity 310,000 cu ft.

(Imperial War Museum)

S.S. (SEA SCOUT) NON-RIGID AIRSHIPS

Construction of these small airships, used chiefly for searching narrow channels such as Dover Straits and the Irish Narrows, began in March 1915, and 36 were supplied to the RNAS. The first Sea Scout base was established at Capel (Folkestone) on 8 May 1915 and the second at Polegate (Eastbourne) on 6 July 1915. By the end of 1915 there were five S.S. airships at Capel and three at Polegate. The airships S.S.1, 2, 3, 7, 8, 9, 10, 10A, 12 to 20, 23, 24 and 25 were fitted with a B.E.2b type car. S.S.28 to 39A had a Maurice Farman type car and S.S.27, 40, 41 and 42 an Armstrong Whitworth type car. The Sea Scout illustrated has a B.E.2c car.

(Imperial War Museum)

S.S.Z. (SEA SCOUT ZERO) NON-RIGID AIRSHIPS

This improved version of the S.S. airships, known as the Zero, was first built at Capel in June 1916 and the first S.S.Z. was flown to St Pol (Dunkirk) on 21 September 1916. It was originally intended for towing by ships of the Belgian Coast Patrol and by Monitors so as to assist gunnery spotting. Sixteen S.S. Zeros had been delivered by July 1917, and altogether the RNAS received 66, numbered S.S.Z.1 to 20 and S.S.Z..25 to 70 inclusive. The S.S. Zeros were preceded by six S.S.P. airships, numbered S.S.P.1 to S.S.P.6. Two S.S. Twin airships (with two 75 hp Rolls-Royce Hawk engines) were also used experimentally and numbered S.S.T.1 and S.S.T.2. Length, 143 ft. Capacity, 70,000 cu ft.

C. (COASTAL) NON-RIGID AIRSHIPS

Twenty-seven of these airships, numbered C.1 to C.26, entered service with the RNAS. The last of the line, C.26, is illustrated. The Coastal airships had a trefoil section envelope of 170,000 cu ft capacity and had an endurance of 11 hr at 45 mph. The Coastal type was first ordered in June 1915 and the first airship assembled at Kingsnorth in September 1915. The first RNAS airship station with Coastals was Pembroke, commissioned in January 1916, from whence the first Coastal flight took place on 9 June 1916. Other Coastal airship stations were commissioned at Pulham (February 1916), Howden (March 1916), Longside (March 1916), Mullion (June 1916) and East Fortune (August 1916). On 6 September 1916 experiments were conducted in the refuelling of an airship from a ship, using C.1 and the light cruiser *Canterbury*. Coastal airships were used for patrols off Land's End, the mouths of the Humber and the Forth, north of Aberdeen and off the Norfolk coast. It is on record that one of these airships served continually for over two years, in that time flying a distance of over 66,000 miles. Power was provided by two Sunbeam engines of 150 hp or other types of similar power, and a crew of five was carried. Maximum speed was about 50 mph and the cruising endurance 24 hr. Length 195 ft 6 in.

C STAR (COASTAL STAR) NON-RIGID AIRSHIPS

This designation was used to signify the Coastal airships which had been improved and modified. Airships so modified were identified by the star on the envelope, as in C Star 1 illustrated. Length, 218 ft. Capacity, 210,000 cu ft.

N.S. (NORTH SEA) NON-RIGID AIRSHIPS

Twelve of these airships, the last military non-rigids to be made in Great Britain, were built for the RNAS. They were numbered N.S.1 to N.S.12 and had a trefoil section envelope of 360,000 cu ft capacity. First ordered in January 1916, the North Sea type was ready in February 1917 and N.S.1 was delivered to Pulham, where in June 1917 it flew 1,500 miles during a 49½ hr flight. The North Sea airships were from July 1917 concentrated at East Fortune, but there were numerous difficulties with the power transmission gear, and they could not be used with the Fleet in the manner originally intended. In 1919 N.S.11 set up an endurance record for non-rigid airships by remaining airborne for 101 hr during a cruise of 4,000 miles. The normal duration of the North Sea airship was about 24 hr and the maximum cruising speed about 58 mph. Power was provided by two 240 hp Fiat or two 250 hp Rolls-Royce engines. Length, 262 ft. Capacity, 360,000 cu ft.

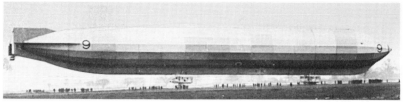

RIGID AIRSHIP R.9

Built by Vickers Ltd at Barrow-in-Furness, the R.9 made its first flight on 27 November 1916 and was delivered to Howden on 4 April 1917. It was used chiefly for training by the RNAS. Four 150 hp Wolseley Maybach and one or two 250 hp Maybach engines. Length, 530 ft. Diameter 53 ft. Gas capacity, 889,500 cu ft. Maximum speed, 45 mph. Maximum range, 1,615 miles.

RIGID AIRSHIP R.23

Built by Vickers Ltd at Barrow-in-Furness, the R.23 was delivered to Pulham on 15 September 1917. It had four 250 hp Rolls-Royce Eagles (one in each of the forward and aft cars and two in the centre car) and attained a speed of 55 mph. In 1918 the R.23 was used for a series of experiments in carrying its own defensive fighter aeroplane for launching in flight. Two Sopwith 2F.1 Camels (N6622 and N6814) of No.212 Squadron were used and one of them can be seen in the photograph. The first successful drop was by N6814 flown by Lt Keys on 6 November 1918.

(Imperial War Museum)

RIGID AIRSHIP R.24

This airship, generally similar to the R.23, was built by Beardmores at Inchinnan, Renfrew, and was delivered to East Fortune on 28 October 1917. It was used for training by the RNAS.

(Imperial War Museum)

RIGID AIRSHIP R.25

Another airship in the '23' class, the R.25 was built by Armstrong Whitworth at Barlow, Selby, Yorkshire, and was delivered to the RNAS station at Howden on 15 October 1917.

(Imperial War Museum)

RIGID AIRSHIP R.26

R.26 was the first of five more '23' class airships ordered for the RNAS in January 1916 and was built by Vickers at Barrow-in-Furness. Four 250 hp Rolls-Royce Eagles. Length, 535 ft. Diameter, 53 ft. Gas capacity, 997,640 cu ft. Maximum speed, 52 mph. Maximum range, 1,895 miles.

RIGID AIRSHIP R.27

One of the two airships of the '23X' class to be completed, the R.27 was built by Beardmores at Inchinnan, Renfrew. The other two '23X' airships (R.28 by Beardmore and R.30 by Armstrong Whitworth) were cancelled after the capture of the German Zeppelin L33 in September 1916.

RIGID AIRSHIP R.29

Sister-ship of the R.27 in the '23X' class, the R.29 was built by Armstrong Whitworth. Four 300 hp Rolls-Royce Eagles. Length, 539 ft. Diameter, 53 ft. Gas capacity, 990,500 cu ft. Maximum speed, 55 mph. Maximum range, 1,056 miles.

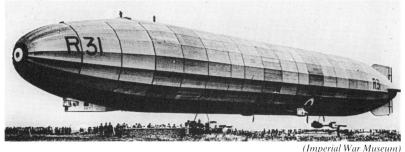

RIGID AIRSHIP R.31

The R.31 and R.32 were built by Short Bros at Cardington on the principles of the wooden Schütte-Lanz airship of German origin. They had five or six 250 hp Rolls-Royce Eagle engines and 1,500,000 cu ft capacity. Length, 614 ft 6 in. Diameter, 66 ft. Maximum speed, 71 mph. Maximum range, 2,000 miles.

RIGID AIRSHIP R.33

R.33's design was based on that of the German airship L33 which came down at Little Wigborough in Essex on 24 September 1916 after being damaged by gunfire. It was built by Armstrong Whitworth and served with the RNAS at East Fortune and Howden and went on to serve with the RAF until 1927. In 1925 and 1926 it was used for air launching experiments with a D.H.53 Humming Bird lightplane and Gloster Grebe fighters. Five 250 hp Sunbeam Maori IV. Length, 643 ft. Diameter, 78 ft 9 in. Gas capacity, 1,958,553 cu ft. Maximum speed, 60 mph. Maximum range, 4,815 miles.

RIGID AIRSHIP R.34

R.34 was the last rigid airship to be used before airships were abandoned by the Admiralty at the end of 1919. It was a sister-ship of the R.33 and was built by Beardmores. In July 1919, R.34 made the first airship crossing of the Atlantic, flying from East Fortune, Scotland, to Long Island, USA, a distance of 3,130 miles in 108 hr 12 min. The return flight, helped by favourable winds, occupied only 75 hr 3 min. This historic flight was the first return crossing of the Atlantic by aircraft of any kind. The R.34 was commanded by Major G H Scott, AFC.

Five 250 hp Sunbeam Maori IV. Length, 643 ft. Diameter, 78 ft 9 in. Gas capacity, 1,958,553 cu ft. Maximum speed, 60 mph. Maximum range 4,815 miles.

APPENDIX C

A list of aircraft-carriers, assault ships and seaplane-carriers of the Royal Navy 1913–90

This list does not include warships which have carried small numbers of aircraft for launching from a turret-platform, or from a catapult. In November 1918 over 100 aircraft were being carried in ships of the Grand Fleet other than aircraft-carriers. Twenty-two light cruisers had been fitted with aircraft launching platforms and all battleships and battle cruisers carried a two-seater aircraft on the forward turret platform and a single-seat fighter on the aft turret platform.

At the start of the war in September 1939, the FAA had 115 catapult aircraft in warships as well as 225 aircraft in aircraft-carriers.

Note on MACships

In addition to the ships listed in the following pages, the FAA also operated Swordfish from the rudimentary flight decks of converted merchantmen during the period 1943–45. These grainships or tankers continued to operate as merchantmen whilst also carrying three or four Swordfish for anti-submarine duties.

The following is a full list of MACships: *Empire MacColl, Empire MacAlpine, Empire MacAndrew, Empire MacRae, Empire MacKendrick, Empire MacCabe, Empire MacCallum, Empire MacDermott, Empire MacKay, Empire MacMahon, Empire MacOma, Adula, Alexia, Acavus, Amastra, Ancylus, Miralda, Gadila* and *Rapana*.

NAME	DESCRIPTION	COMMISSIONED	REMARKS
Activity *(ex-Empire Activity)*	Escort Carrier 14,250 tons 15 aircraft	May 1942	British-built
Albatross	Seaplane Carrier 6,000 tons 9 aircraft	1938 to RN	Originally built for Royal Australian Navy. Operated FAA Walrus squadron, W. Africa and Madagascar, 1939–1943
Albion	Light Fleet Carrier 26,118 tons 36 aircraft	May 1954	First with mirror landing aid, autumn 1954. Converted as 2nd commando carrier, 1961. Sold 1973.
Ameer (ex-*Baffin's*)	Escort Carrier 11,420 tons 24 aircraft	June 1943	*Smiter* class (lease-lend). Returned to USA in 1946.
Anne	Seaplane Carrier 4 aircraft	1915	Former French steamer
Arbiter (ex-*St Simon*)	Escort Carrier 11,420 tons 24 aircraft	Sept 1943	*Smiter* class (lease-lend). Returned to USA in 1946.
Archer (ex-*Mormacland*)	Escort Carrier 12,000 tons 20 aircraft	Nov 1941	*Archer* class (US-built). Returned to USA in 1946.
Argus	Fleet Carrier 17,000 tons	Sept 1918	First with flush-deck. Formerly *Conte Rosso*. Embarked first air torpedo-bomber squadron (Cuckoos) 19 October 1918. Still operational 1942. Scrapped 1947.
Ark Royal	Seaplane Carrier 7,450 tons 10 aircraft	1915	First to be fitted exclusively for seaplane carrier operations. Later renamed *Pegasus*.
Ark Royal	Fleet Carrier 22,000 tons 70 aircraft	Dec 1938	Sunk 13 Nov 1941.

NAME	DESCRIPTION	COMMISSIONED	REMARKS
Ark Royal	Fleet Carrier 49,950 tons 60 aircraft	Feb 1955	First with deck-edge lift and operational steam catapult. Re-commissioned Feb 1970 after 3-year re-fit. Was only RN carrier capable of operating Phantom aircraft. Withdrawn late 1978. Scrapped in 1980.
Ark Royal	Light Carrier 19,500 tons 20 aircraft	May 1985	Third carrier in *Invincible* class (originally known as 'through-deck cruisers'). First built with 12° ski-ramp.
Atheling (ex-*Glacier*)	Escort Carrier 11,420 tons 24 aircraft	July 1943	*Smiter* class (lease-lend). Returned to USA in 1946.
Attacker	Escort Carrier 11,000 tons 15–20 aircraft	Oct 1942	*Attacker* class (US-built). Returned to USA in 1946.
Audacity	Escort Carrier 10,200 tons 8 aircraft	July 1941	Originally *Empire Audacity*, converted from German merchant ship *Hanover*. Sunk 21 Dec 1941.
Avenger	Escort Carrier 12,000 tons 20 aircraft	Mar 1942	*Archer* class (US-built). Sunk 15 Nov 1942.
Battler (ex-*Mormactern*)	Escort Carrier 11,000 tons 18 aircraft	Apr 1942	*Attacker* class (US-built). Returned to USA in 1946.
Begum (ex- *Bolinas*)	Escort Carrier 11,420 tons 20 aircraft	Nov 1942	*Smiter* class (lease-lend). Returned to USA in 1946.
Ben-my-Chree	Seaplane Carrier 4 aircraft	1915	Formerly Isle of Man packet. Launched first air torpedo attack (Short seaplane) in Aegean 12 Aug 1915. Sunk 11 January 1917.
Biter	Escort Carrier 12,000 tons 20 aircraft	May 1942	*Archer* class (US-built). Became French *Dixmude* in 1945.
Bulwark	Light Fleet Carrier 26,113 tons 16 helicopters	Oct 1954	Angled deck. Converted as commando carrier in 1959. Scrapped in 1984.

NAME	DESCRIPTION	COMMISSIONED	REMARKS
Campania	Seaplane Carrier 20,000 tons 10 aircraft	Apr 1915	Ex-Cunard liner; 200 ft flying-off deck for 10 trolleyed seaplanes. Sunk Nov 1918.
Campania	Escort Carrier 16,000 tons 18 aircraft	Mar 1944	British-built. Scrapped in 1955.
Centaur	Carrier 25,760 tons 45 aircraft	Sept 1953	First carrier with operational angled deck. Scrapped in 1972.
Chaser (ex-*Mormacgulf*)	Escort Carrier 11,000 tons 18 aircraft	June 1943	*Attacker* class (US-built). Returned to USA in 1946.
City of Oxford	Seaplane Carrier 1 aircraft	1914	Served with No.64 Wing, Alexandria.
Colossus	Light Fleet Carrier 18,400 tons 36 aircraft	Dec 1944	To French Navy as *Arromanches* in 1946.
Courageous	Fleet Carrier 26,500 tons 48 aircraft	Feb 1928	Sunk 18 Sept 1939.
Dasher	Escort Carrier 12,000 tons 20 aircraft	July 1942	*Archer* class (US-built). Sunk 27 March 1943.
Eagle	Fleet Carrier 26,400 tons 21 aircraft	Feb 1924	First with offset super-structure. Formerly *Almirante Latorre*. Sunk August 1942.
Eagle	Fleet Carrier 49,950 tons 75 aircraft	Oct 1951	Modernised in March 1955. Scrapped in 1978.
Emperor (ex-*Phybus*)	Escort Carrier 11,420 tons 20 aircraft	1943	*Smiter* class (lease-lend). Returned to USA in 1946.
Empress	Seaplane Carrier 4 aircraft	Aug 1914	Converted Channel packet
Empress (ex-*Carnegie*)	Escort Carrier 11,420 tons 20 aircraft	Aug 1943	*Smiter* class (lease-lend). Returned to USA in 1946.
Engadine	Seaplane Carrier 4 aircraft	Aug 1914	Converted Channel packet. Launched seaplane at Battle of Jutland.

NAME	DESCRIPTION	COMMISSIONED	REMARKS
Fearless	Assault Ship 12,120 tons	Nov 1965	Embarked six Wessex troop-carrying helicopters. Served Falklands 1982.
Fencer	Escort Carrier 11,000 tons 15–20 aircraft	Mar 1943	*Attacker* class (US-built). Returned to USA in 1946.
Formidable	Fleet Carrier 29,240 tons 31 aircraft	Nov 1940	Scrapped in 1953.
Furious	Fleet Carrier 22,450 tons 33 aircraft (originally 8 aircraft)	June 1917	Ship on which Dunning's Pup made first landing on a ship under way in August 1917. Modernised 1918 and 1925. Scrapped in 1945.
Glorious	Fleet Carrier 26,500 tons 48 aircraft	Oct 1929	Sunk 8 June 1940 off Norway.
Glory	Light Fleet Carrier 18,400 tons 32 aircraft	April 1945	*Colossus* class. Served in Korean War 1951–53. Scrapped 1961.
Hermes	Seaplane Carrier 3 aircraft	May 1913	Parent ship of Naval Wing, RFC. Sunk Nov 1914.
Hermes	Carrier 12,900 tons 15 aircraft	May 1923	World's first aircraft-carrier built as such. Sunk April 1942 in Indian Ocean.
Hermes (ex-*Elephant*)	Light Fleet Carrier 27,800 tons 28 aircraft	Nov 1959	Converted to commando carrier in 1973. Joined Falklands task force, 1982. Sold to India 1985.
Hunter (ex-*Trailer*)	Escort Carrier 11,000 tons 18 aircraft	Jan 1943	*Attacker* class (US-built). Returned to USA in 1945.
Illustrious	Fleet Carrier 28,210 tons 31 aircraft	May 1940	Modernised in 1948 and 1951. Scrapped in 1956.
Illustrious	Light Carrier 19,500 tons 20 aircraft	Mar 1983	Initially classified as 'through-deck cruiser' *Invincible* class.
Implacable	Fleet Carrier 32,110 tons 54 aircraft	Aug 1944	Modernised in 1948 and 1951. Scrapped in 1955.

NAME	DESCRIPTION	COMMISSIONED	REMARKS
Indefatigable	Fleet Carrier 32,100 tons 54 aircraft	May 1944	Modernised in 1950. Scrapped in 1956.
Indomitable	Fleet Carrier 29,730 tons 48 aircraft	Oct 1941	Modernised in 1948–50. Scrapped in 1955.
Intrepid	Assault ship 12,120 tons	Mar 1967	Embarked six Wessex troop-carrying helicopters. Served Falklands 1982.
Invincible	Light Carrier 19,500 tons 20 aircraft	July 1980	*Invincible* class embarking Sea Harrier and Sea King aircraft. Joined Falklands task force, 1982.
Khedive (ex- *Cordova*)	Escort Carrier 11,420 tons 20 aircraft	Aug 1943	*Smiter* class (lease-lend). Returned to USA in 1946.
Magnificent	Light Fleet Carrier 19,500 tons 34 aircraft	Apr 1948	To Royal Canadian Navy. Returned RN 1957. Scrapped July 1965.
Manxman	Seaplane Carrier 2,174 tons 10 aircraft	1916	Formerly Isle of Man packet.
Nabob (ex-*Edisto*)	Escort Carrier 11,420 tons 20 aircraft	Sep 1943	To Royal Canadian Navy. Scrapped in 1977.
Nairana	Seaplane Carrier 3,000 tons 8 aircraft	Sept 1917	Same class as *Campania* and *Vindex*.
Nairana	Escort Carrier 16,000 tons 18 aircraft	Dec 1943	To Royal Netherlands Navy in Feb 1946.
Ocean	Light Fleet Carrier 18,400 tons 33 aircraft	Aug 1945	First jet (Vampire) to land on carrier on 3 Dec 1945. Served at Suez in 1956. Scrapped in 1962.
Patroller (ex- *Keeweenaw*)	Escort Carrier 11,420 tons 20 aircraft	Oct 1943	*Smiter* class (lease-lend). Returned to USA in 1946.
Pegasus	Seaplane Carrier 3,000 tons 9 aircraft	Aug 1917	Formerly Great Eastern steamer *Stockholm*.
Pegasus	Depot Ship	—	Re-named from *Ark Royal* in 1935.

NAME	DESCRIPTION	COMMISSIONED	REMARKS
Perseus (ex-*Edgar*)	Ferry Carrier 18,040 tons	Completed March 1944	Intended as *Colossus* class but completed as aircraft maintenance ships.
Pioneer (ex-*Mars*)	Ferry Carrier 18,040 tons	Completed May 1944	
Premier (ex-*Estero*)	Escort Carrier 11,420 tons 21 aircraft	Nov 1943	*Smiter* class (lease-lend). Returned to USA in 1946.
Pretoria Castle	Escort Carrier 23,500 tons 21 aircraft	Apr 1943	Training Carrier. Scrapped in 1963.
Puncher (ex-*Willapa*)	Escort Carrier 11,420 tons 20 aircraft	Feb 1944	*Smiter* class (lease-lend). Returned to USA in 1946.
Pursuer (ex-*Mormacland*)	Escort Carrier 11,000 tons 18 aircraft	June 1943	*Attacker* class (US-built). Returned to USA in 1946.
Queen (ex-*St Andrew*)	Escort Carrier 11,420 tons 20 aircraft	Dec 1943	*Smiter* class (lease-lend). Returned to USA in 1946.
Rajah (ex-*Prince*)	Escort Carrier 11,420 tons 20 aircraft	Jan 1944	*Smiter* class (lease-lend). Returned to USA in 1946.
Ranee (ex-*Niantic*)	Escort Carrier 11,420 tons 20 aircraft	Nov 1943	*Smiter* class (lease-lend). Returned to USA in 1946.
Ravager (ex-*Charger*)	Escort Carrier 11,000 tons 15–20 aircraft	Apr 1943	*Attacker* class (US-built). Returned to USA in 1946.
Raven II	Seaplane Carrier 4 aircraft	1916	Former French steamer
Reaper (ex-*Winjah*)	Escort Carrier 11,420 tons 20 aircraft	Feb 1944	*Smiter* class (lease-lend). Returned to USA in 1946.
Riviera	Seaplane Carrier 4 aircraft	Aug 1914	Converted Channel packet.
Ruler (ex-*St Joseph*)	Escort Carrier 11,420 tons 20 aircraft	Dec 1943	*Smiter* class (lease-lend). Returned to USA in 1946.
Searcher	Escort Carrier 11,000 tons 15–20 aircraft	June 1942	*Attacker* class (US-built). Returned to USA in 1945.

NAME	DESCRIPTION	COMMISSIONED	REMARKS
Shah (ex-*Jamaica*)	Escort Carrier 11,420 tons 20 aircraft	Sep 1943	*Smiter* class (lease-lend). Returned to USA in 1945.
Slinger (ex-*Chatham*)	Escort Carrier 11,420 tons 20 aircraft	Aug 1943	*Smiter* class (lease-lend). Returned to USA in 1946.
Smiter (ex-*Vermilion*)	Escort Carrier 11,420 tons 20 aircraft	Jan 1944	*Smiter* class (lease-lend). Returned to USA in 1946.
Speaker (ex-*Delgada*)	Escort Carrier 11,420 tons 20 aircraft	Nov 1943	*Smiter* class (lease-lend). Returned to USA in 1946.
Stalker (ex-*Hamlin*)	Escort Carrier 11,000 tons 15–20 aircraft	Dec 1942	*Attacker* class (US-built). Returned to USA in 1945.
Striker (ex-*Prince William*)	Escort Carrier 11,000 tons 15–20 aircraft	Apr 1943	*Attacker* class (US-built). Returned to USA in 1946.
Thane (ex-*Sunset*)	Escort Carrier 11,420 tons 20 aircraft	Nov 1943	*Smiter* class (lease-lend). Returned to USA in 1946.
Theseus	Light Fleet Carrier 18,400 tons 33 aircraft	Feb 1946	Served in Korean War 1950–51 and at Suez 1956. Scrapped in 1960.
Tracker (ex-*Mormacmail*)	Escort Carrier 11,000 tons 15–20 aircraft	Jan 1943	*Attacker* class (US-built). Returned to USA in 1945.
Triumph	Light Fleet Carrier 18,400 tons 24 aircraft	May 1946	*Colossus* class. Served in Korean War 1950. In 1953 became officer cadet training ship. Scrapped 1981.
Trouncer (ex-*Perdido*)	Escort Carrier 11,420 tons 20 aircraft	Jan 1944	*Smiter* class (lease-lend). Returned to USA in 1945.
Trumpeter (ex-*Lucifer*)	Escort Carrier 11,420 tons 20 aircraft	Aug 1943	*Smiter* class (lease-lend). Returned to USA in 1946.
Unicorn	Maintenance Carrier 20,300 tons 36 aircraft	March 1943	Re-designated Ferry Carrier in June 1953. Scrapped in 1959.
Venerable	Light Fleet Carrier 18,400 tons 24 aircraft	Jan 1945	To Royal Netherlands Navy as *Karel Doorman* in 1948.

NAME	DESCRIPTION	COMMISSIONED	REMARKS
Vengeance	Light Fleet Carrier 18,400 tons 35 aircraft	Jan 1945	To RAN. Sold Brazil 1956.
Victorious	Fleet Carrier 31,790 tons 31 aircraft	May 1941	Rebuilt with angled deck in 1957. Scrapped in 1969.
Vindex	Seaplane Carrier 7 aircraft	Sept 1915	Formerly Isle of Man packet. First landplane take-off from ship by Bristol Scout Nov 1915.
Vindex	Escort Carrier 16,830 tons 18 aircraft	May 1943	British-built
Vindictive	Seaplane Carrier 9,996 tons 6 aircraft	Oct 1918	Formerly light cruiser *Cavendish*. First operational catapult take-offs from its deck in 1925.
Warrior	Light Fleet Carrier 18,400 tons 24 aircraft	Jan 1946	To Royal Canadian Navy. Sold to Argentina in 1958.

Fighter Catapult Ships

Fighter aircraft (generally Sea Hurricanes) catapulted from merchant ships were widely used for convoy protection between 1941 and 1943. Although the majority of these ships (known as CAM-ships) had a Merchant Navy captain, operated under the Red Ensign and had RAF pilots supplied by the Merchant Ship Fighter Unit at Speke, five ships (*Ariguani, Maplin, Michael E, Pegasus* and *Springbank*) flew the White Ensign, had RNR Captains and exclusively Fleet Air Arm pilots. They were known officially as 'Fighter Catapult Ships'.

The first pilot catapulted (in a Sea Hurricane) was Sub-Lieutenant M A Birrell, RN, from the ship *Michael E* in May 1941.

APPENDIX D

A list of ships of the Royal Navy (other than aircraft-carriers) embarking helicopters

In 1990 the Royal Navy had about 60 ships (frigates, destroyers and auxiliaries) carrying helicopters, mostly for anti-submarine warfare duties.

NAME	TYPE OF SHIP	HELICOPTERS CARRIED
Active	Type 21 Frigate	One Lynx
Alacrity	Type 21 Frigate	One Lynx
Amazon	Type 21 Frigate	One Lynx
Ambuscade	Type 21 Frigate	One Lynx
Andromeda	*Leander* class Frigate	One Lynx
Argonaut	*Leander* class Frigate	One Lynx
Argus	Royal Fleet Auxiliary Aviation Training Ship	Six Sea Kings
Ariadne	*Leander* class Frigate	One Lynx
Arrow	Type 21 Frigate	One Lynx
Avenger	Type 21 Frigate	One Lynx
Battleaxe	Type 22 Frigate	Two Lynx
Beaver	Type 22 Frigate	Two Lynx
Birmingham	Type 42 Destroyer	One Lynx
Boxer	Type 22 Frigate	Two Lynx
Brave	Type 22 Frigate	Two Lynx or one Sea King
Brazen	Type 22 Frigate	Two Lynx
Brilliant	Type 22 Frigate	Two Lynx
Bristol	Type 82 Destroyer	One Lynx
Broadsword	Type 22 Frigate	Two Lynx
Campbeltown	Type 22 Frigate	Two Lynx
Cardiff	Type 42 Destroyer	One Lynx
Charybdis	*Leander* class Frigate	One Lynx

NAME	TYPE OF SHIP	HELICOPTERS CARRIED
Chatham	Type 22 Frigate	Two Lynx
Cleopatra	*Leander* class Frigate	One Lynx
Cornwall	Type 22 Frigate	Two Lynx
Coventry	Type 22 Frigate	Two Lynx
Cumberland	Type 22 Frigate	Two Lynx
Edinburgh	Type 42 Destroyer	One Lynx
Endurance	Ice Patrol Ship	Two Lynx
Exeter	Type 42 Destroyer	One Lynx
Fearless	Helicopter Assault Ship	Six Sea Kings
Fort Austin	Fleet Replenishment Ship	Four Sea Kings
Fort Grange	Fleet Replenishment Ship	Four Sea Kings
Glasgow	Type 42 Destroyer	One Lynx
Gloucester	Type 42 Destroyer	One Lynx
Hecla	Survey/Patrol Ship	One Lynx
Herald	Survey Ship	One Lynx
Hermione	*Leander* class Frigate	One Lynx
Hydra	Survey/Patrol Ship	One Lynx
Intrepid	Helicopter Assault Ship	Six Sea Kings
Jupiter	*Leander* class Frigate	One Lynx
Liverpool	Type 42 Destroyer	One Lynx
London	Type 22 Frigate	Two Lynx
Manchester	Type 42 Destroyer	One Lynx
Newcastle	Type 42 Destroyer	One Lynx
Norfolk	Type 23 Frigate	Two Lynx
Nottingham	Type 42 Destroyer	One Lynx
Olmeda	Fleet Replenishment Ship	Two Sea Kings
Olna	Fleet Replenishment Ship	Two Sea Kings
Olwen	Fleet Replenishment Ship	Two Sea Kings
Penelope	*Leander* class Frigate	One Lynx
Phoebe	*Leander* class Frigate	One Lynx
Scylla	*Leander* class Frigate	One Lynx
Sheffield	Type 22 Frigate	Two Lynx
Sir Bedivere *Sir Galahad* *Sir Geraint* *Sir Percivale* *Sir Tristram*	Logistic Landing Ships each capable of operating one helicopter and stowing a second.	

NAME	TYPE OF SHIP	HELICOPTERS CARRIED
Southampton	Type 42 Destroyer	One Lynx
York	Type 42 Destroyer	One Lynx

Future helicopter-carrying ships due to enter service during the 1990s include three additional *Duke* class Type 23 Frigates (including *Argyll*) and three additional *Broadsword* class Type 22 Frigates.

APPENDIX E

Fleet Air Arm Squadrons in 1990

In December 1990, the Royal Navy had an estimated total of around 340 aircraft in service, comprising 240 helicopters and 100 fixed-wing aircraft, including training and second-line aircraft.

Disposition by squadrons is shown in the following table:

SQUADRON	EQUIPMENT	SHORE BASE
No. 800	Sea Harrier Mk. 1	RNAS Yeovilton
No. 801	Sea Harrier Mk. 1	RNAS Yeovilton
No. 810	Sea King Mk. 6	RNAS Culdrose
No. 814	Sea King Mk. 6	RNAS Culdrose
No. 815	Lynx Mk. 3	RNAS Portland
No. 819	Sea King Mk. 6	RNAS Prestwick
No. 820	Sea King Mk. 6	RNAS Culdrose
No. 826	Sea King Mk. 5	RNAS Culdrose
No. 829	Lynx Mk. 3	RNAS Portland
No. 845	Sea King Mk. 4	RNAS Yeovilton
No. 846	Sea King Mk. 4	RNAS Yeovilton
No. 848	Sea King Mk. 4	RNAS Yeovilton
No. 849	Sea King Mk. 2	RNAS Culdrose
No. 899	Sea Harrier Mk. 1 Sea Harrier Mk. 4 Hunter Mk. 8	RNAS Yeovilton
No. 702	Lynx Mk. 3	RNAS Portland
No. 705	Gazelle Mk. 2	RNAS Culdrose
No. 706	Sea King Mk. 5	RNAS Culdrose
No. 707	Sea King Mk. 4	RNAS Yeovilton
No. 750	Jetstream Mk. 2	RNAS Culdrose
No. 771	Sea King Mk. 5	RNAS Culdrose
No. 772	Sea King Mk 4	RNAS Portland

Other units: FRADU at Yeovilton with Falcon 20s, Canberras and Hunters, Flying Grading Flight at Roborough with Chipmunks, Communications Flight at Northolt with BAe 125 and Yeovilton Station Flight with Lynx, Gazelles, Jetstreams and Chipmunks.

Additionally, Royal Marines operate Army versions of Lynx and Gazelle with 3rd Commando Brigade Air Squadron.

Fleet Air Arm Museum

It would seem inappropriate in a volume devoted to the history and development of British Naval Aircraft not to record some details of the magnificent Fleet Air Arm Museum which is open to the public as a permanent record of the achievements of British Naval Aviation.

Situated at Royal Naval Air Station Yeovilton, (2 miles east of Ilchester on road B3151) the FAA Museum was first established in 1964 and has since developed into one of the finest aviation museums in the world. It has over 30 aircraft on permanent display as well as over 20 airframes in reserve and five or more under active restoration. Most interesting of all, perhaps, is the very active Fleet Air Arm Historical Flight which has in its possession Sea Hawk, Firefly and Swordfish aircraft which give regular shows at airfields all over the country during the summer flying season.

Details follow of the aircraft which can be seen at the FAA Museum, together with those in storage or under restoration.

TYPE	YEAR OF MANUFACTURE	SERIAL NUMBER
Blackburn Buccaneer S.1	1963	XN957 (ex-736 Squadron)
Blackburn N.A.39	1958	XK488
Chance Vought Corsair IV	1944	KD431 (ex-768 Squadron)
D.H. Sea Vampire I	1945	LZ551
D.H. Sea Venom F.A.W.21	1955	WW138
D.H. Sea Vixen F.A.W.2	1966	XS590 (ex-892 Squadron)
Douglas Skyraider A.E.W.1	1951	WT121 (ex-849 Squadron)
Fairey Albacore I	1940	N4389 (representing 827 Squadron)
Fairey Fulmar II	1939	N1854
Fairey Gannet A.E.W.3	1960	XL503 (ex-849 Squadron)
Fairey Swordfish II	1943	HS618 (represented as P4139)
Gloster Sea Gladiator	1939	N5903 (represented as N2276 ex-804 Squadron)

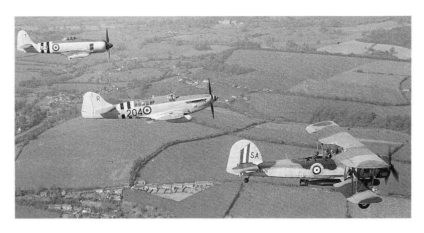

The Swordfish, Firefly and Sea Fury (lost 1989) which appeared regularly at air shows all over the United Kingdom in the 1970s and 1980s. (*Royal Navy*)

The famous Swordfish LS326 which is always a popular item when it makes an appearance at air displays. (*Royal Navy*)

TYPE	YEAR OF MANUFACTURE	SERIAL NUMBER
Grumman Avenger E.C.M.6	1947	XB446
Grumman Hellcat II	1944	KE209
Grumman Martlet I	1940	AL246 (ex-804 Squadron)
Hawker Sea Fury F.B.11	1950	WE726 (represented as WJ231 ex-802 Squadron)
Hawker Sea Hawk F.G.A.6	1954	WV856 (ex-781 Squadron)
Hiller H.T.1	1953	XB480 (ex-705 Squadron)
McDonnell Douglas Phantom F.G.1	1966	XT596
North American Harvard III	1943	EX976
Short S.27	Replica of 1912 type	
Sopwith Baby	1915	Composite of 8214/8215 represented as N2078
Sopwith Camel	Replica of 1917 type	Represented as B6401
Sopwith Pup	Replica of 1917 type	Represented as N6452
Sopwith Triplane	Replica of 1917 type	Represented as N5492
Supermarine Attacker F.1	1951	WA473 (ex-736 Squadron)
Supermarine Scimitar F.1	1959	XD317
Supermarine Seafire XVII	1945	SX137 (ex-759 Squadron)
Supermarine Walrus I	1938	L2301
Westland Dragonfly H.R.5	1953	WN493 (ex-705 Squadron)
Westland Wasp H.A.S.1	1965	XS527
Westland Wessex H.A.S.3	1968	XP142 (ex-737 Squadron)
Westland Wyvern T.F.1	1947	VR137

Fleet Air Arm Historic Flight

Fairey Firely A.S.5	1948	WB271
Fairey Swordfish II (two)	1942–43	LS326 and W5856
Hawker Sea Hawk F.G.A.6	1954	WV908

Hawker Sea Fury T.20 WG655 was destroyed in a forced landing near RNAS Yeovilton on 14 July 1990.
Also D.H. Tiger Moth (T8191) and North American Harvard (EZ407) in storage at Lee-on-Solent.

TYPE	YEAR OF MANUFACTURE	SERIAL NUMBER

In storage or under restoration

Blackburn Skua (wreckage only)	1939	L2940 (ex-800 Squadron)
D.H. Sea Vampire T.22 (nose section)	1953	XA127
Fairey IIIF (parts only)		
Fairey Barracuda II (wreckage only)	1942	DP872
Short Type 184 (fuselage only)	1915	8359
Westland Whirlwind H.A.R.3	1961	XG574

Reserve Collection at Wroughton

D.H. Sea Vampire T.22 (XA129), Fairey Firefly T.T.4 (VH127), Fairey Gannet C.O.D.4 (XA466), Gloster Meteor T.7 (WS103), Percival Sea Prince T.1 (WP313), Saro P.531 (XN332), Westland Wessex H.A.S.1 XS881) and Westland Whirlwind H.A.R.1 (XA864).

On Loan to other Museums

D.H. Sea Vixen F.A.W.1 (XJ481), Douglas Skyraider A.E.W.1 (WV106), Fairey Gannet T.2 (XA508), Fairey Gannet T.5 (XG883), Gloster Meteor T.T.20 (WM292), Hawker Sea Hawk F.G.A.6 (XE340), Saro P.531 (XN334), Supermarine Scimitar F.1 (XD220), Westland Dragonfly H.R.1 (VZ962), Westland Wasp H.A.S.1 (XT427) and Westland Whirlwind H.A.S.7 (XG594).

Enemy Aircraft Collection

Aircraft representing ex-enemy air forces which the RNAS or the FAA engaged in past conflicts include an Albatros D V and Fokker Dr I Triplane (both replicas) and a Pucara captured in the Falklands.

APPENDIX G

British Naval Aircraft
on charge 1914 to 1990

This table shows the total number of aircraft (excluding blimps and airships) on strength with the Royal Naval Air Service and the Fleet Air Arm between 1914 and 1990, with associated flight or squadron strengths.

In general, *total* numbers are shown, including reserves and trainers, etc, but equivalent first-line strength is indicated where the data is available.

YEAR	TOTAL AIRCRAFT	SQUADRONS OR FLIGHTS
1914 (Aug)	93	
1915	1,050 (354 first-line)	3 Squadrons
1916	1,599	7 Squadrons
1917	2,851	22 Squadrons
1918 (April)	2,949	69 Squadrons
1920	50	1½ Squadrons plus 6 Flights
1922	78	14 Flights
1924	128	19 Flights
1930	144	24 Flights
1932	146	26 Flights
1935	175	15 Squadrons
1938	251	15 Squadrons
1939 (Sept)	340 (233 first-line)	20 Squadrons
1940	278 first-line	28 Squadrons
1941	296 first-line	42 Squadrons
1942	485 first-line	61 Squadrons
1943	671 first-line	83 Squadrons
1944	1,135 first-line	102 Squadrons
1945 (Aug)	11,300 (1,336 first-line)	117 Squadrons (plus training squadrons and fleet requirements units)
1953		53 Squadrons (27 first-line plus 17 second-line and 9 RNVR)
1957	520	30 first-line Squadrons
1967		28 Squadrons (16 first-line plus 12 second-line)

YEAR	TOTAL AIRCRAFT	SQUADRONS OR FLIGHTS
1973		19 Squadrons (11 first-line and 8 second-line)
1977		26 Squadrons (15 first-line and 11 second-line)
1978	516	19 Squadrons (9 first-line and 10 second-line)
1980		17 Squadrons 8 first-line and 9 second-line)
1990	340	21 Squadrons (14 first-line and 7 second-line)

APPENDIX H

I wish to acknowledge the invaluable assistance I have received from consulting the following works and, indeed, the sheer pleasure of reading many of them, especially the highly individualistic narratives.

Beaver, Paul. *The British Aircraft Carrier.* Patrick Stephens, 1982
Beaver, Paul. *Encyclopaedia of the Fleet Air Arm since 1945.* Patrick Stephens, 1987
Brown, David. *Carrier Operations in World War II, Vol. 1.* Ian Allan, 1968
Brown, David. *The Seafire.* Ian Allan, 1973
Brown, David. *Carrier Fighters.* Macdonald, 1975
Brown, David. *H.M.S. Eagle.* Hylton Lacy, 1972
Brown, Eric. *Wings on My Sleeve.* Airlife, 1961
Brown, Eric. *Wings of the Navy.* Jane's, 1980
Bruce, J M. *Sopwith Pup.* Albatros, 1986
Bruce, J M. *Sopwith 2F.1 Camel.* Albatros, 1987
Bruce, J M. *Morane-Saulnier Type L.* Albatros, 1989
Bruce, J M. *Britain's First Warplanes.* Arms & Armour, 1987
Bruce, J M. *Nieuport Aircraft.* Arms & Armour, 1988
Cameron, Ian. *Wings of the Morning.* Hodder & Stoughton, 1962
Cathcart-Jones, Owen. *Aviation Memoirs.* Hutchinson 1935
Draper, Christopher. *The Mad Major.* Air Review, 1962
Friedman, Norman, *Carrier Air Power.* Conway Maritime Press, 1981
Friedman, Norman, *British Carrier Aviation.* Conway Maritime Press, 1988
Gamble, C F Snowden. *Story of a North Sea Air Station.* Oxford University Press, 1928
Gibson, M. *Warneford VC* (FAA Museum 1979)
Hallam, T D. *The Spider Web.* William Blackwood, 1919
Hanson, Norman. *Carrier Pilot.* Patrick Stephens, 1979
Harrison, W A. *Swordfish Special.* Ian Allan, 1977
Harrison, W A. *Swordfish at War.* Ian Allan, 1988
Hezlet, Sir Arthur. *Aircraft and Sea Power.* Peter Davies, 1970
Hoare, John. *Tumult in the Clouds.* Michael Joseph, 1976
Horsley, Terence. *Find, Fix & Strike.* Eyre and Spottiswoode, 1943
Humble, Richard. *Aircraft Carriers: the illustrated history.* Michael Joseph, 1982
Ireland, Bernard. *The Rise & Fall of the Aircraft Carrier.* Marshall Cavendish, 1979
Jackson, Robert. *Strike from the Sea.* Arthur Barker, 1970
Johnstone, E G. *Naval Eight.* Signal Press, 1931
Kemp, P K. *Fleet Air Arm.* Robert Jenkins, 1954

Kilbracken, Lord. *Bring Back My Stringbag.* Peter Davies, 1979
Lamb, Charles. *War in a Stringbag.* Cassell, 1977
Layman, R D. *The Cuxhaven Raid.* Conway Maritime Press, 1985
Longmore, Sir Arthur. *From Sea to Sky.* Bles, 1946
Longstaff, Reginald. *The Fleet Air Arm.* Richard Hale, 1981
Milne, J M. *Flashing Blades Over the Sea.* Maritime Books, 1980
Moore, John. *The Fleet Air Arm.* Chapman & Hall, 1943
Newton, Don. *Taranto.* William Kimber, 1959
Nicholl, G W R. *The Supermarine Walrus.* G T Foulis, 1966
Nowarra, Heinz. *Maritime Aircraft of the 1914–18 War.* Harleyford, 1966
Partridge, R T. *Operation Skua.* FAA Museum, 1983
Poolman, Kenneth. *Escort Carrier.* Ian Allen, 1972
Poolman, Kenneth. *Catafighters.* William Kimber, 1970
Poolman, Kenneth. *Ark Royal.* William Kimber, 1956
Poolman, Kenneth. *Illustrious.* William Kimber, 1955
Popham, Hugh. *Sea Flight.* William Kimber, 1954
Popham, Hugh. *Into Wind.* Hamish Hamilton, 1969
Profile Publications. No. 13 Sopwith Pup
                       No. 31 Sopwith Camel
                       No. 44 Fairey IIIF
                       No. 56 Fairey Flycatcher
                       No. 73 Sopwith Triplane
                       No. 74 Short 184
                       No. 121 Sopwith 1½ Strutter
                       No. 126 Hawker Sea Fury
                       No. 139 Bristol Scout
                       No. 212 Fairey Swordfish
                       No. 221 Supermarine Seafire
                       No. 224 Supermarine Walrus
                       No. 240 Fairey Barracuda
                       No. 254 Fairey Fulmar
Rawlings, John. *Pictorial History of the Fleet Air Arm.* Ian Allen, 1973
Rochford, Leonard. *I Chose the Sky.* William Kimber, 1977
Samson, C R. *Fights and Flights.* Benn, 1930
Sturtivant, Ray. *FAA at War.* Ian Allan, 1982
Sturtivant, Ray. *Squadrons of the Fleet Air Arm.* Air-Britain, 1984
Sturtivant, Ray. *Fleet Air Arm 1920–39.* Arms & Armour, 1990
Till, Geoffrey. *Air Power & the Royal Navy.* Jane's, 1979
Tillman, Barrett. *Avenger at War.* Ian Allan, 1979
Tillman, Barrett. *Corsair.* Patrick Stephens, 1979
Tillman, Barrett. *Hellcat.* Patrick Stephens, 1980
Tillman, Barrett. *The Wildcat.* Nautical & Aviation Pub Co, 1983
Williams, Ray. *Fly Navy.* Airlife, 1989
Winton, John. *The Forgotten Fleet.* Michael Joseph, 1969
Winton, John. *Find, Fix & Strike.* Batsford, 1980

Index